Sylvia H

ALSO BY
ROBERTA TEAGUE HERRIN AND
SHEILA QUINN OLIVER

*Appalachian Children's Literature:
An Annotated Bibliography* (McFarland, 2010)

Sylvia Hatchell

The Life and Basketball Legacy

Roberta Teague Herrin *and*
Sheila Quinn Oliver

McFarland & Company, Inc., Publishers
Jefferson, North Carolina

ISBN (print) 978-0-7864-6791-4
ISBN (ebook) 978-1-4766-4249-9

LIBRARY OF CONGRESS AND BRITISH LIBRARY
CATALOGUING DATA ARE AVAILABLE

Library of Congress Control Number 2021021201

Front cover image: Sylvia uses the golden scissors to cut down the net
after defeating Duke to win the ACC Championship, March 9, 2008.
Photograph courtesy Jeffrey Allan Camarati, UNC Sports Information

Printed in the United States of America

*McFarland & Company, Inc., Publishers
Box 611, Jefferson, North Carolina 28640
www.mcfarlandpub.com*

Contents

Acknowledgments

by SHEILA QUINN OLIVER

Writing a biography of Sylvia Rhyne Hatchell required assistance from many individuals and institutions. Friends, family members, players, and colleagues recalled fond memories of Sylvia and gave valuable advice. The vast amount of information we gleaned from research, conversations, phone calls, and emails would fill several volumes, but we are limited in time and scope.

Among the individuals who provided information on countless topics, we must first thank Judy Stroud of Hendersonville, North Carolina, for suggesting that Sylvia's life would make a compelling story. Judy first met Sylvia when they both worked in Pat Summitt's summer basketball camps and has considerable experience in women's basketball. She was the head basketball coach at Boiling Springs High School in Spartanburg, South Carolina; North Greenville University in Tigerville, South Carolina; and Western Carolina University in Cullowhee, North Carolina. She served as regional adviser of NCAA officials in the Southeast and is currently the coordinator of officials in the South Atlantic Conference and the associate coordinator of officials for the Big South, Colonial Athletic, and Southern conferences. When discussing our interest in writing a biography about a notable women's basketball coach she said, "Lots of folks know Pat Summitt at the University of Tennessee, but few know Sylvia Hatchell. Sylvia's accomplishments rank up there with Pat's in women's college basketball, but she has never received the recognition. Why don't you write about her?" So to Judy Stroud, we say thank you for initiating this exploration of Sylvia Rhyne Hatchell's life and career.

We gratefully acknowledge the generosity and kindness of the dozens of other individuals who provided information, verified details, and read multiple drafts.

The insightful readers who proofed the manuscript and offered valuable suggestions for improvement are Carolyn Allen, Susan Carson, Dr. Tony Cavender, Mary Ann Fore, Kathy Hajnal, Ruth Hausman, Janet Knight Linder, Dr. Dalene Vickery Parker, and Mary Webb Quinn.

Sylvia's family contributed treasured memories of her life. Sylvia's sister, Phyllis Rhyne Cooley, was generous with her time and could be counted on to supply accurate and in-depth information about the Rhyne and Shepard families. Additionally, Sylvia's husband Sammy and son Van, ever accessible and willing to share stories about the Hatchell family, made immense contributions to the biography. Sylvia's family members Amanda Cooley, Barbara McCall, Karen Rhyne, Mary Rhyne, Ralph Rhyne, Ronnie Rhyne and friends Phil Cherry, Patsy and Rick Davis, Paula Ryan, and Earl Walters were equally generous in sharing their memories.

Michael Hawkins, associate athletic director for communication services at Francis Marion University, is the ultimate professional, and his assistance was crucial to our research. He was generous with his time and remarkable in his patience. We went back to him time and time again, and he graciously shared his knowledge and his repository of photographs and documents.

Linda Hayes and Tim Dargin gave us insight into the history of schools in the South Carolina Lowcountry, specifically the historical significance of the Rosenwald school, and referred us to historians at the Darlington County Historical Commission. Pat Gibson High-Moore shared information about Pearl Moore.

When stymied by medical terminology, we relied on nurses Jill Nunamaker Cooke, Dianne Glover, Jill Humphries, and Jackie Koss for professional and accurate explanations.

Diane Brady Fetzer, Joel McCracken, Larry Miller, and Kathy Streeter Morgan lent historical insights into women's basketball, baseball, and men's basketball. Sports enthusiasts Dr. Ralph Bland and Dr. Russell Wayne Brown gave advice on documenting game statistics. Dr. Don Johnson and his son Matt Johnson provided information on baseball, spring training, and Dick Williams. Bryant Stokes shared his memories of playing basketball for Coach Sammy Hatchell at James F. Byrnes Academy.

Torben Ross, principal of Hunter Huss High School, gave information on naming the high school basketball court in Sylvia's honor.

Jane and Charlie Sams provided significant historical information on the "Hold the Rope" story.

Troy Geiser explained the automated Shoot-A-Way device and told us that Sylvia was one of the first coaches of women's basketball to purchase a Shoot-A-Way to improve the performance of her players.

Wayne Roberts and Raymond Massey of Blue Ridge Log Cabins provided detailed information and about the construction of Sylvia's mountain cabin.

Edith Quarles gave us contact information for Sylvia's first school principal, Mr. Tommy Northern.

The Honorable Jesse B. Caldwell, III, provided valuable assistance with documenting a source.

Joyce Fitzpatrick of Fitzpatrick Communications supplied valuable details about the 2019 NCAA Final Four basketball tournament.

University of North Carolina, Chapel Hill employees provided critical information and media passes to UNC basketball games. From the biography's inception, Sylvia's administrative assistant, Jane High, was an enthusiastic supporter of the project and always willing to help. Assistant directors of athletic communications Bobby Hundley and Mark Kimmel promptly answered our requests for information and provided access to UNC games.

Tracey Haith, an ACC coordinator, supplied valuable information about Sylvia's committee work and Amy Ufnowski, associate director of communications, supplied media passes to ACC tournaments.

Carol Alfano shared information about Sylvia's service to the Women's Basketball Coaches Association (WBCA), and Tip Tucker Kendall, director of membership strategy with the WBCA, supplied archival records of Sylvia's stint as WBCA president and her committee memberships.

We relied on staff at several institutions for accuracy in photo captions: the Francis Marion University Alumni Association, the University of North Carolina General Alumni Association, Winthrop University Alumni Association, and the University of Tennessee Alumni Association. Susie Trentham, director of advancement services and planned giving coordinator at Carson-Newman University, was a tremendous help in locating the names and addresses of members of the 1974 Carson Newman women's basketball team.

Without the assistance of librarians and archivists, completion of this biography would have been impossible. For providing information about 4-A girls' basketball, a special thank you goes to the school library media specialists at East Mecklenburg High School, Garinger High School, and West Charlotte High School in Charlotte and Hunter Huss High School in Gastonia.

Librarians Margaret Collar of the E.N. Zeigler South Carolina History Room at the Florence County Public Library and Jim Holland of the Cleveland (NC) County Public Library lent accurate information about Sylvia's and Sammy's families.

For an historical perspective on Sylvia's hometown, we relied upon Jennifer Motszko of the UNC Greensboro Archives, the Gaston County Museum in Dallas (North Carolina), the Gaston County Parks and Recreation Department, and the Gaston County Public Library.

Libraries are vital to research, and we are grateful to the following: the Charles C. Sherrod Library at East Tennessee State University and the Johnson City Public Library in Johnson City, Tennessee; the Charleston County Public Library in Charleston, South Carolina; Richland County Public Library in Columbia, South Carolina; the Sandor Teszler Library at Wofford College; the Spartanburg County Public Library; the University of South Carolina-Upstate Library in Spartanburg, South Carolina; the Transylvania County Public Library in Brevard, North Carolina; and the H.J. Lutcher Stark Center for Physical Culture & Sports which holds the Jodi Conradt Papers at the University of Texas at Austin.

For permissions to use photographs held in their respective archives, we thank Adam Cavalier, director of athletic communications at Carson-Newman University; Dana Hart, president of the Women's Basketball Hall of Fame; Michael Hawkins, associate athletic director for communication services at Francis Marion University; the Rev. Roger Mathis, Unity Baptist Church; Herbert Ragan, archivist at the William J. Clinton Presidential Library; and Matt L. Zeysing, historian at the Naismith Memorial Basketball Hall of Fame.

We appreciate the personal photo rights granted by Jeffrey Camarati, director of photography at the University of North Carolina, Sylvia and Sammy Hatchell, and Russell Oliver.

Preface

by Roberta Teague Herrin

Sylvia Hatchell is one of the most successful women's college basketball coaches in the history of the sport. She has won more than 1,000 games and three national championships in three different college athletic associations. She is among the generation of women who were pioneers in women's athletics, who fought for the opportunity to play sports and to have the same opportunities as men. Her life story resonates with many women who grew up before 1972, the year that Title IX was enacted into law. Sylvia, her college peers, her coaches, and her early players were girls who loved sports but had little opportunity for organized competition, so they honed their skills on playgrounds and in backyards. They were tomboys, "girls who played with boys." At the top of the list is Pat Head Summitt. Others include Sylvia's senior-year college coach Sharron Perkins Bilbrey and dozens of Sylvia's early players, such as Pearl Moore, Daphne Donnelly, and Kim Slawson. These women and thousands like them tolerated a wide range of attitudes and perceptions, from awe to fear to outright bigotry.

The first half of the 20th century produced outstanding women athletes, such as Babe Didrikson Zaharias, but even they were considered anomalies. When Zaharias died on September 28, 1956, at age 42, the loss to sports, in general, and to women's sports, in particular, was felt globally. Among the many tributes to this amazing athlete was sportswriter Arthur Daley's "A Remarkable Woman," published in the *New York Times* on September 30, 1956. Daley praises "the Babe" as a woman who never took shortcuts, lived by the rules, and worked obsessively to perfect her golf game. Daley quotes this line from her autobiography: "Before I was even in my teens, ... I knew exactly what I wanted to be when I grew up. My goal was to be the greatest athlete that ever lived." Daley calls this a "strange confession" and her ambition "odd" because—in his words—"the best woman athlete in almost any sport is about on a par with a schoolboy champion."[1] Sylvia Rhyne was four years old when Daley's tribute to "the Babe" was published, and though she was not old enough to read his *New York Times* column, there is no doubt that such biased attitudes shaped her life.

Women's sports in American culture are marked by complexity, myth, stereotypes, and incongruities. For example, early women's athletic organizations opposed commercialization of women's sports. The Association for Intercollegiate Athletics for women (AIAW) tried to ban financial scholarships for female athletes and deliberately promoted ideals that were counter to the National Collegiate Athletic Association (NCAA), which did not govern women's sports until the 1980s. AIAW leaders hoped to avoid what they perceived as the "evils" of men's collegiate athletics and to emphasize academics and leadership in young women as opposed to money and star status. This attitude would change when Title IX was enacted in 1972.

Title IX was one of the 1972 Education Amendments to the 1964 Civil Rights Act. It dictated that "no person in the United States shall, on the basis of sex, be excluded from participation in, be denied the benefits of, or be subjected to discrimination under any education program or activity receiving Federal financial assistance."[2] Title IX was originally created as an anti-discrimination civil rights law that guaranteed equal access to education, regardless of gender, but the implications for athletics soon became obvious. The legislation made clear that violations of Title IX could result in the loss of Federal funding for research and financial aid. A high number of low-income students, including athletes and minorities, depended on Basic Educational Opportunity Grants (BEOG), which were created as part of the 1972 Higher Education Amendments and later renamed Pell Grants. Loss of this funding stream would decimate enrollments of all students, not just athletes. Schools had no choice but to support women's sports.

The changes brought about by Title IX were met with enthusiasm and resentment. Women were mostly supportive, but men feared what their programs stood to lose. So much emphasis had been placed on men's sports that it was hard for athletic departments to conceive of the full implications of the new law. Consequently, the impact of Title IX was colossal but slow. A 1973 lawsuit ended the AIAW ban on women's scholarships.[3] Even so, Sylvia's alma mater did not award a scholarship to a woman until 1977, when women's basketball became a varsity sport at Carson-Newman. According to Christopher Jones, Carson-Newman had awarded men's scholarships for decades, and in 1935–1936, doubled the number of $100 men's scholarships from 12 to 24.

In the 21st century, some still agree with Arthur Daley's observation that "the best woman athlete in almost any sport is about on a par with a schoolboy champion." Consider this example from February 26, 2000: The Duke men's basketball team was playing St. John's in Cameron Indoor Stadium. Two Duke students, Jen Feinberg and Sarah Bradley, were checking credentials at the stadium media entrance and asked to see CBS announcer Billy Packer's press pass. He responded, "You need to get a life. Since when do we let women control who gets into a men's basketball game? Why don't you go find a women's game to let people into?" Feinberg and Bradley wrote a protest letter to CBS Sports president Sean McManus, who was, ironically, a Duke alumnus.[4] According to *USA Today*, McManus e-mailed both women to say CBS "stands against bias of all sorts." CBS advised Packer "that any comments contrary to the network's policy will not be tolerated" and stated that Packer would apologize. When asked about the incident, Packer responded, "If those two girls have a problem with me, they should call me up. I'm easy to find, or they should've told me at the time." Feinberg said that at the time she was so "stunned" she "couldn't think of anything to say." Later, Packer wrote the girls: "I am sorry you were offended by my comments.... It was never my intention to disparage Duke University or its students. Please accept my apology."[5] They accepted the apology, but it escaped no one's notice that Packer did not apologize for his words; he was merely sorry that they were "offended."

A more recent incident involved Carolina Panthers quarterback Cam Newton and female journalist Jourdan Rodrigue. The *New York Times* reported that when Rodrigue asked Newton a question about Devin Funchess' "route running," he smiled and said, "It's funny to hear a female talk about routes."[6] Condemnation of the remark was immediate. Mike Persinger described Newton's reaction as "unfortunate and out of line."[7] The Dannon Company pulled its sponsorship of Newton. These two incidents, 17 years apart and 63 years after Daley's observation, demonstrate that the impact of Title IX has been colossal but slow.

Without question, Title IX has fostered exponential growth of women's athletics over 48 years, but as women's basketball evolves at all levels—middle school, high school, college, and professional—its status has not yet achieved parity with men's basketball in TV coverage, in coaches' salaries, or in professional women players' salaries. Recently, the scale has tipped in an unexpected direction. In a *CBS This Morning* broadcast on April 19, 2019, Norah O'Donnell cited surprising statistics. In 1972, 90 percent of "coaches of female basketball teams were women." In 2019, that figure has dropped to 41 percent. And "nearly eighty percent of all college athletic directors are men." O'Donnell asked Muffet McGraw, head women's basketball coach at Notre Dame, "Why is the number decreasing?" McGraw contended that increased coaches' salaries in women's sports are attracting higher numbers of men—an unintended and perhaps counterproductive result.[8]

This ironic consequence of Title IX is but one change in women's basketball during Sylvia's lifetime. Other shifts are noteworthy. In the age of social media, the Black Lives Matter, racial conflict, and helicopter parents, Title IX has stepped out of the spotlight. Political correctness, a heightened sensitivity to the power of words, and player empowerment have claimed center stage. It is a good thing that women have found their voice, but voices are most effective when they are raised and heard in the context of trust. Because Sylvia Hatchell values relationships above everything else, she is quick to trust, to believe that she and others have communal bonds based on a common purpose. This trait made her an excellent coach whom players considered a "second mom" and a friend. This trait is the underpinning of her character. She is just Sylvia: plain, down-to-earth, unpretentious, passionate, vocal, trusting. But at the end of her career, that trust was broken—sacrificed, perhaps, to unintended consequences of Title IX, raised voices, player empowerment, and shifts in academic values and standards.

Today's young women are indebted to the female athletes and coaches of Sylvia's generation who forged a path, who begged and fought for opportunities to play sports. Title IX was not a magic solution, and the complexities of its application are often baffling, but it moved women's basketball from the neighborhood playground to college gymnasiums and professional arenas. Peggy Birmingham, Sylvia's freshman-year college coach, believes that without Title IX, collegiate women would still be competing as clubs or extramural activities: "All they were interested in was men's football, basketball, and baseball," but "if the truth were told," Birmingham continues, "Title IX helped men's sports, particularly the 'minority sports,' which got more money and publicity and recognition because of the emphasis on equal access, parity, and ratios." Without it, women such as Sylvia Rhyne Hatchell and Pat Head Summitt would never have had the opportunity to influence thousands of young lives, male and female. Without it, their dreams would have lain fallow in the backyards and on the playgrounds of America. But their legacies are vulnerable. If their achievements are forgotten, the loss to all women will be tragic.

1

Becoming Sylvia

Sylvia Rhyne Hatchell is a Tar Heel—by birth and by choice. The roots of her family tree reach to the far western corners of North Carolina, and her upbringing in a close-knit, 1950s Carolina mill town made her who she is. Except for her college days in Tennessee and her first job in South Carolina, she has lived her entire life in the state, and for 33 years she wore Carolina blue and white, the colors of the University of North Carolina at Chapel Hill.

Sylvia Jean Rhyne was born in Gaston Memorial Hospital at 4:18 p.m. on February 28, 1952, to Veda Elvira Shepard Rhyne and Carroll Costner Rhyne. Family stories disagree about how her parents met. One version says that they met at a tent revival in Gastonia, where Veda lived. Another says they met at Temple Baptist Church, which Veda attended. The one common detail of the story—that they met at a church activity—is important, for church would be the center of their lives. Veda and Carroll married on June 7, 1947, and their first child Phyllis was born in 1948. On the day Sylvia left the hospital in 1952, Phyllis waited in the car with Aunt Catherine Rhyne (Boggs), eager to take the seven-pound, seven-ounce baby to their house at 505 Bessemer City Road, next door to Veda's father and stepmother—Van Buren and Eathel Shepard. It was a small, frame house with 1,000 square feet—a front porch, living room, kitchen, two bedrooms, and one bath. Later, Sylvia and Phyllis would be joined by two brothers—Ralph, in 1956, and Ronnie, in 1957.

Veda and Carroll were a typical 1950s, middle-class, working couple who valued education but never earned college degrees. Veda graduated from Gastonia High School (now called Ashbrook High School) in 1942 and finished one year of business college. Carroll's education was interrupted in the eleventh grade, when an appendectomy caused him to drop out of Dallas High School. The military rejected him because he had scoliosis, so he was spared World War II. In 1960, he attended adult night school to earn his General Education Diploma (GED), and a couple of years later, Carroll was helping Phyllis with difficult algebra problems. Carroll held a variety of jobs. When Sylvia was born, he worked at Sunrise Dairy in Gastonia. Later, he owned an ESSO service station on Bessemer City Road, very close to their home and church. When he sold the service station, he became an apprentice at Southeastern Precision Tool and Die and eventually worked for AMP Inc.

Living next door to her grandparents Shepard, Sylvia was a frequent visitor, running in and out of their house as though it were her home, too. "I stayed at my grandparents' house as much as I stayed at home," says Sylvia. For one thing, the Rhynes did

Sylvia Rhyne pulling Radio Flyer wagon, 1953. Courtesy Sylvia Hatchell.

not have a telephone, so they went to Eathel and Van Buren's house when they needed to make a call on the party line. The Shepards' house had a big front porch where neighbors gathered on summer evenings. Sylvia would crawl up on the glider-swing beside her grandmother Eathel, lay her head in her lap, and beg, "Rub my back." Eathel would oblige as Sylvia lay there long into the night, gently rocking in the glider, dozing, and listening to the adults. Then her parents would carry her home and put her to bed.

Van Buren was a powerful influence in Sylvia's life. Affectionately called "Vannie," he was much loved and respected in the neighborhood and was especially attentive to children, engaging them with a sense of playfulness that was also instructive. He made a contest out of simple tasks: who could plow the straightest garden row or finish hoeing a row of corn first. He challenged them to peel an apple without breaking the peeling. Then, before he cut open the apple, he would ask them to guess whether it had an odd number of seeds or an even number. At that age, they hardly knew the difference between "odd" and "even" and had no idea that they were learning math. Vannie was skilled with his hands and could repair or build anything. He and Sylvia's father refurbished old bicycles for the children, who never got new ones, not even at Christmas. Vannie took the grandchildren with him on construction jobs, where Sylvia learned about woodworking, building, and tools.

Vannie was head of the Extension Department at Unity Baptist Church, a position that required him to visit elderly and shut-in community members and take them copies of LifeWay's *Home Life* magazine, a monthly publication launched in 1947 and still available today. Between the ages of six and twelve, Sylvia and her friends accompanied Vannie on these visits. Watching him, she learned how to be personable and sociable—how to visit and "be" with people. She recalls the Davis Trio, a church singing group composed of two brothers and a sister—Thornton, Floyd, and Polly—who were blind. At first, she was afraid for them to run their hands over her hair and face, but she came to understand that this was how they "saw" her. Later, she was part of the Unity Baptist youth group, which visited shut-ins, continuing the tradition begun with her grandfather Vannie.

The Rhyne family quickly outgrew the house on Bessemer City Road where Sylvia, Phyllis, and Ralph had to share one bedroom: Sylvia and Phyllis in a double bed and Ralph in a twin bed. Their baby brother Ronnie slept in a crib in their parents' room, but Ronnie soon outgrew the crib. In 1961, her father, his oldest brother Jacob, and her grandfather Vannie, built a new, three-bedroom brick home at 504 Oliver Street, directly behind their Bessemer City Road house. In the new house, the sisters had their own room, though they still shared a full-sized bed and a dresser. Sylvia and Phyllis had different priorities and conflicting perspectives on housekeeping. On her side of their blue room, Sylvia had a box that contained everything she loved: her baseball bat, glove, basketball, and football. Phyllis' treasures consisted of dolls and books, and her side of the room was orderly and clean. She frequently chastised Sylvia for her messiness, and just as often, their mother would say, "Y'all need to clean up this mess."

From their house on Oliver Street, they could see the steeple of Unity Baptist Church, two blocks away. Vannie, Eathel, and Veda were charter members of this church, which was the core of the Rhyne family's social and spiritual life. If the doors were open, Sylvia says, "We were there." They attended Sunday morning and evening services and Wednesday prayer meeting. "There was no getting out of it," explains Ralph. Sylvia could run to the church in less than two minutes—and often did. Carroll was a deacon, and Phyllis played piano and organ for services. Then Veda became a church employee. She was working as a secretary at Wix Accessories, a company that manufactured filters for cars, trucks, and large equipment, when the Reverend Gwaltney came to their home to offer her the position of church secretary. Seven-year-old Sylvia got so excited that she spilled Kool-Aid on Gwaltney, a *faux pas* that did not affect his offer. For more than 20 years, Veda was the church secretary and treasurer, handling all the usual responsibilities, including the church bulletin, which was printed on a mimeograph machine kept in their living room. First, Veda made a stencil on a typewriter and loaded it onto the fluid-filled cylinder. Then Sylvia and her friends turned the crank to rotate the drum and print the bulletin. As church treasurer, Veda was responsible for the sizeable offering. Sylvia observed her mother closely and learned the importance of following protocol. The offering was never kept in their home, for example. Immediately after church, Veda took it to the bank's night-deposit drop; on Monday morning, she went to the bank and counted the money in the presence of witnesses. The message to Sylvia was clear: Money is not to be handled carelessly; money is serious business.

Left to right: Phyllis, Ralph, Sylvia, and Ronnie Rhyne on the Shepards' front porch at 507 Bessemer City Road, circa 1961. Courtesy Sylvia Hatchell.

The Rhyne family walked to Unity Baptist Church for Sunday morning services, which bored Sylvia. She enjoyed Sunday School, but she squirmed through the Rev. W.F. Woodall's sermons. Woodall had replaced Gwaltney in 1960, and though she respected him, she preferred to draw pictures—especially house plans—on the church bulletin while he preached. Sylvia learned life skills from the Reverend Woodall: the importance of being organized, showing compassion, and fostering good in people. Even as a child, she appreciated his work ethic, his sincere interest in people, and his ability to build relationships. Under the Reverend Woodall's leadership, the church grew, and Sylvia recognized that "the Lord used Reverend Woodall's talents to serve the community."

After church, the family walked home for a big Southern, Sunday dinner of fried chicken or cubed steak, coleslaw, potato salad or creamed potatoes, deviled eggs, macaroni and cheese, green beans, biscuits—always biscuits—and sweet iced tea. Then they loaded into the Chevrolet and drove to Dallas to visit Sylvia's paternal grandparents, Anna Maude and Quince Rhyne, a mere seven miles or 20 minutes from Gastonia, but to them, it was a long trip. On one trip to Dallas, Sylvia's father surprised her. After they turned off NC State Route 321 and got to Cloninger Road, her father pulled over to the side and said, "'Sylvia, get over here. Drive.' I was like,

'REALLY?' He said, 'Yeah.' And my mama yelled, 'CARROLL! CARROLL!'" Sylvia was barely twelve years old, but her father often let her and the other children drive the final mile or so down the dirt road.

Sunday at the Rhyne family home was crowded with visiting aunts, uncles, and cousins, who engaged in all sorts of games and play: basketball, softball, football, tag games such as Red Rover and Red Light, and—of course—Cowboys and Indians. The big, noisy Rhyne clan hiked in the woods and climbed trees and played on swings hanging from the trees—tire swings, rope swings, grapevine swings. On summer Sundays, they played in the nearby creek and caught lightening bugs if they were still there at dusk. They rode horses, and they rode bicycles. And in the warm weather, everyone sat outside, talked, and often made ice cream in a hand-cranked churn. The children put a towel over the churn and took turns sitting on the top or cranking the handle, which was Sylvia's favorite part. Occasionally, a local young man, William C. Friday, would drop by. He later became the first and longest-serving president of the University of North Carolina system (1956–1986). He had been best friends with Maude and Quince's son Ralph, who was killed in World War II. At the end of the day, Sylvia's family headed back to Gastonia for the Sunday evening church service.

From a young age, Sylvia was a full participant in church activities, and every summer, she attended South Mountain Baptist Camp at Connelly Springs, on Highway 18, mid-way between Morganton and Shelby. In August 1961, when Sylvia was nine, she became a Christian at this camp and was later baptized in the church that her grandfather Vannie helped found. She returned to South Mountain Baptist Camp every year, and at age 16, she worked there as a counselor and general assistant. She still maintains strong ties to the camp and helped create the annual Unity Baptist Church/South Mountain Baptist Camp Retreat, which is held annually during the last week of August.

Like many young girls in Southern communities, Sylvia joined the Girls' Auxiliary, a Baptist organization for young women that had a strong presence in the 1950s and 1960s. Founded in 1913 by the Baptist Women's Missionary Union (WMU), Girls' Auxiliary emphasized missions education. Sylvia was attracted to the challenge it offered for setting and reaching goals. In this case, the goal was to become Queen-Regent-in-Service, the highest level of achievement. Sylvia's personal *Intermediate Girls' Auxiliary Manual* shows that advancement through the "Forward Steps" required reading, memorization, research, Bible study, community engagement, and reflection. True to form, Sylvia advanced through all the steps—Maiden, Lady-in-Waiting, Princess, Queen, Queen-with-a-Scepter, and Queen Regent—and was crowned Queen-Regent-in-Service.

In the Rhyne household, school was a near-second to church, and Myrtle School was just three blocks west of their Oliver Street home. Sylvia, Phyllis, Ralph, and eventually Ronnie walked to school and literally *ran* home at noon for lunch, as did many of the neighbor children, including Debbie Morrow, Kathy Whiteside, and Jerry Thomas. Being able to walk home for lunch is but one difference between school in the 1950s and 1960s and school in the 21st century. Another difference is that students frequently had to repeat a grade for failure to master the curriculum. Jerry Thomas recalls that "there was no such thing as passing to a higher grade without earning it. Either you did your subjects and passed your tests, or you stayed back sometimes one or two or three grades." Two members of his and Sylvia's eighth-grade class at Myrtle School were 16 years old.

Sylvia's life unfolded in a safe, working-class neighborhood filled with children her age, all of whom played outdoors every possible minute in all weather. The Rhynes owned a television, but the children rarely watched the two or three channels it received. Sylvia wanted to be outdoors doing, not sitting: bike riding and swimming; playing football, basketball, baseball, softball; pitching horseshoes; and roller skating on the outdoor basketball courts at Myrtle School. Sometimes Sylvia and Phyllis skated together, but Sylvia spent most of her time with Debbie Morrow and Kathy Whiteside, who lived across from their first house at 505 Bessemer City Road. Debbie was a tomboy like Sylvia, so they hurried home from school, changed clothes, grabbed the basketball, and ran back to the schoolhouse to play until dark. If the girls weren't playing basketball, they were usually in the creek behind Debbie's house. They cut grapevines that hung from the trees and made swings for riding back and forth over the creek. They played "Tarzan and Jane" in the woods. Though they were tomboys, they enjoyed the same interests as other eight- and nine-year-old girls—and they looked like typical 1950s little girls. They wore dresses to school and church. In summer they could wear shorts for play, and in the winter, they could wear long pants—but *under* their dresses. As Debbie puts it, "Sylvia had a girlie side to her as well." They made aluminum foil crowns, covered with stars, and aluminum foil scepters and pretended to be princesses. But Sylvia did not have the typical interest in dolls, and, later, makeup and clothes would be eclipsed by sports.

Coronation of Sylvia as Queen-Regent-with-a-Scepter, Girls' Auxiliary, Unity Baptist Church, 1967. Left to right: Ernest Crenshaw, Sylvia Rhyne, and Lisa Hovis. Courtesy Sylvia Hatchell.

Sylvia's parents were socially conservative, but in Debbie's and Kathy Whiteside's homes, radio station WAYS 610 AM out of Charlotte—known as BIG

WAYS 61—was always on, playing the popular late-fifties music. They also owned a stereo. "That's where I fell in love with the Four Seasons," says Sylvia, "and the Ray Conniff Singers." Kathy's mother loved Ray Charles, the Temptations, and the Four Tops and sang their songs while she worked around the house. Sylvia and Kathy and Debbie danced. They danced with each other, and they danced holding on to the door knob. They did the Watusi, the Twist, the Peppermint Twist, and the Mashed Potato. Sylvia expressed her growing love of music through physical activity—dancing—the medium that came most naturally to her.

Debbie was also one of the many neighborhood children who played all sports, not just basketball. When they didn't have enough players for two baseball teams, they played Rolly-Bat. Arguments were routine. One player would say, "You cheated!" or "The ball bounced over the bat and didn't hit it!" When they played in Sylvia's back yard, Veda had to be the referee, sticking her head out the back door to settle disagreements. On summer evenings, the Rhynes' back yard would be full of kids, as many as 15. On more than one occasion when Veda was inside cooking supper, she heard the familiar sound of a baseball shattering glass, but when she looked out the kitchen window, there was not a kid in sight—they had all scattered at the noise. It happened so often that Carroll kept spare glass in his workshop.

Though Sylvia "ran the neighborhood" on her bike, her parents never worried about her. They expected her to stay out of trouble and come home before it got fully dark, and the children did not run wildly and unsupervised through the community. Their parents held them to strict behavior codes. They could not curse or use off-color language. They had to show consideration by asking permission to visit with other children and by honoring curfews. If Sylvia's mother told her to come home in one hour, she obeyed. Parents gave the children almost unlimited freedom but kept close watch. Debbie's father would come by the schoolyard and say, "You girls need to get on home—it's getting dark." Debbie's mother had a distinctive whistle, and the children knew to go home when they heard it. Their *Leave-It-to-Beaver* neighborhood undoubtedly had its problems, but the children were unaware of them.

In Sylvia's family, play was secondary to work. Her father believed in gender equity before it became politically correct: "Forget that you're a girl—you *will* hoe your row of corn." The Rhynes and Shepards had a vegetable garden that was legendary. Phyllis, Sylvia, Ralph, and Ronnie hoed and pulled weeds in the mornings before they were allowed to play. Sylvia used the Merry Tiller to plow between the rows, eager to finish so she could head for the park. "I'll do the tilling," she said. "Somebody else can do the hoeing." She liked to walk barefoot behind the tiller, feeling the soft dirt between her toes. When the garden "came in," they shucked corn and picked green beans and tomatoes. Ralph remembers having to string and break bushels of green beans, which they put up in the freezer, along with the corn and other vegetables. Sylvia also had household chores. She helped Veda cook supper, and Phyllis cleared the table and washed the dishes. The Rhyne children had to cut the grass with a motorized push mower. Saturday was cleaning day, when they swept the floor, vacuumed the rugs, and dusted the furniture. They also helped Carroll wash the car on Saturday, a task they relished because they liked playing in the water.

Sylvia's work ethic evolved into an entrepreneurial spirit. "I was always looking for ways to make money," she says. She took orders for groceries from the neighbors and rode her bike to Kenley's Grocery, a small neighborhood store. Mr. Kenley helped her select the items from her lists and bagged the groceries, which Sylvia loaded in her bicycle basket and delivered. Neighbors rewarded her with a nickel. Vannie had a pear tree in the back yard, and in late summer and early fall when the pears were ripe, Sylvia came home for lunch, gathered pears in a paper sack, took them back to school, and sold them to her classmates, two for a nickel. Sylvia canvassed the neighborhood asking for discarded magazines, from which she cut coupons: "Then I would take them to the store and turn them in for candy." She occasionally babysat, but she did not like that job. In summertime, "before I was really big enough to push a lawn mower," she says, "I had two or three yards to cut at a dollar a yard." Later, she had a small riding mower: "I mowed everybody's yard in the neighborhood." On hot Gastonia afternoons, Sylvia went to the park and solicited orders for Coca-Cola, Orange Crush, Cheerwine, Sun Drop Cola (bottled in Gastonia), and Grape Ne-Hi. Then she rode her bike to the store, where Mr. Kenley again helped fill her order. When she delivered the drinks, the kids gave her a few pennies extra for her effort, usually enough to buy herself a drink and have a little profit.

In the 1950s and 1960s, it was also common for children to pick up drink bottles that littered the roadside and cash them in for the two-cent deposit. Sylvia was no exception. She would gather up a few dozen bottles and take them to Mr. Kenley's store. Her efforts netted pennies and nickels, which don't seem like much, but a nickel in 1959 would be the equivalent of $0.47 in 2020. "Now I've always been tight," says Sylvia. "My daddy was like that. My daddy would drive across town to save a penny on gas. I've always been a wheeler-dealer because you can negotiate for anything. And when I see something I want, I usually get it—and at a great price." When she got older, she put to good use the skills she learned from her grandfather Vannie. By the time she was fifteen, she knew how to sand wood floors, lay tile, mix mortar, lay brick, and shingle a roof. In the summers, she painted houses. "You know, it's not just about the money. When you can do stuff, it gives you confidence. I don't have to have a lot of money to be happy, but I like making money. I like the challenge of it, the negotiating. It's sort of like winning."

In a 2000 interview with Emily A. Colin, Sylvia revealed that her goal at age eight or nine was "to play football for the Green Bay Packers."[1] She appeared to be destined for such a career, with her fierce competitiveness and no-holds-bared approach to *anything* athletic. She became legendary for a church softball game at Rankin Lake when she was 11 or 12. It was Sylvia's turn at bat. She walloped the ball and tore out for first base, which was blocked by Mr. H.M. Freels. Sylvia ran straight toward him and hit him so hard that he turned a flip and landed in the creek. He was unhurt, but she suffered severe pain in the jaw, and the doctor said it was dislocated, but years later, an X-Ray showed that her jaw had been broken. The accident left her with a slightly-crooked smile but made her a much-desired teammate for the boys. Jerry Thomas describes her as "a tomboy-type person; she was more or less like one of the guys." Every day, neighborhood boys knocked on the door and asked her to come out and play. No matter what the sport, they wanted Sylvia on their team.

With the onset of puberty, Sylvia had to make annoying adjustments. When the time came for a training bra, Veda took her to Sears on a Friday afternoon, and Sylvia's reaction was, "I do not want this. This is not what I want." She was particularly upset because her Sunday school class was going bowling the next morning. Sylvia left for the Saturday expedition thinking, *I cannot bowl with this thing on.* In many ways, she matured late. Consistent with 1950s parenting, Veda never expressly told her the "facts of life." One Sunday night before Sylvia was to leave the next day for South Mountain Baptist Camp, her mother came into her room and said, "Sylvia, you're going to be around older girls at camp, and you will be exposed to new things. You will hear girls talking about topics you may not understand." That was it. That was the extent of Sylvia's formal sex education. She remembers the specific Sunday night when she came home from church and found blood on her panties. Her first thought was *Oh! My Gosh!* She called to her mother and begged, "Oh, no! Don't tell Daddy!" Being a tomboy and a daddy's girl, she did not want him to know that she had crossed the threshold from childhood to womanhood. She was somewhat prepared for puberty because her friends had bras and menstrual periods, but she was stunned when it happened to her.

Developing breasts and the arrival of menses changed her sports routine. From an early age, she had played tackle football with the neighborhood boys, but suddenly her mother insisted that she play touch football. Sylvia was furious, but because she was a good player, the boys still wanted her on the team, so she shifted to the quarterback position. She learned to throw a football well, and she was somewhat protected by the no-tackling rule. Puberty did not interfere with basketball, so she focused on that sport. The school had outdoor basketball courts with chain-metal nets, not nylon; on many days, Sylvia was the only girl out there playing basketball. Her dad would drive by in the car, and toot the horn, which she took to mean, "I'm proud of my girl." She and Ralph and Ronnie played one-on-one in their back yard. Being left-handed, she had a pretty good little bank shot that she could make from the corner. When the weather was bad, they used the indoor basketball court in the Hunter Huss High School gym. Technically, they broke into the gym, climbing in through a window, but the maintenance man never reported them because they never abused or destroyed property. "All I remember during the sixth, seventh, and eighth grades," says Jerry Thomas, "is being on the basketball court every afternoon. We all just stayed on the court all the time, Sylvia included, religiously every day." Thomas remembers Sylvia as being "just as good as, if not better than, the guys." Even after Sylvia moved on to high school, she continued to "hang out" on the court with the neighborhood boys during the summer. Says Thomas, "She fit right in with the guys."

In the summer, when the Rhynes' garden was in full growth and the kids couldn't play there, they moved to the vacant lot that the church owned—known as the Myrtle School-Unity Baptist Church Park. They played baseball and Pickle, but these games were a problem for Sylvia. First, she did not own a glove and had to borrow one from the boys. Second, she was left-handed. On her eighth birthday, Sylvia went with her parents to visit their friends the Badgers. Mr. June Badger was the director of Gastonia Parks and Recreation and a basketball referee. As she and her parents were getting ready to leave, Mr. Badger left the room, and her daddy said, "Sylvia, I think Mr. Badger has something for you." He came back with one hand hidden behind him, and as he brought his hand around to the front, she saw a left-handed baseball glove. Sylvia treasured that glove. She slept with it. She put her baseball inside the glove, and wrapped twine around it to make a pocket for the ball.

Despite the old adage that "equipment is everything," Sylvia's new baseball glove didn't change the 1950s–1960s culture. She had to learn hard lessons, and one of them was that to compete successfully in a boy's world, she would have to lose with grace but keep her passion and determination. All the boys in her neighborhood played Little League Baseball. These were the same boys that Sylvia played with year-round, but she was barred from the games because she was a girl. Mr. Mack Hanna coached Little League baseball and would let her practice with the boys, but she could not play. Undaunted, she attended all the Little League games, usually hitching a ride with the boys' mothers. She often waited by the road and flagged down Ronnie Christopher's mother Leila on her way home from work at DANOCA (an acronym for Dallas [DA], North [NO] Carolina [CA]). Sylvia kept the scorebook in the dugout and cheered for the local boys' team, hiding her disappointment that she could not join them on the field. Little League bylaws were eventually amended (after 57 lawsuits), and girls were finally allowed to play in 1974, but by that time, Sylvia had finished college.

Not being able to play baseball, Sylvia found other opportunities for athletic competition. At the Myrtle School-Unity Baptist Park and nine other parks around town, the Gastonia Parks and Recreation Division sponsored a variety of activities, from crafts to horseshoes. On the Fourth of July, the city brought together winners in all areas of competition from the ten parks to compete at Lineberger Park for a city championship. When Sylvia was 12, she won the horseshoe-pitching contest for Myrtle School-Unity Baptist Park, so she competed with the other nine winners—all boys and men—in the horseshoe pitching contest. She beat everyone and won the top prize, a free pass to the city swimming pool for the rest of the summer. Jerry Thomas was stunned that Sylvia could even throw a horseshoe, much less win a tournament: "Man! She is so competitive."

In the fifth and sixth grades, Sylvia got her first opportunity to compete against other girls in the Tri-Gra-Y Girls Basketball League, sponsored by the Gastonia YMCA. At the 1962 Tri-Gra-Y banquet, Sylvia won the trophy for the highest scorer in basketball for the entire league, but when she left grade school and was too old for the Tri-Gra-Y program, she had no opportunity to continue competing with girls. Because she had limited transportation, she probably could not have participated in a Tri-Hi-Y program in Gastonia even if one had existed. Though she tried to get schools and community leaders to create girls' teams, she had no success. One problem was that few girls wanted to play. Other than Sylvia, girls in the neighborhood, including her sister Phyllis, didn't want to play sports, and by this time, Debbie Morrow had moved from Bessemer City Road.

Because Sylvia had to settle for being *near* competitive sports, she tried out for the cheerleading squad in the eighth grade and was named captain—she *had* to be in charge. It was foreign to her nature to be on the sidelines, rooting for other players rather than being in the thick of the game, but this was her only way to be part of the boys' world of sports. This was one of the most critical periods of her life: "I wondered why I wasn't a boy. You know, I just loved sports and I loved to compete. I just thrived on it. And I wanted to play so bad, but I could not do it because I was a girl." Looking back at that time, Sylvia is not bitter: "Well, that's the way it was then." Today it is more than acceptable—even *desirable*—for women to work out and to train and condition their bodies, but in the 1950s and 1960s, most girls shunned the unflattering label "tomboy." In eighth grade, Sylvia beat her boyfriend Mike Ellis in the high-jump contest, and Mr. Whitesides, her teacher and coach, said, "Sylvia, you're not supposed to beat your boyfriend!"

Sylvia completed grade eight at the neighborhood Myrtle School and, in the fall of 1966, entered Hunter Huss High School, a large, new, 4-A school in Gastonia. Hunter Huss fielded football, basketball, baseball, track, golf, and tennis for boys, but it offered girls no opportunities for organized, competitive sports—not softball, not even track. Sylvia was devastated that she would have no opportunity to play sports, though surrounding 1-A, 2-A, and 3-A high schools fielded girls' teams. She had one possibility. In Dallas, where her grandmother Maude Rhyne lived, Dallas High School had a girls' basketball team. Her grandfather Quince Rhyne had died of a stroke on September 14, 1965, and her grandmother lived alone, so it made sense to Sylvia that she should live with her grandmother Maude and attend Dallas High School in order to play basketball. Her parents said, "No." Even though she could easily have traveled the seven miles between Gastonia and Dallas to come home on weekends, they didn't want to break up the family.

Consistent with her positive attitude, Sylvia accepted their decision and made the best of a situation that disfavored girls. Ironically, her high-school physical education teacher, Mrs. Dorothy Baxter, had enjoyed greater opportunities for formal athletic competition than were available to Sylvia. Baxter attended the small North Brook High School in Lincoln County that had only 29 students in her 1946 graduating class, but the school had a girls' basketball team, and Baxter played half-court, three-on-three basketball.[2] In the 20 years between her high-school experience and Sylvia's, opportunities for girls dwindled. Sylvia's generation fell victim to a movement that began in the 1920s and 1930s to bar women from competitive athletics because women were considered unfit for strenuous physical activity. In 1952, the North Carolina State School Board Association enacted the rule that "there shall be no regional or State championship games for girls." In the spring of 1953, the North Carolina General Assembly officially banned a state high-school championship for girls.[3] The 1960s gradually reversed attitudes toward women and competitive athletics, but the change did not come soon enough for Sylvia. Hunter Huss High School added girls' softball in 1974–1975 and girls' basketball in 1975–1976, but by then, Sylvia had earned two college degrees and had landed her first coaching job. The state of North Carolina did not reinstitute a girls' basketball tournament for all divisions (1-A through 4-A) until 1977. According to Sylvia, "That's just the way it was then."

At Hunter Huss, Sylvia's only opportunity for athletic activity was physical education classes, or "PE," as it was called. Junior and senior girls, who had met their PE requirements could work as student assistants, checking the roll, supervising the dressing room, making sure the girls were dressed on time, and leading the 15–20 minutes of calisthenics prior to the day's scheduled activity. They worked without pay or academic credit, mainly to avoid study hall, but Sylvia's motive was different. She loved the activity. Dorothy Baxter remembers Sylvia as a good student and a good athlete whom the students respected and obeyed. Aware of Sylvia's passion for sports, the principal, Mr. Barkley Robbins, gave her permission to go into the gym when it was empty, shoot basketball, practice drills, or snag some willing boy for a contest of H-O-R-S-E. She never turned down a pick-up game.

In the 1950s and 1960s, many southern industries, businesses, and textile mills sponsored baseball leagues for men and softball leagues for women as a way of building community and developing company loyalty. Sylvia's athletic talent came to the attention of these industrial teams in Gastonia. The women's softball teams sometimes practiced or played after the Little League games concluded, so the women saw Sylvia practicing with the boys, keeping their score books, and shagging balls. When she came of age, they recruited her. She played for Firestone Mill for four years and for Hope Plastics even longer, though she never worked for either company. She filled in at any position, wherever they needed her. During these years, she played slow pitch softball with exceptional women athletes, who were role models and leaders, trying to make opportunities for themselves and for the young women who would come after them. Doris Bradshaw, Nancy Holloway, "Sam" Holloway, and Kate Bradley are four whom Sylvia remembers.

Other than these softball players, there were few women athletes with whom Sylvia could identify. She knew about Babe Didrikson Zaharias and was vaguely aware of Chris Evert and Billie Jean King. She was also vaguely aware that there were women competing successfully in the Greenville and Winston-Salem textile softball leagues, but the local press and media did not feature these women prominently, so she turned to men's sports, especially the University of North Carolina (UNC) men's basketball team and coach Dean Smith. The heated rivalry between UNC and Davidson (coached by Lefty Driesell) piqued Sylvia's interest, as did UNC men's basketball guard Larry Miller. The men's basketball games were sometimes broadcast on TV, so she began to watch and learn from Miller's court play and Dean Smith's coaching style.

Despite the disappointment of not being able to play high-school sports, Sylvia's outgoing nature and upbeat attitude prevailed. She "fit in" with her peers. She was required to wear a dress or skirt every day—to church, to school, everywhere except working around the house or playing sports. Skirts and blouses were "in": blue pleated skirts, checked skirts, Oxford blouses, and Madras. "A year or two after I got out of high school they started *letting* girls wear pants to school," says Sylvia, "and I was like, why didn't they do this when I was in school?" She also fit in socially. In her senior year, she played the role of Vera in the class play *The Thread That Runs So True*, which was based on Jesse Stuart's 1950 autobiographical book by the same title.

According to Sylvia, the "macho guys" were perhaps threatened by an athletic girl: "That's the way it was then; you almost had to choose between being popular and being athletic, but I loved sports." Fortunately, *she* did not have to choose. Her winning personality balanced her athletic interests and "tomboy" reputation. She was popular in high school, dating several boys but not getting serious: "I just wanted lots of friends." On one December Friday night, she had two dates with two different young men. First, she went with Billy Mack Hanna to a Presbyterian Youth Group wiener roast and hay ride, held at 5:30 because it was winter and days were short. Billy Mack took her home by 8:30, in time for her next date with Steve Buchanan, a young man from her Unity Baptist Church Youth Group. Steve finished his shift at Sears and picked her up at 9:15 for a Christmas party that didn't start until 9:30 because many of the young people worked at Sears during the holidays. Billy Mack and Steve never knew that she went out with both of them on the same Friday night.

Though Sylvia was popular, she was a traditional "good girl." In summer, she and eight or ten girls, chaperoned by their mothers, went to Myrtle Beach. Some of the girls and their boyfriends went to the Beach Club or the Magic Attic at the Pavilion and danced to the music of Major Lance, Billy Stewart, The Delfonics, Archie Bell and the Drells, and Jerry Butler. Though she loved to dance, Sylvia never went: "I was a late bloomer. I was very conservative." At the beginning of her senior year, she met Charlie Frederick on one of the Myrtle Beach trips. Charlie attended Garinger High School in Charlotte, and Sylvia dated him all that summer and for the next two years. They attended ice hockey, football, and basketball games, as well as the Charlotte Hornets baseball games. Charlie filmed local sports events and was a runner for the sportscaster at WSOC-TV Channel 9 in Charlotte. Sylvia went along and then accompanied him to the studio as he manually edited and spliced the film for the 11:00 p.m. sports news. Computers didn't exist, so she helped him post scores manually on the boards, stood to the side, and watched the sports news, which concluded at 11:30; then Charlie took her home in time for her midnight curfew. "I loved that," says Sylvia. "Most girls would have hated it, but I loved it. A lot of people say they didn't enjoy high school, but I had fun."

Sylvia got her drivers license on the day she turned 16, February 28, 1968, and officially entered the work force that summer. Her first real job was at Tom's Barbeque on Bessemer City Road, which was close enough to her home that she could walk to work. She ran the cash register, served drinks, and bagged orders for $1.00 an hour. Her shift was from 4:00 p.m. to the 11:00 p.m. closing, and then she had to help clean up. During the week of July 4, she worked as much as seventy hours. The next summer, she got a job at DANOCA Industries, which made children's clothes in sizes newborn to 6X for Sears. In her first summer, she was trained to run the commercial sewing machines, and she sewed on bindings; in her second year, she sewed on cuffs. Her regular shift began at 7:00 a.m. and ended at 3:00 p.m., but because she wanted to earn as much money as possible, she also worked on Saturdays from 8:00 a.m. to 1:00 p.m., when workers got paid time-and-a-half. She also noticed that most workers took "smoke breaks." She didn't smoke, so she kept on sewing while the other workers enjoyed their cigarettes. In addition to her minimum wage of $1.40 an hour, Sylvia also earned an additional sum per piece of work that she completed—a system called "production" or "piecework." Workers who achieved high production levels were given better work bundles, such as smaller sizes to sew, which meant that they could complete more pieces within their shift and earn more money.

At DANOCA, Sylvia honed more than her work ethic and got a different sort of education, the kind that a teenager doesn't get in school. For one thing, the work was grueling and dull. She could not imagine spending her life sewing cuffs and bindings on children's clothes. She was also intrigued by some of the older women who had worked at DANOCA for a long time, especially one who wore leather and rode a Harley-Davidson motorcycle. Such women were different from the mothers in her neighborhood and church. The close camaraderie and familiarity among the older workers, male and female, fostered off-color jokes, pranks, and sexual innuendos that were foreign to Sylvia. Though she was intrigued, she was also a little put off by the "shenanigans," as she calls it, and never told her mother about this "educational" feature of her summer job.

Sylvia thought everybody grew up the way she did—in a safe community with a stable home that fostered her unique personality, irrepressible spirit, entrepreneurial bent, athleticism, and strong values. She was wrong. When she became a coach and learned the details of her players' home lives, she realized that her upbringing was anything but the norm, a realization that strengthens her gratitude for a "great childhood" in a West Gastonia neighborhood that exists no more. Today it is a large suburb of Charlotte with a population exceeding 76,000, but in the 1950s and 1960s, it was a small mill town of fewer than 50,000. Robert Ragan's *History of Gastonia and Gaston County, North Carolina* (2010) recounts the growth and demise of the textile industry in Gastonia, called the "City of Spindles," a town divided into two groups: mill owners and management on the one side, and the working class on the other. In describing the Grand Cotton Festival (1939–1941 and 1946), Ragan writes, "The normally hardworking city was transformed as if by magic into the gaiety of festival life each June, and its laboring people forgot the drudgery of factory work, if only for a short while."[4] Seventy percent of the population—the "laboring people"—worked in the textile mills or in related machine shops. Sylvia's family and community numbered among these, not the "prominent" textile executives and their "beautiful" ladies, who were crowned Kings and Queens of the Cotton Festival. No "Grand Festival" or "gaiety" could magically supplant the "drudgery of factory work." On the other hand, they didn't aspire to escape their working-class status. Sylvia's family was not affluent but was enterprising, hardworking, and comfortable. They valued their simple and secure life in a blue-collar community that shaped Sylvia into a competent, hardworking, strong, spiritual woman.

2

Honing Her Skills

After graduating from Hunter Huss High School in 1970, Sylvia was destined for college—there was never any question. College was her parents' goal, and she wanted to please them, so she chose Carson-Newman, the small, private, Baptist institution in Jefferson City, Tennessee, that Phyllis had attended. Carroll did not accompany Sylvia and her mother on the ritual going-off-to-college trip to Jefferson City. Being a "daddy's girl," Sylvia shared many of Carroll's interests and was his close companion, so he wanted her to live at home and attend Gaston College, a two-year school. He even tempted her with the promise of a car if she stayed in Gastonia, but she said, "No, I'm going to Carson-Newman." In the fall of 1970, she and Veda drove to Tennessee alone.

Sylvia moved into Burnett Hall and immediately "clicked" with her roommate, Phyllis Alred (Braddock), from Knoxville. Though Phyllis was an art major, she and Sylvia got along "like two peas in a pod." They came from families with a similar work ethic, values, and religious beliefs. Phyllis was impressed by Sylvia's friendly, genuine manner: "She's like a good pair of house slippers. You could just slip in and be very comfortable." Sylvia never put on airs or tried to be anything but herself. She was competitive, but also a team player, and she had a great sense of humor—always laughing, always fun with her "unique little country expressions." Phyllis was also impressed with Sylvia's love of beach music, which by then had extended to rhapsody and doo-wop and groups such as The Dells, music Phyllis had never heard of. Being a Dallas Cowboys fan, Sylvia plastered their dorm room with posters of quarterback Roger Staubach. Though Phyllis was athletic and followed sports, she did not follow women's basketball. She knew that Sylvia's first love was basketball, but during their three years as roommates, she never attended a single women's game. She preferred to watch the men play. "Back then it was the BOYS' basketball team, the BOYS' baseball team, the BOYS' football teams," she says. "I really don't remember much about the girls' teams."

Sylvia's first basketball coach, Peggy Birmingham, remembers her as "one of the most popular girls on campus." Her friend Gracie Woolwine agrees: "One of the great things about Sylvia was that she was everybody's friend. The guys just went crazy over her, and it wasn't a romantic kind of thing. It was just that she was their buddy." Sylvia was easy and relaxed "but smart as a whip." She always had something going, was always thinking up something to do, such as a cookout at Cherokee Lake. Her lively social circle included dorm mates Bitha Creighton (Wodrich) and Barbara Mitchell

(Moody) who lived on the first floor of Burnett Hall—or First Floor Hell North, as they called it. Life for young women at Carson-Newman was "pretty strict," says Gracie. "I don't think the guys had any [curfews], so they were out running around, but we had to be in the dorm." There was little to do other than go to Cherokee Lake or drive to Morristown or Knoxville for hamburgers. Students at Carson-Newman were not allowed to dance on campus. Gracie says, "You couldn't use the D word," but "folk dances" in Butler-Blanc Gymnasium eventually became acceptable.

Tuition at Carson-Newman was expensive for Sylvia's parents, who—in her words—were "just common workers." She had a National Defense Student Loan and worked all four years as the women's intramural director—for $400 a semester. "I had to do it," she says, "because it cost so much to go to school there." As director, she advertised on campus for intramural teams and organized equipment and schedules for volleyball, basketball, badminton, and softball. She set the pairings for games and intramural tournaments: "I remember going around and putting up flyers in all the dorms. We put up signs in the gyms and on the bulletin boards in all the buildings." Then she arranged for captains and dorm leaders to take charge. Freshmen played sophomores; juniors played seniors. Sororities and dorms competed against each other. It was the perfect job for a "tomboy."

Intramurals kept her busy, but basketball was her passion, and for the first time she played organized, competitive basketball. The Lady Eagles took their motto—To Soar with the Eagles—from Isaiah 40:31 (KJV): "But they that wait upon the Lord shall renew their strength; they shall mount up with wings as eagles; they shall run, and not be weary; and they shall walk, and not faint." It was an apt motto, because they struggled to survive. They had no budget, no scholarships, and no salaried coach. Libby Hudson (Gardner), a PE teacher at Carson-Newman, had coached the women's basketball team before Sylvia arrived, but she opted out of this "extra" assignment that came with no salary. Under Hudson's leadership, the team had built momentum and wanted to continue, so they searched for a coach and found Peggy Birmingham, a graduate of Union University in Jackson, Tennessee, and a graduate assistant (GA) at the University of Tennessee at Knoxville (UT). As part of her assistantship, she drove to Jefferson City every other day to teach three PE activity classes, including tennis and fencing. She agreed to coach the Lady Eagles because she liked basketball and had coached church league teams.

Title IX did not exist in 1970, so schools were not obligated to offer equal opportunities for men and women. While men's sports, particularly football, had expansive budgets and paid staff, Sylvia's basketball team struggled for basic support. They traveled to away games in school vans, but Birmingham says, "We used our own gas money." Occasionally, the college gave each player a meal allotment of fifty cents, which would buy a hamburger, fries, and a drink. The girls sometimes pooled their money for McDonald's or Dairy Queen meals, or sometimes the cafeteria would provide sack lunches, which were included in their meal plans. There was no such thing as a budget for warm-up jerseys. The girls bought their own shoes and socks, and the Student Council gave them money for athletic tape. Wanting to be recognized off the court as the Lady Eagle Women's Basketball Team, the girls bought green fatigues from the Army salvage store in Knoxville and put their initials on the back, right pockets using iron-on letters. Sylvia's teammates teased that her initials, S.R., stood for "south rear." The Lady Eagles had orange and blue uniforms, which they had to wear for both basketball and volleyball, the only other sport available to the Carson-Newman women. Sylvia wore number ten. Gracie Woolwine suggests that "female athletes today don't know how good they have it. They don't know what it's like to put your pennies together and buy a T-shirt and everybody go in the same room and iron your number on so you can play." Gracie recalls that one of Peggy Birmingham's PE classes took up money to buy gas so the women's basketball team could play in a tournament.

According to Birmingham, Sylvia was one of the greenest freshmen she had ever seen—enthusiastic, focused, eager, but green: "She didn't know a thing about basketball, but she wanted to learn. She was very receptive and had so much ENERGY!" Birmingham's team was not allowed in Holt Field House, the "men's gym." Instead, they practiced every afternoon from 3:00 to 5:00 in Butler-Blanc, an old, small gymnasium reserved for the women. Birmingham pushed the girls hard. Traditionally, women had played half-court, three-on-three basketball, and then the game changed to include two "rovers" who could cross the half-court line and run the full court. In 1971–1972, women's collegiate basketball officially made the transition to a full-court game. The Carson-Newman Lady Eagles were playing five-on-five, full-court basketball in 1970–1971, but not all schools had made the change, so sometimes they had to accommodate an opponent who still played three-on-three. (The transition was effected state by state, and Oklahoma was the last state to convert in 1995.)

Coaching Sylvia's college team was difficult. Some of the women had played in high school, but most had not, so Birmingham had to start with the basics, such as dribbling. The girls also had to learn a whole new set of rules for full-court play, which was much more demanding than half-court play, so Birmingham had to focus on conditioning. Being a jogger, she ran with the team at least a mile a day. Finally, having to switch between the two systems created confusion. For example, when playing three-on-three, Sylvia was a rover, and when she got a defensive rebound, she would shoot at the opponent's goal. Birmingham would shout, "Sylvia, that's two points for the other team!" Sylvia had to learn to dribble the ball all the way to the other end of the court—to her team's offensive goal. When she tried to run with the ball, Birmingham would yell, "You got to dribble or pass—you can't just take off and run with it!" When she was closely guarded, she would go into the backcourt, not understanding backcourt violations in full-court basketball. Birmingham would yell, "Backcourt! The ball goes to the other team, now!" For a student as motivated and enthusiastic as Sylvia, this type of coaching was frustrating, but she was a quick learner. Birmingham says, "She never made the same mistake twice, and she rarely made serious mistakes in game play." She was a team player, a good passer, and got many assists, though she was barely 5'6" and had to work hard for every goal, rebound, steal, and block. Always a starter, playing guard and forward, she developed a solid shot from the wing.

Sylvia was the team leader, the "motivator and energizer." She may have been "green," but she was an excellent athlete and a "real hustler," according to Birmingham: "She was the first one in the gym, and the last one out. She hated losing, but she was a good Christian and a good sport on and off the court. She gave 110 percent."

Sylvia's personality was the spark plug. She wanted the team to have a good time, and she "always had something going." For example, she ate onions or garlic before a game to keep opponents from guarding her. She claimed that these stinky foods calmed her nerves and the smell helped her with rebounds because no one would get close to her. Gracie says that it may have been hard on the opponents, but "the rest of us had a hard time, too." Bitha recalls that Sylvia ate onions routinely: "If she wanted a snack, she would get an onion, peel it, salt it, and eat it." Gracie concurs: "I've never seen Sylvia back away from a meal. She likes to eat. I can remember when she would study late at night, she would fix tuna fish and put onions in it. The whole hall would smell."

Always looking for a way to build team spirit, Sylvia discovered that Birmingham's birthday was March 16, so she called Birmingham's mother on the sly and collected childhood photographs. Sylvia and the team converted them to a slide presentation, drove to Knoxville, and surprised Birmingham at her apartment. They brought a slide projector, screen, birthday cake, and a gift: a pair of green Army fatigues with "COACH" written on the back, right pocket in iron-on letters. Says Birmingham, "I wore those forever, and when they wore out I wore them for shorts. We were just so proud of them." Birmingham took pride in being tough. "I believed in discipline and hard work and was not their friend, so I was shocked when they appeared at my apartment."

Under Birmingham's leadership, Sylvia got her first taste of college competition. The Lady Eagles played eight games and ended with a four-four record against teams such as Hiwassee College, the UT Nursing School, and Cleveland State Community College. Of course, UT was their primary rival, being just 25 miles away. On February 9, 1971, in Sylvia's freshman year, her team lost to UT 46–33, and when UT hosted the Tennessee Collegiate Women's Sports Federation's (TCWSF) Eastern District Tournament (February 26, 1971), they beat Carson-Newman 52–37.

Though women's basketball was on the cusp of national recognition and parity with men's programs, not all regions and states had equal opportunities. Sylvia was fortunate that Tennessee had a strong women's basketball tradition, even though its strength was relative compared with men's basketball. Otherwise, her life and career may have taken a different path. Nashville was home to Nashville Business College which dominated Amateur Athletic Union (AAU) championship play throughout the 1960s. In 1968, Betty Wiseman had founded a women's basketball program at Belmont College in Nashville, which was one of the first women's programs in the entire southeast region. Between 1973 and 1977, Wiseman coached the Belmont women to four consecutive appearances in the National Women's Invitational Tournament. Says Birmingham, "It was a different time. There were no governing conferences, and women's college teams played business teams. We didn't care whether our opponents were big or little, junior college or private college, or a major university such as UT. We were just glad that we had an opportunity to play."

Sylvia admits to "just having a good time" during her first semester: "I was just 'in college.' My grades were shaky, mostly C's. Phyllis had gone to school there—my parents wanted me to go to college—all that stuff." At Christmas she went home thinking, *I'll go back and finish this year out because my parents expect me to, but I'm not sure if this college thing is what I want to do.* When basketball season kicked into high gear after Christmas, her attitude changed. She learned that some of the seniors on the basketball team (Gracie Woolwine and Mary Edna Glover) were going to UT as GAs the next year—as Peggy Birmingham had. She began to see Birmingham not just as her coach but as a mentor and to see possibilities for her own future. Sylvia thought, *I can do this, too. This is what I want to do. I want to go to the University of Tennessee and be a GA.* During her second semester, she became motivated and focused, and for the rest of her career at Carson-Newman, she excelled, making the Dean's List and graduating with honors. Says Sylvia, "Peggy was such a tremendous influence, simply because I could see what somebody else was doing. I told my freshmen players, if you don't have goals, if you don't have a target, you don't have anything to aim for. Peggy was it for me."

At the end of the 1970–1971 academic year, Birmingham finished her master's degree at UT. She hoped to become a full-time professor and women's basketball coach at Carson-Newman. Everyone had expected the PE department to expand the next year, with new opportunities for women, but the college experienced financial shortfalls, and faculty positions were cut. The college had a winning football team, so all the football coaches were retained, but two of the women's positions were eliminated. Disappointed, Birmingham took a job with Southwest Baptist College in Bolivar, Missouri, coaching women's basketball and tennis.

On November 4, 1971, Sylvia lost her beloved grandfather Vannie, who died of a cerebral hemorrhage. Sylvia had also lost her only mentor, Peggy Birmingham, and the Lady Eagles were without a coach for the second time in two years, so they searched for yet another volunteer. They found Mike Snodderly, who was interested from the start. Snodderly knew basketball. He grew up in Spray, North Carolina, and attended Morehead High School in Leaksville, where he played basketball on the 1965–1966 undefeated North Carolina state championship team. Snodderly had a half scholarship to assist Coach Gene Mehaffey with the men's basketball program, but he had never even coached men before, much less women: "I understood men a whole lot better than I did women."

Snodderly agrees that Sylvia and most of her teammates "had never had serious coaching," but Linda Gay Blanc and her sister Nancy were exceptions, having played in high school. Several girls had potential, despite their different levels of preparation, so he emphasized conditioning: "I'm going to run you so hard that when we're coming down the stretch in the second half, you're going to have more energy than the other team." One or two girls quit before Snodderly had the chance to develop "even a semblance of a team," but Sylvia never complained. Snodderly recruited male Carson-Newman students who had played high-school basketball to scrimmage against the women's team. "They absolutely wore the girls out because the girls didn't know anything about running fast breaks." (The tradition of women's teams scrimmaging against men is today regulated by the NCAA.) "It was almost like coaching a high-school girls' team," says Snodderly, "so I had to have a different mindset from the approach I would have taken with a men's team." Most of the girls were serious about the game, and "Sylvia was *so* into listening to whatever I said—especially when it had to do with strategy." In Snodderly's opinion, "Sylvia was a better defensive than offensive player because she absolutely did not mind getting into somebody's face! She had one of the most aggressive attitudes." Sylvia was "all arms and legs. More importantly, she would *move* her arms and legs, which you have to do to play good defense."

The women continued to play in the old-fashioned Butler-Blanc Gymnasium, which had a walking track or balcony around the upper perimeter, and the basketball court wasn't even regulation-size but "two-thirds to three-fourths of the length of a regular basketball court." Snodderly jokes that the balcony made defense easy: "You didn't have to guard anybody in the corner because the walking track would block the shot for you." Occasionally the women's basketball team was allowed in Holt Field House where they could play on a regulation-size court. On those occasions, "they were somewhat intimidated," says Snodderly, by its size and, what seemed to them, its state-of-the-art furnishings. For example, the backboards in Holt Gymnasium were glass; in Butler-Blanc, they were wooden—and old.

Sylvia was an exceptional student of the game: "Once she understood what needed to be done, nothing could stop her." Snodderly observes that "some players had more athletic ability than Sylvia, but she was goal oriented and would try to accomplish what I asked her to do. She knew that if she followed instructions, good things would happen for our team." Sylvia was never afraid to ask questions, even at the risk of frustrating him, after he had explained something two or three times: "Sylvia was one of the few that would just keep asking until *she understood*." Her intensity in practice was remarkable: "She was not afraid to sweat, and she had no fear of work—no fear of work at all."

Though Birmingham and Snodderly describe Sylvia's Carson-Newman team as inexperienced, untaught, and lacking the fundamentals, most other area college teams were little better, so the Lady Eagles continued to compete fairly well against Knoxville College, Milligan College, Lincoln Memorial University, and Tusculum College. Under Snodderly's coaching, Sylvia's team faced Hutson's UT Knoxville team twice in the 1971–1972 regular season and lost both games: 51–45 and 71–41. In the Tennessee College Women's Sports Federation (TCWSF) Eastern District Championships, Carson-Newman lost a third time to Hutson's UT team 45–39. In Sylvia's junior year, Margaret Hutson's UT team again beat the Carson-Newman women (56–50) in the TCWSF Eastern District Tournament and went on to win the title. Says Snodderly, "We were competitive against those schools. They had much better athletes and more depth than we did, but my girls were well-disciplined."

Snodderly recalls a game at Milligan College, which is 82 miles east of Carson-Newman, near Johnson City, Tennessee. He did not think that his Lady Eagles could beat Milligan, because they had barely practiced as a team, but they did. After the game, one of the players ran out of the locker room and said, "Hey! They've got an indoor swimming pool." Every girl "took off running," says Snodderly. They locked the doors so that no one else could get in, and every girl jumped into the pool—uniforms and all. They came out soaking wet with their hair dripping. They had no clothes to change into—no warm-up jerseys—so they loaded back into the vans for the return trip to Jefferson City, wet but happy.

Sylvia was the team lynchpin—the one whom the other players trusted, the "go to" person who handled conflicts, says Snodderly: "When Sylvia came to me, I knew something was up, and Sylvia was the spokesperson." Snodderly recalls one instance that highlighted how little he knew about women. One of his starters was slacking off, and Snodderly yelled at her. During the water break, Sylvia approached him and said, "Coach, you shouldn't be so hard on that girl." Snodderly asked, "Why not? Her mind is not in the game, and you, of all people, Sylvia, know that is one thing that burns me up." Sylvia said, "She's sick, Coach." Snodderly came back with "Well if she's sick, tell her to go to her dorm. Is she running a fever?" Sylvia answered, "No." Snodderly's irritation began to show: "'Sylvia, you're not making sense.' She got this exasperated look on her face and got real quiet, and just as she said, 'Coach, she's having her period,' it hit me—hard. But the thing was, it was Sylvia whom the other players sent to talk to me—not the girl, not her best friend, but Sylvia." Snodderly's experience with men's teams had not prepared him for this.

Snodderly coached the Lady Eagles for two years and graduated at the end of Sylvia's junior year. On the day of the All-Sports Banquet, which honored the men's football, baseball, and basketball teams, Sylvia went to him and said, "Coach, we need you to be at the banquet tonight." Snodderly had no reason to attend because he played no sport. Sylvia insisted: "No, you got to show up, Coach. Show up, Coach." He donned a sport coat and tie, went to the banquet, and sat with the women's basketball team during dinner. He was shocked when he heard Coach Mehaffey say, "And now, I'm going to recognize Sylvia Rhyne and Bitha Creighton, representing women's basketball." Snodderly panicked. He had not bought trophies for the team, not even a most-valuable-player trophy, because women's basketball was not a varsity sport and, as far as he knew, would not be acknowledged at the banquet. The girls earned "Eagle Club points" and could achieve "letters," but they could not be recognized at the All-Sports Banquet. Snodderly was stunned to learn that *he* was being honored, not the girls. Sylvia presented him with a plaque of appreciation because his efforts had meant so much to the team, and they wanted him to be recognized at the banquet. Says Snodderly, "It blew me away. I was embarrassed—humbled—I didn't know how to respond. They paid for the plaque out of their own money—it sure didn't come out of the school's money like it did for all the men's trophies." Sylvia was the "ring leader" in this gesture of appreciation. Snodderly believes that "even back then, when she was just learning the game, she had her priorities right, and her humanity shone through. That touched me more than you could ever know." Looking back, Snodderly realizes that Sylvia has used everything she learned from her Carson-Newman coaches. "She was a sponge, making sure she understood the game so she could explain it to her players somewhere down the road."

During her first two years at Carson-Newman, Sylvia was a happy "gym rat" enjoying competitive basketball for the first time and loving college life, but she did not have a car and sometimes regretted turning down her father's offer to buy her one if she would attend Gaston College. To get home from Carson-Newman, she had to hitch a ride with a fellow student who was driving to North Carolina. At the end of her sophomore year, she came home for the summer and said to her father, "I'm not going back to school without a car. I'll work all summer; I'll save every penny. But I want you to help me get a car." Sylvia had earned her Water Safety Instructor certification at Carson-Newman, so she worked as head lifeguard at the Wesley Acres Swimming and Racquet Club for $75 a week. She kept just enough for gasoline and hamburgers and saved the rest. At the end of the summer, she had $750, the equivalent of $4,629 in 2020.

As the fall semester neared, she and her father searched for a car. She tried out a Nash Rambler and a mint green Mercury Comet with a push-button gear shift. It needed new tires and a thorough going-over, but it was the best deal for the money. Carroll told her to go back to college, and he would have the car ready for her next time she came home. On her next visit, she expected to see the car sitting in the driveway, but it was not there. She rushed into the house and asked, "Mama, where is my car?" Veda said, "Well, your daddy has your car, but he's not here right now." Soon after, he showed up in a light blue Volkswagen. Sylvia asked, "Daddy, where is my car." And he said, "Here it is!" She couldn't believe it. She was expecting a Comet. Instead, she got a Volkswagen, the most popular car in America with college students. The icing on the cake was its Carolina blue paint—Sylvia's favorite color and the Hunter Huss High School colors, too. The car had spoke wheels and a wood-grain steering wheel. It was lovely. It cost more than the $750 Sylvia had saved, but her father paid the balance.

Having a car improved Sylvia's junior and senior years at Carson-Newman, especially when her schedule became complicated by academic obligations, such as student teaching, and her first coaching job. Talbott Elementary, a small, rural school in Jefferson County, needed a coach for sixth-, seventh-, and eighth-grade girls. Talbott was a tobacco community, seven miles outside Jefferson City but close enough to the college that Sylvia could easily commute. She was set. She was a coach with a salary of $200. Mr. Thomas (Tommy) Northern, the principal, recalls that Sylvia "got into it. She did a good job." After practice with the Lady Eagles, she drove to Talbott in her Carolina blue Volkswagen to work with the middle-school girls. She was hooked. "I remember her bringing that little VW bug up to Talbott from Jefferson City," recalls Mr. Northern. "We knew she had ability. The girls liked her a lot and she had good success. We felt fortunate to have her." Under her leadership, the team blossomed, and Sylvia's love for basketball and coaching blossomed as well: "The Talbott team was good," she says. "We had a blast." Talbott Elementary was not part of a conference but played other schools in Jefferson County. Their record for the year was 16–4, and three of the girls made All-County.

When Snodderly left Carson-Newman at the end of Sylvia's junior year, the women's basketball team was again without a coach. Sharron Perkins (Bilbrey), a graduate of Emory & Henry College in Emory, Virginia, replaced Snodderly as the third women's basketball coach in four years. Like Peggy Birmingham, Perkins was a GA at UT and commuted to Carson-Newman to teach PE activity classes. When she took on Sylvia's Carson-Newman team, she had only two years' experience under the new system. She relied on John Wooden's *Practical Modern Basketball*, published in 1966, and she looked to her father, a Tennessee basketball official, who taught her the wheel offense. Perkins remembers Sylvia as "wide-open—just as wide open as she could be. Always full-force. Lots of energy, lots of drive, lots of fun to be around."

It is not surprising that in the four years Sylvia played basketball at Carson-Newman, her team had three volunteer coaches. And given that the team had no financial support, their intercollegiate competitive play is a testament to the players'

1974 Carson-Newman Women's Basketball Team. Left to right: Vicki McGaughey, Linda Gay Blanc, Vicki Brumley, Sally Miles, Sandra Ramsey, Hazel Wilkey, Sylvia Rhyne (No. 10), Ann Kyle, Sherry Bell, Donna Newry, Coach Sharron Perkins. Courtesy Carson-Newman Sports.

and coaches' passion for sport. Sylvia's Carson-Newman team never competed on a national level, but each year they vied with nearby sister institutions, large and small, for the opportunity to win the TCWSF Tournament. Add to this achievement Sylvia's success with the Talbott middle-school team. She finally had a taste of competitive women's basketball.

Sylvia's time at Carson-Newman exceeded her expectations for college life. Except for her freshman year, when her grades were "barely passing," she was a good student who took school seriously, had good study habits, and never struggled academically. She was also thrifty, and few of her peers had ready cash, so they looked for ways to make a little spending money. She, Phyllis, Bitha, and a group of their friends frequently drove to Knoxville and sold their blood to the Blood Bank for $10 cash per pint, which would be worth about $60 today. With this spending money, they could buy a pair of jeans at The Bottom Half on Cumberland Avenue for $5.00. On one occasion, Sylvia bought a pair of hip-hugger, bell bottoms that were white, red, green, and blue striped. With the remainder of their $10, they ate at Zippy D's, the only hamburger joint in Jefferson City. Sylvia liked to pile the onions on her hamburger, without consideration for her friends or her date.

Sylvia had an active social life and dated several boys in college, both at home and at Carson-Newman. She continued to date Charlie Frederick, who drove to Jefferson City to visit a couple of times during her freshman year, and she saw him during Christmas breaks, when she still accompanied him to sports events for WSOC-TV in Charlotte. When she returned to Gastonia for holidays and vacations, she always had a job and met new people through work. She met Charlie Morrow, who attended Ashley High School, and except for his smoking habit, Sylvia enjoyed his company: "We had a great time—I just really had a good time going out with him because he was a lot of fun."

In her sophomore year, Sylvia got to know Bob Strunk, one of the men who later scrimmaged with the women's team. He shared her love of basketball and spent as much time in the gym as she did, so they began to date steadily the next year. Bob was the only child of parents who lived in Somerset, Kentucky, and his grandfather was a minister, so his values meshed with Sylvia's. Peggy Birmingham describes Bob as "a tall, good-looking boy with a big car; he and Sylvia loved to go to Cherokee Lake and take everybody on picnics." During summer vacations they went their separate ways and dated other people. Sylvia came home to Gastonia and her usual summer job at Wesley Acres Swimming and Racquet Club, eventually becoming the manager. Meanwhile, Bob was a counselor and, eventually, the assistant director at Ridgecrest Boys Camp near Black Mountain, North Carolina. When Bob had a free day, he drove to Gastonia to see her. Their relationship grew, so they decided that during their junior-year spring break (1973), they would drive to DeLand, Florida, to visit Bob's maternal grandparents and to meet other Carson-Newman spring-breakers at Daytona Beach. Veda disapproved. Sylvia argued her case: "Mama, there is nothing wrong with this. There are other people riding with us, and we're going to stay with his grandparents. His grandfather is a retired minister, for goodness' sake!" Veda was not persuaded. "She didn't tell me I couldn't go," says Sylvia. "She just said she didn't think that I should. It was the only time I ever did something she did not want me to do."

Sylvia, Bob, and two other students left Carson-Newman in Bob's father's Cadillac, and all was well until they reached Unadilla, Georgia, on I-75, about 45 miles south of Macon. There the car broke down. Bob called his father in Somerset, Kentucky, who sent a mechanic to diagnose the problem: a cracked motor block. The car could not be driven, so the four college students boarded a Trailways bus. The driver stopped in Ocala, Florida, for fifteen-minutes, just enough time for Sylvia and Bob run to a nearby hamburger "joint," but when they came outside, burgers in hand, they saw that the bus was gone: "Everything we had was on that bus. Bob had some money in his pocket, but he didn't have a lot." They had to hire a taxi to chase the bus 27 miles to its next stop. Sylvia recalls that "it cost a lot of money, and Bob had to pay." Back on the bus, Sylvia kept thinking, *My mama told me not to do this*. Eventually, they made it to DeLand and Bob's grandparents lent them their car. They drove to Daytona Beach for two days and spent a day in Orlando. Bob's father, on the other hand, had to drive to Unadilla and tow the Cadillac back to Kentucky. Sylvia and Bob had to hitch a ride back to Carson-Newman with some of their spring-break friends. When she was back on campus, Sylvia thought, *Lord, I will never, ever again do anything my mama tells me not to do.* "I thought she had put a curse on me. And I never told her about it. I never told her what all happened."

Peggy Birmingham says that Bob Strunk treated Sylvia "like a queen." For example, he took her to the World Series in 1972. Bob had been a batboy for the Red Sox minor league spring training camp (March 1965), in DeLand, Florida. At that time, Dick Williams was a minor-league manager, and he and Bob must have developed a friendship because seven years later, when Williams was managing the Oakland A's, Sylvia and Bob were his guests for the Cincinnati games in the 1972 World Series—a heady experience for Sylvia, especially because Williams led Oakland to defeat the Cincinnati Reds and win the Series.

Sylvia thrived on sports and competition at all levels. A November 10, 1972, article about intramurals in the Carson-Newman student paper, *The Orange & Blue*, shows that she distinguished herself in football. In a match between two sororities, the Callies and the Hyps, Sylvia "made herself a legend to exist forever in the Callie-Hyp history books." The article misspells Sylvia's last name as "Rhine" and makes a pun with "rhino": "Miss Rhine, referred to hereafter as Rhino was present all over the field running around girls, over girls, and frequently right through them in claiming interceptions, tackles or touchdowns, in what may be described as one of the greatest 'one-woman' shows in the history of WFL (Women's Football League)."

Sylvia's final semester at Carson-Newman was busy. In addition to playing basketball and coaching, she was completing the student-teaching requirement at the Tennessee School for the Deaf in Knoxville. Sylvia and three other classmates carpooled to Knoxville every day in her Volkswagen, leaving Jefferson City at 7:00 a.m. and returning in time for her to practice basketball and coach the Talbott team. The student teachers observed the regular teachers and learned sign language without formal instruction: "I just learned," says Sylvia, but they communicated at the most basic level. She worked with children of all ages but mostly high-school grades, teaching rhythm, folk dancing, and gymnastics. Sylvia "took to it" enthusiastically: "It was one of the best experiences of my life."

At Christmas in her senior year, Bob visited her in Gastonia, proposed marriage, and gave her a diamond ring. Sylvia accepted. "It was the thing to do," she says. Her sister Phyllis was married, her roommate Phyllis Alred had married, and everybody else was getting engaged. She and Bob didn't set a wedding date because he still had to complete his senior year at Carson-Newman. Oddly, Sylvia and her college friends recall little about her engagement. Perhaps their intuition led them to proceed with caution. When Phyllis Alred got married, Sylvia roomed with Maureen Walling during her senior year. Maureen would be involved many years later in Sylvia's continued relationship with Strunk.

Sylvia graduated *cum laude* from Carson-Newman on May 10, 1974, with a Bachelor of Science in Physical Education, Health, and Recreation. Uncertain of her future, she came home to Gastonia for the summer. Her goal was to attend graduate school at UT, a dream she attributes to Peggy Birmingham. There was one glitch: She could afford to attend UT only if she was awarded a GA, which would pay in-state and out-of-state tuition along with a monthly stipend. She was accepted to graduate school at UT but was not offered an assistantship right away, so she continued her usual summer routine, which included playing softball for Hope Plastics. An August 17, 1974, issue of the *Gastonia Gazette* reports that Sylvia led the hitting—"three singles in four trips"—in the first round of the State Class C Women's Slow-Pitch Softball Tournament to beat Shuford Mills (in Shelby) 9–5.[1]

Sylvia also applied for teaching positions and was called for an interview with Mr. Robert Falls, Assistant Superintendent for Personnel in Gaston County Schools. On the day of the interview, she was backing her Volkswagen out of the driveway when the mail carrier, Gene Fox, pulled up to the Rhyne mailbox and blocked her in. She stopped and walked back to visit and take the mail. As she stood there, chatting and flipping through envelopes, she spied a letter addressed to her from the University of Tennessee. She tore it open and read the first line: "The Department of Physical Education at the University of Tennessee would like to offer you a graduate assistantship." Standing there in the driveway, she shouted, "Yes! Yes! Thank you, Lord!" She ran inside, called the school board office, and told Mr. Falls' secretary, "I won't be coming in for my interview because I'm going to graduate school at the University of Tennessee!"

In the fall of 1974, Sylvia entered a whole new world. With a population of 175,000, Knoxville was much larger than Gastonia, and UT enrolled 29,000 students, in contrast to Carson-Newman's 1,676. Another change was that Sylvia lived in Sutherland Apartments, not a dorm, located a couple of miles from campus, but she still had two roommates from Carson-Newman: Peggy Hudson, a PE major, and Leslie Spears, a library science major. Sylvia adjusted quickly, settled in with other students and faculty, and made friends. On the first day of classes at UT, Sylvia met Pat Head (Summitt) and Judy Wilkins (Rose). Pat Head was a native of Tennessee, a graduate of the University of Tennessee at Martin, and would become the winningest coach in men's and women's basketball history. Judy Wilkins was from Blacksburg, South Carolina, a graduate of Winthrop College in Rock Hill, and would serve as Director of Intercollegiate Athletics at UNC Charlotte for 28 years. But in 1974, they were young women learning to make their way in graduate school, unaware that their lives would be forever bound together.

At UT, Sylvia was a PE major, specializing in elementary-school fitness. Her assistantship had a work requirement of 20 hours a week, so she was assigned to the Knoxville City Schools, under the supervision of David Huntsinger. In the mornings, she went to class. In the afternoons she worked in the public schools because Knoxville City Schools didn't have full-time elementary PE teachers. In addition to her work assignment, Sylvia found other opportunities for athletic activity. Pat Head was training to strengthen her knee after a recent surgery so she could compete in the 1975 Pan-American Games, and Sylvia often accompanied her during these training sessions. As a GA, Pat was asked to coach the women's basketball team because Margaret Hutson had taken a leave of absence. Sixty girls wanted to play basketball—too many—so Pat asked Dr. Nancy Lay, Coordinator of UT Women's Intercollegiate Athletics, if they could have a junior varsity (JV) team. Dr. Lay gave permission, and Pat tapped Sylvia to coach the JV team. Judy would help Pat with the varsity team, and Sylvia would assist. Because she wanted to learn everything about basketball, Sylvia attended every varsity practice with Pat and Judy. Her JV team had no budget and wore the varsity team's old uniforms, but they ended the year with eight wins and two losses.

Regardless of their win-loss records, these women were pioneers in women's basketball, and they seized upon any opportunity for competition. Some colleges and universities labeled women's athletic teams "extramural"; some called them clubs. Even at UT, there were no scholarships, no lettering, no recognition, and no budget. Many coaches paid expenses out of their own pockets. Sylvia knew she was lucky to be associated with Pat Head, and her graduate-school experience at the University of Tennessee was one of the happiest times of her life. She was completely on her own, earning money, earning a master's degree, and coaching basketball. Pat, Judy, and Sylvia had different backgrounds, but the three became good friends, on and off the court. For example, Judy taught Sylvia the Shag: "Judy was a Winthrop girl," says Sylvia, "and all the Winthrop girls knew how to Shag."

At Carson-Newman, Sylvia had learned how to study and earn good grades, and these skills served her well at UT because their coursework was serious, and they had good teachers, such as Dr. Lay, who became their academic mentor. Sylvia, Pat, Judy, Susan Phillips, and Debbie Rollins studied together in the Hoskins Library on Cumberland Avenue every night from 6:30 or 7:00 to 9:00, when Sylvia or Pat would look at her watch and say, "It's time." They all knew what that meant: It was time for Krispy Kreme Doughnuts, "Hot. Now." They closed their books and drove to Krispy Kreme at 2626 Magnolia Avenue for hot doughnuts, fresh out of the fryer, and they didn't eat one or two. They ate six apiece.

In addition to their coursework, they were determined to learn as much as possible about women's basketball. On March 19–21, 1975, for example, Sylvia and Pat attended the Association for Intercollegiate Athletics for Women (AIAW) Tournament at James Madison University in Harrisonburg, Virginia. Sixteen teams competed for the title, with Delta State, Immaculata, Cal State-Fullerton, and Southern Connecticut State making up the semi-final round. Delta State beat Immaculata (90–81) to win the championship. This tournament gave Sylvia her first taste of women's basketball competition at the national level.

Sylvia was in her element in graduate school, but there was one snag: her relationship with Bob Strunk. While she was in her first year at UT, Bob was a senior at Carson-Newman, finishing his undergraduate degree. He visited Sylvia a couple of times a week and was well liked among her friends, but in the fall of 1974, he was assigned to Rush Strong School, in Strawberry Plains, Tennessee, to complete his student-teaching requirement. There he met a girl whom he wanted to date, so he and Sylvia broke their engagement, and she returned his diamond ring. Sylvia was not as broken-hearted as one might expect, particularly because Strunk could be clinging, and she craved independence. But Strunk's infatuation with the other girl faded, and he was not ready to give up on Sylvia, so one night he appeared at her door with a recording of the Jim Croce song "Time in a Bottle." He wanted to marry her. Against her better judgment, she agreed that they would "get back together." Today, she doesn't remember whether she agreed to wear the diamond ring—again—and doesn't remember whether they were officially engaged when she completed a master's degree at the University of Tennessee. Her focus was elsewhere.

Sylvia was scheduled to graduate in August 1975, so during the summer she began to look for a job. As early as May or June, Pat Head was already set on her career path. Margaret Hutson had decided to pursue a doctoral degree at Ole Miss and would not return as the UT women's basketball coach. Hutson unknowingly created one of basketball's greatest dynasties: The University of Tennessee at Knoxville offered the position to Pat Head. In her first year as the official head coach (1975–1976), the Lady Vols competed in the first Tennessee State Tournament, held in Jackson, Tennessee, at Union and Lambuth colleges, and they ended the season with a 16–11 record. As the saying goes, "The rest is history." It would be more than 30 years before the UT women's team would again lose 11 games in a season—2008–2009.

While Pat was preparing for her first season as the UT head coach, Sylvia learned that Roane State Community College had an opening for a women's basketball coach. Pat recommended her: "You get that job," said Pat, "and we'll get an apartment together." Sylvia was granted an interview that went so well she was called in for a second meeting with the athletic director. Though she had not signed a contract, she felt confident about the job and did not search further. Roane State was located 42 miles west of Knoxville, so she and Pat looked for an apartment within easy driving distance of both campuses—Pat going east; Sylvia going west. Then Sylvia got disappointing news: Roane State would hire a man as the women's basketball coach—Andy Landers. He was Sylvia's age and was just finishing a degree at Tennessee Tech in Cookeville. In his four years at Roane State, Landers led the women's basketball team to an 82–21 record. In 1979, he moved to the University of Georgia, where in 36 seasons he coached the women's basketball team to 862 wins and 299 losses.

Sylvia earned her Master of Science in Physical Education from the University of Tennessee Knoxville on August 23, 1975, an accomplishment that the *Gastonia Gazette* reported a month later. She did not attend the graduation; she was too busy trying to find a job. Bob Strunk had entered graduate school at Eastern Kentucky University, so he urged her to find a job nearby. She explored a number of opportunities and found a position as recreation director for a special needs facility, but she knew it was not the right fit. She wanted a coaching position. It was late-August; the lease on her apartment was running out; she was unemployed; and she did *not* want to move back home.

In the UT physical education office there was a clipboard where job openings were posted. Sylvia checked it almost every day though Bob kept pressuring her to take the job in Kentucky. At the last minute, the clipboard posted an opening for the head women's basketball coach at Francis Marion College in Florence, South Carolina. With barely two weeks before the beginning of the fall 1975 semester, Sylvia interviewed with Athletic Director Gerald Griffin who also coached baseball. He and Sylvia toured campus in his green car: "I think it was a Plymouth. Oh, my gosh! That thing was so old and beat up and just junky.... I thought, *Man! I can't believe he is putting me in this car.*" Griffin then escorted her to the interview with Dr. Walter D. Smith, the founding president of Francis Marion, but she left campus without an offer. Two days later, he offered her the job. She had no place to live, so Becky Short (whose parents were good friends with Veda and Carroll) let Sylvia sleep on her sofa. Later, Tom Davidson, the Francis Marion assistant baseball coach, helped her find an apartment in neighboring Quinby at 126 Dogwood Lane, an address that would be significant during her Francis Marion tenure. Her father moved her belongings from Gastonia to Quinby in his truck, which broke down in Camden, further complicating this major life transition. Sylvia was still driving her Carolina blue Volkswagen.

3

Becoming a Coach

Originally an extension campus of the University of South Carolina (USC-Florence), Francis Marion was created in 1970 and gained university status in 1992. In 1973 the school organized a women's basketball team, which competed in Division II of the Association of Intercollegiate Athletics for Women (AIAW). The women's team played its first official game on January 4, 1974, under coach Gayle Baker, whose one-year record was 16–4. Sherril York coached the Lady Patriots in 1974–75 and ended the season 11–11. Then it was Sylvia's turn.

Sylvia immediately "took to" her job. In her first year, she not only coached women's basketball but also taught outdoor recreation, tennis, and folk dance. She was the cheerleading sponsor and directed women's intramurals. Fran Ellis reported in the *Florence Morning News* that Sylvia created six Flag Football teams for women—a "first" for Francis Marion.[1] Though she had a full schedule, she continued to work off campus during summer terms because her salary was so low—$9,200 annually for a nine-month contract. In the summer of 1976, she returned to Gastonia to run the Wesley Acres Swimming and Racquet Club and attended the National Aquatic School at Camp Rockmont, North Carolina, to earn her Water Safety Instructor Trainer certificate (WSIT). Her instructor was the remarkable and nationally-known Ruth Rogers Magher, who died on February 4, 2013, at age 94. Magher described Sylvia as an excellent teacher and swimmer: "She could swim on her back and talk at the same time!" So in her second year at Francis Marion, she added WSIT instructor to her list of duties.

Sylvia liked Francis Marion. For one thing, everything was new, from the buildings to the academic and sports programs. Unlike older colleges, such as Carson-Newman and the University of Tennessee, the college did not have a long history of men's programs, so women's programs were created on a par with men's. "What the men had, the women had," says Sylvia. Because of the new facilities, the quality players, and the budgets, the women's basketball program fared much better than programs at schools where the women were struggling to catch up. Francis Marion athletic facilities and the gym were excellent, but there were no dormitories, which made recruiting difficult, so she recruited heavily from the local high schools because these players could live at home and commute. Others lived at Patriot Place, a private apartment complex across from the school, or in trailer parks, which were plentiful in Florence. Sylvia told Bob Gillespie with *The State* that she "wore out four cars" driving South Carolina roads, searching for talent.

Sylvia did not have a "cushy," well-paid job. She washed the uniforms, drove the bus, and swept the floor. "If it got done," she says, "I did it." In a 1979 interview with the *Greensboro Daily News*, Sylvia said that except for the few, limited scholarships, her annual budget for Francis Marion women's basketball was $4,000. When she started a basketball camp in 1980, she designed the logo for the T-shirts, made her own silk screen, and printed the shirts on her dining room table. Francis Marion refused to allow her to hold the camps on campus, so for three years she ran week-long, off-campus, day camps for as many as 125 girls. She rented the Southside Middle School gymnasium for two years and the adjacent South Florence High School for one year, and she hired local high-school coaches at $100 a week. Finally, in 1983, Francis Marion allowed Sylvia to hold residential basketball camps on campus.

In 1975, Sylvia met Coach Kay Yow, NC State head women's basketball coach, at a coaching clinic at Peace College in Raleigh. Immediately recognizing a sister spirit in Yow and being moved by her inspirational and motivational message, Sylvia introduced herself after Yow's speech. She learned that Yow's NC State team had a contract with Pro Keds, so Sylvia later called her to ask how she could make a similar arrangement or at least get shoe discounts for her players. Yow returned her call the next week, asking for the Lady Patriots' shoe sizes. Then came an unexpected gift: Francis Marion's team colors were red, white, and blue, and NC State colors were red and white, so Yow shipped Sylvia enough red and white sneakers to outfit her entire team, using part of her contract allotment. A strong friendship was thus begun between two women who understood the struggle for equality in women's sports. In 2009, Sylvia told Tim Crothers, "We were both little girls dreaming big dreams, ... but even our dreams were never as big as what actually happened."

The only glitch in Sylvia's professional and personal life was Bob Strunk. During her first year at Francis Marion, they continued to see each other steadily. Once a month, she flew to Lexington, Kentucky, where he was in graduate school, and once a month he came to Florence. In 1976, Bob finished a master's degree in recreation at Eastern Kentucky University and took a teaching job at Pamplico High School in Pamplico, South Carolina, so he could be near Sylvia.

At the same time, Sylvia found a rental house, with an option to buy, at 202 Magnolia Drive, very near her Dogwood Lane apartment. Still responsible for the lease, she sublet the apartment to Bob Strunk and moved into the house. She soon discovered that having Bob "just around the corner" was not ideal; she felt smothered by his possessiveness. During the year he was at Eastern Kentucky, Sylvia had enjoyed a great deal of freedom, and though they had seen each other twice a month, Bob arrived in Florence as an outsider. He wanted her to spend every minute with him, and she felt crowded—stifled: "I couldn't do this and this and this, and I couldn't do that." They fought and argued for the whole next year. She remembers a night in May, the spring of 1977, when a good friend, Larry Bartol, took her to dinner. Bartol was a New York Life Insurance agent, so they had dinner and talked about insurance policies. When they returned to campus, Bob was waiting at Sylvia's car and confronted Larry. She was furious: "Whoa, whoa, whoa, whoa! We've been talking insurance! This is a friend of mine, and you're not going to cramp my style like this!" Bob was preparing for Ridgecrest, where he would spend the summer as the assistant director, so she told him, "This is just *not* going to work. This is not what I want." Sylvia uses the old cliché, "I loved him, but I wasn't *in love* with him." She knew she would never marry him and felt it was unfair not to be honest. Bob suggested, "Let's just take some time off for the summer."

Bob left for Ridgecrest, and Sylvia "was just so relieved." That summer, she worked at a number of basketball camps, including two with Pat Head. Sylvia maintained her relationship with Head's summer basketball camps even into the 1980s: "If I was doing USA basketball or whatever, I would fly in to Knoxville for a day or two. I didn't miss any of her camps." Sometimes she taught clinics on the fast break, footwork, defense, or ball handling; other times, she supervised a camp league. In addition to Pat's basketball camps, she worked at Campbell College and Belmont Abbey in North Carolina; at Carson-Newman, her *alma mater* in Tennessee; and at Billie Moore's UCLA camp at San Jose State. Sylvia "was really into basketball!"

The night she and Larry Bartol had dinner and talked about insurance, he had asked her whether she and Bob Strunk were "still together." She said, "Yeah, we are, but I don't know how much longer it's going to last." Larry told her that if she and Bob broke up, he would like for her to meet a friend of his who played basketball in the same summer league, someone she might "have a whole lot in common with." When she and Bob parted company for the summer, she let Larry know that she was ready to date other people. A few months earlier, Larry had introduced her to Sammy Hatchell in Shoney's Restaurant. Sylvia merely said "Hello" and kept on going, never giving Sammy a second thought, but he remembers the incident as a slight: "When he introduced me to her, she acted like I didn't exist. I wasn't real pleased."

With Bob gone for the summer, Sylvia was free to pursue her own interests and activities, so on a June evening in 1977, she and her roommate Rhonda Beam (Avant) attended a summer league men's basketball game at McClenaghan High School. As they were watching the game, Sylvia saw Larry on the court and remembered their previous conversation. She began to watch the game with a different kind of interest: *Now, who is it that he wants me to meet? Which player?* She narrowed the options to two players: Jud Drennan and Sammy Hatchell, whom she barely remembered. The *Florence Morning News* reported that "Sam Hatchell led all the scores with twenty-six points."[2] Sylvia, however, was less interested in the score than in Sammy's physique: "Sammy," she says, "was not really that big, but I thought, *That guy has got good looking legs!*"

When the game was over, Larry invited Sylvia and Rhonda to join him and Sammy at Pizza Hut and formally introduced Sylvia to Sammy for the second time. By the end of the evening, Sylvia was still not impressed, but a couple of days later, Sammy invited her to a coaching clinic at the Holiday Inn in Sumter, South Carolina. He picked her up at 7:30 a.m., and they spent the day attending lectures and taking notes. The clinic ended at 5:30; they drove back to Florence and stopped at Shoney's: "We went in and got a booth, and we sat there and we ate and we talked," says Sylvia. "We sat there for probably two and a half to three hours. Just sat there, talking about everything." He took her home, and she thought, *Well, this will be it. I'll never see him again.* But two days later, he called again. "We got to be good buddies," says Sylvia. "Hanging out with each other and talking. We just enjoyed each other's company."

Carl Davis (Sammy) Hatchell was the son of Leo and Faye Hatchell. He grew up on a farm in Evergreen, a small town eight miles outside of Florence, attended Southside High School (a 3-A school), and played basketball and baseball. The Southside baseball team won the state championship five years in a row, and Sammy was on two of the winning teams. In 1974 Sammy earned the B.S. degree in physical education from Mars Hill College in North Carolina. After graduation, he returned to Florence and took a job at James F. Byrnes Academy, grades K-12, where he taught physical education and coached basketball, football, and golf. His love of sports matched Sylvia's. Leo Hatchell, Sammy's father, was a World War II naval veteran and, according to Sylvia, a "Renaissance man. He could do anything, and I just loved him. We were buddies." When Sylvia and Sammy met, his mother Faye was nearing the end of a long battle with cancer that began when Sammy was a child.

Sylvia and Sammy began dating steadily, so before her trip to Billie Moore's camp at San Jose State in early August, she called Bob Strunk to tell him she had met someone: "If you get a job offer somewhere else, take it. Don't come back here for me. It's not going to work." She left for California thinking he would take a job elsewhere, but when she returned home, there was Bob's car at the Dogwood Lane apartment. Her heart sank. Immediately, he knocked on her door expecting a warm welcome. She said, "No, Bob. I told you it was over. We can be friends, but it's over." Undaunted, he continued to call, and she continued to say, "NO!" Sylvia's parents liked Bob, and her brothers adored him, so they did not understand why she refused to marry a man who was nearly perfect. Bob held a commanding presence when he entered a room; he could easily engage strangers in a conversation. "He was almost too perfect," says Sylvia. "He was a great guy." Sammy knew that Bob was back, so he kept his distance and gave Sylvia her "space" because he assumed that she and Bob would get back together.

In early October, Bob came by to tell her that he was moving closer to Pamplico where he was teaching, some 20 miles away, so the Dogwood Lane apartment would again be vacant. Sammy was living at home with his parents, which was a 30-minute drive to Byrnes Academy, but the apartment was barely two blocks away. When Bob moved out, Sammy moved in. Sylvia had lived at 126 Dogwood Lane for a year; Bob lived there a year; and then Sammy moved in. Unlike Bob, Sammy allowed Sylvia her independence and treated her like an equal. Their comfortable, mutually supportive bond was growing; they had a common interest in coaching basketball; and now Sammy was living "just around the corner."

In 1978 significant changes came to Sylvia's life. On February 9, 1978, her last living grandparent died—Anna Maude High Rhyne—at age 86. Her roommate Rhonda got married that year, and Sylvia was a bridesmaid. At the rehearsal dinner, she met Mrs. Sylvia Strickland, and they became immediate friends. Mary Lou, Mrs. Strickland's daughter, says that from the first moment they met, they connected: "My mama adored Sylvia—that was everlasting." Eventually, Mrs. Strickland took a job at Francis Marion as secretary to Dr. Joseph Heyward, director of the Smith College Center, which housed the gym, the cafeteria, and the swimming pool, so she worked in the same building as Sylvia. Another good friend was Eleanor Rogers Burns, the assistant counselor in Student Affairs. Eleanor loved basketball, and Sylvia fed her passion for it: "Sylvia can turn anybody on to it. You get around her, and it's just contagious."

Eleanor fed the Lady Patriots in her home and sometimes accompanied Sylvia on trips to Gastonia, stopping at Hamrick's in Gaffney. "Sylvia would stop at every hole in the wall because she loved a deal. If it was a yard sale or a barn or whatever," says Eleanor. "Oh, she would look at any kind of trinket."

Sylvia and Sammy enjoyed the summer of 1978. She managed the swimming pool at the Country Club of South Carolina in Florence. During the mornings, she taught swimming, and Sammy took graduate classes at Francis Marion. At noon, he joined her for lunch at the Country Club grill, and in the afternoons, "we would just hang out at the pool until it closed," says Sylvia. Sammy played softball almost every night, and she went along. After spending so much time together, Sammy was ready to get serious, but she was reluctant. One night, they drove around for four or five hours and talked about their futures and whether they were truly serious about each other. Sylvia remained non-committal. Sammy took her home and said, "OK, I guess I'll see you—maybe." He went back to his apartment, thinking, *It's over.* The next day, Sylvia went home to Gastonia to think: The situation with Bob was complicated. On the other hand, she and Sammy had "something special," and she didn't want to ruin it. But her biggest question was whether a commitment to Sammy would derail her personal goals. After a long weekend in Gastonia, she drove back to Florence and called Sammy immediately: "Let's go do something tonight." He was shocked, but he said, "OK," and soon decided it was time to get married.

Sammy proposed on Sunday night, December 10, 1978. They went to a movie in Florence, and when Sammy brought her home, he caught her off guard: "We got out of the car and walked up on the porch, and as we were getting ready to go into the house, he grabbed me and turned me around. He looked at me and said, 'What do you think about getting married? We spend a lot of time together. We enjoy each other.'" Sylvia still hedged: "There's a lot of things I want to do, whether it be coaching a college team or USA basketball, and if that is not what you want for me, then we shouldn't be married." Sammy assured her, "I want you to be your own person—do your own things." Sylvia trusted his response, and from that moment they were unofficially engaged, but at Christmas, he presented her with a ring making it official.

Their engagement announcement and photograph appeared in the May 6, 1979, *Gastonia Gazette*, and on June 16, two years after she met Sammy, they were married on a rainy Saturday night in Immanuel Baptist Church in Florence—not in Unity Baptist Church in Gastonia because Sammy's mother Faye was too ill to travel. The first stop on their honeymoon trip was a Holiday Inn in Santee, and for her honeymoon night Sylvia had packed a "box of goodies—her nighties," as Sammy called them. When it was time to "dress" for bed, she realized that she didn't have the luggage key, so Sammy had to break the lock. Once open, the "box of goodies" revealed a teddy. She teased Sammy, "Take a good look. You'll never see me wearing one of these things again."

They honeymooned in Florida, driving all the way to Daytona Beach and then to Orlando. They went to Gatorland, Sea World, Disney World, and Epcot. Sammy was a huge NASA fan, so they closed out the week at Cape Canaveral and the Kennedy Space Center. Immediately upon returning home, basketball took center stage again: They went to a week-long basketball camp at Campbell, where Sylvia had worked in

Wedding of Sylvia Rhyne and Sammy Hatchell, June 16, 1979. Left to right: Carroll and Veda Rhyne, Sylvia and Sammy Hatchell, Faye and Leo Hatchell. Courtesy Sylvia Hatchell.

previous years. Then they moved into the house at 202 Magnolia Drive, which Sylvia had been renting with Sharon Sturgeon and Rhonda Beam. They wanted to buy the house, but it didn't pass the inspection. Rather than make the necessary repairs, the owner sold it to them "as is" for $20,000. Leo Hatchell lent them $8,000, and they assumed a $12,000 loan, with a monthly payment of $143. Their first home was a three-bedroom house on a 100' × 200' lot, with a single garage and a big fenced backyard with tall pines and azaleas. It had a large, open living area and a nice master bedroom, two smaller bedrooms, and one and a half baths.

The two coaches settled into married life, learning how to fit into each other's families and pursuing their individual interests. In 1976, Sammy and five other men had organized a band called Hav-N-Fun, which played gigs mostly in North and South Carolina, but occasionally they traveled to Georgia and Virginia for weddings, private parties, golf tournaments, and clubs. Sammy played guitar and sang. They covered a variety of music genres, including beach music, which was popular in both Florence and Myrtle Beach, where Sylvia and Sammy visited often, so they decided to take Shag lessons, building on Judy Wilkins' instruction in graduate school. There was also a Shag club in Florence. After Sylvia and Sammy were first married, she didn't like his being away every weekend, leaving her alone, but Sammy's absence on Friday and

Saturday nights gave her more time with her mother-in-law Faye. They often went to the Mandarin Chinese restaurant in Florence and sometimes they saw a movie. Sammy says Sylvia was "very good with my mama. It was hard for Mama at the time," dealing with cancer. Faye died on September 10, 1981, at age 56.

Summer basketball camps continued to be important to Sylvia, so she was eager to involve Sammy. He joined her at the Campbell camp and at Pat's UT camp, where he met many of her basketball friends and saw a different side of his wife, especially at Pat Summitt's UT camp in 1982—the year of the Knoxville World's Fair. (Pat had married R.B. Summitt in 1980.) At Francis Marion Sylvia was "straight-laced and hard-nosed. I was Coach Hatchell. I was walking the line every step of the way, and I made my players do the same." But away from Florence, and in the company of her old friends, she "cut loose." In 1982 Sammy saw the group in rare form. He said, "I've been letting you come over here *by yourself!*" He enjoyed the camaraderie and revelry. He liked the professional development—learning new ideas, meeting colleagues, and networking—but he never developed Sylvia's "love" for basketball camps: "I remember thinking, *Here I am training someone else's players when I could be training my own!*"

While Sylvia was settling into married life, her passion for basketball was growing, and she was developing a winning program. When she arrived at Francis Marion in the fall of 1975, she inherited a team with a previous-year record of 11–11. Right off, she began to look for talent and struck gold when coach Anne Long from Wilson High School called her about a player named Pearl Moore who had graduated from Wilson in 1975. Moore enrolled in Anderson Junior College (now Anderson University), which had an excellent women's basketball team coached by Annie Tribble, but she was homesick, so after one semester, she transferred to Francis Marion. The move made her a hometown star.

Sylvia's first season as the Francis Marion head coach was a success. The Lady Patriots lost twice to instate rival Clemson but defeated South Carolina twice—a Division I school. They went to the AIAW Division II Regional playoffs, where they lost to her former coach Peggy Birmingham's Union University Lady Bulldogs 90–71. The Patriots went on to the AIAW National Small College Women's Tournament at Ashland, Ohio, and lost in the fifth-place game to Southeastern Louisiana 81–70. They finished sixth out of 16 teams and ended the season 23–9. Upon their return to Florence, the South Carolina House of Representatives passed a resolution honoring the team's accomplishments, and the mayor of Florence, C. Cooper Tedder, presented Sylvia with a key to the city.

In the 1976–1977 season, Francis Marion defeated South Carolina three times. Moore hit her stride and began to dazzle fans and the media with her double-digit scores. In a February 3, 1977, away game against rival Clemson, she had the flu, and Sylvia didn't want her to travel with the team, but she went anyway because they would be playing against her former coach Tribble, who had moved to Clemson in 1976. Despite Moore's 44 points, Francis Marion lost the game 83–70 but won the next Clemson matchup 83–82. The Lady Patriots were faring well against larger, instate rivals. Sylvia continued to face *her* former coach as well. For the second year in a row, she squared off against Peggy Birmingham in the AIAW Small College Regional

Tournament in Florence, but the Lady Patriots prevailed, beating Union 79–74. Birmingham says, "Sylvia was just ecstatic, yelling, 'I beat my coach! I beat my coach!'" Francis Marion then advanced to the AIAW Small College National Tournament in Pomona, California, where they lost in a consolation-bracket game (59–49) to Tarkio College, a Presbyterian institution in Missouri. Frances Marion ended the 1976–1977 season 21–11.

In 1977–1978, Sylvia's Lady Patriots lost three games each to Clemson and South Carolina by slim margins. The loss to Clemson on January 16 was a heartbreaker but, again, the two-point margin indicated that the team was competitive. Sylvia hoped—again—to win the AIAW Small College National Tournament, especially because Frances Marion hosted the event on March 22–25. As with previous years, her team advanced through the state tournament in Aiken, South Carolina, and the regional competition in Bridgewater, Virginia. Back on their home court, Moore did her part to help the Lady Patriots win the championship, scoring 60 points in the March 22 game against Eastern Washington State College, setting an all-time AIAW record, and giving the Lady Patri-

ots a 114–71 win, but they lost to Shorter College in the consolation-bracket game 83–80 and ended the season 22–11.

In 1978–79, the rivalry with Clemson continued. Pearl Moore scored 22 points in the matchup on December 9, 1978, but the Lady Patriots lost 118–64, the harbinger perhaps for a disappointing season. The team did not advance beyond the AIAW regionals, despite the talents of Moore. On March 10, 1979, she scored 42 points in the AIAW Small College Regional Tournament in Louisville, Kentucky, giving the Lady Patriots the 81–75 win over UT Chattanooga in the consolation game. Francis Marion ended the season 19–11, but Moore had made history. She set the all-time women's collegiate scoring

Sylvia coaches courtside, Francis Marion vs. Clemson, January 16, 1978. Left to right: Rosita Fields, Sylvia Rhyne, Martha Williamson, Pearl Moore, and Referee Bill Stokes. Courtesy Francis Marion Sports.

record of 4,061 points in an era when the three-point field goal did not exist, a record that still stands. Moore was Sylvia's first player to be drafted by a professional team— the New York Stars in the Women's Professional Basketball League (WBL), which folded in 1981.

The Francis Marion season ended, but Sylvia didn't slow down. She gained valuable experience as assistant coach to Chris Weller, from Maryland, for the East All-Star team in the third annual Hanes Underalls All-American Basketball Classic, held in the Greensboro Coliseum, on March 31. The West All-Star team was coached by Jody Conradt, from the University of Texas, and Sonja Hogg, from Louisiana Tech. Sylvia and Weller thought they had a good chance to win the Classic, with players such as Holly Warlick. Another East team member was Nancy Lieberman, from Old Dominion, who had little practice time with her East teammates. "Of course, we had to put her in there," says Sylvia, "because she was National Player of the Year," but the West team proved too powerful for the East and trounced them 90–62.

Around this time, Sylvia decided to get a dog, a Cock-a-Poo that she named Sassafras. "Sass" rode everywhere with Sylvia in her Navy blue MGB convertible: "I would put the top down and we would ride around. She would lie on my shoulder and look out." When Sylvia traveled, Sammy took care of Sass, who resented her absences. "You talk about moody," says Sylvia. "I'd come back home, and she would have nothing do to with me. She would pout and be mad at me for days."

Sylvia began her fourth season at Francis Marion, 1979–1980, with a husband and a new dog, with experience coaching some of the top players in the country, and with new recruits, such as Daphne Donnelly from Mullins High School, in Marion County, South Carolina. The eleventh of 12 children (seven girls and five boys), Donnelly spent her free time playing ball in the back yard. According to Bob Gillespie with *The State*, "she was 5-11 by the time she was 12," and her brothers "taught her to play like a boy." Fred Senter, Donnelly's high-school coach, told Gillespie, "She's the best I ever coached in 48 years.... Offense, defense, ball-handling ... and competitive. She'd spit in your eye to beat you." Sylvia gave Gillespie an equally colorful description: "On the court, ... Daphne was mean as a snake." Coach Senter told Gillespie that it was a challenge to get college coaches to recruit his Mullins girls, but Sylvia visited often, and she was outspoken about her intent: She wanted Donnelly "bad" and was worried when she saw USC Coach Pam Parsons at Mullins games. But Donnelly and Sylvia hit it off. Having the opportunity to play for a college 30 miles from her home appealed to her, so she signed with Francis Marion. In her first year, she led the team to a 20–8 season and a national ranking of No. 18.

The rivalry with Clemson took a back seat to an emerging and greater threat— the College of Charleston Cougars. The Lady Patriots went up against the Cougars four times in 1980–1981. First came a win on January 19 (74–70) followed by a loss five days later (66–62). On February 7, Francis Marion got another win (66–56) in the title game of the Winthrop Invitational Tournament but lost to the Cougars in the AIAW Small College Regional Tournament (70–65) on March 13. Though Francis Marion did not advance to the national tournament, the team finished the season at 27–5. They had been ranked No. 5 nationally and finished at No. 12.

The 1981–82 season was pivotal for Sylvia, largely because her Lady Patriot team was special. In addition to Donnelly, Sylvia had recruited top-notch players, such as 5'6" Melanie McLeod, whom she describes as "a really good, smart point guard," and 6'3" Cassandra Bishop. Gwen Canty was the wing guard, and the three-player was Lynette Mickle. "She was a great shooter," says Sylvia. "If we had had the three-point shot at the time, she would have really been good. We didn't have a whole lot of depth, but we were good." They were not good enough to beat Clemson or Kay Yow's Wolfpack, however, who trounced Francis Marion Patriots 103–70 on November 28, 1981. After the game, the Wolfpack players ridiculed the Patriots, so Donnelly, Mickle, and McLeod, made a pact: Next year, NC State would go down!

But their real nemesis was the College of Charleston. The Lady Patriots finished the year with a 27–7 record, and the College of Charleston Cougars accounted for six of the total 34 games. In the regular season, they lost to the Cougars twice, 85–79 and 93–82. Then they defeated the Cougars twice, first by a slim margin in the Winthrop Invitational Tournament (83–82) and again in the South Carolina AIAW state championships at Newberry, South Carolina (97–70). Their fifth face-off was in the AIAW Division II regionals on the Cougars' home court in Charleston, which the Lady Patriots lost 81–80. The loss robbed them of an automatic bid to the AIAW Tournament, but they won an at-large bid to the first and second rounds of the AIAW Division II National Tournament in Edmond, Oklahoma. In round one, they handily defeated Colorado College (91–54). In the second round, they squeaked by Central State University (91–87), and advanced to the Final Four.

Unlike today's NCAA tournament brackets, there were sixteen total teams, or four regional groups of four, and the winners of those four regions came together for the Final Four, hosted by the College of Charleston with Athletic Director Joan Cronan as the tournament director. The 1982 Final Four teams were Francis Marion, North Dakota State, William Penn, and the College of Charleston. On Saturday, March 27, Francis Marion was up against William Penn, whom they defeated 84–70. Sylvia, Sammy, and the team were staying at the elegant Francis Marion Hotel, and the next day, Sunday, March 28—the day of the championship game—tournament organizers moved them to the Sheraton Hotel. Sylvia interpreted this *faux pas* to mean that Joan Cronan's management team expected Francis Marion to lose and did not reserve rooms for them beyond March 27. Sammy remembers that "Sylvia got all fired up about that." She agrees: "I was furious. It actually helped because I was so mad, and I used it as ammunition for the players." When the Lady Patriots met the College of Charleston for the AIAW Division II National Championship, it was their sixth face-off in the 1981–1982 season. In the final game on their home court, the College of Charleston was heavily favored to win, but fired up by a number of events—from the NC State slight to Sylvia's ire at being forced to change hotels—Sylvia's Francis Marion team defeated them by a score of 92–83 to become the 1982 AIAW National Champions.

In a 2012 interview, Cronan said she did not remember the hotel snafu: "Heavens, no. I wouldn't have done that." In all likelihood, there was a simple mistake with the reservations, but Sylvia capitalized on it. The rivalry between Francis Marion and the College of Charleston was intense, and when Cronan left in 1983, Charleston led the series by one game—15–14: "It was a neat, neat rivalry," says Cronan. "If you look

Francis Marion 1982 AIAW Championship Team. Back row, left to right: Michelle Avignone, Lynette Mickle, Manager Wayne Williams, Cassandra Bishop, Rebecca LaGrant, Coach Sylvia Hatchell. Middle row, left to right: Daphne Donnelly and Jackie McDuffie. Front row, left to right: Melanie McLeod, Gwen Canty, Miriam Pittman. Courtesy Francis Marion Sports.

at AIAW and what all happened, I think it was amazing for the College of Charleston and Francis Marion, two small schools from South Carolina, to have succeeded at the national level. It is a real tribute to those schools and to the coaches." In Cronan's opinion, "Sylvia was a great recruiter of great athletes and had the ability to bring out the best in those great athletes."

Compared with today's NCAA Championship celebrations, the Lady Patriots' 1982 AIAW National Championship celebration was low key. The players were ecstatic with the win, a first for Francis Marion, an institution that was barely 10 years old. Defeating rival College of Charleston was even sweeter. Francis Marion held a celebration, but there were no embroidered hats, no T-shirts, no rings. Sylvia wanted the players to have rings, so she canvassed the town and solicited nearly $2,000 to buy them. She took the team and her staff to a restaurant at South of the Border, the I-95 truck stop and tourist attraction on the North Carolina/South Carolina State Line. Mrs. Strickland came along. Because of her close friendship with Sylvia, she was considered "one of the team." She played the ukulele while they all sat around and sang; then Sylvia presented their rings. Following the 1982 AIAW championship, Sylvia and her team were presented to the joint South Carolina House and Senate, and on April 15, 1982, Governor Richard Riley presented her with the Order of the Palmetto, the top civilian honor in South Carolina.

Still riding the championship wave in the summer of 1982, Sylvia began her 13-year association with USA Basketball and the Olympic Games as a court coach in the National Sports Festival (renamed the U.S. Olympic Festival in 1986) in Indianapolis, Indiana, July 23–31. Her responsibilities included organizing drills on the court and managing the tryouts for the four teams. Sylvia then served as head coach of the South Team which went 4–0 in the competition, defeating Juliene Simpson's West Team 74–64 to win the Gold Medal. She had "gotten her foot in the door," as she says.

When Sylvia returned to coaching in the fall of 1982, the organizational structure of women's basketball had changed. The 1982 AIAW championship was its last. In the 1980s, the NCAA began including women's teams, and many AIAW programs joined the NCAA. Francis Marion, however, joined the National Athletic Intercollegiate Association (NAIA), so Sylvia began the 1982–1983 season in a new league and with new talent. She had lost Michelle Avignone, Cassandra Bishop, Harriett Bonnoitt, and Jackie McDuffie from her championship team but had recruited Kim Slawson (Hawkins). Slawson had lived in Europe for 13 years and learned to play basketball with her brothers in Aviano, Italy. When her father retired from the Air Force in late 1979, the family moved to South Carolina, and Kim joined the Summerville High School basketball team as a junior. When Sylvia heard about this 5'7" shooting guard, she traveled to Summerville to see her play and offered her a scholarship. Slawson was also recruited by NCAA schools Clemson, South Carolina, and Georgia Tech, but she "felt real comfortable" with Sylvia and "thoroughly enjoyed" the small Francis Marion community because she "really didn't like big places." Slawson says that Sylvia "was great. She was like my second mom. When things went wrong you could always go to her. If you got homesick, she would be your mom; she understood. She would call home for you anytime—her door was always open whether she was at home or in her office. And academics were very much a priority with her."

In 1982–1983, Francis Marion earned a 23–7 record, with new recruits Kim Slawson and Sharon Brailey, sophomores Gwen Canty and Rebecca LaGrant, junior Melanie McLeod, and seniors Daphne Donnelly and Lynette Mickle. The Donnelly-Mickle-McLeod pact held firm; they were determined to beat NC State, an NCAA Division I team, and—miraculously—they did (85–81) on December 18, 1982. Donnelly told Bob Gillespie, "We had such unity, we all got along well.… We felt, 'This is our year.'" Sylvia's fired-up team was expected to win the 1983 NAIA Tournament. They faced Campbellsville in the Area 7 Tournament on March 9, a team they had easily defeated in Charleston on March 11, 1982 (107–56), but playing on Campbellsville's home court made a difference. In 2008, both Donnelly and Sylvia recounted for Bob Gillespie their disappointment, which to this day is vivid and painful. According to Donnelly, the game was "taken away" from Francis Marion "by the referees." Sylvia agrees: "She's exactly right; we got cheated.… That's my worst loss in 34 [now 46] years coaching." Francis Marion led the game at Campbellsville, Kentucky, only to lose 105–103 in double overtime. Five of Sylvia's players—Brailey, Canty, Donnelly, McLeod, and Slawson—fouled out. Two players—Mickle and J. Alston—ended the game with four fouls each. The box scores show that Francis Marion players had been called for 35 fouls to Campbellsville's 22. "[Campbellsville] got half their points at the free throw line," remembers Donnelly. "Afterward, the refs celebrated with the

[Campbellsville] team," recalls Sylvia. "The host team provided the refs back then. There wasn't a lot you could do."

Kim Slawson (Hawkins) remembers the game as "almost surreal. You see plays going against you and you're thinking, *OK. All right. Don't worry about that.* But it just seemed to continue. Just obvious calls—blatant, bad calls against us." Slawson says Sylvia "stayed calm," but after the game, she saw "defeat" in her face for the first time: "We should have beat this team, and the officials were not going to let us win. Period." Sylvia told the team, "We just have to refocus, step back from the game for a little while, and get ready for the next season." "That's all she could say," says Slawson. "She handled it the best way she could. That was a hard one to swallow because we should have won, and we didn't have the opportunity to take care of business ourselves. Someone took it away from us." Sylvia agrees:

> We would have won the whole thing because we were loaded. We had a big lead, and we were fast breaking like crazy, and then the referees, all local Campbellsville guys, started fouling us out. Even though we finished the game in double overtime, ... we still lost by only two points. I mean we got cheated. Cheated, cheated, cheated. Big time. That was the most devastating game I have ever coached.

Sylvia went back to the hotel room, ran a big tub of water, and cried: "I was just so upset and so mad, I remember crying all night long. That's one of those lessons about life not always being fair." Slawson was a freshman, but Donnelly was a senior, and finishing her college career on such a note was disappointing. Still, Donnelly had much to be proud of. In her four years with the Lady Patriots, she averaged 19.9 points and 12.2 rebounds per game and was a three-time All American. During Donnelly's tenure with Francis Marion, the team lost only 27 games and won 97. She ranks third in Francis Marion scoring history, with 2,403 points, and first in rebounds, with 1,472. Michael Hawkins, associate athletic director for media relations and marketing at Francis Marion University, told Bob Gillespie, "It was a time when players with her abilities didn't all go to Division I [schools]. She could've played anywhere." Sylvia agrees: "Those Francis Marion teams would be able to play in the ACC.... We beat South Carolina, Clemson, NC State, all of them. After a while, we couldn't get anyone to play us." Sylvia's memory isn't exact, however. In 1981–1982, her Lady Patriots lost to Clemson (92–79) and in 1982–83 to South Carolina (95–89), but she left Francis Marion with an 11-year winning record against South Carolina.

Sylvia hated losing. In 2009, she told Tim Crothers, "When I first started coaching and we'd lose, I wouldn't sleep a wink, and I applied for a job at UPS because I hated losing so much.... I'll never forget one day Kay [Yow] telling me, 'Don't get too up with the wins and don't get too down with the losses. You've got to persevere. You may have to count to ten. Bite your tongue. Whatever it takes. But you've got to persevere.'"

Sylvia took Yow's advice and persevered, getting right back to basketball in the summer of 1983. From July 1 to 11, she assisted Jill Hutchinson, of Illinois State University, as head coach for Team USA in the World University Games, which are held every two years to showcase top college athletes. In 1983, the Games were held in Edmonton, Canada, and opening ceremonies were on July 1—Canada Day—which is the equivalent of Independence Day for the United States. Prince Charles and

Princess Diana opened the Games, celebrating also the 14th anniversary of Charles's investiture as Prince of Wales and Diana's birthday. Laurie Watson wrote, "In an emotional moment that brought tears to the eyes of the princess, the crowd rose in unison to sing 'Happy Birthday' to Diana, who turned 22" on July 1. When Charles and Diana visited the British delegation in the Games Village, Sylvia snapped dozens of photos of "Princess Di." More importantly, she and Hutchinson led Team USA to a 5–1 record. They defeated Hong Kong in the first round 134–23. In the fourth game, the U.S. team lost to Romania (85–71) but came back to beat Romania in the medal round (83–61) for the Gold, the second Gold Medal for women's basketball in the University Games, the first being in 1979. The win somewhat compensated for the devastating end to Sylvia's 1982–1983 season.

As Sylvia's reputation grew, she became a South Carolina personality who came to the attention of Strom Thurmond, U.S. Senator from South Carolina. In 1983, she received a call from Nancy Thurmond, who wanted to visit Sylvia at Francis Marion. Sylvia says, "I was just a little pee-dunky doodle coach, you know? She called me up and wanted to come see me. I said to myself, *Why does Nancy Thurmond want to come see me?*" Around four o'clock in the afternoon, on the appointed day, a black Rolls Royce arrived at Francis Marion. Out stepped a beautiful, blond woman, the former Miss South Carolina who married Thurmond in 1968 at age 22 when he was 66. She invited Sylvia to have breakfast with Senator Thurmond at his Columbia office. Sylvia accepted the invitation, wondering all the while, *Why on earth are they interested in* me? When she arrived at the South Carolina State House, an attendant greeted her and took her up to the suite where they had breakfast with a small, select group. She and Senator Thurmond talked casually, but nothing of any consequence happened. She had a pleasant day, but she left still wondering, *What are they after?* She was soon to find out. When Thurmond was gearing up for the 1984 U.S. Senate campaign, his assistant called her to ask for an endorsement. There was no pressure, and Sylvia declined to endorse Thurmond because she wanted to keep out of the political fray. Nothing more came of it.

Sylvia began the 1983 fall semester with the Campbellsville wound somewhat healed and with more determination to succeed than ever. Always searching for ways to improve, she put into practice a team-building technique she learned from Jill Hutchinson while coaching the World University Games in July. At the beginning of basketball season, she gathered the players, assistant coaches, and staff in the locker room and gave each person a large sheet of butcher paper, crayons, and magic markers. Sylvia asked each player to divide the paper into four parts representing team goals, individual goals, her favorite toy as a child, and what she wanted to be doing in five years. Players could use words, but she preferred that they draw pictures. Then they stood in front of everyone in the room and explained their drawings. The experience was intense. As each player shared her goals and dreams, other players listened closely and learned personal—sometimes intimate—details about the young women who would be their closest companions for the next year and beyond. Sylvia and her staff discovered each player's unique personality, insight that helped them guide and mentor the young women. The connection between a childhood toy and a winning basketball team may not be immediately obvious. This activity, however, opened a window into players' childhoods and family lives, few of which were as idyllic as Sylvia's wholesome 1950s upbringing. At the end of the activity, Sylvia asked them to display their drawings permanently in the backs of their lockers as reminders of who they are, their goals, their dreams, the women they will become, their places in the world, and their places among their teammates. She found this activity to be so effective that she used it throughout her career.

Sylvia needed strong team-building techniques because she had lost seniors Daphne Donnelly and Lynette Mickle, and she had nine freshmen. Fortunately, she had five strong returning players: sophomores Annette and Jeannette Alston and Kim Slawson; junior Gwen Canty; and senior Melanie McLeod. The team gelled and ended the year with an unbelievable 28–5 record. They beat Limestone (77–62) to win the District VI Tournament and advanced to the Orangeburg round of District VI play, where they defeated the College of Charleston (86–61) and Erskine (82–62). For the NAIA Bi-District XI playoff game, Sylvia's Lady Patriots had home-court advantage against Berry College. Berry coach Brenda Paul recalls, "I came rolling in with my kids to Florence. Sylvia called me up and said, 'Brenda Paul, you got your kids taken care of?'" Brenda said, "Yeah." Sylvia then invited her out, and the two opposing coaches, vying for a chance to advance to the national tournament, spent the night on the town. "We go dancing that night with her radio guy and Sammy," says Paul. "They just took me out. Now, we're supposed to be playing each other the next day for a chance to go to the national tournament!" Francis Marion beat Berry 83–71, and today Paul still jokes, "SHE WON! I think it was a plot!" Paul captures something of the camaraderie and good will that characterized women's tournament play 36 years ago that no longer exists: "Now, you know—you can't do this now." On the other hand, the Campbellsville defeat probably couldn't happen today, either.

The win over Berry sent Sylvia's Lady Patriots to the NAIA National Quarterfinals in Cedar Rapids, Iowa, which would be comparable to the NCAA Sweet 16 today. South Carolinians took note that Francis Marion again had a shot at a national title. Bob Marcum, the athletic director at the University of South Carolina, flew out to watch Sylvia's team defeat St. Ambrose (81–68) on March 14. A win against Portland in the second round on March 15 would send them to the semifinals, but they lost (91–79) and had to settle for the FCA Sportsmanship Award.

In 1984, the Olympics were held in Los Angeles, July 28–August 12, and once again, Sylvia was involved as a member of the events staff. She may have had the attention of powerful political leaders such as Strom Thurmond, but she had so little money that during her stay in L.A., she and two other staff members slept on the floor of UCLA assistant coach Colleen Matsuhara's apartment in Culver City. Sylvia was first assigned to the USA men's basketball team and worked in the locker room area, preparing chalk boards, making sure they had water and towels or anything the players or head coach needed. Security was tight for the elite, star-studded team with players such as Michael Jordan, Patrick Ewing, Chris Mullin, Steve Alford, and Wayman Tisdale. Sylvia worked with Jordan and with Bobby Knight, the men's USA basketball coach, and she carried the American flag to lead the USA men's basketball team onto the Forum Floor for their first game against China, which they won 97–49. Knight led the USA men's basketball team to an 8–0 record, defeating Spain 96–65 to win the Gold Medal.

Pat Summitt coached the 1984 USA women's basketball team with Kay Yow as her assistant. At that time, Sylvia knew Yow from basketball clinics and the 1975 gift of shoes from NC State to Francis Marion, but they did not know each other well. Pat and Sylvia were the same age and had known each other for 10 years. At age 42, Kay was their senior by at least a decade, but during the Olympics, Sylvia and Kay became "good buddies." When the women's team played in the Forum, it was Sylvia's job to assure that Yow's good-luck earrings were ready at courtside—Yow wore them only during the games. Sylvia, Pat, and Kay rarely had free time, but when they were not working, they attended other games and ate or shopped together. On one occasion, they watched the Olympic women's volleyball competition, held in the Long Beach Arena. Another time they went to the San Diego Zoo. On another occasion they went to the Chart House restaurant at Marina Del Rey. "I didn't have a lot of money," says Sylvia, "so when we went to places like the Chart House, I would get a salad because I couldn't afford a filet mignon or lobster. But that didn't matter. I was just glad to be there." On another day, Pat Summitt, Kay Yow, Jody Conradt, Sue Gunter, and Sylvia went to the Gold Mart on the corner of Sixth and Hill in downtown L.A. These were the pioneers of women's basketball, and Sylvia was honored to be in their company. "It was a perfect day for me," says Sylvia, "because that was the world I wanted to be in." Summitt and Yow led the USA women's basketball team to victory over South Korea and won the Gold Medal.

Despite her winning record (210–74), one national championship to her credit, and Olympic experience, in 1984 Sylvia made less money than high-school coaches in Florence County. Her entrepreneurial bent helped—for a short time, she had a balloon shop, and she filmed weddings to augment her salary. Eventually, the low pay forced her to look for another job. Having observed Sylvia's Lady Patriots in the Cedar Rapids NAIA Tournament, Bob Marcum invited her to apply for the South Carolina head women's basketball coaching position. The women's program had suffered a national scandal involving Coach Pam Parsons' relationship with a female player, followed by a difficult transition through two women's basketball coaches. During the interview period, a reporter asked her what her dream job would be. Somewhat off the cuff, Sylvia answered, "head women's basketball coach at UNC." USC did not like that response. After the interview, she told Sammy that she was unsure whether she would have taken the job had they offered it to her. Except for the budget, her program and situation at Francis Marion were superior to the program at the University of South Carolina.

In the summer of 1984, Francis Marion hosted the South Carolina AAU Tournament. Sylvia was sitting in the stands watching a game when Andrew Calder sat down with her. Sylvia had known Calder since 1981. He grew up in McBee, South Carolina, where his father, A.J., owned Ridgeview Farms and coached boys' and girls' basketball, football, and baseball at McBee High School. A.J. Calder also served on the Chesterfield Board of Education and the South Carolina Board of Education. Being the child of an educator and politician, and having been raised on a peach farm, Calder had a work ethic that equaled Sylvia's. In 1979, he became the girls' basketball coach at McBee, where his father had coached, and won a state championship in 1981. As he and Sylvia sat in the stands, the conversation eventually turned to UNC women's basketball. Sylvia said, "That's my dream job." Calder said, "I'll tell you what. If you ever get that job at North Carolina, I'll come be your assistant." Sylvia responded, "That sounds good to me."

Going into the 1984–1985 season, the Francis Marion women's team was ranked No. 8 in the NAIA. Melanie McLeod had graduated, but Gwen Canty returned as a senior; Annette and Jeannette Alston and Kim Slawson were returning juniors. Sylvia picked up another promising freshman in Tracey Tillman, from Society Hill, South Carolina. Tillman had been recruited by several schools, but Sylvia trumped them all when she asked Tillman whether she wanted to be a little fish in a big pond or a big fish in a little pond. In a 2012 interview, Tillman said, "You know, I did want to be a big fish in a little pond. I really did." Another factor was that she was "a real home-body" and wanted to stay close to home.

In early-season play, Francis Marion had good success and won games with wide margins, defeating Newberry 87–44; Morris 118–32; and High Point 110–75. On January 19, 1985, Sylvia's Lady Patriots suffered a close loss to USC-Spartanburg (90–86) and an even closer loss to Fayetteville State on January 26 (69–67). In the Winthrop Invitational, they lost to their arch-nemesis College of Charleston by three points (74–71) but 11 days later, defeated them in regular play 91–66. Because the team was strong, Sylvia entered post-season play feeling hopeful about their chances to advance in the NAIA Tournament. On February 26, the Lady Patriots easily defeated Limestone 97–68 in the first round of the NAIA District Six Tournament to advance for the third consecutive year to the second round in Orangeburg, South Carolina.

In the first game, Francis Marion went up against the College of Charleston for the third time that season and delivered their arch-nemesis a 20-point defeat (88–68). The win gave Sylvia's team confidence going into the game against Claflin the next day. In her 10 years at Francis Marion, Sylvia's record against Claflin was 9–2, and her Lady Patriots had squeaked by Claflin (85–82) just two weeks prior to the tournament game. Still, she was confident and did not expect Claflin to execute a 3–2 zone: "Our outside shooting was terrible," she says, "and we couldn't break the zone." Claflin defeated Francis Marion 75–66 to end Sylvia's chances for another shot at a national title: "When that game was over, I was just devastated. The season was over." Though Francis Marion finished the year with a stellar 26–4 record, Sylvia still remembers that 1985 loss to Claflin and still blames herself: "We should have gone further [in the tournament]. That was bad coaching on my part." A bright spot was that Tracey Tillman was named to the NAIA All-American Third Team for the 1984–85 season, an honor that foretold good things for the Lady Patriots.

In the summer of 1985, for the third time in four years, Sylvia was selected as an assistant coach at the national level. Vivian Stringer, head coach of women's basketball at the University of Iowa, would lead Team USA in the World University Games, which were held in Kobe, Japan, July 24–August 4. Sylvia was "really impressed" with Japan, especially its progressive, conservative, and space-conscious features. She had not previously seen the use of card keys to manage the consumption of electricity. In the first game, the USA women's basketball team defeated the People's Republic of Korea 108–81, and took easy wins over Yugoslavia (77–51) and Great Britain (77–36). In the fourth game, USA beat China with the slimmest margin of the Championship series (83–78) but won easily over Canada in game five (85–61). USA was favored to win the Gold Medal, but, says Sylvia, "the chemistry just wasn't good with the players, a couple of whom had ongoing issues," and events surrounding the championship game were "discombobulated." The timing was not good: a two-hour practice and a meal before the game. *This is crazy*, she thought. On game day, she wants her players to "have their legs." Whatever the reason, USA lost the championship game to the Soviet Union (87–81) and came home with the Silver Medal. For Sylvia, "That was the only USA trip that was not just off the charts." All of the other experiences and opportunities at this level exceeded her expectations, including the people, the venues, the activities, but the 1985 World Championships "was the only trip where I was just glad to get home."

While Sylvia was away from home for long stretches of time, Sammy made good on his promise that he would not stand in the way of her career. He never once complained about her absences. Sylvia describes him as quiet, confident, and secure, qualities that gave her the freedom to pursue her career and dreams without guilt or conflict: "I could put myself into coaching and what I needed to do. And the fact that he was so supportive of me meant the world to me. It meant so much. I can't say enough good things about the fact that he was so understanding."

Disappointed with a Silver Medal, Sylvia returned to Florence, a patient husband, a pouting Sassafras, and her upcoming 1985–1986 season, which was life-changing in every respect. Sylvia says she "had the whole team back. That was a really good group." Annette and Jeannette Alston and Kim Slawson were seniors. Tracey Tillman was a sophomore. The Francis Marion team played eight non-conference games before the end of 1985, losing only once to Division I East Carolina 75–65. But all was not perfect. In December of 1985, Bob Strunk entered Sylvia's life again. She had stayed in contact with him, and by the time she and Sammy announced their engagement in 1978, Strunk was the assistant men's basketball coach at Clemson under head coach Bill Foster. In 1983, Strunk became head men's and women's basketball coach at Tusculum College in Greeneville, Tennessee. It was not unusual for Bob to call, so Sylvia was not surprised when Mrs. Strickland pulled her out of practice to take a call from him just before Christmas in 1985. Sylvia went up to her office and shut the door for privacy.

Bob was sobbing into the phone. He recounted a host of recent disappointments. Tusculum College had terminated his contract at the end of the 1984–1985 season. Bob had applied to be the full-time director of Ridgecrest Boys Camp, where he had worked as an assistant director for years, even when he and Sylvia were undergraduates at Carson-Newman, but he did not get that job. Instead, he took a position as area director of the Upper East Tennessee FCA. Finally, Bob was devastated when a romantic relationship with a woman ended. Sylvia talked with Bob for a long time, and when they ended the conversation, he seemed composed.

Shortly after Christmas, her senior-year roommate at Carson-Newman, Maureen Walling, called her late at night to ask, "Have you heard anything about Bob?" Sylvia briefly told her about their recent conversation. Then Maureen relayed the sad news that Bob had committed suicide. Sylvia was in shock—utter disbelief. She lay awake until the next morning, when she called the athletic department at

Carson-Newman. The staff confirmed the story. Then she called Bob's parents. His mother was inconsolable. Sylvia had thought he was calm and composed at the end of their phone conversation. She realized that he had been reaching out, and she had done her best to listen and comfort him. Over the next weeks, she examined and re-examined her relationship with Bob, asking herself what she could have done differently: Perhaps he would still be alive if she had married him. Sammy quickly reassured her: "You would have gotten a divorce."

Bob's suicide came just before basketball season heated up. Beginning in January 1986, the Lady Patriots lost only one game, to their long-time foe, the College of Charleston, on January 18 (77–76). According to Kim Slawson, "It was a good rivalry, and Sylvia did not like losing to the College of Charleston. That was not an option. We had to practice immediately when we got back home from Charleston. We knew it, and we would just go in there and, yes ma'am, we practiced." Francis Marion was the No. 1 team going into the NAIA District VI playoffs. They averaged 93.9 points a game and maintained a scoring margin of 27.3, the highest in the nation. Sylvia told Dave Kelly, with *The State*, that her 1986 Lady Patriots could "compare with the best we've had." She was right. The team cruised through matchups against Newberry College (104–60) and Limestone (104–35), but on March 1, they had to face Claflin, who had robbed them of the NAIA District title in 1985. Sylvia told Kelly that the 1985 loss to Claflin made the team "more determined," and that the Lady Patriots had not yet played to their full potential: "I still feel we can play better than we have lately." Again, she was right. They defeated Claflin 83–71 to win the NAIA District VI title, and then knocked out Georgia Southwestern 96–70 to win the NAIA District VI regional championship. For the second time in five seasons, Sylvia's Lady Patriots were off to a national championship tournament, this one in Kemper Arena, Kansas City, Missouri. Sylvia and her team stayed at the Crown Plaza, and this time they did not have to change hotels.

On March 14 and 15, 1986, Francis Marion's women played back-to-back games and won both: Dominican College 109–41 and Wingate 89–71. The win over Dominican was the largest margin of victory in NAIA history and gave Francis Marion a three-way tie with Claflin and Oklahoma City for most field goals in a game (47). With one day's rest, the team then faced Georgia Southwestern in the semifinals (for the second time in 12 days). Again, the team won by a solid margin 91–77. Sammy had told Sylvia that if she made it to the Final Four, he would fly out for the championship game. Sylvia called with the good news—"We made it!"—but the bad news was that her team would play the next day, March 18. To keep his promise, Sammy drove to Charlotte in the middle of the night and caught an Eastern Airlines red-eye direct flight to Kansas City. Sylvia sent someone to the airport to pick him up—she was too busy preparing for her second shot at a national title.

In the championship game, the Lady Patriots faced the perennial powerhouse Wayland Baptist College, a private school in Plainview, Texas, that had a rich history in women's basketball. Kim Slawson was Francis Marion's point guard. As a senior, Slawson remembered the sting of the 1983 loss to Campbellsville in her freshman year, but the Kansas City tournament was different: "The officiating was great. I couldn't complain about the officiating at all, for all of 1986." The Wayland Baptist

Flying Queens "were the team that was supposed to beat everybody, with a long, outstanding winning record" says Slawson, who came down with the flu but played one of her best games: "I said, 'Thank you, Lord, for giving me the flu.'" The game was close. Sylvia encouraged the team, "Keep on going—just keep on going. You're doing fine." Slawson says, "It was back-and-forth. You know, we made mistakes; then we would come back; then they would come back." Jeannette Alston scored 23 points and Slawson 22, a career high. According to the *Aiken Standard*, Alston "converted a three-point play with 5:53 left in the game. She then stole the ball and drove the length of the court for a layup to start Francis Marion on a 12–3 spurt that gave the Lady Patriots a 68–59 lead with 2:17 left." Slawson remembers that "Near the end, Sylvia called a time out and said, 'Now this is it. You seniors, this is it. What are you going to do? You've come this far! What are you going to do?'" Francis Marion beat Wayland Baptist 75–65. Slawson says that "both teams played their hearts out. Coach Hatchell just motivated us more, and we took home the trophy." Tracey Tillman made a combined 53 rebounds in the four tournament games and was named MVP.

The 1986 NAIA national championship celebration was bigger than the 1982 AIAW festivities. According to Sammy, everyone was "in celebration mode," and he and Sylvia went out to eat with the team. Then Sylvia had to take him straight to the airport to catch the Eastern Airlines red-eye back to Charlotte because he had to work the next day. Sylvia lifted the team curfew, and most of them stayed up all night, except for Slawson: "I showered and went to bed. I was sick." They flew out the next day, and when the plane reached its altitude, the pilot announced, "We would like to welcome on board the 1986 NAIA National Champions Francis Marion College." Everyone on the plane applauded. "We felt pretty proud," says Slawson.

They landed at the Florence airport, loaded onto vans, and a crowd followed them back to campus. "Everybody was at Francis Marion," says Slawson. "Everybody you could think of was there. We were tired, but we were so excited. All those people didn't have to be there, but they came out to welcome us." Slawson credits Sylvia with their dedicated fans: "The community was just fantastic. Coach Hatchell is one of the great communicators. She had everybody on our side—during our regular season, the games were packed. To be honest, with the caliber of fans we had, I think even if we had lost they would still have been there."

The 1986 championship earned Sylvia an even greater level of respect. On April 9, Governor Riley presented her a second Order of the Palmetto. On April 10, Sylvia's team was honored with Lady Patriots' Day, which included a key to the city of Florence. The team also led the Palmetto Balloon Classic parade on May 2 in Camden. Her Francis Marion Lady Patriots were scheduled to play UNC the following season, but after she won the championship, UNC head women's basketball coach Jennifer Alley called her to cancel the game. Sylvia was disappointed because she believed her team had a good chance to beat UNC.

Sylvia's championship season did not end on this high note, however. She attended the NCAA Division I women's basketball Final Four, on March 28 and 30, in Lexington, Kentucky, and stopped in Somerset to visit Bob Strunk's parents. She and Mrs. Strunk sat at the kitchen table, remembering the past and piecing together the sequence of events in Bob's last few days. She visited with the Strunks several hours, had dinner with them, and then made her way to Lexington. That was the last time she saw them. Mrs. Strunk died within two years: "I really think she died from a broken heart," says Sylvia.

Sylvia coached and taught at Francis Marion for 11 years, and though she credits much of her success and happiness to those years, when she won two national championships and married Sammy, she was underpaid. In 1986, with a record of 272–80, two national championships, and a master's degree from the University of Tennessee, her annual salary was $20,000. But Sylvia believes in work, and she gave Francis Marion good effort: "I've always said there are people who go to work and there are people who get things done. Some people just go to work, but don't get anything done." But she was also a realist, so she explored a variety of coaching opportunities. She interviewed twice at Winthrop, a Division II school, which had five different women's head coaches between 1975 and 1986. When Debbie Yow stepped down as head women's basketball coach at Florida in 1985, Sylvia interviewed for that position. But neither Winthrop nor Florida was the right fit.

Her interview for the women's basketball coaching position at Division I Indiana was "different." She did not understand why she was asked to meet with men's basketball coach Bobby Knight, but she speculated that Athletic Director Ralph Floyd wanted him to "size her up." Or perhaps it was because of the Olympic events staff experience in 1984, when Knight coached the USA men's basketball team. In cases such as these, says Sylvia, "I frequently eliminated myself, because I wasn't going to go just anywhere." When she detected an attitude of "We're Indiana—you're Francis Marion," she knew she was wrong for the job.

Sylvia's interview with Texas A&M was much more positive than the Indiana experience. She verbally agreed to take the job if they could find a position for Sammy. They flew Sammy to College Station and offered him a graduate assistantship, with the possibility of being an assistant baseball coach. Following Sammy's visit, they offered Sylvia the job, but the day before the official announcement, they called to say that giving Sammy a graduate assistantship would violate their nepotism policy. So Sylvia said, "No. I'm not coming." Sammy supported Sylvia totally during this period: "If the shoe had been on the other foot, and I had big schools coming after me, I would have wanted to do it. So I told her to 'go for it.'" Sammy says that none of these schools "were the right fit for her." And, then, the perfect fit presented itself.

4

Living Her Dream

In 1986, Sylvia's world changed with a series of unexpected events. After winning the NAIA national championship, she was named NAIA (Phyllis Holmes) national Coach of the Year. Following that honor, she and Marianne Stanley (head women's basketball coach at Old Dominion) were named assistants to Kay Yow, head coach for the Goodwill Games and FIBA World Championships for Women, both to be held in Moscow in the summer of 1986. The opportunity that affected her life most dramatically, however, was the opening for a head women's basketball coach at UNC. In May of 1986, a reporter from the *Florence Daily News* called Sylvia and asked, "Coach, are you sitting down?" She answered, "'No, but I will.' I sat down in a rocking chair, and he said, 'The North Carolina job just came open. Jennifer Alley just resigned.'" Sylvia was shocked to learn that Alley was leaving UNC women's basketball after nine years with a win-loss record of 179–104 overall and 70–36 in the ACC Conference: "I was like, WOW!" In 1985–86, the Tar Heel women's basketball team had earned a record of 23–9 in the ACC and had made it to the NCAA Sweet 16.

In the Maymester while Sylvia, Mrs. Strickland, and a group of friends were at Myrtle Beach, Beth Miller, the UNC Senior Associate Director of Athletics, called to ask if she was interested in the job. Sylvia immediately answered, "Yes!" and her already packed schedule was ratcheted up several notches, but she thrived on the bustle and excitement: "You talk about having fun!" She and Yow scouted players and competition, attending events and games in the United States and abroad. In May, Sylvia served as Head Court Coach for the U.S. Trials at the Olympic Training Center in Colorado Springs. In June, Sylvia, Yow, and Stanley trained the team at the Van Der Meer Tennis Center and Sea Pines Academy Gym on Hilton Head, South Carolina. Interestingly, Dick Weiss had reported in July of 1985 that both Yow and Stanley were being considered for the position of head women's basketball coach for the 1988 Olympics. If there was any rivalry, the three women never acknowledged it. In fact, Stanley remembers the collegiality, the support of USA Basketball (which was "as good as it gets"), and their "great working environment."

The first ever Goodwill Games were held in Moscow, July 5–20, 1986. Ted Turner created the Goodwill Games in 1986 as an alternative to the politically controversial Olympic Games, which had been boycotted by a number of nations in 1980 (including the United States) and again in 1984 (the Soviet Union). In her biography of Kay Yow, MaryEllen Williams says that Turner spent $50 million to create the games, which "rivaled any Olympics" in "size and grandeur."[1] The U.S. women's team defeated

Yugoslavia in the first game (72–53), followed by Brazil (91–70), Czechoslovakia (78–70), and Bulgaria (67–58). Cheryl Miller, Anne Donovan, and Teresa Edwards led the scoring for Team USA. Then they faced the undefeated Soviet Union in the championship game, which they won 83–60.

Kay Yow and Sylvia agreed not only on basketball strategy; they were also devout Christians who could not resist an opportunity that presented itself when they were sightseeing after the championship game. According to a November 12, 1986, *New York Times* article, Kay Yow was "approached" on Red Square by a woman they called "Iya," who "asked for medical supplies, including multivitamins and a certain prescription drug." Yow reported that she had an oversupply of multivitamins for the team and a "huge bottle" of the requested prescription. When Yow later gave Iya these items, she expressed a need for Ukrainian-language Bibles, a request Kay and Sylvia took seriously.[2] They returned from Moscow with a Gold Medal and a two-week window before they had to leave for training camp and then for Moscow a second time for the World Championships. A November 11, 1986, AP story reported that during their short time back in North Carolina, Sylvia and Kay "collected the items Iya and her father said they needed." According to this story, Sylvia identified Iya as part of a Moscow "Baptist underground" that needed not only Bibles but also "food and clothing."[3]

During the two weeks when she was back in the United States, Sylvia interviewed with UNC athletic director John Swofford for the position of head women's basketball coach. Swofford knew exactly what he wanted in a coach: Someone who knew the game and could teach it; someone with a proven track record; and someone who had the character and the values to match the University of North Carolina's academic standing. Swofford's final test was "Would I want my son or daughter to play for that person?"

Sylvia was not the only candidate for the job. Phil Lee (Vanderbilt); Charlene Curtis (Radford); and Sylvia's fellow assistant coach Marianne Stanley (Old Dominion) were among the other interviewees. "And I was at little Francis Marion," recalls Sylvia. At the time, she and Stanley did not know that they were competing for the job. Not even Kay Yow knew that Stanley had applied, so Sylvia's focus was strictly on the interview: "I remember talking with Mr. Swofford, and before I left I leaned across his desk, and I said, 'Mr. Swofford, I don't care what you pay me—I want this job.'" Swofford says, "I don't think I ever interviewed a potential head coach at Carolina that wanted the job more than Sylvia did. It truly was her dream job."

Immediately after her UNC interview, Sylvia, Stanley, and Yow went to U.S. national team camp at Eastern Michigan State to train Team USA for the World Championships. At the training site, Sylvia and Yow shared a dorm suite, and one afternoon, they found a pink telephone message taped to the door: "Call John Swofford." Sylvia showed it to Kay, who drew a deep breath. There were no phones in dorm rooms, so Sylvia had to go downstairs to the resident assistants' office to make the call. Swofford offered her the job, she accepted on the spot, and went back upstairs and gave Kay the news. After training the U.S. National team in Michigan, the three of them boarded a plane for Finland, their first stopover, and at 4:00 p.m. on July 30, while their international flight was sitting on a runway during a two-hour delay at

O'Hare in Chicago, UNC held a press conference announcing that Sylvia Hatchell had been appointed the new UNC head coach. She missed her own press conference announcing to the world that she had realized her dream.

One of Sylvia's first tasks as the new UNC women's basketball head coach was to build her staff. She immediately called Andrew Calder: "Andrew, do you remember sitting in the stands at Francis Marion, watching an AAU basketball game, and you said if I ever got my dream job at UNC, you would come be my assistant?" Andrew remembered. She continued, "Well, I got the job. Will you come?" At that time, Calder was a volunteer assistant to Bill Foster with the University of South Carolina men's basketball team. He agreed without hesitation and packed for Chapel Hill. Calder's reputation as a coach had grown since he and Sylvia first met, and in 1985 he was named AAU National Coach of the Year for the Under 19 Boys' Team.

While Calder was moving to Chapel Hill, Yow, Stanley, and Sylvia were in Moscow for the tenth World Championships for women. The games were held August 8–17, 1986, in three Soviet Union venues (Vilnius, Minsk, and Moscow). On August 1, 1986, before the Championships began, Sylvia sent her parents a postcard: "Greetings from Russia! We play Taiwan tomorrow. If we win the championship then we get Gold Rings." She then added a poignant comment: "Check on Sammy for me. He's a little nervous about moving to Chapel Hill and going back to school."

The Taiwan game gave the United States an easy victory. Yow's team defeated Taipei 105–52. In succession, they handily defeated Czechoslovakia (89–61), Hungary (78–63), Australia (76–50), China (99–74), and Canada (82–59). According to the USA Basketball official website, both the USA and Soviet teams "cruised to the semifinals untouched." Having been defeated by USA (83–60) in the Goodwill Games in July, the Soviet Union "wanted revenge," and USA wanted "proof" that their win "was no fluke." Again, the USA team won the Gold Medal, beating the Soviet Union (108–88) for the second time in a month.

They were also pleased to deliver the Bibles and other items they had collected for "Iya" and the secret or "underground" churches. Sylvia says they gave the Russians tennis shoes, blue jeans, hosiery, and toiletry articles: "I left every pair of tennis shoes I had and a boom box." Sylvia, Yow, and Stanley returned home at the end of August in 1986 with Gold Medals from both the Goodwill Games and the World Championships. Only then did Sylvia learn that she and Stanley had competed for the UNC head coach position, but she had other, more pressing concerns: "When I got back, it was a whirlwind. I had jet lag so bad, but I had to get to North Carolina within three days." The Francis Marion fall semester had already begun, so she had to vacate her office immediately. Eleanor Rogers Burns remembers that the Francis Marion community was disappointed to lose Sylvia, but "very happy for her. With her success, we knew she wouldn't stay on. And she never forgot us." When Sylvia walked out of her Francis Marion office for the last time, Mrs. Strickland handed her a CD recording of Michael W. Smith's "Friends Are Friends Forever," and "she just bawled," says Sylvia. "She sobbed, 'Oh, what am I going to do without you?'"

Sylvia's departure from Francis Marion had no legal complications because she was still on a year-to-year contract. The college issued a press release announcing a farewell reception for her in Smith College Center on Wednesday, August 20, from

7:00 to 9:00 p.m., three days after the conclusion of the World Championships in Moscow. The press release recounted her successful eleven years, beginning with her first career win over Voorhees College (88–62) on January 14, 1976, but it also mentioned the bitter 1983 double-overtime loss (105–103) to Campbellsville.[4] Sylvia remembers that she "cried and cried. And I don't cry much." *Lord, have mercy*, she thought. *What am I doing? You know I love this place and these people. Sammy and I are so happy here. What am I doing?*

Sylvia's official contract with UNC was effective August 1, and she was nearly three weeks behind. Sammy had resigned his coaching job at Byrnes Academy when she accepted the UNC job, so while she was traveling the globe for the Goodwill Games and the World Championships, the burden of the transition from Florence to Chapel Hill fell to Sammy. "I wasn't there," says Sylvia. "That was tough because he had a lot on him—just being there by himself." Sylvia's contract included moving expenses, but they didn't have a house, so Sammy found an apartment and moved a chest of drawers, a mattress (which they put on the floor), two forks, two spoons, two knives, a few clothes, and the ironing board and iron. On top of everything else, Sylvia did not have the opportunity to announce her departure to her Francis Marion players in person. Her UNC career was off to a late start, and she felt out of sync: "I was so green. I didn't know anybody. I had been in a world where I was Queen Bee, and I was starting over where nobody knew me."

Her new assistant coach, Andrew Calder, arrived in Chapel Hill before she did, and having him in place made her transition easier. Still, she says, "when I think back to that time, I wonder, *How did I ever do that?*" Her salary nearly doubled from $20,000 to $36,000, but because Sammy wasn't working, their income did not increase. Almost immediately, Sammy started looking for a house and found something suitable in Durham, not far from Duke, at 3620 Manford Drive. The price was $87,050, but they had not sold their house in Florence, so they had no cash for a down payment. Sylvia took $10,000 out of her South Carolina retirement account for a down payment: "It was the worst financial decision I ever made," she says. When they were in a better financial situation, she tried to buy back nine of her eleven total years in the South Carolina retirement system. She was shocked that the original $10,000 she had borrowed would cost her $157,000 to buy back into the system. "At the time," she says, "we needed it, but it was a bad financial decision."

A bright spot was the September 19, 1986, announcement that Kay Yow would be the coach of the 1988 USA Olympic women's basketball team, pending official confirmation. Immediately, she announced her choice of assistant coaches: her sister Susan and Sylvia Hatchell. Sylvia was elated to have a third shot at an international Gold Medal, and she believed she could assist Yow while also meeting the challenges at UNC, but she didn't expect what came next.

On Sunday, November 9, 1986, Kay Yow spoke to the congregation of Morris Chapel United Methodist Church in Walkertown, North Carolina, and revealed that she and her staff took Bibles and other items to Moscow when they coached the World Championships. The news spread quickly. On November 11, the Associated Press reported that Bill Wall, head of USA Basketball, was "concerned and embarrassed": "A basketball team representing the United States and visiting another country simply is not the place for this, no place for this at all.... This was the coach of our national women's team, and we chose her to coach the next Olympic team. I am very concerned." There was speculation that Sylvia and Kay's actions might "jeopardize" Yow's confirmation as the 1988 Olympic coach. Sylvia downplayed the incident: "The smuggling was 'very low key,' she said. 'No one lost any perspective. We were there, first of all, to win basketball games. Kay kept cool about it.'"[5] A UPI version of the story—also on November 11—reported that "Yow and her assistants never thought the smuggling would jeopardize the team or embarrass the United States." Sylvia said, "We thought, 'Why not? There's nothing to lose.'" The same UPI story quoted Yow as saying, "I have to believe the Lord placed me in the Soviet Union this summer.... I have learned since I returned that people have been arrested for taking religious material in there. The maximum sentence is 20 years for that."[6] By Wednesday, November 12, the story had made it to the *New York Times*, which reported that Bill Wall appeared "to be more troubled than the Russians themselves. A spokesman for the Soviet Embassy in Washington said ... that he strongly doubted his Government would comment on 'such a minor incident.'"[7] Nothing more came of it, and in February 1987 Yow was formally approved as the 1988 Olympic women's basketball coach for Team USA.

Sylvia had realized her dream, but the dream job was a high-profile coaching position that demanded near perfection. She accepted the job in late July, so she had missed the recruiting cycle for that year and had to coach a team of players whom she did not sign—much less know. Sylvia could have raided her Francis Marion team for players, especially Tracey Tillman, who was good enough to play for UNC but would have had to sit out a year. Sylvia told Tillman that if she wanted to move up to the next level she could: "But I didn't really try to talk her into it. I didn't try to take any of those kids." The Lady Tar Heels' win-loss record through January 28, 1987, was encouraging—12 wins and 6 losses—but then Sylvia's personal life was dealt another blow.

On Friday, January 30, 1987, Sylvia traveled with her team to Maryland and had just checked into the hotel when Mary Lou Strickland Garnett called with devastating news. After a year in remission, her mother's cancer had returned. In 1986, Mrs. Strickland had been diagnosed with colon cancer. Mary Lou, pregnant with her first child Molly, kept Sylvia apprised of her mother's progress through two surgeries, a battery of treatments, and a good outcome—remission. Now the cancer was back, and Mary Lou said the doctor in Florence, South Carolina, "gave up." He told the family, "There is no more I can do." Sylvia's response was immediate: "No, no! We are NOT giving up!" She told Mary Lou to bring Mrs. Strickland to North Carolina: "I'll get you an appointment with an oncologist at the UNC Cancer Center."

On Saturday morning, January 31, before the Maryland game, Sylvia called Dr. Timothy Taft, who recommended a top surgeon. Her Tar Heels lost the game to Maryland 82–71, and she returned to Chapel Hill with a heavy heart but with a strategy. Within four short days, Mrs. Strickland had an appointment with a world-class physician—Dr. Ben Calvo—at the Lineberger Cancer Center. On Thursday morning, six days after Mary Lou had called Sylvia in Maryland, he removed a large tumor from the liver, but Mrs. Strickland was not cancer free and had to endure a long treatment regimen. During this period, when she and Mary Lou made the trip to Chapel Hill, Sylvia insisted that they stay with her: "That's how Sylvia is," says Mary Lou.

In Sylvia's first year at UNC, the Lady Tar Heels enjoyed a winning season: 19–10 overall and 9–5 in the ACC. Her Lady Tar Heels made it to the ACC Tournament semifinals, losing—ironically—to Kay Yow's NC State team 70–63. Their appearance in the NCAA Tournament ended in the second round with a loss to Marianne Stanley's Old Dominion team (76–58) on UNC's home court. Unfortunately, the 1986–1987 team lost three seniors—three excellent players—and only one freshman joined the team. After that, says Sylvia, "the well was dry."

In the summer of 1987, Sylvia focused on recruiting and building her team while still scouting for USA basketball, but she took time out to enjoy a summer afternoon in Pat Summitt's swimming pool. While she was enjoying the water, someone handed Pat a cordless phone. It was Nora Lynn Finch, the NC State associate athletic director, with devastating news: Kay Yow had been diagnosed with breast cancer. "I remember that like it was yesterday," says Sylvia. She and Pat climbed out of the pool and called Kay, who reported that she was scheduled for immediate surgery, followed by chemotherapy. Sylvia faced a tough decision: She realized that Yow's diagnosis would affect scouting and travel for the 1988 Olympics. She needed to focus on building her own UNC women's program, but she also needed to honor her commitment to Yow as her assistant Olympic coach. During 1987, Yow underwent the surgery and extended treatment while Sylvia and Susan Yow scouted players for Team USA. While Kay recovered, Sylvia and Jill Hutchinson scouted their Olympic competition at the European Championships, held in Cadiz, Spain, September 4–11.

When the UNC 1987–1988 basketball season got under way, Sylvia's Lady Tar Heels struggled. She was not accustomed to losing games, much less losing seasons, and she had thought that the 1986–1987 record might be her lowest, but 1987–1988 was worse. The team fell to sixth place in the ACC regular season, with a record of 4–10. Remarkably, three of its four conference wins were against their close rivals; they beat Duke twice (66–65 and 68–64) and NC State once in double-overtime (75–74). They finished the season 10–17 overall and were knocked out of the first round of the ACC Tournament by Wake Forest (61–53). For the first time in six years, the Lady Tar Heels did not get a bid to the NCAA Tournament.

Coping with a deteriorating, high-profile basketball program and cancer in two of her best friends, Sylvia nevertheless established a normal home life. When she and Sammy lived in Florence, they often drove one hour to Myrtle Beach for supper and rode around looking at property. They rented beach houses for vacations and talked about how they would love to own their own place. In March of 1988, their dream found them. Out of the blue, Sammy's father Leo called to say he knew a man who wanted to sell his house at the beach. After work one day, she and Sammy drove to Cherry Grove in North Myrtle Beach to see the house, and the next day she negotiated the purchase.

The house quickly became their get-away sanctuary, a place they could relax and forget about the pressures of coaching and teaching, and a place for intimacy and romance. On a May morning, Sylvia was lying on the couch at the beach house and thought, *Something ain't right—I don't feel normal—something is different*: "People laugh at me for saying this, but I knew immediately that I was pregnant. Something was different. I mean, really!" Indeed, she was pregnant. "I'm telling you," she says, "if it hadn't been for the beach house, Van would never have been here." Children had not been uppermost in their minds. "We were very happy," says Sylvia. "We were just so into each other." She has always believed that events happen as they are meant to: "But, to be honest, I just didn't think I could get pregnant." In August, they invited Leo and stepmother Inez to the beach house and shared the news: "We are going to have a baby." Leo looked puzzled and said, "This year?" Sammy said, "It only takes nine months."

Sylvia's pregnancy did not alter her commitment to assist Kay Yow in coaching Team USA in the 1988 summer Olympics, so in June she traveled to Kuala Lumpur with Yow and her sister Susan to scout their Olympic competition at a Malaysian tournament. Sylvia was six weeks pregnant and having morning sickness. Upon their return home, they trained the USA women's basketball team at the Air Force Academy in Colorado Springs where Sylvia finally told the team that she was pregnant: "Before and after practices, the girls would all touch or rub my stomach for good luck." Team USA was strong. Coach Yow made difficult and controversial decisions in the final selection process, cutting a few players because they were not a good fit, including University of Southern California Cheryl Miller, who had played on the 1984 Jones Cup and Olympic teams, both of which won Gold Medals. The selection process produced a strong team with good chemistry. Because there was not one star player to carry the load, every team member knew she had to "step up." "It was a great team," says Sylvia.

The Olympics were held in Seoul, South Korea, September 9–29, 1988. Sylvia, Kay, and Susan worked well together. "We worked hard," says Susan, "and there wasn't a time that we weren't focused on what we were about." Susan understood her place: "Sylvia was Kay's right-hand person, and I was the next person in line." They also had a good time. They practiced at the U.S. Army Garrison (Yongsan) where they could get American hamburgers. They cruised the famous Itaewon shopping district, where Sylvia found bargains too good to pass up: "I'm telling you, things were dirt cheap." She bought all her Christmas gifts, including a right-handed baseball glove for her unborn baby. But one of Sylvia's most vivid memories was a private tour of the demilitarized zone between North and South Korea, led by a four-star general, for Sylvia, Kay, Susan, Maria Shriver, and Tom Brokaw.

Despite her pregnancy, Sylvia felt great and gained very little weight. Her staff would ask, "Where do you get all that energy?" At home, she had been in an energized nesting mode, cleaning out closets and rearranging furniture: "I was just busting with energy." She continued to be the team talisman: Before games they rubbed her belly for good luck. In the preliminary round, Team USA defeated Czechoslovakia (87–81), Yugoslavia (101–74), and China (94–79). Eight teams competed in the semi-final round on September 27, when USA was paired against the Soviet Union. USA's 102–88 win sent them to the final round against Yugoslavia—again—whom they defeated 77–70 to win the Gold Medal.

Sylvia returned from the Olympics and had to "hit the ground running again," because her own 1988–1989 season was gearing up. But a month later, at Thanks-

Left to right: Barbara Gill, Sylvia Hatchell, Kay Yow, and Susan Yow at the 1988 Olympics, Seoul, South Korea. Courtesy Sylvia Hatchell.

giving, she was in Hawaii with her UNC women's team for the Rainbow Wahine Classic. "When I was pregnant, I traveled the world three times: Kuala Lumpur; Seoul, Korea; and Hawaii, with no complications." While Sylvia was training Team USA, traveling the globe, and winning a Gold Medal in Seoul, Sammy was finishing his master's degree at UNC, just 18 months after entering graduate school in January 1987. At the end of the summer of 1988, he earned the Master of Arts in Teaching and found a job coaching basketball and softball and teaching physical education at Meredith College in Raleigh, a top-ranked private, independent women's college, founded in 1891. The Meredith women's basketball team had won three games in 1986–87 and two games in 1987–88, but Sammy felt he could turn the program around, so in the summer of 1988, he faced two new challenges: fatherhood and a losing basketball team.

Sylvia's UNC women's basketball team continued to struggle. They did not fare well in the 1988 November Rainbow Wahine Classic in Honolulu, Hawaii, but in non-conference play, they lost only two games and won seven, beating teams such as Indiana, Alabama, UCLA, and Minnesota. Though eight months pregnant, Sylvia's energy did not wane and her court-side manner did not alter. On January 4, 1989, she traveled with the team to South Carolina, who beat her Tar Heels 98–71. Down by 19 points with nearly nine minutes to go in the second half, referee Tommy Salerno gave Sylvia two technical fouls. She told Lezlie Patterson with *The State*, "Can you believe he called two technicals on me—an 8½-month pregnant woman?" Sylvia thought the baby would arrive before her January 14 game against Georgia Tech. It did not. Amid her and Sammy's hectic lives, she believed that she could "arrange" the birth with lit-tle disruption for her struggling team. The official due date was January 22, and Syl-via's obstetrician, Dr. Nebel, agreed that if she had not delivered by then, he would induce labor.

January 22 came and went. Sylvia felt no labor pains, so Dr. Nebel agreed to induce labor on Tuesday morning, January 24, 1989. She and Sammy drove to Durham County General Hospital, still discussing names. When she discovered that Sammy had left his video camera at Meredith College, she was furious; she wanted a video of the birth. At the hospital, Sammy called Annette Alston, whom they had hired as their nanny and helpmate. (Annette and her twin Jeannette had played on the 1985–1986 NAIA Francis Marion championship team.) Annette picked up a video camera from Meredith and delivered it to Sammy.

Hospital staff checked Sylvia in and assigned her to a comfortable birthing suite: "They hooked me up, and by 7:00 a.m., I was watching the contractions on the moni-tor, and I'm thinking, *Okay. I'm tough. I can take pain.*" Sylvia prides herself on a cer-tain degree of stoicism: "You know, really, nothing much ever bothered me. I had never taken medicine my whole life. I just thought, *Put on your big girl panties and deal with it.* I'm not real sympathetic with complainers, to be honest with you." Her attitude was about to be adjusted.

She settled in, watching the contractions on the monitor, and gradually the pains increased. "I could feel them coming, and then I'm like, 'Oh, God!'" Dr. Nebel said, "When it gets to be too much, we'll give you an epidural." In a short time, she said, "'Uhmmm, I think I might be ready for that epidural.' So I rolled over on my side, and they put the needle in my spine. 'Well,' I said, 'Is this thing supposed to work? Cause it's not working.'" Dr. Nebel determined that the epidural was effective on one side only. So they had to start over and repeat the procedure; this time it worked. "But," says Sylvia, "it made me so numb I couldn't feel anything at all. Then they said, 'You've dilated enough, and you need to start pushing.' I never once felt the urge to push, and the nurses were telling me, 'Push! Push! Push!' I don't ever remember my water break-ing. I'm thinking, *What's this thing about water breaking? There's no water—nothing has broken here.*"

Sylvia followed orders, breathing and pushing, breathing and pushing, harder and harder. The second epidural made her nauseated: "Every time those contractions would come—and I'd see them on that monitor—everyone in the room would yell, 'Push! Push! Push!'" And every time she pushed, she threw up. By 1:30 in the after-noon, she was exhausted and began losing consciousness in between contractions. She heard someone say, "I can see the head. I can see the head. He's got a head full of hair." She shot back, "Just grab that head full of hair and pull him out! Yank him out of there!" By 4:00 p.m., she still had not delivered. Dr. Nebel came in to evaluate Sylvia's condition, and when he stepped to the side of the bed, she "grabbed him by the throat. He probably still has the claw marks around his neck. I said, 'Dr. Nebel, you've got to do something for me, and you've got to do it NOW!'" He said, "Take her to the oper-ating room." From the beginning of her pregnancy, she had made it clear that she did not want a Caesarian birth, a C-Section, because the recovery time would keep her off the basketball court. She begged, "Please don't cut me open."

In the operating room, Dr. Nebel performed an episiotomy: "They cut me bad. But they didn't do a C-section." At 4:33 p.m. on January 24, 1989, her son was born. Sylvia heard "waaaah—waaaah. It was not a scream—more like a little Billy-goat." Then they laid him in her arms, and she saw that full head of hair. He was a big baby, 8 pounds, 11 ounces. They chose the name Van Davis: "Van" for Sylvia's grandfather, Van Buren Shepard, and "Davis" for Sammy's maternal grandfather, Sam Bailey Davis. As planned, Sammy recorded the birth: "The video is somewhere around the house," he says, suggesting that they have not viewed it often, if at all.

After the birth, neither mother nor son were out of the woods. Dr. Nebel stitched up the episiotomy, and Sylvia was moved from the operating room to a regular hospital room. The difference between the birthing suite that she occupied at 7:00 in the morning and the hospital room she was assigned at 5:30 in the afternoon was stark. Sylvia thought, *Where's my nice room? I've gone from the Marriott to Motel 6.* As the effects of the epidural and other medications wore off, she "got the shakes. So here I was in that hospital bed, and I would be talking to somebody, and all of a sudden I would start shaking and I couldn't stop." Still, her focus was on the 7:00 p.m. NC State game that she was missing. At 6:00 p.m., an hour and a half after the birth, she was able to talk via speaker phone to her team from her hospital bed. Their conversation was broadcast on radio station WCHL in Chapel Hill.

After her speaker-phone conversation, Sammy left her to join his father Leo and stepmother Inez in the waiting area. Leo was so excited by the prospect of his first grandchild's birth that he came to the hospital in a suit and tie, "like he was going to church on Sunday morning," as Sylvia describes it. He and Inez sat in the hospital all day, waiting for Van to be born. Sammy said, "Daddy, you could at least have dressed casual." They were standing in the hallway talking when they saw nurses running toward Sylvia's room. Sammy asked, "What's going on?" They pushed him out of the way. After the day's trauma, he couldn't imagine what else might go wrong, but Sylvia was lying on the floor unconscious. A nurse had helped her to the bathroom, and—as Sylvia describes it—"I just wiped out." The next day, Sylvia and Van were resting in her hospital bed when the UNC women's basketball staff came to visit, including Andrew Calder. In Sylvia's absence Andrew had coached the game against NC State, which the Wolfpack won 86–69. Keeping the focus off the loss, Sylvia began describing the difficult birth, and as Andrew listened, he broke out in a sweat: "The next thing you know," remembers Sylvia, "he has passed out. And the nurses are coming in with cold packs and cold towels, wiping his face, and waving smelling salts under his nose."

The birth of a new Tar Heel was widely announced. Both *USA Today* (January 26) and the *New York Times* (January 25) carried the story, but the cleverest announcement was generated by Sylvia herself. She borrowed the idea from Rick Strunk, the Sports Information Director at Lenoir-Rhyne. It appeared in *The State* (Columbia, South Carolina) on January 26, 1989: "Coaches Sylvia and Sammy Hatchell have officially signed their first recruit, Van Davis Hatchell, who was born at 4:23 Tuesday at Durham County General Hospital." The article stated that the "signing ended nine months of speculations and intense negotiations." Sammy added that he and Sylvia "made the initial contact, but most of the labor for this one was on Sylvia's part.

She literally stayed with this kid for nine months and deserves a lot of credit." The announcement ended with speculation that "there will be no shortage of babysitters."[8]

Annette was Van's nanny for six months. When she left Chapel Hill to play professional basketball in Oslo, Norway, the Hatchells turned to another Francis Marion friend, Deneene Herring, who had been Sylvia's scorekeeper when Francis Marion won the NAIA national championship in 1986. According to Van, Deneene "had a big, big hand in raising me, especially in the early years. I would say that she had almost as much of an impact as my parents did because we were always together." From the night of his birth, Van was part of the UNC women's basketball family. He was a good baby, so sometimes Sylvia took him to the office and laid him in the corner of the sofa. She put a towel around his neck and positioned the bottle in the towel so he could nurse.

After Van's birth in January, Sylvia again turned her attention to her struggling team. Beginning in January 1989, however, the team won only one game in regular ACC play against Duke (93–92), then lost 14 consecutive games, settling for eighth place in a conference with nine members. Their only win after Duke was against non-conference Mount St. Mary's (116–92). They lost to Maryland in the first round of the ACC Tournament, ending the season 10–20 overall and 1–13 in the ACC: "We were struggling," says Sylvia. "Oh my gosh—that was when the team was just terrible." She told herself that if she had not become involved in USA Basketball and the Olympics, she "could have gotten the team going sooner. Bigger, faster. It took me longer to get things going than I had planned. But I felt like I was making the right decisions." For one thing, through USA Basketball, she made connections in the coaching world that would never have been open to her otherwise. Most importantly, she had kept her promise to Kay Yow.

By March, she needed a break from basketball, so instead of watching March Madness on television one Sunday afternoon, Sylvia took a ride and came upon an Open House on Knotty Pine Drive in Durham County. Van was six months old, and Deneene had come to live with them, so they needed more room. The house was larger than their Manford Drive home and closer to campus, so when the builder offered the Hatchells a good deal, they accepted it and moved into their third home in 10 years: 6917 Knotty Pine Drive.

Sylvia looked to the summer and fall of 1989 for respite, but she was balancing enormous responsibilities: trying to rejuvenate and build her team, being a new mother, hiring a new nanny, buying a new house, and moving. Sylvia was gearing up practices, getting ready for the season: "In December I was just exhausted—just zonked. I felt so tired and thought, *Well, I'm anemic.*" Her doctors found nothing, and she kept saying, "I have no energy. I just want to sleep all the time." Her doctors ordered still more tests and, by Christmas, she had a diagnosis: mononucleosis. She was 37 years old, had a new baby, was responsible for one of the most high-profile women's basketball programs in the country, and needed all the energy she could muster, but she had mono, an infection that usually affects teens and young adults.

Mononucleosis took its toll on Sylvia. It was the end of January before she started feeling "decent," and her team continued to struggle. The 1989–1990 season was one of her worst, with a conference record of three wins and 11 losses. The next season (1990–91) was equally horrible. UNC won two ACC games and lost 12. Despite her struggling team, Sylvia continued to focus on women's basketball beyond UNC Chapel Hill. In December 1990, she and Gina Markland, the women's basketball coach at Coastal Carolina, created the Coastal Carolina Classic Tournament at Myrtle Beach. The two had met at Pat Summitt's basketball camps in Tennessee when Sylvia was still at Francis Marion. According to Markland, Sylvia was the impetus for creating the tournament: "She kept saying, 'We need to do a North and South Carolina basketball tournament.' So, I decided I would try to do it." In the beginning, the Classic was limited to eight teams, but later teams came from everywhere— Nebraska, Iowa, Northern Illinois. It evolved into a double-header day for women's college teams,

Van Hatchell, Deneene Herring, and Sassafras, 1991. Courtesy Sylvia Hatchell.

and the tournament name has gone through several iterations. Sylvia calls it the Holiday Classic and acknowledges there is confusion about the name: "We'll call it WHATEVER, just so long as people come."

For *whatever* reason—Olympics, Coastal Carolina Classic, Sylvia's personal life—the UNC women's Tar Heels were last in the ACC for three consecutive years. Sylvia admits that these were dark days. One of the lowest points in her career came on January 29, 1991, when the Durham *Herald-Sun* ran a story with a huge color photograph of Sylvia talking to her point guard Emily Johnson on the sideline. The headline read "Black Cloud in Blue Heaven," and the story continued in double columns on the inside. Sports writer Jim Furlong detailed her losses and contrasted her losing record to winning records of other UNC women's varsity teams: soccer, field hockey, track, swimming, volleyball, and softball. He attributed Sylvia's last-place ranking in the ACC and her 32 losses in 36 ACC games to "unproductive recruiting, several season-ending injuries, frequent poor shooting and a lack of outstanding talent." She was devastated. No one had ever written such negative things about her. Furlong had interviewed UNC athletic director John Swofford, who described the UNC women's basketball program as being in a "building mode," not "weak." He insisted that there was no move to dismiss Sylvia, who was working on a year-to-year contract at that time. Furlong also interviewed Sylvia, who defended her record and her team, emphasized their academic strength, and called for patience. He concluded the article with Sylvia's plea, "Give me a little more time."[9]

Swofford's positive comments were of no comfort, and she felt that Furlong was on a witch hunt, hoping to get her fired. She had landed her dream job, had a great marriage and a two-year-old son, but she got the message: She couldn't fail. Chapel Hill was not a fun place to be when she was losing: "The UNC community and the media treat losers like lepers," she says. She reached out to her friends, such as Judy Stroud, trying to recruit her as an assistant coach. Stroud, who had left coaching and gone into the insurance business, understood Sylvia's distress and encouraged her, telling her that "times would roll around in her favor—that times would change.... You just have to recruit the kind of athletes that you had at Francis Marion—it will turn around.'"

Sammy, more than anyone else, empathized with Sylvia's public humiliation and her sense of defeat. Sylvia prayed: "I am doing everything right, Lord. I'm doing it the right way, but it just seems like nothing is working. Am I not supposed to be here?" Another disappointment came at the end of the 1990–91 losing season. Sylvia was hoping to be selected as the 1992 women's basketball Olympic coach, especially after helping Kay Yow bring home the Gold in 1988. Instead, she lost the position to Theresa Grentz at Rutgers. Sylvia realized that her record at UNC raised questions; still, it was another blow to her already wounded ego. Coached by Grentz, the USA women's basketball team brought home the Bronze Medal in the 1992 Olympics.

One rainy night following Furlong's article, the women's team was lifting weights after practice, and Sylvia dropped in. As she was leaving the weight room in Kenan Fieldhouse around 5:30 p.m., the early winter darkness matched her state of mind. She ran into John Swofford who knew that she was desperate—she had hit her all-time emotional and professional low. He put his arm around her as they walked out and said, "You are *my* coach, and I *believe* in you." Then he got in his car and drove away. "That was my endorsement," says Sylvia. "That's all I needed, right there, and I just wanted to work day and night, and I wanted to be successful for him. I wanted to win so badly for him." She went back to her office in Carmichael that night and worked until early morning: "I wanted to prove that he had not made a bad hire—that I was the right choice and right decision." Beginning that night, recruitment became her passion. She knew that if she *didn't* recruit top players who were also strong academically, if she *didn't* turn the UNC women's basketball program around, she would be fired, a tough realization for a woman who had rarely failed at anything.

The *Herald-Sun* article came at the point when Sylvia and her team were on the brink of becoming winners. Though they won only two ACC games that year, their overall record was 12 wins and 16 losses, an improvement over the 1988–89 overall record of 10 wins and 20 losses. Sylvia says, "We were working unbelievable hours. But recruiting wasn't good; academics were not good; everything was off. Sometimes you have to walk before you can run; sometimes you have to crawl before you can walk. We had to crawl and walk a little bit before we ever could even think about running." The team began to improve academically and started making small advances, but its coach was still in despair. During that summer, when Sylvia and her family went to the beach, she walked the shore alone for hours, asking herself, "What are we going to do?" And she prayed: "God you put me at UNC. What's going on here? Something's got to change. I'm doing everything I can. I'm busting my behind. I can't do any more. What's going to happen here?" Then the answer came. She decided to "put things in God's hands," relax, and not worry about the negative publicity or the threat of failure. She would "chill out" and not put extra pressure on herself by worrying and fretting. She said to herself, *God has everything in His control. I'm going to go out there and have fun.* In the fall, she returned as a rejuvenated leader who enjoyed coaching and refused to let public opinion rattle her. She believed that "God had a plan."

Part of that "plan" may have been a key recruit for the 1991–92 season, Charlotte Smith. Charlotte's uncle David Thompson played on the 1974 NC State men's basketball team, coached by Norm Sloan, that won NC State's first national championship. Basketball was in her DNA. She began playing in seventh grade and first met Sylvia in 1989 when she was a junior at Shelby High School in Shelby, North Carolina, playing power forward.

Another recruit for the 1991–92 team was Stephanie Lawrence from Morrow High School (Morrow, Georgia), which won three consecutive girls' state championships, largely because of her success with the three-point shot (49.7 percent). In a 2017 interview, Lawrence said she was highly recruited but didn't "have any idea" where she would attend college. She considered Stanford and Ole Miss. Twenty-two coaches visited her home in a three-week period, but Sylvia Hatchell and Andrew Calder "sold the dream" for what they wanted to accomplish. Lawrence says,

> I fell in love with the vision that Coach Hatchell had for the program. At the time, they were at the bottom of the ACC. During the recruiting process, I had many other coaches tell me, "I don't know why you're looking at UNC because if she doesn't win this season she's gonna get fired." I decided to ignore that advice and go with my gut. That was where I really needed to be, and God intended me to be there for some reason.

When the 1991–92 preseason rankings were published, both the AP Poll and Coaches' Poll picked UNC to be last in the ACC, as it had been for three straight years. Sylvia Crawley and Tonya Sampson returned as sophomores. Sampson was the 1990 North Carolina High-School Player of the Year. Tonya "got it," says Sylvia's brother Ralph, "and it was like flipping a switch." The team began to gel. Sammy says, "They just took off." At the end of the 1991–1992 season, the team ranked third out of nine ACC teams and lost to Virginia (74–55) in the semifinals of the ACC Tournament. This performance boosted them to the NCAA Tournament, for the first time since 1987. In the first round, played on their home court, they defeated Old Dominion (60–54), a win that sent them to the second round of the NCAA Tournament in Miami, Florida, where they lost to Miami (86–72). The Lady Tar Heels finished the season 9–7 in the ACC and 22–9 overall.

Sylvia needed more talent. In the 1992–93 season Crawley and Sampson were returning juniors; Charlotte Smith and Stephanie Lawrence were sophomores. Though Sylvia was confident in those players, she kept searching. Then, in the spring and summer of 1992, a strong possibility came to her attention—a great track athlete named Marion Jones from Thousand Oaks, California, who was also a good basketball player. The UNC head track coach, Dennis Craddock, wanted to know if Sylvia had any interest in bringing her to UNC to consider both sports. Sylvia's answer was "Sure!" Assistant track coach Curtis Frye and Sylvia's assistant Fred Applin went to California for a home visit with Marion.

Marion Jones liked what she heard from Frye and Applin, so she chose UNC for one of the five official visits to campuses allowed by the NCAA. Jones's interest in other universities was primarily for track, but she also had a strong desire to play basketball. When Marion Jones and her mother visited UNC, Sylvia and Craddock asked right off, "Marion, what do *you* want to do?" Jones answered, "I want to do both sports." The home visit, the campus visit, and the meeting with Sylvia and Craddock were convincing. Jones committed to UNC before she left the gym. According to NCAA rules, Jones's primary sport at UNC had to be basketball; track would be secondary. Sylvia and Craddock knew that the World Championships were on the horizon, followed by the Olympics. At the outset, they all agreed that Jones could redshirt a year for the World Championships. Sylvia assured her, "Whatever you need to do—we will do that." In November 1992, Jones signed a letter of intent with UNC.

In the interim, good recruiting began to pay off. The 1992–93 team got off to a great start, winning its first nine games. Tonya Cooper, Tonya Jackson, Kim Rouse, Maja Vukojcic, and Julie Wight were freshmen; Gwendolyn Gillingham, Stephanie Lawrence, Carrie McKee, Charlotte Smith, and Jill Suddreth were sophomores; juniors included Sylvia Crawley and Tonya Sampson. Toni Montgomery was the only returning senior. By February 6, 1993, the team was 18–2 overall, and Sylvia was enjoying her best season since arriving at UNC. On February 9, 1993, she traveled with the team to Virginia, where her Tar Heels suffered their third loss of the season (73–67). The bus ride home was long, and she arrived in Chapel Hill late: "I remember I came in at 3:00 a.m. on February 10. As I walked in the front door, Sammy came down the steps and said, 'My dad had a heart attack and died tonight.'" After a couple of hours of sleep, Sammy left for Florence to be with Inez and the family. Ironically, Sylvia was already scheduled to be in Florence to be inducted into the Francis Marion Hall of Fame on Saturday, February 13. She and Sammy had planned to take four-year-old Van and make it a family weekend with Leo and Inez, but they decided that Van was too young for a funeral, so Sylvia stayed back to tell him that his grandfather had died: "I remember sitting Van down and talking to him about Pop Pop, that he had gone to heaven."

Though Van was only four, he had developed a good relationship with his grandfather Hatchell because Sylvia and Sammy allowed Van to spend overnights and weekends with him. Van vividly remembers Leo's taking him to an auction in Evergreen and buying a Bart Simpson doll with a pull-string in the back and a repertoire of obnoxious Bart-Simpson comments: "My mom hated Bart Simpson, the bad kid who talks back to his parents. Here she sends me to my dad's dad, and she comes to pick me up, and I've got a Bart Simpson doll that is just as big as I am." Van recalls that "it was only a few months before Bart 'went away.'" As Sylvia was leaving for Leo's funeral service in Florence, Van handed her a Valentine, signed in his own handwriting, and asked, "Mama, will you give this to Pop Pop to take with him to heaven?" Before the casket was closed, Sylvia slipped the Valentine into Leo's hand. The next day, she was inducted into the Francis Marion Hall of Fame.

The Hatchells' marriage proved strong enough to withstand life's ups and downs. At different institutions, the two coaches struggled to build winning traditions. While Sylvia suffered under a "black cloud in blue heaven," Sammy fought his own uphill battle to develop a strong women's basketball program at Meredith College. In his first year as coach, 1988–89, the team won 14 games, and 17 in 1989–90. In 1990–91, they again won 17 games, 14 in 1991–92, but in his fifth year (1992–93), the team won 19.

Sylvia's Tar Heels were also improving and ended the 1992–93 season with an ACC record of 11–5 and 23–7 overall. The team tied for second place in the regular ACC season but lost to Maryland (75–61) in the ACC Tournament semifinals. Again, they got a bid to the NCAA Tournament—an at-large bid and a first-round bye— and they had home-court advantage in the second-round game against Alabama. The game was a nail-biter, but UNC advanced with a 74–73 win. This victory sent Lady Tar Heels to the Mideast Region semifinals—the NCAA Sweet 16—for the first time since 1986, which was Jennifer Alley's last game as the UNC Women's Basketball Head Coach. This was Sylvia's first trip to the NCAA Sweet 16 as a head coach, and her opponent was none other than Pat Summitt, who had won three national titles in the previous six seasons. The No. 4 seed UNC Lady Tar Heels met the No. 1 seed Tennessee Lady Vols on March 25 in Carver-Hawkeye Arena in Iowa City, Iowa. UNC came within one point early in the first half, but the Lady Vols led all the way and got a decisive 74–54 victory. Sylvia told the press that Tennessee's strength was the deciding factor: "We just got manhandled at times.... On this level strength is more of a factor than skill."

Despite the loss, Sylvia's trip to the NCAA Sweet 16 was, indeed, sweet, and Jim Furlong's 1991 article began to lose its sting. With her strong roster of players, Sylvia's Tar Heels looked promising, and Van was growing fast. In 1993, he entered kindergarten at Cresset Christian Academy, a private Baptist school in Durham. Sylvia spent as much time with him as her schedule allowed and took him with her whenever possible, to practices, to basketball camps, and to games. Sylvia never worried about him. "Van was like me," she says. "He was raised by a village with a lot of people around him. You just make sure you surround yourself with good people." One day, Van was talking to Sylvia about other children's mothers and observed that she was different. She said, "Well, Van, your mother is not a typical mom." She thought that he viewed basketball as taking her and Sammy away from him because their obligations to their teams often meant that they couldn't be with him.

Van settled into kindergarten, with a teacher he loved—Jane High—so Sylvia turned her focus to the basketball court and her new recruit, Marion Jones, whom Sylvia describes as "the ultimate" coachable athlete: "She was off the charts in every aspect—athleticism, competitiveness, leadership." Jones loved basketball because it is a team sport, and track is strictly individual. Sylvia's definition of a great athlete is not one who excels, but one who raises everyone around her to a higher level: "That's what Jones did. She was used to competing in track at the highest level; that was the only way she knew how to function. She would not lower herself to somebody else's standards." Sometimes a good athlete will adjust her skills to the level of lesser players because she wants to fit in. "Marion made everybody come to *her* level," says Sylvia.

Another indication of Jones's leadership was her selflessness. According to Sylvia, "It was all about the team. It was never about her. She was unselfish, and everybody 'bought into her.'" Her confidence was backed by performance; as a consequence, the team believed in her. She had raw talent. When the coaches demonstrated a move, they had to do it only once: "I can remember the day that she got nailed on a screen, and we just stopped in practice, and I said, 'Marion, when you get a screen like that, just spin off of it.' And I showed her how to rotate her body. 'Spin off of it, and always roll towards the ball.' Next time, she did and did it better than anyone I've ever seen do it." Sylvia had coached excellent players before, such as Pearl Moore: "Pearl was a good athlete, had great skills, and was a basketball pioneer. She played basketball *all* the time." But Jones was Babe Didrikson quality. Sylvia says she was "a world class athlete. Quickness. Anticipation. Her competitive spirit was off the charts."

After a few days of practice, Sylvia called Jones into her office and said, "'Marion, I'm going to make you a point guard.' She looked at me like I had lost my mind, but she said, 'Whatever I can do to help the team.'" Jill Suddreth, from South Caldwell High School near Hickory, had been the starting point guard in 1992–93. Going into the 1993–94 season, Suddreth was a junior and a solid, fundamental player who had won Most Improved Player honors in her freshman and sophomore years, but Sylvia felt that the team needed a stronger point guard to transition to a higher level. Jones was it.

Sylvia called Suddreth to her office to tell her that Marion Jones was going to become a point guard. Then she did the unthinkable. She said, "Jill, I need you to help us train Marion, to make her to best point guard she can be. And that's what's best for our team." Suddreth's face betrayed her thoughts, but all she said was, "OK." Sylvia inferred more from that "OK" than mere consent, but Suddreth came through. She told Marjo Bliss, with the *Charlotte Observer*, "To be honest, it hasn't been easy; it's been a difficult transition." But she added, "I realize I've got to do what I've got to do in order for us to win.... I've got to accept my role."[10] Stephanie Lawrence recalls that Marion Jones "definitely brought us a different dynamic" and a "different level of point guard. I don't think in the ACC there had ever been a point guard like her— her arm-length, her speed, her ability. She was really a game-changer for us." Suddreth earned Sylvia's unqualified respect because she did what was asked of her and what was best for the team. As for Jones, Sylvia says, "I probably have had the ultimate experience of coaching an athlete like Marion Jones. Because she was just off the charts in every aspect. That's one of the greatest blessings of my life."

Coming into the 1993–94 season, the team had lost one freshman (Julie Wight) and one senior (Toni Montgomery) and gained two freshmen: Lori Gear and Marion Jones. Otherwise, the 1992–93 team was intact, and Sylvia knew it was special. When Jones came in as the point guard, her competitive spirit spread throughout a team that was already passionate and forceful by nature. They loved playing basketball, and they all got along. They had good chemistry. Sylvia explains that chemistry is like the wind: "You cannot see it, but you sure can feel it and see results of it."

The chemistry was palpable, but Stephanie Lawrence believes that Sylvia's emphasis on strength training also gave the Lady Tar Heels an edge. Remembering the Sweet-16 loss to Tennessee, Sylvia worked with the UNC strength staff to develop a higher level of physicality in the team. According to Lawrence, the team worked hard: "We really put an emphasis on strength and conditioning that year: power lifting, squats, leg presses, maxing out. If you were bench pressing 155 pounds, the next time you stepped into the weight room the staff wanted you to press 165 pounds. It made a huge difference." Preseason rankings were No. 9 in the AP Poll and No. 10 in the Coaches' Poll. The Lady Tar Heels won the Carolina Invitational Tournament, the Citrus Sports Holiday Classic, and the ACC/Big Ten Challenge. In early conference play, they lost only one game to Virginia—at home on January 12 (77–75). By mid–January, they had risen in the polls to No. 7. On February 9, on its home court, Virginia defeated UNC a second time—83–74. The Lady Tar Heels ended the season at 14–2 in the ACC.

The 1994 ACC Tournament was held in the Winthrop Coliseum, Rock Hill, South Carolina. On March 5, Sylvia's Tar Heels won easily over Georgia Tech (78–55) but squeaked by Clemson (65–64) the next day. On March 7, they again faced Virginia in the ACC Tournament final—the team that had dealt them their only two losses in regular season. This time, Sylvia's team was motivated to win. She remembers the locker room before the game:

> I was talking to them about going out and playing for the championship. Marion was staring at me like daggers coming through my body. That kid was so focused and so intent looking at me. She did not even blink, and tears were rolling down her face. When I saw that, I knew we had that game. With my point guard sitting there, and she is that focused and intense, all I thought was, *Sylvia, you just need to sit over there. Don't over coach and don't get in the way. Don't get in the way.*

Sylvia stayed out of the way and let her team do the work. They defeated Virginia 77–60 to win the ACC Championship—UNC's first ACC title since 1984 and Sylvia's first ever.

A week later, on Sunday, March 13, 1994, the team came to Sylvia's house to have lunch and watch the NCAA pairings, which were broadcast on ESPN at 12:30 p.m. She was in the kitchen with her staff and assistant coaches helping prepare the food, and Van was with the players in the living room, "showing off," according to his father: "He ended up trying to stand on a basketball. Of course it rolled out from under him, and he landed on his left arm. It hurt him really bad, so he went up to bed." Sometime later, Sammy went to check on him and found a little boy in severe pain: "I went into the garage and found a short piece of board and splinted his arm." Van stayed in bed while everyone else focused on the pairings: With a 32–2 overall record, UNC was the No. 3 seed in the East bracket and had home-court advantage for the first round and second rounds, where they would face the No. 14 seed Georgia Southern. Leaving the players in celebration mode, Sylvia went up to Van's room to inspect the arm. It was badly swollen, so Sylvia, Sammy, and Van departed for Chapel Hill Pediatrics, leaving the team, assistant coaches, and staff to clean up after lunch. When the doctor saw the arm, he sent them to the emergency room. Van's left arm was, indeed, broken.

During NCAA Tournament time, the buzz around Chapel Hill is usually about men's basketball, but 1994 was different. On March 22, Celeste Whittaker reported that local radio stations and shops were cheering on the Lady Tar Heels. Sylvia was thrilled: "People always said that there was no way that you could have a great women's team at a school that is known so much for its men's basketball team.... I never believed it. I think it's been an asset playing at the same school. The men's team gets so much recognition, and the women's team gets added recognition because of them." Whittaker said that memorabilia for the UNC women's team was at a premium. The Shrunken Head shop, described as "a shrine for the men's basketball team," was selling "T-shirts and posters for the women's team as well." Shrunken Head owner Shelton Henderson said, "Lady Tar Heel shirts are selling very well. I've had to reorder two or three times already.... When they make it to the Final Four, we'll have those shirts ready, too."[11]

With home-court advantage in the first and second rounds of the NCAA Tournament, the Lady Tar Heels won an easy game against Georgia Southern (101–53). Four days later, they faced the No. 6 seed, Old Dominion, who was enjoying an 18-game winning streak and was the only thing standing between UNC and the Sweet 16. It was a battle to the finish. The Newport News *Daily Press* described the game as "physical" and "bloody": "Several UNC players left the contest temporarily because of blood on their uniforms. Senior forward Tonya Sampson, who went to the locker room several times, finally changed uniforms, replacing her No. 34 with jersey No. 55."[12] With less than a minute to play, UNC led by 12 points, and at the 40-second mark, UNC's Charlotte Smith went up for an offensive rebound and "was dragged to the floor," according to Jeff Drew. A fight broke out between Smith and Old Dominion's Beth McGowan. Both players were ejected, and conflicting news reports variously blamed both players. NCAA rules prohibited the head coaches from any appeal and from making comments to the media. Sylvia told Drew, "Charlotte got up and stepped away and the little girl [McGowan] went after her.... You've got to understand that I'm not allowed to say any more. I want to coach [on] Thursday."[13] UNC won the game (63–52) and a trip to the Sweet 16 at Rutgers in Piscataway, New Jersey, but they would have to play without their top rebounder and star forward because NCAA rules required a one-game suspension for Smith.

On March 24, UNC faced off against Vanderbilt—without Charlotte Smith. She was at courtside, anguishing over that one-game suspension for fighting, but the UNC bench was deep, and Smith's teammates stepped up, including Gwendolyn Gillingham who normally averaged about nine minutes a game. On this night, Gwendolyn competed against her sister Heidi, a Vanderbilt Commodore senior who had helped lead the Commodores to the 1993 Final Four, just six months before their father was killed in a plane crash. Without Smith, and with a grieving Gillingham, UNC nevertheless persevered, winning a close game (73–69) and their first trip to the Elite Eight.

On March 26, they faced none other than Geno Auriemma's No. 3 Connecticut Huskies in the Elite Eight. Auriemma had coached the Lady Huskies since May 1985 but had yet to win a national title. Connecticut had a seven-point edge with about 17 minutes to go, but Sampson and Smith ignited a run that the Huskies couldn't match. UNC defeated Connecticut 81–69 to earn a trip to the Final Four, the first ever for UNC women's basketball—and for Sylvia. The team had validated Shelton Henderson's confidence and his investment in Lady Tar Heels T-shirts. Milton Kent ended his March 27 account of the game with a fitting comment: "And so, Chapel Hill will have a representative in the Final Four, but not the one it was counting on."[14]

USA Today dubbed the 1994 NCAA regional finals as "the end of an era and the start of something new." After paying homage to previous players who "had flash and flair and could play an up-tempo game," Ray Glier wrote, "But never have four teams showed up in the Final Four with a style that represents the changes taking place in the women's game." The Final Four teams—Alabama, Louisiana Tech, Purdue, and North Carolina—"prevailed with ball-hawking defense by their guards, strong overall defense by the whole team, and ability to make quick, accurate passes in transition." In other words, women's teams were beginning to play more like men's teams. He believed that UNC was not "one-dimensional" but gave the edge to Purdue and picked the Lady Techsters to win it all.

The AP Poll ranked Sylvia's Tar Heels No. 4 nationally; the Coaches' Poll ranked them No. 1. According to Kelli Anderson, the team was "alternately considered overrated and underappreciated" going into the Final Four, which was held at the Coliseum in Richmond, Virginia, a site close enough to Chapel Hill to attract hundreds of UNC fans. Sylvia and the team traveled three hours by bus, joined by Sammy, Deneene, and Van, wearing a cast on his left arm. Even Dorothy Baxter, Sylvia's high-school PE teacher, went to the tournament. Friends who could not attend, such as her Carson-Newman coach Sharron Perkins Bilbrey, watched the games on television. On Saturday, April 2, the UNC women got a fairly easy win over Purdue (89–74) and would face Louisiana Tech in the championship game the next day—Sunday, April 3. Louisiana Tech was a worthy opponent, looking for a third national title after eliminating Pat Summitt's Lady Vols in the Mideast semifinals (71–68) to earn a berth in the Final Four. Then the Lady Techsters squeaked by Alabama (69–66) in the semifinal game on Saturday. The back-to-back semifinal and championship games did not go without comment. Lorraine Kee used the phrase "looming lunacy" to describe the women's NCAA schedule and chalked it up to "growing pains": "The women, unlike the men, square off in the semifinals Saturday and the championship Sunday. The back-to-back games are a concession to CBS Sports." Sylvia had less than 24 hours to prepare for the national NCAA Championship game—the game of a lifetime.

April 3, 1994, was Easter Sunday. An already fired-up team raised the emotional level several degrees when it decided to hold a worship meeting. The players "spread the word through the hotel that we were having a devotional that morning." The result was a "packed room full of people worshipping and sharing testimonies. It got a little carried away," wrote Victor Lee, and Sylvia "had 15 minutes to get ready for the team bus to the game." In a 2012 interview, Sylvia explained, "They were all standing around holding hands in a circle. Charlotte Smith's daddy was a preacher. Sylvia Crawley's mother started talking, and finally I looked down and I thought, 'I got to get dressed. I'm not going to have time to get ready for the game.'" The clock was ticking toward the 3:45 p.m. tipoff.

The locker room was equally emotional. Lawrence recalls that Sylvia "talked about having faith and being able to accomplish something you've never seen before. Believing in something that is not visible, that your eyes have not seen, but you really believe you can be there and do that." Lawrence says,

> I started getting emotional and had tears running down my face. I looked up, and right across the circle from me was Marion Jones, and she had tears streaming down her face. I think that was a validation of "We are here. This is about to happen." I thought that was a really special moment—an insight into the locker room that most people never get to see.

To say that Sylvia's Lady Tar Heels arrived on the court keyed up and ready to play would be an understatement, but the Louisiana Tech Lady Techsters, coached by Leon Barmore, were defending a 25-game winning streak. UNC controlled the opening tipoff, and Stephanie Lawrence scored first—a beautiful three-pointer. UNC did not score again for four minutes. The game was intense and physical. Marion Jones was quickly called for three personal fouls and went to the bench at 5:30 into the game, where she stayed for the rest of the first half. Jill Suddreth played only two minutes but earned praise from CBS color analyst Ann Meyers for her poise.[15] But both teams looked sloppy. Smith was frustrated by the Lady Techsters' defense and forced her shots; UNC handled the ball poorly and made unnecessary turnovers. With 32 seconds remaining in the half, Louisiana Tech led 32–30, but Sampson stole the ball, drove to the basket, and made a two-point layup to tie the score 32–32. UNC had trailed most of first half, but Sampson's effort gave UNC an emotional edge going into halftime.

In the second half, Jones was back in the game, but she came off the bench "cold" and never regained her momentum. The other UNC players stepped up. Charlotte Smith immediately gave UNC the lead with a two-point layup. UNC was more aggressive on the boards, but with 6:50 to go, Pam Thomas gave Louisiana Tech a one-point lead and held on to it until Smith scored to tie the game at 53 with 2:36 to go. UNC again tied the game with 34 seconds left; then with 14 seconds on the clock, Thomas made a 16-foot jump shot to take the lead 59–57. Tonya Sampson got the ball after the inbounds pass and missed a layup that would have tied the game 59–59. After a crazy scramble for the ball on the rebound, a jump ball was called, and the possession arrow went to UNC. CBS's Ann Meyers was critical of Sylvia for failing to call a timeout to set up a final play.[16] The clock had ticked off 10 seconds, and UNC was left with 0.07 seconds to inbound the ball and make a basket. Stephanie Lawrence had difficulty inbounding the ball but wisely followed Sylvia's instructions and signaled for a timeout. Sylvia called Play 30. Charlotte Smith would later tell Bob Lipper that she heard her coach, but the words "didn't sink in," so she "whispered" to Sylvia Crawley, "What's Play 30?" With 0.07 seconds left, Stephanie Lawrence made a long inbounds pass from under the UNC basket to Charlotte Smith on the right wing. Charlotte's 20-foot, three-point lob made a perfect arc and swished through the net, giving UNC the win, 60–59, and its first NCAA Women's Basketball Championship. The player who had been sidelined for fighting on March 20 had effected a miracle on Easter Sunday.

Every news clip and media report highlighted Charlotte Smith's miracle shot. Pat Summitt told Richard Walker, "In my 20 years of coaching, I don't know if there's been a more exciting finish. People all over the nation were shocked and ecstatic."[17]

Andrew Calder asked Steve Politi, "Has there ever been a bigger shot?" Writing for *Sports Illustrated*, Kelli Anderson called it "one of the most exciting conclusions to an NCAA Championship game." Smith "didn't even get to see her game-winning three-pointer fall through the net." She said, "I just prayed and shot, ... then the mob hit me." UNC forward Carrie McKee, was quoted as saying, "That shot by Charlotte wasn't hard work, that shot wasn't luck.... That shot was God." Nobody could believe it. To this day, Dorothy Baxter still gets excited in the retelling: "Oh, Lord! I was a wreck. I WAS A WRECK. It was some game." Sharron Perkins Bilbrey, Sylvia's Carson-Newman coach, agreed: "My son and I were watching it together, and I was praying for her, and I said to myself, *I know Lord, that she is going to give You all the glory if she wins this championship.*" Sylvia's comment to a courtside reporter amid the chaos proved Bilbrey correct: "Thank You, Lord, thank You."[18]

The stress of playing intense games on consecutive days and the drama of winning a national championship left everyone exhausted, but they had to return to Chapel Hill that night. Some players drove back to campus with their families, but most were on the bus with Sylvia, Sammy, Van, and Deneene as it left Richmond for the three-hour trip. They needed to stop for dinner, and because Charlotte Smith sank the winning shot, Andrew Calder let her decide where the team would eat. She chose McDonald's, so their bus driver, "Super Dave" Harder, who drove the men's team for 27 years, headed for the "double arches" coming out of Richmond on I-95. On road trips, players were usually restricted to five or six dollars for a meal, but this time, Sylvia told them, "You can get anything you want!" Stephanie Lawrence recalls, "We went crazy and got ice cream sundaes and milk shakes—all the things that we couldn't get normally on our budget." Sylvia cherishes her photograph of Super Dave surrounded by the team wearing their national championship hats—in McDonald's. After the meal, Sylvia was so tired that she fell asleep on the bus: "Sammy couldn't believe I was asleep, but I can go to sleep anywhere."

Players and coaches wondered whether there would be a celebration of their NCAA Championship. According to Vic Dorr, players didn't expect "the raucous revelry that greeted the Tar Heels' successful pursuit of the men's title in 1993," but they hoped for some sort of recognition. Tonya Sampson said, "I'll drive my car down the road and blow the horn if I have to."[19] Just outside of Durham, as the bus approached the intersection of NC Routes 15–501 and Garrett Road, a highway patrolman was waiting with blue lights flashing. Sylvia thought they had come upon an accident, but he was their escort to campus. As Super Dave pulled the bus onto South Road and stopped at Carmichael, around 11:30 p.m., they were met by at least 300 people. Bob Cole reported that hundreds of fans celebrated along Franklin Street: "They had launched rolls of toilet paper into the trees, a tradition normally reserved for big wins by the men's team." Sylvia told Bob Cole, "When the players saw all that toilet paper, they knew they had arrived."

The next day a formal celebration was held in Carmichael. Sylvia had told her players that if they won the national championship, they could paint her hair blue. They did. Some players got in line two and three times to spray blue color on her hair. To this day, Sammy regrets that his father died the year before Sylvia won the national championship: "He would have been so proud."

When a blue-haired Sylvia left the basketball floor after the celebration, John Swofford was waiting for her at courtside with the promise of a raise. Even Swofford was surprised by the national championship. "I would like to tell you I wasn't," he says, "but I was a little surprised.... I knew that Sylvia was building a program that was going to have a national presence, and that was what we wanted when we brought Sylvia in, but in '94 I can't tell you that I expected it." Says Swofford, "It truly was the highlight of my seventeen years as the UNC Athletic Director." Swofford would agree with Charlotte Smith's assessment that winning a national championship puts a team, coach, and university on a whole new level: "It puts you amongst some of the greatest in the history of the game." Says Smith, "There are not that many coaches who have won a national championship, let alone a national championship on every level." The NCAA women's basketball championship was the first for UNC and for the ACC. It gave a tremendous boost to the development of women's basketball.

In three years, the team that was ranked last in the ACC—a team that was, Sylvia admits, one of the worst in America—became national champions and brought to Chapel Hill the prized NCAA Division I Tournament Trophy for women's basketball. It is proudly displayed in the Women's Basketball Museum in Carmichael Auditorium, home to the UNC women's basketball program, and it bears a brass plate engraved with "UNC—NCAA CHAMPIONS—1994." Sylvia prizes this symbol of success, but she also keeps the alternate brass plate that was prepared in case Louisiana Tech won the final game. That plate is engraved with "LA TECH—CHAMPIONS—1994." The memento is a reminder of what the outcome would have been had Charlotte Smith missed that final shot. Victory can be won by hard work and good coaching, but it can also be capricious. During the celebrations and amid all the accolades, Sylvia quietly acknowledged to herself that the win was for John Swofford. She never forgot that dark, January night when he put his arm around her and said, "You are *my* coach, and I *believe* in you."

The annual women's basketball banquet in 1994 was held in the Carolina Club in Alumni Hall of the George Watts Hill Alumni Center. Because of the NCAA National Championship, at least 600 people attended. It is customary for the team members to speak at this annual event, when the team's successes are celebrated and athletes' individual accomplishments are recognized. When it was Jill Suddreth's turn, Sylvia wondered what she would say and remembers Suddreth's comments to this day: "I can say that every day I got up and worked out with Marion Jones to make her the best point guard in the country so that our team could win a national championship. And because I did that, I have a national championship ring on my finger for the rest of my life." Sylvia's respect for Jill soared that night, and—this time—Sylvia did not have to solicit money for rings. Immediately following the championship game, every player was given a standard NCAA Championship ring, with the NCAA logo on oval-cut black onyx, bearing the words "National Champion." Later, every player received a personalized ring bearing the player's name, the team record, and the UNC logo—paid for by UNC.

When the UNC women's basketball team received an invitation to the White House to meet President Clinton, Sylvia, her mother, Van, Sammy, the staff, and team left for Washington, D.C. Her father didn't go, and she's not sure why: "Probably because he didn't like Bill Clinton," she says with a laugh, "or probably because he didn't want to fly." On Wednesday, July 27, they met President Clinton in the East Room at 2:30 p.m. Senator Jesse Helms and Congressmen Valentine, Lancaster, Price, and McMillan were among those present. According to Sylvia, the players were "overwhelmed" to be in the presence of Senators, Congressmen, and President Clinton.

The President made brief remarks about the championship game and Sylvia's short-lived blue hair; he then made more serious comments about academics and athletics:

> The thing I have always admired about the University of North Carolina is it's been [*sic*] a place that emphasized both academics and athletics and other extra-curricular activities. And it's demonstrated to the country that it is not necessary to make a choice and that there's something to be said for learning how to compete, to work on a team, to put aside your own personal ambitions for what is best for a group, and that an institution like the University of North Carolina, which I had the opportunity to join in celebrating its 200th birthday just a few months ago, can really set a standard for the entire country.[20]

Sylvia responded with "Mr. President, as coach of the University of North Carolina Lady Tarheels [*sic*], we would just like to say when you get in a pressured situation and there's less than a second on the clock, just keep your cool, don't panic, and always believe that you can win. And most of all, go for the win, not the tie." Clinton laughed at this comment; then Sylvia presented him with a UNC women's blue and white basketball jersey, bearing the numeral 1 and lettered "H. Clinton" for Hillary Clinton.[21] As the President chatted with Sylvia, she was impressed by how much he knew about the team: "He commented about individual players by name, and he knew their numbers, their stats, and the qualities and characteristics of certain players. He knew how the game had ended. I was impressed that he knew that much about my team. I thought, *Boy, somebody has briefed him really good*." Later she learned that he has a phenomenal memory, but still, she says, "you think about something as small as meeting a basketball team in the Rose Garden or East Room and what it means in the larger day of a President."

Sylvia also noted that Clinton was charmed by Gwendolyn Gillingham, a 6'7", good-looking girl with long blonde hair. Gwendolyn was striking in a short, sleeveless white dress with a round neck, and President Clinton took note. "We have pictures of Gwendolyn with Clinton," says Sylvia. "He has his arm around her and is looking up at her. The President was mesmerized." An August 15, 1994, posting on People.com validates Sylvia's perception of the exchange between the President and Gillingham: "'All my life I've been looking for a woman as tall as I am,' joked 6'4" Bill Clinton at a July 27 White House ceremony for the UNC women's basketball team. He found her in Gwendolyn Gillingham, the NCAA Championship team's 6'7" center."[22] When the Monica Lewinski scandal broke in late 1997, Sylvia reflected on her earlier suspicions and thought, *No wonder he was hitting on Gwendolyn*.

The White House visit validated Sylvia, her staff, and the team. It affirmed their struggle. "We kept believing in what we were doing. I knew we were doing the right things," says Sylvia. It took five years—from 1987 to 1992—to build a program and lead her players to develop the qualities that resulted in success. When UNC won the NCAA national championship, Tonya Sampson and Sylvia Crawley, whom Sylvia had recruited, were seniors, and they remembered the lean years. In 1996, both players

Sylvia presents President Bill Clinton with H. Clinton # 1 basketball jersey. Courtesy William J. Clinton Presidential Library.

joined the professional ranks—Crawley went to the Colorado Explosion and Sampson to the Portland Power in the now-defunct American Basketball League (ABL).

Swofford made good on his promise to reward Sylvia's success. On October 8, 1994, Wendy Parker reported that UNC gave Sylvia a "$30,000 salary increase in July," bringing her salary to $90,000 and making her the "highest-paid women's coach at UNC" and the "third-highest-paid coach of a women's sport in the ACC." Sylvia speculates that before the raise, she was the *lowest* paid coach in the ACC. Virginia's Debbie Ryan was first at $188,800, and Maryland's Chris Weller was second at $110,000. NC State's Kay Yow earned $85,000. The same *Journal-Constitution* article reported UNC men's basketball coach Dean Smith's 1994 salary as $147,000. Parker also commented that "until three years ago," the women Tar Heels "were ACC doormats."[23]

The NCAA trophy meant a great deal more than money to Sylvia and her program, however. According to Noah Bartolucci, enrollment in her 1994 summer girls' basketball camp rose to 3,000, and she turned away nearly 1,000 applicants because the camp was at capacity. The boys' basketball camp enrolled fewer than 2,000—and this in a town "where men's hoops overshadow, well, just about everything." Seven of Sylvia's players were coaches and counselors in the camp, including Marion Jones. The girls, ranging from age 9 to 17, treated the Lady Tar Heels like superstars, Tonya Cooper told Bartolucci: "But with us staying in the dorm with them, being around them, they realize we're just like them." In truth, a major goal of Sylvia's camps is to provide young women with chances she didn't have—such as basketball camps—and to help them realize that they, too, can live their dreams.

In the summer of 1994, Sylvia did not "rest on her laurels" but took the international spotlight again, coaching the USA women's basketball team in the Jones Cup, which is held annually in Taipei, Taiwan. The official USA Basketball website describes the 1994 Team USA action as "Packing more excitement and drama than a Godzilla movie," with a "one point win over the defending champion [Republic of China-Cathay Life], three come-from-behind victories and a 90–89 overtime win over South Korea in the gold medal game." Sylvia came home with yet another Gold Medal.

5

The Dream Deferred

At home, Sylvia had an understanding husband who helped her parent Van, a typical little boy in an atypical family of coaches and basketball players. Not many children grow up with two parents who are coaches, but Deneene Herring was a strong, balancing influence and taskmaster. Van's childhood, like Sylvia's, included work. "I took the trash out; I took the recycling out; I did laundry." Early on, Van learned the word "no." When he begged for a kitten, Sylvia's response was an emphatic "NO! I don't like cats, and Sammy doesn't either. I said, 'NO cats! NO kittens!'" While the cat-question was being deliberated, Sylvia lost her beloved Sassafras, who was 16 years old and had been part of her life since before she met Sammy: "I'm telling you, that about killed me when we put that dog to sleep." With Sassafras gone, and partly to make up for not getting Van a kitten, they got a beagle named Scooter. He was Van's dog—Scooter and Sylvia did not bond. Van says it's because they had "very similar personalities—set in their ways, very stubborn." Sylvia says, "Now I like dogs, but Scooter was a hunting dog. He wouldn't listen to you."

Having good care and supervision for Van freed Sylvia to focus on basketball. Following the high of the NCAA Championship, the Tar Heels' 1994–1995 season began with mixed predictions. The preseason AP Poll ranked the UNC women's team at No. 7. Mechelle Voepel wrote, "Some publications didn't even put the Heels in the top 10," but Voepel argued that Sylvia's team had the "talent and depth" to win a second NCAA title. Bill Worrell of Tennessee Tech told Voepel, "North Carolina is just one sweet basketball team. I've seen Tennessee and Louisiana Tech, and I have to say I think North Carolina is the No. 1 team right now."[1] The Lady Tar Heels had lost seniors Sylvia Crawley and Tonya Sampson, but their star lineup of Stephanie Lawrence, Marion Jones, and Charlotte Smith returned, along with Tonya Cooper, Tonya Jackson, Carrie McKee, Lori Gear, Gwendolyn Gillingham, and Jill Suddreth. Marion, of course, was the point guard. In addition, three freshmen joined the team: 6' 3" Nicole Walker, her 6'4" twin Sheneika Walker, and 5'11" Tracy Reid. In her senior year of high school (1993), Tracy Reid was an All-Star player at Miami Central, was named Miss Florida Basketball, and was named National Player of the Year by the Downtown Athletic Club of Columbus, Ohio. She had planned to make campus visits to Clemson, the University of Florida, Georgetown, Kentucky, and Syracuse. UNC was not even on her list. Then she met Sylvia at a Nike All-Star game in Hampton, Virginia: "Sylvia made an impression on me. Because of how she approached me, because of that Southern hospitality—the way she was and everything—I thought, *I'll at least look at UNC and take a visit up there."* Reid struggled with the decision but eventually signed with UNC.

In November, Tracy and her teammates played in the Rainbow Wahine Classic in Honolulu, Hawaii, and defeated three teams in three consecutive days to win the tournament. Charlotte Smith continued to shine; on December 4 in a 113–58 rout against North Carolina A&T, she became the second collegiate women's player to dunk a basketball in a game. On December 21, they beat East Tennessee State University 106–72 to win the Holiday Beach Classic in Myrtle Beach. Between November 25 and January 22, they won every game. Then they met Duke on January 25 and lost a heartbreaker—74–72.

Two days later the announcement came that Sylvia had been selected as head women's basketball coach of the summer 1995 World University Games in Fukuoka, Japan, August 24–September 3. Though she had assisted Jill Hutchinson in 1983 and Vivian Stringer in 1985, she had never served as a head coach for the World University Games. But she had to keep her focus on the present season, not on an international competition eight months into the future. Following the January 25 loss to Duke, two more losses came at the hands of Virginia. After that, the Lady Tar Heels lost only one other regular-season game—a double-overtime dogfight with NC State (88–86), and then on February 25 they had a sweet victory over Duke—85–57—which boosted their confidence for post-season play. They finished 12–4 in the ACC for second place.

By ACC Tournament time, their national ranking had fallen to No. 11, but their performance exceeded their ranking: They beat Wake Forest (71–51), NC State (90–71), and Duke (95–70) in three consecutive days to win the ACC Tournament. Charlotte Smith earned her second ACC Tournament MVP Award, and the *Atlanta Journal-Constitution* dubbed Smith and Jones the "common-name consortium" who led the championship rout against Duke. Sylvia told the press, "We are peaking at the right time…. I think we can play even better, and that's what we're going to do as we go into the NCAA [Tournament]."[2] Their wide margin of wins in the three ACC Tournament games seemed to bear out Voepel's NCAA repeat prediction. Sylvia's team entered the tournament as the No. 3 seed in the West Region. Marion Jones was "eager": "I want to go to California," she told the press. She was looking forward to playing in the West Regional semifinals, held in Los Angeles, near her home town in Thousand Oaks. She had not been home for a year.

The first and second rounds of the NCAA Tournament were played in Chapel Hill, and Sylvia's UNC team took advantage of their home-court momentum, defeating Western Illinois (89–48) in the first round and Seton Hall (59–45) in the second, for a berth in the NCAA Sweet 16. The game demonstrated UNC's depth—12 players scored. Charlotte Smith fouled out of the Seton Hall game, but the team picked up the slack. On March 19, the *New York Times* noted that the Seton Hall "victory also made Coach Sylvia Hatchell the first in school history to achieve 30 victories in successive seasons." She responded with her usual candor and humility: "I might have been the first Carolina coach to be last in the A.C.C. [*sic*] three years, too."[3] Marion Jones got her wish. The Tar Heels traveled to Los Angeles on March 21 for the West Regional semifinals in Pauley Pavilion, where they met No. 2 seed Stanford on March 23. This was Sylvia's third trip to the NCAA Sweet 16.

On game day, the intensity was high. Sylvia described the Stanford matchup as comparable to a Final Four, but with a two-year record of 63–6, her team was confident. They would rely on their quickness up and down the court, but Stanford had the advantage of size. According to the *Herald-Sun*, Sylvia expected Stanford to "play physical" and acknowledged that they were "probably the biggest team we've seen" who could match the UNC running game.[4] Stanford led at halftime (36–31) and "came out firing" in the second half, according to Dave Trimmer.[5] UNC cut the lead to four points with 28 seconds on the clock, but they committed critical fouls (Charlotte Smith had earned her fourth foul with nearly 20 minutes to go), and Stanford excelled at the free throw line in the final seconds. Though they fought hard, and Stanford coach Tara VanDerveer praised their "heart," Sylvia's Tar Heels lost 81–71. The seniors were devastated. There were floods of tears. Gwendolyn Gillingham, Stephanie Lawrence, Carrie McKee, Charlotte Smith, and Jill Suddreth had played their last game.

Despite this disappointment, Sylvia attended the Final Four in Minneapolis, where she assumed her position as second vice-president of the Women's Basketball Coaches Association (WBCA), the first stage of a four-year commitment. She told the press, "I'll be busy every day.... That will be good to keep my mind off things.... I think, more than anything, I am realizing what we did [in 1994] and what it meant." Indeed, she did keep busy. An April 1, 1995, Associated Press story focused on the controversy over pay equity during the WBCA Convention, following the Final Four in Minneapolis. According to the story, "32 percent of Division I women's basketball coaches earn in excess of $60,000, compared to 88 percent of coaches of men's basketball." Sylvia has always refused to compare women's and men's coaching salaries, but some of her colleagues did not hesitate to speak out. In 1995, WBCA president-elect Linda Hill-McDonald was "embroiled in a contract dispute" with the University of Minnesota, and Marianne Stanley had just lost her suit against the University of Southern California. Tara VanDerveer argued that the inequities in salaries and support for men's and women's programs sent the message that women's programs are of less value than men's and that the outcome is predictable: "If you have two farmers and you give one a tractor and one a plow horse, the outcome is obvious." VanDerveer continued, "When I sat down at the table, my parents didn't give my brother steak and my sisters hot dogs."[6] According to Melissa Murphy, Sylvia and former WBCA president Rene Portland represented the organization during Title IX hearings before Congress on May 9, 1995.[7]

One of Sylvia's long-time dreams was to be head coach for an Olympic team. After winning the 1994 NCAA Championship, her national status rose, and her extensive experience with USA and Olympic basketball made her chances for the 1996 Olympics look promising, but by 1995, Olympic rules for head coaches had changed, requiring a college coach to take a sabbatical from his or her coaching job to focus strictly on the Olympics. Sylvia's competition included Iowa's Vivian Stringer and Stanford's Tara VanDerveer, who was not only willing to give up coaching her team for a year, but also agreed to move to Colorado Springs. The selection of VanDerveer as the coach of the 1996 USA Olympic women's basketball team was announced in April of 1995. Sylvia told the press the only thing she could: "Tara is an excellent choice and she'll do a fantastic job." She was disappointed, but she respected the decision.

Having lost her bid to coach the 1996 U.S. Olympic team, Sylvia turned her attention to the World University Games in the summer of 1995. Trials for the U.S. team were held at the Olympic Training Center in Colorado Springs, May 18–25, and Marion Jones became a factor. When Jones signed with the Tar Heels in 1993, Sylvia and Dennis Craddock had promised her that they would support her track interests, so Marion had always intended to redshirt for the 1995–96 basketball season. Immediately following the 1995 NCAA Tournament loss to Stanford, she went back to California and began training with her former track coach, Elliott Mason, to compete in track and field in the 1996 Summer Olympics. In her 2004 autobiography, Jones says, "I'd barely begun my return to form when I got a call from Coach Hatchell. The U.S. team was going to the World University Games, and the team wanted me at point guard. Would I be interested?" Jones saw the opportunity as a "dilemma" but felt the experience would look good on a resume and may help boost her to a spot on a future Olympic national team. "I had to accept," she says. "There was never a doubt that it was the right decision." Jones planned to compete in the World University Games and then announce the decision to redshirt. It was a good plan, but on August 10, she broke the fifth metatarsal bone in her left foot while practicing with the team in Colorado. "I was diving for a loose ball at the same time as my teammate Katie Smith, who managed to land on my left foot. I knew it was broken right away."[8] Jones had to drop out.

In Fukuoka, Japan, Team USA was favored to win the Gold, and their early games supported the predictions: three quick and easy victories over the Ukraine (93–54), Mexico (100–78), and South Korea (108–58) to advance to the quarterfinals round against Japan, whom they defeated 108–64. In their next game, Charlotte Smith and Sylvia Crawley led the charge against Yugoslavia to win 76–58, which meant they would play Russia in the semifinal game. Again, Charlotte Smith came through, earning a double-double (14 points and 14 rebounds) to help Team USA defeat Russia 101–74 and advance to the championship game. With six easy victories to their credit, Team USA faced unbeaten Italy in the Gold Medal game on August 31. With 7:39 left, Italy outscored the USA 17–7 to win the Gold Medal (73–65). Sylvia had to settle for Silver. She credited Italy's game plan, defense, and physical play: "We should have won the championship game," says Sylvia. "We played just really, really bad. We should have won it but..."

Back at UNC, Marion Jones was nursing a major foot injury and contemplating her future. Dennis Craddock told Jim Furlong that she was finding it difficult to decide whether to redshirt for the 1995–1996 season. Craddock said that Jones was the "probable 'heir apparent' to Jackie Joyner-Kersee as the USA's top women's long jumper." Jones waited until September to announce that she would sit out the 1995–1996 basketball season and devote an entire year to track.[9] Sylvia's UNC women's team had lost its star point guard—its cornerstone—along with five seniors. The Lady Tar Heel team consisted of eight returning players and six freshmen. The preseason rankings plummeted. As the season progressed, their ranking dropped to No. 25.

The black cloud from 1991 reappeared in blue heaven, and the magic began to wear off of UNC's talented point guard, whose life quickly became fodder for the media and frustration for Sylvia. Though Jones was not a member of the team, she was still a student at UNC and stayed in touch with her basketball "family." Accompanied by a man named C.J. Hunter, she went to Myrtle Beach to watch her team compete in the Christmas Holiday Beach Classic, December 19–21, 1995. Jones didn't have a drivers license. "Marion's mother was really very, very strict on her," says Sylvia, and "Marion couldn't even drive a car, so C.J. brought her down to Myrtle Beach." At the time, Sylvia did not know Hunter, who was in his first year as an assistant UNC track coach. After one of the games, around 11:30 p.m., Sylvia got a call saying that Jones, Hunter, and another girl were at the police station in Aynor, South Carolina. Hunter had been stopped for speeding on the way back to Chapel Hill, and he was driving on an expired Colorado drivers license.

Sylvia sent two team managers to Aynor to pick up Jones: "I gave them keys to the car, and I said, 'I don't really care what you do with C.J. but bring Marion back *here*. Marion can spend the night with us in the hotel, and we'll make arrangements tomorrow to get her back to Chapel Hill.'" Then she went to bed. At breakfast the following morning she asked, "Where's Marion?" The staff "turned and rolled their eyes." They had picked up Jones, Hunter, and the other girl as Sylvia instructed. One staff member was driving Hunter's car, but five miles outside of Aynor, Hunter made him stop, asked him to get out of the driver's seat, took the steering wheel, and drove off with Jones and her friend. Sylvia said to herself, *This is not good.*

Hunter had come from the University of Colorado to join the UNC track staff, and, like Jones, he had Olympic aspirations. Marion writes in her autobiography that she first met C.J. in the weight room when she was "rehabbing" her broken foot. They quickly became "buddies" and "got along famously." Sylvia quickly became suspicious: "C.J. knew that Marion was destined for stardom, so he got in tight with her through the training."

Back in Chapel Hill, Sylvia called Dennis Craddock to report a violation of the NCAA no-fraternization rule between staff and players. Jones and Hunter thought they had succeeded in keeping their relationship quiet, but shortly after the Aynor, South Carolina, episode, Dennis Craddock called Hunter in "and told him he had to quit or be let go." According to Jones, he quit: "He wasn't a big fan of Coach Craddock anyway,"[10] so he took a job at St. Augustine's in Raleigh, and Marion moved in with him. In January, Sylvia began her own investigation and found that Hunter had a wife and two children in Colorado and that he was identified as a "deadbeat dad." Hunter was a UNC employee, seven years older than Jones, and married, hardly a suitable companion for a young woman whose goals included Olympic Gold Medals in track. Sylvia talked with Jones's mother and then took Marion to lunch:

> I can show you the booth where we sat. We went to this little hole-in-the-wall place because I knew no one else would be there, and we sat in this booth, and I sat across from her and begged her, "Marion, look. You have a wonderful future. C.J. has a wife and two small children." I said, "He has too much baggage. You do not need this. You can have any man in this world that you want, eventually. You've got an unbelievable future; you do not need this right now. This is not good for you. Plus, think about what you're doing to his family, to those two small children."

Sylvia then visited with Marion's mother, who was "on the same page," but from that point her relationship with Marion was severed. "I had done all I could do," says Sylvia, "and so had her mama. We just had to back off."

On January 5, 1996, Kimberly Rae Kendrick Hunter, of Arvada, Colorado, filed for divorce from Cottrell J. Hunter. Then tragedy struck. On that same day, Marion Jones again broke the metatarsal bone in her left foot during running drills in UNC Fetzer Gymnasium. The re-injury was devastating. Not only had she given up basketball for a year; now her dream for an Olympic Medal in 1996 evaporated. The degree to which this stress and controversy negatively affected the women's basketball team will never be known, but the Christmas Beach Holiday Classic was the beginning of a losing season. After January 1996, the team won only two games: Georgia Tech (88–72) and NC State (76–65). A 13–14 overall record and an even 8–8 in the ACC brought out the black cloud. The UNC women's basketball season ended with an ACC Tournament quarterfinal loss to Clemson (67–49), and for the first time since 1992, the Lady Tar Heels did not get an NCAA Tournament bid.

The 1996 summer Olympics were held in Atlanta, July 19–August 4, and Tara VanDerveer led the U.S. women's basketball team to defeat Brazil (111–66) for the Gold Medal. Sylvia's disappointment at not being selected as the 1996 Olympic women's basketball coach could have been rekindled, but she faced bigger problems: C.J. Hunter's influence on her star point guard. Jones was unable to compete in the 1996 Olympic games, but from the stands, she watched Hunter finish seventh in the shot put. On July 31, amid the Olympic competition, the *Orlando Sentinel* reported that Hunter owed his ex-wife Kimberly Kendrick almost $6,000 in child support and $10,000 because of "tax problems ... and other obligations."[11]

For the 1996–1997 season, Sylvia had lost seniors Tonya Cooper and Tonya Jackson, but Marion Jones rejoined the Tar Heels. Even so, the Lady Tar Heels were ranked No. 25. Sylvia believed that her team was better than the rankings, but she faced a tough situation. Though C.J. Hunter had been forced to leave the UNC track coaching staff, he remained a looming presence, a fixture in the top rows of Carmichael Auditorium, watching Jones at every practice or game. "As soon as practice was over, she did not go back to the locker room or interact with her teammates. She couldn't get to him fast enough, and they were gone," says Sylvia.

During the early part of January 1997, while Sylvia was struggling with the Jones-Hunter dilemma, her longtime friend Sylvia Strickland was losing her battle with cancer. In May 1995, she had retired from Francis Marion, and her health continued to decline throughout 1996. Mary Lou describes the week of her mother's death as "just real freaky." Mary Lou, her husband, and daughter Molly were living with Mrs. Strickland in Florence, trying to maintain the house and keep her comfortable. On Wednesday, January 15, Mary Lou was outside hanging clothes on the line when something caught her attention, and she turned around. There stood Sylvia, saying, "My schedule was clear today, and I just thought I needed to come spend some time with your mama." No one had called her to report Mrs. Strickland's weakened state. Though it was peak basketball season, she came and visited several hours with her friend and "just talked." "It was awesome," says Mary Lou, "because I know that meant a lot to Mom.... As busy as Sylvia was, she came."

Mrs. Strickland died two days later, on Friday, January 17, 1997. Sylvia had a game at Duke the next day, which her team won 87–73. Then she drove back to Florence for the funeral, which was held on Sunday, January 19, because Mary Lou believed her mother would have wanted to be buried "on the Lord's day." Sylvia gave the eulogy and brought Hope Kelly from Cresset Baptist Church to sing "Friends Are Friends Forever," the song by Michael W. Smith that Mrs. Strickland gave to her when she walked out of her Francis Marion offices for the last time in 1986. Immediately afterward, Sylvia drove straight to Clemson for a Monday night game, which her team won 75–63.

Sylvia's Lady Tar Heels achieved a record for the 1996–97 season that outmatched their early rankings. They ended the season 29–3 overall and 15–1 in the ACC, losing only once on February 17 to rival NC State 84–77. In the ACC Tournament in Charlotte, they beat Wake Forest, Duke, and Clemson to win the title and a bid to the NCAA Tournament. Their ranking rose to No. 4, and they were the top seed in the East Region, with home-court advantage in the first two rounds. They defeated Harvard and Michigan State for a trip to the Sweet 16, but there was a cost: Jessica Gaspar tore her ACL in the Michigan State game and was on the bench when they faced George Washington in Columbia, South Carolina. George Washington was the Atlantic 10 champion and played a half-court running game. Coach Joe McKeown said he did not want to "get into a 40-minute transition game" with UNC. He didn't. Sylvia's Lady Tar Heels struggled without Gaspar. They shot 28 percent from the floor and did not score in the last 4:45 of the game, posting their lowest score of the season in the 55–46 loss.

Alongside this abrupt and disappointing end to their season, there was a bright spot: Tracy Reid was selected as the ACC Player of the Year and was named to the Kodak and Associated Press All-America team. At the Kodak All-American banquet, Sylvia noticed that Tracy never touched her food—"She did not eat one bite." When Sylvia asked her about the evening, Tracy confided that she was daunted by all the silverware; she did not know which fork to use. In a 2014, interview, Tracy said, "I came from the inner city. I didn't want or need for anything, but I (and a lot of players) just don't get out to settings where you are sitting with three or four forks in front of you, a dessert spoon, and this or that type of glass." Tracy's embarrassment prompted Sylvia to act, and she vowed that no UNC women's basketball player would ever again be intimidated by forks and glasses. She enlisted her good friend Cecelia Grimes to teach an etiquette class, which so impressed Tracy that she kept Grimes's etiquette book with her: "I would study it." Afterward, when she had a formal dinner at the Chancellor's home, she was comfortable and confident. Now, as a coach at Miami Central Senior High School, she teaches etiquette to her players: "I always mention Coach Hatchell and how she took me and all the players under her wing and made sure we were ready for the real world—not just basketball but situations where you don't want to be embarrassed."

In the summer of 1997, Van was eight—old enough to go to summer camp—and Sylvia and Sammy disagreed about where he would go. Sammy had attended Camp Seagull at Arapahoe, North Carolina, on the Neuse River, near the Pamlico Sound. "He loved it," says Van. Sylvia wanted Van to attend Camp Rockmont, a Christian, nondenominational boys skills camp in Black Mountain, North Carolina, where she earned her WSIT certificate in 1976. Sylvia won out. Van attended Camp Rockmont two weeks every summer, from age 8 to 16: "It really did have a big impact on my life. It was one of those places where people didn't know about my background and who Mom was. It was a place where I feel like I got to grow."

Van was happy at camp, and Sylvia's summer was quiet, but the Marion Jones story continued to affect the Lady Tar Heels in the 1997–98 season. Because Jones had redshirted in 1995–96, she had one more year of eligibility and could have played in 1997–98, but she opted out. Sylvia blames C.J. Hunter for the decision. Jones's absence on the court was a blow, but returning seniors included the Walker twins, Nicole and Sheneika, and Tracy Reid. Sylvia had also snagged Juana Brown from Memphis, one of the top five recruits nationally. And then there was Nikki Teasley, the number one recruit out of high school who joined the team as a freshman. The *Atlanta Journal-Constitution* predicted that Teasley "might make some in Chapel Hill forget a little about Jones." Sylvia compared her with Magic Johnson.[12]

With this new talent and her stable of veteran players, Sylvia's Lady Tar Heels began 1997–98 with a preseason ranking of No. 5 and were picked early on as NCAA Tournament contenders, right up there with No. 1 ranked Tennessee. In preconference play, UNC lost one game to Florida (68–48) in the Hall of Fame Tipoff Classic and won ten, including an overtime 82–78 win over UCLA. Their star seemed to be rising, and on January 22, the No. 11 Lady Tar Heels beat Kay Yow's No. 8 NC State Wolfpack (67–64) to give Sylvia her 500th win. The seventh woman to reach this milestone, Sylvia commemorated the event by giving engraved briefcases containing $500 each to her three assistant coaches—Andrew Calder, Ann Hancock, and Emily Murphy—and four staff members—videographer Shannon Spencer, secretary Joan Nipper, nanny and camp coordinator Deneene Herring, and public address announcer Jan Boxill, whose role in UNC women's basketball would become more prominent over the next two decades. When Sylvia was asked if the win was "any sweeter" because it was against NC State, she answered, "Heck no. I would rather have won it against Virginia." Her team had already missed two good opportunities to give Sylvia her 500th win, first on January 15, when they lost in triple overtime to Virginia 105–100, and three days later when they lost to Maryland 84–62. Sylvia credited her 500th win to the players: "Heart. It was just heart that won it…. We were down by 10, we didn't fall apart. We just bore down and played harder." An AP wire story said, "Tracy Reid and Jessica Gaspar made sure she got [the win]."[13]

In her senior year, Reid was taking a strong leadership role and earning the spotlight as a stand-out player. After a win over Coastal Carolina (74–45), Reid told the press, "Sometimes it's difficult to maintain your focus when you're winning by a lot…. There were things we did out there tonight that will cost us if we do them against Clemson." Reid was no doubt remembering their recent January 2 loss to Clemson (77–63) and anticipating their next matchup on February 1, which they won 80–59. Sylvia, too, may have been remembering her losing years at UNC and the 1991 Durham *Herald-Sun* article that crowned a low point in her life, but on January 31, 1998, the day after UNC so handily defeated Coastal Carolina, the *Herald-Sun* ran another long article on UNC women's basketball. After Sylvia's 1994 NCAA

Championship and three ACC Tournament titles (1994, 1995, and 1997), sports writer Jim Furlong offered a different perspective from his 1991 "Black Cloud in Blue Heaven." This time, the headline read, "Born to Coach" and featured another color photograph of Sylvia with the caption "Intensity Personified." The article included interviews with her parents, whose anecdotes demonstrated that Sylvia truly was "born to coach." Sammy contributed a perspective that showed the human, caring side of Sylvia, such as her mothering instincts and her devotion to Van. Furlong featured players' comments, such as Tracy Reid's: "I am 14 hours away from home [Miami], and she is my mother away from home. She took me under her wing." Players also highlighted Sylvia's seriousness about the game and their lives, emphasizing her discipline, trust, and high expectations. Andrew Calder assessed her coaching strengths: "Evaluating talent, building unity and her ability to adjust during a game" plus "the ability to motivate."[14] The front pages of these two sports editions are symbols of the lows and highs of Sylvia's career. She kept copies of both these newspapers in her office as reminders that success is hard won and easily lost.

Coinciding with the 1998 Furlong article was Andrew Calder's unforeseen health crisis, which dealt a blow to the team, the staff, and—most of all—to Sylvia, who trusted him implicitly and depended on him as more than an assistant coach: "He is a rock-solid friend." Sylvia first noticed that something was wrong when they were playing in the Myrtle Beach Classic on December 20, 1997. Andrew expressed relief that Christmas vacation was approaching: "I need some time to get myself back together and rest," he told Sylvia. "I'm just burning the candle at both ends." "And he was," says Sylvia. After Christmas, Calder still did not feel well and thought he had a serious case of the flu. He saw a doctor in the Sports Medicine Clinic, got a prescription, and felt better for a couple of days.

On the morning of January 12, Sylvia had dropped Van off at Cresset and arrived at work around 8:15. Andrew, says Sylvia, "always made sure he was there before I was. Andrew has a tremendous work ethic." The UNC women were playing Duke at home that night, so she expected to see Calder already working. Instead, he had his head down on his desk and was trembling. "He raised his head up and looked at me, and he looked awful. I said, 'Come on. I'm taking you to the emergency room right now.'" He was admitted immediately to UNC Memorial Hospital. According to Jim Furlong's *Herald-Sun* account, he was "treated for pneumonia and anemia."[15] According to Sylvia, he was dehydrated and malnourished. By January 20, he felt better and was released.

Ten days later he was readmitted to UNC Memorial. Sylvia visited every day, and she saw little improvement in his condition. He was in the hospital for weeks without a definitive diagnosis. Eventually, a team of physicians diagnosed septicemia, an infection that damaged Calder's aortic valve. On a Sunday night, renal failure seemed imminent, and Sylvia thought he was going to die: "He was hanging on by a thread." She was distraught. Not only was he a staunch friend, he was her loyal assistant. Prior to being hospitalized on January 12, 1998, Calder had never missed a game since joining her staff in 1986. In many ways he was the other half of her coaching psyche. Andrew likes order and perfection, a trait that makes him a demanding coach. He is passionate about two things, basketball and golf, which he plays with consistency and skill. "He's great at teaching, and he's got a great basketball mind. Andrew is a great guy, and he's been extremely loyal to me. He's like my brother. He and I can talk about anything." Furlong quoted Sylvia as saying, "He knows, without asking me, what I am thinking and what I want done."[16] Calder's absence was hard for the players. Senior Tracy Reid told the press, "It's been more difficult than people realize.... Coach Calder has been like a father away from home for a lot of us."[17]

According to Sylvia, Calder is very detailed. "I'm not," she says. Another difference? "I'm more personable about relationships, and he is more private." Sometimes they seemed like a good-cop, bad-cop team. "I don't go after the players like he does. He goes after them hard; when they don't do what he wants them to do, he's pretty rough." Their partnership worked. He did all of the scouting and film work. When his coaching skills came to the attention of the media and other coaches, there was talk about his becoming a head coach. "But he didn't want to be a head coach," says Sylvia. "He liked what he was doing. He loved basketball—the strategy, the film work, and all that. He didn't want to do all the stuff a head coach has to do, such as PR and speaking and handshaking and meetings."

The UNC women's Tar Heels ended the 1997–98 season 27–7 overall and with an 11–5, fourth-place finish in the ACC. They went into the ACC Tournament as a low seed, but they were playing for Calder. "I left his chair vacant on the bench. I wouldn't let anyone else sit there; that was Coach Calder's chair," says Sylvia. The team handily defeated Virginia (76–56) and then faced Duke on February 28, a team that had beaten them by 13 points just 16 days earlier. They squeaked by Duke (56–52), but on March 1, they hammered Clemson (81–50) to win the ACC title for the fourth time in five years. It was the second-worst loss in the history of the ACC Championship, and Jim Davis was furious with Sylvia for leaving her starters in the game until the 1:28 mark. According to the *Seattle Times*, Davis and Sylvia had words after the final buzzer. "He repeatedly pointed to the clock as he made what appeared to be animated remarks." Then he "bowed to the queen" because she was "queen for the day." When Sylvia made no reply, Davis said, "The truth hurts." Sylvia was focused on a different "truth." For the second time in a row, Tracy Reid won the ACC Player of the Year Award and was named to the Kodak and Associated Press All-America team. Nikki Teasley was named the 1998 ACC Rookie of the Year. The only downside to UNC's unlikely ACC title was Calder's illness and absence.

That night, UNC women's basketball boosters held a celebration for the team at Red Hot & Blue, a barbecue chain restaurant on Elliott Road, which has since closed. Before joining the festivities, Sylvia took the ACC trophy to Calder's hospital room. He was scheduled for a heart valve replacement the next morning, on March 2. She told Jim Furlong that she wanted Calder to have "a look at it, so he will feel better in the morning."[18] Calder told Furlong, "'She brought it in, and I was so happy that they had won.... She wanted to leave it, but I wouldn't let her.'" According to Furlong, "Calder wept that night. 'I was happy,' he said, 'but also sad because I couldn't be there.'"[19] Calder's operation was a tremendous success. "It was amazing," says Sylvia. "They brought him back from the recovery room, and I'm telling you, minute by minute you could see him get better. By that afternoon, by three or four o'clock he was like a new person. He had color—he was alert—it was like pouring water on a wilted flower. It was the most incredible thing I've ever seen."

The ACC title earned UNC a No. 2 seed in the NCAA Mideast Region bracket. Playing in Carmichael Auditorium, they won their first-round game against Howard (91–71) on March 13. Aaron Beard reported that Calder attended the second-round game on March 15, "with an attendant," to see his UNC Tar Heels beat Florida International (85–72), but he immediately returned to the hospital.[20] In the Mideast Regional semifinal in Nashville, Tennessee, they beat Illinois (80–74) on March 21, the same day that Calder was released from the hospital, but he was not approved to return to work. The win against Illinois sent Sylvia's Tar Heels to their first Elite-Eight appearance since 1994, and Andrew wasn't about to miss the game. He and his mother Joan were in Nashville for the March 23 face-off between UNC and Tennessee in a packed Vanderbilt Memorial Gymnasium—14,848 in attendance. On orders from his doctors, Calder watched from the stands, not the bench, as UNC fought for another trip to the Final Four, a trip they hadn't taken in four years. The game was so significant to Tennessee that Pat Summitt devoted an entire chapter to it in her book *Raise the Roof*. For Summitt, the game was a notable step toward another championship. For Sylvia, it was a lesson in officiating and the power of intimidating officials.

From the moment she walked onto the court, Sylvia felt that something was amiss. She expected Vanderbilt's Memorial Gymnasium to be a sea of orange and white, and it was. Summitt's Lady Vols were undefeated, "the greatest team that has ever played," some said. The game had all the expected hype and drama of an Elite-Eight matchup between two teams coached by college friends. Sylvia believed that her team was prepared: "I had them ready." An AP story emphasized that the game would also be a contest between two star players: UNC's All-American Tracy Reid and Tennessee's Chamique Holdsclaw, who were friends off the court. Sylvia's record against Summitt was 1–12.[21]

The teams were warming up, and Sylvia was already in position on the bench, but Summitt was absent from the court. Sylvia was stunned: "It's three or four minutes before the game starts, and Pat is not even out there yet. Then all of a sudden, over in a far corner, a door opens, and Pat comes out. This is when I just knew. I thought, *Pat has lost it. She has lost it.* Now, the teams are still out there on the court, and she walks to the middle and stands out there waving regally to the crowd. And I'm thinking, *Pat has lost it.*" Then Summitt took her place with the UT bench at her end of the floor.

Pat Head Summitt was "larger than life," says Sylvia. "Pat was a dear friend. Nobody has done more for the game than Pat Summitt, and I wouldn't have been at North Carolina without her, but I'm just telling you: Ain't *nobody* intimidated the officials more than Pat Summitt." In Sylvia's estimation, the only coach in men's basketball who could match Summitt is Mike Krzyzewski. In the women's game, it's Geno Auriemma, and the intimidation factor is a combination of "a little bit of everything—their status in the game, the referees' fear that if they get certain coaches mad at them, they are going to raise a ruckus and the referees probably won't advance. It's political."

UNC took an early 4–0 lead and kept the score close throughout the first half, but at the buzzer, Tennessee was ahead by six points (33–27). Milton Kent wrote that "North Carolina stormed out of the dressing room at halftime with an 11–2 run to take the lead at 38–35."[22] Sylvia recalls, "We were kicking their butts with 7:35 to go and a 12-point lead." That's when Summitt called a time out and went out on the court to the foul line. "She was shaking her finger in the referees' faces, and I'm thinking, *Give her a technical—come on, give her a technical*! Any referee would have slapped a technical on any other coach, but not on Pat Summitt!" The Lady Vols answered UNC with their own 13–1 run and tied the score at 62. Sylvia was fuming: "Kellie Jolly (Harper) was the Tennessee point guard, and in the last four minutes UT shot sixteen foul shots and we shot four. Why would we foul? We were up by twelve points, why would we foul?" In the second half, Tennessee made 10 of 12 free throws and won the game 76–70. Sylvia was furious: "We should have won that game. There wasn't anything I could do about it. Plain and simple, Pat went out there and intimidated those referees like you cannot imagine."

While Sylvia emphasized intimidation, the media emphasized UNC's near-win. Marcia Smith wrote, "It seemed so improbable that any team would have the athleticism or the spine to stand up and trip top-ranked Tennessee." But UNC "gave the Vols something they hadn't seen from the teams they blew out all season. North Carolina gave Tennessee a game."[23] As a spectator, Andrew Calder witnessed UNC's last game of the season, a bitter defeat by Tennessee—not exactly the way to reduce stress on his first road trip after 51 consecutive days in the hospital. Even without the talents of point guard Marion Jones, who could have played on the 1997–98 team, the UNC women almost made it to the Final Four. In Sylvia's career, the defeat ranks below the 1983 Campbellsville loss, but it still stings—even today.

Sylvia began the 1998–99 season having lost three powerful seniors (Nicole and Sheneika Walker and Tracy Reid), but she had four returning seniors and junior point guard Nikki Teasley. With only two freshmen, the team had considerable experience and seniority. Their prospects looked good, but as the season was cranking up, the Jones-Hunter saga resurfaced. Jones's track career was thriving. She had achieved international stardom, especially in Europe, and was the "darling" of the track world. Then she announced that she and C.J. Hunter were getting married, and the invitations caused something of a kerfuffle. Sylvia was the only UNC women's basketball coach or staff member not invited to the wedding. Though talk spread among team members and coaches and staff, Sylvia kept her own counsel and continued to believe that Hunter's influence on Marion would come to no good end.

Following a home win against No. 10 Clemson on January 4, 1999, UNC's ranking rose to No. 6, but the 87–70 loss to the NC State Wolfpack three days later sent the team into a slide from which it never recovered, despite wins against Maryland (87–58) and Virginia (79–68). Then they prepared to host their perennial foe No. 11 Duke. A week before North Carolina's scheduled game against Duke, Sylvia wrote a letter to *The Daily Tar Heel* lobbying for a sell-out crowd. Her appeal paid off. For the first time, 10,000 fans packed Carmichael Auditorium for a North Carolina women's basketball game, but the outcome was not what she expected. An AP account of the game reported that "The Tar Heels were distracted by the throng when they came onto the court for warmups [*sic*] and lined up 20 minutes too early for the national anthem."[24] Whether the crowd contributed to the Tar Heel jitters or not, Duke dominated the game and held UNC to 30 baskets out of 85 attempts, winning the game

93–71 and handing the Tar Heels their first loss at home since the triple overtime defeat by Virginia (105–100) on January 15, 1998.

Following the humiliating loss to Duke, North Carolina traveled to Atlanta to face unranked Georgia Tech, who had not beaten the Tar Heels since 1993, but this time they handed UNC a 91–84 loss. UNC's ranking fell to No. 14. Still, they persevered and tallied victories over the next three ACC foes: Florida State (87–76), Wake Forest (88–66), and Clemson (76–72). Then, they had to face the Wolfpack for the second time in exactly one month. Following the January 7 loss to NC State in Raleigh, Sylvia concluded her press conference with, "They still have to come to Chapel Hill," suggesting that home-court advantage would boost her Lady Tar Heels. If playing NC State at Carmichael gave UNC any advantage, it was only in the margin of defeat: Kay Yow's Wolfpack outscored the Tar Heels by eight points (79–71) rather than 22.

The Wolfpack was not the only rival to give the Tar Heels grief. On January 22, Duke handed North Carolina their worst home-court defeat since 1991 (93–71). A month later in Cameron Indoor Stadium, Tar Heels suffered another loss to the Blue Devils (88–78) in their final game of the season, but UNC at least kept the final score within ten points. Disappointed but upbeat, Sylvia told the press, "We learned a lot today. Now we know we can play with them. Hopefully we'll meet them in the ACC Tournament."

The Tar Heels finished the regular season at 11–5 in the ACC and defeated Georgia Tech (87–71) and Virginia (83–70) in the ACC Tournament for a chance at the title. In the championship game, they faced Clemson for the third time in three years, and in 1999 Clemson had the edge: its best season ever. Though UNC led by nine points at the two-minute mark in the first half, their offense struggled. Jessica Gaspar admitted, "We kind of just went into a fog offensively for a few minutes at a time." Michael Lewis reported that Clemson "finally slayed its North Carolina demon" with an 87–72 win, and that Clemson coach Jim Davis was elated: "This was just so beautiful, to finally take down the team that's owned us for what seems like a long, long time."

With a second-place ACC Tournament finish, UNC was the No. 4 seed in the NCAA Tournament Midwest Region. They played the first two rounds on their home court, defeating Northeastern (64–55) and No. 5 seed Alabama (70–56). The win against Alabama sent the Tar Heels to the Midwest Regional semifinals in Redbird Arena at Illinois State University—the Tar Heels' sixth Sweet-16 appearance in seven years. Purdue was the No. 1 seed and was an early favorite to win the Tournament. On March 20, 1999, Purdue came out hot and firing, embarrassing the Tar Heels with their lowest score of the season (82–59), especially for a team that came into the Sweet 16 with an average 82.6 points per game. Sylvia's top players were stymied, and she didn't mince words in her post-game interview: "We ran into a buzzsaw." Her only consolation was that Purdue went on to beat Duke in the NCAA title game. Ending the season ranked No. 15 with a 28–8 record and failing to make the Final Four gave Sylvia reason to pause and take inventory of her life and the game. Something needed to change.

6

Changing Her Game

By 1999, Sylvia realized that she did not enjoy coaching as much as she should, though accolades continued to come her way. That year, for example, Carson-Newman inducted her into the school's Athletic Hall of Fame, and she was supremely grateful, but such honorifics did not meet her emotional and intellectual needs as a coach. Her passion had waned. For one thing, she was overcommitted to leadership positions in the ACC, NCAA, WBCA, and USA Basketball. In the ACC she served on the Committee on Officiating (1998–1999) and the Committee on Women's Basketball (1986–1995). In 1996–97, she was president of the WBCA, a four-year commitment. As head Coach of two USA Basketball teams (Jones Cup 1993–1994 and World University Games 1995–1996), she served on the USA Basketball Selection Committee. She valued these opportunities but finally acknowledged that they eroded her time and enthusiasm.

Sylvia needed to "fall back in love with basketball." She began eliminating committee obligations, but her most important steps were returning to the basics of basketball and seeking out male colleagues as mentors. "Nobody," says Judy Rose, "studies the game as much—and through so many different people—as Sylvia does." She has always made it her practice to observe and learn from the best coaches in the country—male and female. In 1999, she felt the need for an intense, focused plan. She selected eight male coaches with whom she visited and from whom she learned. She was persistent. Hubie Brown, former NBA coach and sports broadcast analyst, was not only willing to coach her over the phone, he said, "Send me a plane ticket, and I'll come to Chapel Hill." He spent a day and a half with her staff—without a fee.

As Sylvia puts it, "I went back to the basics of X-ing and O-ing." She went to point guard school at Lynchburg College and was in the gym every session. "Sometimes," says Sylvia, "you just have to go back to the basics." As a result, she changed her coaching philosophy and began to have fun. According to Rose, "Sylvia continues to be a daily student of the game, and that makes an excellent coach" who can communicate analytical skills to her players. Rose says, "Coaching is nothing more than teaching."

While studying the game with male coaches, Sylvia observed a distinct difference between men's and women's attitudes on the basketball court. Women wanted the security of certainty: "We come down the court and we run these plays, and I'm supposed to go here, and I'm supposed to do this, and this is what's going to happen." Women were uncomfortable with a fast pace that demanded quick thinking and action. Sylvia realized she needed to push her players out of their comfort zone, so she developed a variety of offensive and defensive strategies. Players trapped and pressed. They went after their opponent with the fast break. In short, she changed the nature of women's basketball forever to a wide-open, up-and-down-the-court, fast-breaking game. She honed the pressure defense.

What started out as wanting to fall back in love with basketball had a domino effect. Ridding her life of distractions and soaking herself in basketball brought back the passion. As she applied what she had learned, practices became fun; players enjoyed playing; and they caught Sylvia's enthusiasm. The team began to play better—and to win. As Sylvia learned in 1991 with that devastating *Herald-Sun* newspaper article, being number one is important in Chapel Hill. She wanted her Lady Tar Heels to be the team that every other team wanted to beat.

Sylvia approached the 1999–2000 season with new energy, new skill sets, and high hopes. In August, Tracey Williams-Johnson joined the Tar Heel coaching staff as the primary recruiter. Tracey had good connections that would be an asset. Sylvia's team had no returning seniors, but she could count on juniors LaQuanda Barksdale, Juana Brown, and point guard Nikki Teasley. Teasley's 1998–1999 season had been stellar. She led the Tar Heels in scoring and led the ACC in steals. Her 211 assists were an ACC best and set a new Carolina season record. The team began the season with two losses and nine wins, including a big win over unranked Maryland (92–79).

Then the bottom fell out. On January 3, Sylvia's Tar Heels lost to NC State 79–72. Teasley scored 17 points in the game, but she missed 11 of 17 shots, a performance that pushed her over the edge. Four hours after she returned to her room, she called Sylvia to say, "I don't want to be Nikki anymore." Sylvia was unaware that her star player's panic had been building. Teasley took a seven-game leave of absence and worked with a counselor who prescribed medication for depression. Sylvia cited "personal reasons" for Teasley's absence, a phrase that fed the rumor mill and created a media frenzy. What was the cause? Was she suicidal? Was she on drugs? Was she pregnant?

Without Teasley, the team struggled through the month of January, losing six more games, winning only one against Florida State, and dropping from 9–3 to 10–9 before Teasley returned to play. She was back on the court on January 30 when the Tar Heels defeated Maryland a second time 54–49. With Teasley on the team, the Lady Tar Heels won six conference games. Their final game before the ACC Tournament was against Duke, and the 73–64 win—a sweet victory—broke a three-game losing streak against the Blue Devils. UNC ended the regular season 6–7 in the Conference, a record that did not predict their success in the ACC Tournament. They beat Clemson (56–54) and Virginia (67–63) to go up against Duke for the ACC Championship. Teasley scored 31 points and was named MVP, but for all her efforts, Duke won (79–76). A second-place finish in the ACC did not assure the Lady Tar Heels a trip to the NCAA Tournament. John Altavilla, with the *Hartford Courant*, cited the team's "choppy season" and argued that the "residuals and recognition" following the 1994 NCAA Championship "shrink with the failures of each passing year."[1] On the other hand, Teasley appeared to be in top form, and Sylvia felt confident because the whole team had stepped up during Teasley's seven-game absence—especially junior forward LaQuanda Barksdale.

Against the odds, the Lady Tar Heels earned the No. 5 seed in the West Region and traveled to the University of California–Santa Barbara to face Maine, the No. 12 seed, in the first round. Sylvia could empathize with Maine coach Joanne Palombo-McCallie, who was eight months pregnant, but she wouldn't cut her any slack. She did everything possible to win, including lifting the team curfew and practicing at 9:00 p.m. Pacific Time to help the players adjust to the three-hour difference. It paid off. The Lady Tar Heels pulled out a 62–57 win. In the second round, UNC defeated 13-seed Rice (83–50) and went to the NCAA Sweet 16 for a fourth consecutive year.

On March 25, UNC traveled to Portland, Oregon, to face the top-seeded Georgia Bulldogs in the Sweet 16. Sylvia thought she had the edge because the Tar Heels had adjusted to west-coast time while Georgia would be traveling across the country. But it was not to be. Barksdale scored only six points and fouled out with 8:33 left in the game. Teasley hit only three of 19 attempted shots, scoring six points. The Lady Tar Heels suffered a humiliating 83–57 loss, and the *News & Observer* spared no feelings: "The Tar Heels (20–13) amounted to little more than a bug on Georgia's windshield."[2] After this loss, Teasley faltered. Sylvia said she "slacked up with her treatments and took a dive about the middle of April." When she stopped going to class, Sylvia had no choice but to send her home. Teasley would sit out the 2000–2001 season "to get herself straightened out."

Sylvia plowed through this disappointment by reminding herself of a maxim she uses with her players: "It's not about what you gather; it's about what you scatter. Take action, and you will have opportunities." When the UNC Alumni Association asked her to lead a Family Weekend workshop at Camp Cheerio, a YMCA facility just off the Blue Ridge Parkway in northwestern North Carolina, she saw it as an opportunity to "scatter." On the fourth weekend of August she, Van, and Sammy drove up to Camp Cheerio where they met Joseph F. Kirstein and Dr. Jo Ann Hundley, who talked about their land in Black Mountain, North Carolina. Sylvia had always wanted to own mountain land, so a few weeks later, they drove up NC Highway 9 to the Fairview community and pulled off Flat Creek Road beside a small blueberry patch to enjoy lunch. They hiked until late afternoon. Sylvia fell in love with the property, its blueberries, and the hiking path to a lookout. They would make this trip several times, and on every visit, Sylvia's interest grew.

Eventually, Kirstein offered to sell her the 204 acres, but she said, "Joe, I can't afford that land." He suggested that they "work out something," but as much as she wanted it, she kept thinking, *I can't afford that land!* Finally, he offered her a ten-year option: He would finance it, and she would make an annual payment of $75,000 every March. Sylvia thought, *Well, that's nice, but where am I going to come up with $75,000 the first of March every year?*

She pushed this opportunity aside for the time being, stayed in touch with Joe and Jo Ann, and continued to trust that the money to purchase the land would come—if it was meant to be. Meanwhile, she kept living her faith, but in the summer of 2000, that faith was seriously tested. After Van's birth in 1989, she wanted another child and began taking clomiphene, a fertility drug that stimulates the ovaries. She suffered serious side effects, including benign but painful cysts. Dr. Nebel, who had been with her through Van's difficult birth, kept a close watch on her. Sylvia had regular ultrasounds, and an annual CA 125 blood test, which measures the level of cancer antigen 125. In May of 2000, she went in for a routine gynecological exam, and she expected routine test results. She would, in her words, "be-bop" in for the examination and get the usual report: "The cysts haven't grown any," or "they have shrunk some." Then, she says, "I would be-bop out. So I went zipping in there to have that done, and the initial report was reassuring. I heard something like, 'Well, you know—there's a little bit of change, but I think everything is OK.'"

She was scheduled to speak at a Nike basketball clinic in Las Vegas, so on Wednesday, May 10, she boarded a plane at the Raleigh-Durham airport and took her seat beside Dean Smith, who was also speaking at the clinic. Between flights in the Atlanta airport, she had just enough time to check her voice mail from a pay phone. Among all the messages, one stood out: Dr. Nebel expressed concern about her test results and wanted her to see a gynecologist in the oncology department at UNC Hospitals. When she heard the word *oncology*, she thought *cancer*, and she boarded the Vegas flight with that word foremost in her mind: "I sat through that flight to Las Vegas almost numb." After checking into her hotel room, she immediately called Dr. Nebel and got the news that her CA 125 test result was extremely high and she needed to see Dr. Wesley Fowler with UNC Oncology. Sylvia explained that the UNC women's basketball team was leaving the next week for New Zealand and Australia.

When she returned from Las Vegas, she met with Dr. Wesley "Butch" Fowler, chief of gynecological oncology at UNC Lineberger Comprehensive Cancer Center, a facility that would figure prominently in her life for years to come. She underwent additional tests, including an ultrasound, and on May 19, 2000, four hours before she and her family were to board a plane, she got the test results. She remembers Dr. Fowler saying, "This is like at Christmas, when you have a package under the tree and you don't know what's inside it. It looks like we're going to have to open up that package." Then he said, "As soon as you get back here, we've got to do more tests."

She got the news just as she was embarking on "the trip of a lifetime"—a UNC women's basketball summer exhibition tour in New Zealand and Australia. The UNC women's basketball team takes Nike-sponsored international trips every four years, as allowed by the NCAA, per the Nike-UNC contract. According to Sylvia, these excursions are good for recruiting and help build team camaraderie. It's a great experience for the players, many of whom have never been out of the United States, but this trip was special for Sylvia because her entire family was coming along—not just Sammy and Van, but Ronnie, Ralph, Phyllis, and their families—everyone but her parents. Veda told Sylvia, "You're taking my whole family half way across the world. You take care of them." Veda did not know that no one would be taking care of Sylvia.

"The trip of a lifetime," was eclipsed by Dr. Fowler's news, but she kept it to herself, not telling her players, staff, or even Sammy, who had lost his mother to cancer just two years after they were married. Kay Yow, having weathered her own diagnosis 13 years earlier, might have given her encouragement and support, but Sylvia kept the secret even from Kay. Above all, she protected 11-year-old Van from the news.

The group spent two days in New Zealand and then went to Australia, where the women played three exhibition games. According to Tim Peeler, with the *Greensboro*

News & Record, Sylvia "went white-water rafting, scuba diving, and sight-seeing." Her most constant companion was her secret. They returned to Chapel Hill at midnight on Thursday, June 1. As Sylvia and Sammy were going to bed in the early morning hours, she said, "I have something to tell you." This was Sammy's first inkling that anything was amiss. "She explained all of it," says Sammy, including the likelihood that she had ovarian cancer: "It scared me to death." Exhausted from travel and little sleep, Sylvia reported for more tests at 8:00 a.m. on Friday, June 2. Her team of physicians had grown to include Dr. Kelly Ballenger, Dr. John Boggess, and Dr. Linda Van Le, all of whom accepted the possible diagnosis of cancer. For much of the day on Friday, she underwent tests, and the doctors scheduled still more tests for the following Monday. The concern was so great that surgery was scheduled three days later, on Thursday, June 8, 2000.

Sammy, Van, and Sylvia Hatchell after scuba diving, Great Barrier Reef, Australia, May 2000. Courtesy Sylvia Hatchell.

Sylvia recalls, "The day before was just agonizing because you're not sure whether you've got cancer, and you're getting ready to lose all your plumbing that's made you a female for your whole life." Added to that was the realization that she would never have another child. Finally, she shared her secret with someone other than Sammy: "I called my mama on Wednesday afternoon and told her."

Even in this life-altering situation, one of Sylvia's main goals was a quick return to the basketball court: "I begged them not to cut me open unless they had to." She got her wish. The doctors performed a laparoscopic hysterectomy and removed the uterus, cervix, fallopian tubes, and ovaries. Miraculously, the pathologist's report from the preliminary biopsy during surgery showed a benign tumor. Dr. Boggess left surgery immediately to deliver the good news to Sammy: "He came into the waiting room and told me that we had dodged a major, major bullet. He had thought it was ovarian cancer. It turned out that it wasn't. We were lucky—very fortunate." Sylvia's good friend, Dianne Glover (assistant supervisor of PreCare Services at UNC

Hospital) was with Sylvia in the recovery room. "I remember when I was waking up, Dianne was sitting beside me, and she said, 'They didn't have to cut you open, and they don't think it's cancer.'" In the July 19, 2000, UNC press release, Sylvia reported that the first two words she heard after surgery were "It's benign." They were "the sweetest words she could imagine."[3]

When she was released from the hospital on Friday afternoon, after a mere 36 hours, she could hardly believe her good fortune. Back at home, she finally told Van, "They thought I had ovarian cancer." Then she sent Van and Sammy to the North Myrtle Beach house so she could recover in solitude. Deneene took care of her, making up a bed on the sleeper sofa in the den, where she relaxed on Friday night and all day on Saturday. On Sunday morning, Tammy Cates, a friend and Cresset employee, drove her to the beach where she relaxed, rested, regrouped, and recovered. Having lost Mrs. Strickland just three years prior, she dwelt in an extended state of gratitude for her health and her family. She shunned the thought that 11-year-old Van might have had to endure his mother's cancer treatment and, perhaps, death.

The seriousness of Sylvia's situation did not "hit" Van until that Sunday morning. While Tammy Cates was driving Sylvia to Myrtle Beach, Van and his father attended Lakeside Baptist Church, their home church at the beach and one of the churches Van "grew up in." He attended Vacation Bible School there and joined in the Campus Crusade summer projects. They particularly liked the minister. "I can remember it just like it was yesterday," says Van "We got out of church and Dad was talking with the pastor about Mom's surgery. When we got in the car, Dad just broke down crying. It didn't occur to me how serious it was—how much of a big deal it was—until that day."

When Sylvia went in for her first post-op appointment, the doctors were all there—Dr. Fowler, Dr. Boggess, and Dr. Van Le, who, says Sylvia "is the only person I have ever known, who did not know who Michael Jordan was, especially in 2000. I kid her about it all the time." All kidding aside, this trio of physicians emphasized that she was one of the few to come out of this diagnosis with a good result. Sylvia's immediate response to having survived the cancer scare was, "What can I do to help?" Dr. Fowler suggested that she "tell her story so that more women will be checked because ovarian cancer is a 'silent killer.'" She remembered her grandmother Maude Rhyne, who had died from ovarian cancer in 1978. Sylvia says she "didn't realize the statistics were so grim—that most of the time when we find ovarian cancer, it's at stage three or four." Not much is passive with Sylvia, including gratitude. After her brush with cancer, she became one of the Lineberger Center's most dedicated fundraisers and pledged $5.00 for every 2000–2001 UNC women's basketball season ticket sold.

A rejuvenated Sylvia entered the 2000–2001 season with mixed prospects. On the one hand, she had a new assistant women's basketball coach—former player Sylvia Crawley, who had just completed a season in the WNBA with the Portland Fire. Another plus was that Crawley understood Sylvia's brand of Carolina basketball, having been the captain and starting center of the 1994 NCAA Championship team. On the other hand, Nikki Teasley was out for the year. Sylvia would expect leadership from returning seniors LaQuanda Barksdale and Juana Brown who were named preseason candidates for the Naismith College Player of the Year Award. Barksdale had also led the ACC in scoring and rebounding in the previous season. Offsetting these senior leaders were five inexperienced freshmen. Sylvia hoped their height would compensate—especially Candace Sutton at 6'6" and Chrystal Baptist at 6'2". She tapped freshman Joy Hairston to assist sophomore Coretta Brown as Teasley's replacements in the point guard position. Sylvia told the press "that it would be mid–January before this team hit its stride." UNC began the season ranked No. 22 and was predicted to finish fourth in the ACC. Duke was predicted to win the title.

From the outset, the Lady Tar Heels had a seesaw season—sometimes brilliant, often disappointing. The media blamed UNC's inconsistency on the absence of Teasley. William Warnock described the first two weeks of UNC's ACC competition in 2001 as "desultory."[4] On a mission to increase attendance at Lady Tar Heel games and spark interest, Sylvia moved the January 14 matchup with NC State from Carmichael to the larger Dean Smith Center. According to the *Herald-Sun*, Sylvia announced in late fall that she "wanted to break the ACC single-game record, which was set in 1992 when 14,500 saw Virginia beat Maryland in College Park."[5] A second goal was to promote the Lineberger Comprehensive Cancer Center. In a pregame ceremony, she presented a $5,000 check to Lineberger, making good on her promise to donate $5.00 for every season ticket sold. (Only 456 season tickets for UNC women's basketball were sold that year.) Attendance for the NC State game fell far short of a record—7,022 fans filled less than one third of the 21,750 seats. But Sylvia could take heart that the crowd exceeded average attendance (2,009) at the Lady Tar Heels eight home games. Her team also exceeded her expectations. They lagged 36–34 at the half, and when the final buzzer sounded, UNC thought they had won the game 73–71, but Candace Sutton fouled Amy Simpson, who tied the game at 73 with two free throws. In overtime, LaQuanda Barksdale and Coretta Brown took charge, and UNC outscored No. 19 NC State 10 to 4 for the 83–77 win.

When Sylvia got a three-day break in January, she visited the Black Mountain property with Joe and Jo Ann. They were driving back to Chapel Hill in Sylvia's car, and as was customary, she phoned her parents just to check in. It was late, around 7:30 or 8:00 p.m., so she was puzzled when they didn't answer the phone. After dark, they usually stayed close to home, venturing out only to church or the grocery store. She called her brother Ralph, who was not particularly worried but agreed to drive the four miles to Gastonia from his house in Chapel Grove. Within minutes, he called Sylvia with the news: "We found Mama and Daddy at the emergency room. Mama has had a heart attack." On this night, Veda had made supper, and after cleaning up the kitchen, she lay down on the bed. Carroll was sitting in his chair watching the evening news when Veda came into the living room and said she had chest pains. He took her to the emergency room but did not notify any of the children.

Soon, Ralph's wife Karen called Sylvia with an update. Sylvia could hear Ralph in the background saying, "Maybe Sylvia needs to come." By this time, she, Joe, and Jo Ann had made it as far as the Gibsonville exit on I-85/I-40. As usual on these trips to Black Mountain, Joe and Jo Ann had left their car at a gas station at the Hwy 54 exit, so she dropped them off, got on I-85 South, and drove straight to Gastonia in less than two hours: "It's a two and one-half hour drive, and I was flying."

Sylvia spent the night with Veda in the Gaston Memorial Hospital. On Wednesday morning, January 24, Veda appeared to be stable, so Sylvia drove back to Chapel

Hill in time for afternoon practice and a big home game against Duke the next night. Veda's stability was short lived. On Thursday morning, Ralph called Sylvia to report that Veda's right arm was swollen severely from the intravenous beta-blocker, and he was frustrated that no doctor had checked the arm. Around 11:00 a.m., Ralph called again to say, "Mama's arm looks awful. No doctors have been in, and she is suffering." Sylvia felt helpless, so she took action: She called Dr. Stuart Bondurant, Dean of the UNC Medical School. Bondurant immediately called Gaston Memorial Hospital, and Ralph reported to Sylvia that "about eight" doctors had been in to check on Veda, but by the time they examined her, the distended arm was black, and infection had set in. Veda was scheduled for a stent that day, but the procedure had to be canceled. The next hurdle was preventing gangrene and loss of the arm. At 6:00 p.m. on January 25, 2001, Veda went into surgery; Sylvia's game against Duke was at 7:00.

In the first half, UNC suffered a 15-point deficit but fought hard to tie the game at 76 and go into overtime, their second in two weeks. Unfortunately, their 24 turnovers—five in overtime—gave the Tar Heels their second consecutive loss to Duke (92–85) that would ignite a three-year feud between these two Triangle foes. Sylvia was exhausted and emotionally drained, but the night wasn't over: "I hadn't even stepped off the court when Sammy met me and said, 'Come on. We've got to go. They are not expecting your mama to make it through the night.'" Sylvia bypassed the press conference, ran to her upstairs office, grabbed her purse, and they "jumped in the car and took off" for Gastonia. When they arrived, they learned the full story of Veda's condition. While she was having surgery on her arm to relieve the fluid and pressure, she suffered a second heart attack. The doctors put in stents and then dealt with the arm. After hours of surgery, they again told the family, "We don't think she will make it through the night."

The family waited and watched for three interminable days as Veda miraculously improved and was eventually transferred to Belaire Health Care Center for rehabilitation. For the next few weeks, "it was up and down, in and out of the hospital," says Sylvia. "When one thing starts going wrong, it connects to everything else." Even Sylvia's team seemed to be affected—they struggled to gain traction. Every win was erased by a loss. Their victories over Georgia Tech, Wake Forest, and Clemson in double overtime (100–88) were followed by a three-point loss to Virginia. On February 18, the Tar Heels met Florida State at home in a key ACC match-up, which they had to win to get a bid to the NCAA Tournament. They lost 80–78 in their fourth overtime game of the season. Then came losses to their Triangle rivals NC State (84–73) and Duke (72–67). The loss to the Blue Devils was the second of the season and the third consecutive loss in what would become a long succession of losses. The stinger was that the Duke men's team led the mob of Blue Devil fans onto Cameron court to celebrate the win against UNC.

Sylvia tried to keep everyone's spirits high and was conscious of the stress on her father during her mother's touch-and-go recovery. Carroll spent much of his time with Veda at Belaire or Gaston Memorial, so his 76th birthday on February 24, 2001, went relatively unnoticed. Sylvia decided to cheer him up with a new car. He came out of the hospital one night and found a new silver PT Cruiser waiting outside: "He liked those little things," says Sylvia. Carroll and his friends also liked to follow

Sylvia's games. Phyllis recalls an occasion when she took her father to visit Veda, but they had to hurry home to watch Sylvia's game on TV. He got settled in his chair and asked that the telephone be placed where he could reach it. At the end of the first half, the phone rang, and he grabbed the receiver. It was his good friend, Gene Conner, calling to deconstruct the game. They became color analysts, commentators, and play-by-play announcers, analyzing both teams, explaining where the UNC players needed to improve and how Sylvia needed to adjust her game plan. When the second half began, they abruptly hung up. At the end of the game, the phone rang again, and the two arm-chair analysts resumed their commentary. They were as serious as any professionals.

Holding Veda and Carroll uppermost in her thoughts, Sylvia entered the ACC Tournament with the word "miracle" on her mind—for her parents and her team. The Lady Tar Heels were the No. 7 seed, so it would, indeed, take a miracle for them to advance to the NCAA Tournament. William Warnock wrote that an ACC Tournament title would be the obvious way for the Tar Heels to advance to the NCAA, but "the simplest [way] would be to somehow wrangle a personal meeting between Coach Sylvia Hatchell and the NCAA Selection Committee" because the persuasive Hatchell could "talk raccoons out of trees when she feels strongly enough about an issue."[6]

The Lady Tar Heels defeated No. 8 seed Georgia Tech 79–64 in round one of the ACC Tournament. Sylvia was hopeful. In round two, her team would play No. 2 seed Clemson. In the regular season, the Tar Heels had defeated the Tigers twice, and Jim Davis was not keen on facing Sylvia's team a third time, but his fears were unfounded. His Tigers came out on top 75–57. Sylvia's Tar Heels ended the season 15–14 overall and 7–9 in the ACC. Preseason predictions proved partly wrong and partly right: UNC finished seventh in the ACC, not fourth, but Duke won the Conference title. For the first time since the 1995–96 season, Sylvia's Lady Tar Heels did not make an appearance in the NCAA Tournament. "I did not have my All-American point guard," says Sylvia. "That's how important they are to a team." With no commitments for post-season play, she went straight to Gastonia and stayed with her mother for nearly two weeks. Sylvia thought, *OK, I'll give up going to the NCAA Tournament to be here.* "I was upset that we didn't make the tournament, but getting to be with Mama made it OK."

While Sylvia and her Lady Tar Heels struggled, Sammy was achieving his greatest success in his 13th year as the Meredith women's basketball coach. With a 16–7 record in 2001, the team got a bid to the NCAA Tournament, a near-impossible accomplishment. As an independent, Division III college, Meredith was not in a conference, so Sammy thought they would never make an NCAA appearance, but on February 28, 2001, Meredith faced Guilford College. Playing on the opponent's home court and with their home officials, Meredith lost 80–57. At least one Hatchell coach had made a showing in an NCAA Tournament.

Through the summer of 2001, Veda continued to improve, and Sylvia's life returned to the routine of running her summer camps and recruiting. Always a believer in camps, she continued to have a strong hands-on approach, and though Sammy still wasn't as enthusiastic about camps as she was, he was her stalwart assistant. The camps gave her the opportunity to do something she loves—teach basketball

fundamentals—and they also gave her a recruiting edge, especially for North Carolina and South Carolina talent. This edge would spark controversy with a fellow ACC
coach in 2003.

A good example of Sylvia's recruiting technique and "touch" was Jessica Sell. Sylvia and her staff first observed Jessica during the 2000 Beach Ball Classic in Myrtle
Beach. At that time, Jessica was a junior from North Marion High School in Rachel,
West Virginia, so Sylvia invited her to summer Elite Camp in Chapel Hill and then
visited her home in Barrackville, West Virginia, 30 miles southwest of Morgantown,
on September 10, 2001. Sylvia and Tracey Williams-Johnson had an excellent visit
with Jessica and her family. On the morning of September 11, they expected to fly out
of Morgantown to Cleveland, Ohio, for a home visit with another potential recruit,
Barbara Turner. Instead, they—and the rest of the world—were stunned by the developing news that two planes had crashed into the World Trade Center at 8:45 and 9:03
a.m. The news of the terrorist attacks was breaking just as they were leaving for the
Morgantown Municipal Airport. They dropped off their rental car and went to the
terminal, where they learned that all U.S. flights had been grounded. Sylvia quickly
grasped their situation and sent Tracey to retrieve their luggage while she went to get
a rental car. Every traveler was in the same predicament they were, but she got one of
the few remaining automobiles, so they set out for Cleveland and the home visit with
Barbara Turner. As they drove up I-79 toward Pittsburgh, Sylvia said, "Tracey, look
over there. It's just a big black cloud." Later, they learned that the tall plume of black
smoke, visible for many miles, was rising from Flight 93, the fourth terrorist plane
that crashed in Shanksville, Pennsylvania. They drove the 200 miles from Morgantown to Cleveland for the home visit with Turner and then had to drive the rental car
550 miles to Chapel Hill.

Turner would later sign with the University of Connecticut, but Jessica Sell
signed with the Tar Heels. After observing her at Elite Camp and in her home, Sylvia
offered her a scholarship, which she accepted verbally on the spot. Approximately 60
schools recruited Jessica, but she was interested in only one. Says Jessica, "If a letter
came in the mail and it didn't say 'UNC,' I didn't look at it." According to Jessica,

> Sylvia and her staff were warm, good-hearted, good people. From the time Coach Hatch-
> ell and Coach Williams-Johnson walked into my home, I felt that I was part of the family.
> My family could feel it. It was very comforting, and I felt special, cared about, valued. I had
> a smile from ear to ear during that entire process because the University of North Carolina
> really, really made me feel special. And even to this day, I am so humbled and so thrilled
> that I had that opportunity.

Along with Sell, 6'1" La'Tangela Atkinson, the *USA Today* Player of the Year, signed
letters of intent on November 14, 2001. Atkinson played for Lee Central High School
in Bishopville, South Carolina, and was heavily recruited by women's basketball powerhouses, including the University of Tennessee, but she chose UNC. Both would
start the 2002–2003 season.

As the basketball season was gearing up, UNC was renegotiating the Nike
All-School contract, which was renewed on October 15, 2001, for another eight years.
The entire package was approximately $28.34 million. In the early 1990s, Sylvia's
portion of the Nike contract with UNC was $10,000. By 1997, after having won the

1994 national championship, earning two trips to the Sweet 16 and one trip to the Elite Eight, her Nike contract had increased to $50,000 annually. When the contract was being renegotiated, UNC athletic director Dick Baddour had indicated that her portion would be increased, and when she met with him to discuss his proposal, he handed her a sheet of paper with "$75,000" written on it. She never compared the value of her Nike contract with men's basketball coach Matt Doherty's at $500,000; women's soccer coach Anson Dorrance's at $150,000; or football coach John Bunting's at $150,000. Instead, she saw the $75,000 as a "gift": *I've got it*, she thought. *I've got the land.* The Nike payment was made on January 1 of every year, so she annually signed the $75,000 check over to Joe Kirstein. In her view, it was meant to be: "You don't argue with stuff like that."

7

Duke! Duke! Duke!

In the fall of 2001, Nikki Teasley was back as a senior, having taken off a year to "get herself together." Gregg Doyel wrote that Teasley "spent the year working, construction by day and J.C. Penney by night. She kept her game sharp by playing pickup, sometimes driving an hour to an all-night gym in Washington [D.C.] to play against men." She told Doyel, "I only play with women when I have to."[1] Sylvia would start Teasley on the wing, not as point guard, hoping to ease the pressure on her.

Preseason polls picked UNC to be No. 2 in the ACC for 2001–2002, and the media compared Teasley's reappearance with Marion Jones's return for the 1996–1997 season. Perhaps Teasley would propel the Lady Tar Heels to the ACC Tournament title and another the NCAA Sweet 16—at the very least—as Jones did in 1997. Right off, Teasley's hyped return was deflated. In January, she had played briefly in a men's recreation league game, which was a violation of NCAA rules prohibiting outside competition. The NCAA gave her a one-game suspension, but Sylvia went further, keeping Teasley on the bench for three games. She was back on the court when UNC traveled to Storrs, Connecticut, to face Geno Auriemma's UConn Huskies. The media promoted the game as a rematch of the March 26, 1994, contest when UNC defeated UConn for a berth in the Final Four, but UConn beat them on the boards, and they lost 94–74.

By the end of November, the Tar Heels gained their first national ranking in more than a year—No. 24. With wins against Kentucky, Old Dominion, and Wake Forest, their ranking rose to No. 18, but injuries began to plague Sylvia's top players. Teasley suffered from back pain, and Leah Metcalf had tendinitis in both knees. UNC was the highest-scoring team in the ACC, but in the Wake Forest game, Teasley missed 13 of her 20 shots, still in the wing position, not point guard. Gregg Doyel reported that instead of "retreating to her room," as she would have at the peak of her depression, "she went to the gym in defiance and shot 300 jumpers using a ball-retrieving contraption called The Gun. Ideally, the North Carolina staff wants players to make 150 shots against The Gun. Teasley wants 180. That day, she hit almost 200."[2]

When the Lady Tar Heels bested Clemson (89–85), their national ranking rose to No. 17, but Georgia Tech clobbered them (81–62). Following the game, Sylvia apologized for the team's poor performance: "I promise we will get better. We will practice at 6 [a.m.]." She was likely also apologizing for Nikki Teasley's behavior. Following the loss, Teasley was involved in a fracas with a Georgia Tech player, and UNC gave her a one-game suspension for unsportsmanlike conduct, so she was on the bench for the fourth time since her much-hyped return, and Wake Forest beat the Tar Heels 65–64. On January 24, Teasley was back on the court, but Duke trounced them 102–82—the Tar Heels' fourth consecutive loss to the Blue Devils. UNC dropped to No. 24.

In the January 27 game against Virginia, Sylvia made a change that paid off. She shifted Teasley from the wing to her old position as point guard, and UNC won 79–64. Jim Furlong called Teasley the "catalyst,"[3] and the victory sparked an eight-game winning streak that ended on February 24 at the hands of Duke (90–75) in Carmichael Auditorium. To make matters worse, the home-court crowd was one of the largest of the season—7,842—and the game was nationally televised. The Duke victory confirmed preseason polls: UNC ended the season as No. 2 in the ACC, and Duke No. 1.

Even with two losses to arch-nemesis Duke, the Lady Tar Heels had momentum going into the ACC Tournament, and Sylvia was thriving. On January 28, WCHL AM 1360 had launched the Sylvia Hatchell Show, which was broadcast at 6:00 p.m. weekly during conference games, from Red Hot & Blue, the restaurant where the Lady Tar Heels had celebrated their 1998 ACC Tournament championship. On February 28—just two wins shy of her 600th—Sylvia turned 50, and the team gave her a cake with 50 candles. Then they gave her two more cherished gifts in the ACC Tournament: her 599th win against Maryland (78–53) and on March 3, 2002, her 600th win against NC State (58–52). Ironically, her 500th win in 1998 was also against NC State. "The key is I enjoy the 600th just as much as the first one," she told the press. This milestone put Sylvia in "The 600 Club," an elite group of six active Division I women coaches to achieve 600 or more wins, the other five being Jody Conradt (785), Pat Summitt (784), Vivian Stringer (653), Sue Gunter (649), and Sylvia's mentor Kay Yow (625). By ACC Tournament time, UNC's national ranking had risen to No. 11— the best of the season—but the team had to face No. 3 Duke on March 4 in the ACC Tournament title game. For the third time in 2002, Duke handed them defeat (87–80). UNC ended the season 11–5 in the ACC, and three of the five losses were at the hands of Duke. The string of consecutive losses to the Blue Devils increased to six.

With a national ranking and a second-place ACC finish, UNC was the No. 4 seed in the NCAA Midwest Region. The pairings were surprising because UNC was in the same bracket as the top two SEC teams—Vanderbilt (the No. 1 seed) and Tennessee (No. 2). Sylvia had expected Tennessee to be seeded No. 2 in the East Region. Instead, she faced a possible repeat of the 1998 Elite-Eight game against Pat Summitt's Lady Vols. With home-court advantage, the Lady Tar Heels defeated Harvard 85–58 in the first round, but the second-round win against Minnesota came harder. The crowd was small—only 1,965 attendees. UNC lagged for much of the game, but the team rallied to a 72–69 win. It was Teasley's final game in Carmichael, and Margaret Banks, with the *Greensboro News & Record*, wrote that the "postgame celebration was all about Nikki Teasley." Her teammates "hoisted" her in the air, and she "kissed the court" twice. She told reporters, "I'm so glad I came back, ... this is everything I expected— and more."

For the eighth time in ten years, the Lady Tar Heels would compete in the NCAA Sweet 16, this time in Ames, Iowa. Having fractured her right index finger, Teasley played with two fingers taped together and made only one of 14 attempted baskets.

Vanderbilt got the win (70–61). The defeat marked Teasley's final collegiate game and UNC's fifth Sweet-16 loss in eight years. Teasley's return to the Lady Tar Heels did not fulfill its early promise, and they ended the season 26–9. At the annual UNC Women's Basketball Awards Banquet, Teasley was awarded three game balls: one for her 1,500th career point, and two each for her UNC record number of assists and three-pointers. Eleven days later the Portland Fire picked her in the WNBA first-round draft.

With the season behind her, Sylvia shifted her focus to the next year and to Van's growing interest in basketball. During the seventh grade, his attitude toward the sport shifted. For Christmas that year, Sylvia gave him a video game (*NBA Live 2001*) that pushed his interest to a new level. In the fall of 2002, when Van entered the eighth grade, he earned a spot on the Cresset High School JV team and was selected captain, but all was not well. The team was not competitive. Van would not be challenged. His basketball skills would not likely improve, and his interest may wane, so Sammy asked Vern Parsons, the Cresset athletic director, to watch and evaluate a practice session. As a result, Parsons himself decided to coach the JV boys' team in Van's eighth-grade year. Sylvia, Sammy, and Van took heart.

Sylvia was even more hopeful about her own upcoming season—her 17th at UNC. She told the press, "I am more excited about starting practice this year than I've been in a long, long time." She described the 2002–2003 Lady Tar Heels as "very athletic, a real up-tempo team, fun to watch, very balanced." Preseason polls ranked UNC No. 13 nationally and No. 2 in the ACC, and the media speculated that the Lady Tar Heels might be able to bump arch-nemesis Duke from its spot as the three-time ACC Champion. Sylvia had lost only one starter, senior Nikki Teasley. Three freshman recruits were promising: Kenya McBee, from Wade Hampton in Greenville, South Carolina; Jessica Sell, from North Marion High School in Rachel, West Virginia; and La'Tangela Atkinson, who led Lee Central High School to a South Carolina State Championship in 2002. Atkinson was named preseason ACC Rookie of the Year.

Another reason for Sylvia's optimism was former player Charlotte Smith, who joined the Tar Heel staff as an assistant coach in October 2002, when Sylvia Crawley opted to play professional basketball in South Korea. Smith had hit that magic, winning shot in the 1994 NCAA title game, had played professional basketball in Italy, and later spent three seasons with the American Basketball League (ABL). When the ABL folded, Smith was drafted by the Charlotte Sting in the WNBA, and she would continue to play for the Sting while coaching.

The Lady Tar Heels' 2002–2003 season began on November 22 against Davidson, and before the tipoff, UNC athletic director Dick Baddour presented Sylvia the game ball from her 600th win in the previous season. The gesture seemed a good omen. Her Lady Tar Heels came away with the win (68–46), but Sylvia told the media that UNC had improvements to make—they "didn't take care of the ball" and "got outrebounded." These types of comments would reverberate throughout the season. UNC cruised to 12 consecutive wins between December 1 and January 16, but their play was uneven and sloppy, as in their performance against Charleston Southern, coached by former UNC star Stephanie Lawrence Yelton. They got the 84–49 win, but Jim Furlong called the performance "subpar," saying UNC "looked sluggish during the first half, fumbled passes, threw unwise passes, missed several open shots near the rim and missed 13 of 29 free throws."[4]

Meanwhile, Duke—their perennial foe—was on a roll. Nikita Bell was especially frustrated: "Duke. Duke. Duke. That's all we hear…. We'd like people to know we're just as good as Duke."[5] UNC's ranking rose to No. 10, and the next three decisive wins seemed to prove Bell right. Wake Forest fell (86–56). Then it was Florida State's turn (74–53). On January 16, UNC trounced Clemson (77–55) for their 12th consecutive win. After the loss, Clemson coach Jim Davis snubbed Sylvia when she tried to shake his hand and told the media he had "respect for every coach in America except one." He did not identify the "one." Jon Solomon, with the Scripps Howard News Service, wrote that Davis had "long suspected" Sylvia of improper recruiting, especially in the way she used her summer camps. Jim Furlong speculated that Davis was "not happy that UNC has successfully recruited two of the top high school players in South Carolina the last two years."[6] Furlong may have been referring to Ivory Latta, who would start in 2003, or UNC's two South-Carolina freshmen La'Tangela Atkinson and Kenya McBee, but Sylvia had always successfully recruited South Carolina players. In her 11 years at Francis Marion, she built good connections with high-school coaches, so they naturally alerted her to the promising players. Davis issued an apology, which Sylvia accepted and moved on. She had a larger concern: Monday, January 20, when the No. 8 Lady Tar Heels would face No.1 Duke in a nationally-televised battle on ESPN2.

With a 15–1 record, and a 12-game winning streak, Sylvia fought the public perception that her team was taking "an unwilling back seat" to the Blue Devils. On January 20, Carmichael Auditorium was sold out. For the first time in the history of UNC women's basketball, fans were turned away from the gate—300 in all—and the 10,180 fans who packed the arena witnessed a spectacular game. Duke led by one point at the half, but the Lady Tar Heels regained the lead 56–49 with 5:49 left. Duke caught up and took a three-point lead, but Leah Metcalf made a three-pointer to tie the game at 61. When Duke's Wynter Whitley fouled Nikita Bell at the buzzer, Sylvia thought they would have a chance for the win at the foul line, but because the game was televised, instant-replay was available. Officials consulted monitors on the sideline, and referee Sally Bell ruled that time had expired prior to the foul. The game went into overtime, and Duke took over. The final 78–67 victory was Duke's 29th consecutive win in the ACC. Sylvia cited her team's poor performance at the foul line: "If we just made some foul shots … we would be celebrating right now." But she didn't stop there. She told Gregg Doyel, "Duke's tough." And then she added, "They're so lucky…. One-tenth of a second can make a difference…. Maybe they're having all their luck early in the season. Sooner or later, it's going to run out."[7] UNC was then 15–2 and Duke was 17–0, but the Tar Heels had the worst free-throw record in the ACC.

Sylvia had no time to lick her wounds. Three days later, her team was at Western Michigan, in near-zero weather, for a 79–76 win that set UNC on an eight-game winning streak. Their national ranking rose to No. 7. Leading up to the second faceoff with Clemson on February 16, the Jim Davis snub was again in the news. The media wouldn't let it die. Wendy Parker, with the *Atlanta Journal-Constitution*, wrote, "If

Hatchell has a sense of humor, maybe she ought to greet him before the game wearing a 'He Hate Me' jersey," a reference to former NFL and XFL player Rod Smart, who wore his nickname He Hate Me on his jersey. Parker then gave the Tar Heels a backhanded compliment: "[U]nlike in past seasons, these Tar Heels aren't a band of chaotic freelancers but are playing some terrific and entertaining team basketball."[8] Sylvia did everything possible to generate enthusiasm and momentum for her team. The buzz around Carmichael was that Senator Elizabeth Dole would be the honorary UNC coach for the Clemson game, and Sylvia had lobbied for a sell-out crowd, but it was not to be. An ice storm moved in. Dole canceled her appearance, and a mere 331 fans showed up to watch the Lady Tar Heels beat the Lady Tigers 70–66.

UNC had won 20 of their last 21 games, a pretty good record for a coach that had been playing without a contract since July—and the only ACC women's basketball coach to have won a national championship. On Monday, February 17, 2003, the lapse was rectified. Sylvia signed a new contract through 2008 that assured her a base salary of $160,000 plus $25,000 for expenses. With the $75,000 Nike supplement and other incentives, the total salary exceeded $270,000. UNC athletic director Dick Baddour praised her winning record and the graduation rate of her players, which was 3 percent higher than UNC students in general.

The new contract came just three days before Sylvia's Lady Tar Heels would face then-No. 2 Duke for the second time, but the rematch would be on the Blue Devils' home court. Duke's only loss of the season had been to then–No. 1 Connecticut on February 1 before a sold-out crowd of 9,314 in Cameron Stadium, a loss that switched the No. 1 and No. 2 spots. Another sell-out was anticipated for this rematch of old Triangle foes. UNC's ranking had risen to No. 6, and the game was nationally televised on Fox Sports South. Lady Tar Heel Jennifer Thomas told the media that this was a battle "for bragging rights," not "revenge," but she also said that UNC wanted to prove to themselves that they were "the No. 1 team in the ACC." Cameron Indoor Stadium was near capacity, and Duke fans savored a UNC meltdown—an embarrassing 97–63 drubbing. Sylvia's January 20 prediction that Duke's luck would run out came back to bite her. Even the *Charlotte Observer* latched on to the word "lucky" to headline the game report.[9] Duke coach Gail Goestenkors said simply, "We kicked their [hind quarters]." She told Gregg Doyel, "Some people think we've been lucky over the course of the season. We wanted to prove that we do have some skill, and we are a pretty good team."[10] With this loss, UNC dropped two points to No. 9. They went into the ACC Tournament with a 26–4 record, and Duke accounted for two of the four losses.

The ACC Tournament opened on March 7 in Greensboro. As expected, Duke was the No. 1 seed, UNC No. 2, and for all the Lady Tar Heels' strengths, their free-throw percentage was still lowest in the ACC—60.2. In the first round on March 8, UNC defeated Clemson (80–71) for the third time in 2003. Still fanning the fire between Sylvia and Clemson Coach Jim Davis, Carroll Rogers reported that Davis "shook her hand and patted her left shoulder." In the semifinals, UNC knocked off Virginia (88–78) on the same day that the UNC men upset Duke (82–79) in their last game of the regular season. Sylvia told the media that her team took heart from the men's victory and would "give it everything we've got." She also said she would "pray a lot."

The Greensboro Coliseum was sold out for the ACC Championship game—11,126 fans. Initially, the Tar Heels kept the score close and led 31–25 at the half, but the lead slipped away. Sylvia did, indeed, give it everything she had. According to Jenna Fryer, she screamed so much, yelling at her players to "play defense," that she lost her voice in the second half. With 4:49 left in the game, she had a sideline "temper tantrum," arguing a non-call with an official that drew a technical foul. Duke's Iciss Tillis said that the call fired up the Blue Devils: "I think a technical can help the other team, as well, and I think we knew we had the game wrapped up then." Fryer reported that "Tillis laughed at Hatchell as the UNC coach jumped up and down and screamed and waved to the UNC fans to get up and demand better play or better calls or something."[11] At the end, Sylvia admitted that her team missed too many layups and got boxed out. Again, the free-throw line was UNC's enemy—Duke outscored them 28–9. The final 77–59 score said it all. According to Ed Hardin, Sylvia wanted Duke: "More than anything else in the world, she wants to beat Duke."[12] UNC had lost nine straight games to the Blue Devils—their last win against Duke had been on February 27, 2000.

UNC ended the ACC Tournament with a 27–5 record overall and was 13–3 in the ACC—the three ACC losses being, of course, at the hands of Duke. The big question was whether the two teams would meet a fourth time in the NCAA Tournament. Duke was the No. 1 seed in the Midwest Regionals. UNC could face Duke again only if both teams made it to the Final Four, a possibility that wasn't such a long shot. The *Atlanta Journal-Constitution* wrote that the Tar Heels were "always packed with Final Four-caliber talent" and "capable of beating anybody," but also "subject to being upset early. Supremely athletic, tremendous on the boards and deadly in the open court."[13]

UNC was the No. 3 seed in the Mideast Region in Boulder, Colorado. Sylvia questioned the site selections and the bracket. If UNC won the first-round game against No. 14 seed Austin Peay (from Clarksville, Tennessee), they would possibly have to play lower-seeded Colorado on its home court. She also questioned the bracket because the team that won the first two Mideast games would then go to Knoxville, and—with certainty—have to face Pat Summitt's Lady Vols on their home court.

The prediction that UNC could suffer an early upset almost came true in round one. Austin Peay had won 22 straight games. UNC had the top rebounding percentage in the nation but had not played a game in 12 days and seemed rusty. The game was surprisingly close. Jim Furlong wrote that Sylvia's Tar Heels "barely avoided a major upset" and called their offensive performance "lackluster."[14] UNC survived, thanks to Nikita Bell whom Sylvia called the "spark." Bell was so exhausted she was taken to the locker room and given oxygen in the mile-high altitude. She told Chris Shelton that she did not remember the final two minutes of the game.

Sylvia's concern about the site selection proved valid. In the second round on March 24, the Lady Tar Heels faced the lower seeded Colorado (No. 6) on its home court. Attendance was surprisingly low—only 4,645 fans showed up in the 11,064-seat arena. Colorado shot 49 percent from the floor, in contrast to UNC's 36 percent, but fouls and free throws decided the game. Colorado hit 31 of 39 at the foul line; UNC made 9 of 16. Jeff Jacobs with the *Hartford Courant* asked, "Was a 39–16 free-throw discrepancy in favor of Colorado caused by the Tar Heels' physical demise in high altitude? Or intimidating officials?" In short, UNC was outplayed and lost 86–67.

At a Division I school, Sylvia was expected to compete at a high level in the NCAA Tournament. At an independent, Division III school, Sammy just felt lucky to get a second near-impossible bid to the Division III NCAA Tournament in 2003. With an 18–6 record, his Avenging Angels traveled to Ashland, Virginia, for a first-round game against the Randolph-Macon Yellow Jackets. They lost 77–74. Still, it could be said that there were not many households where the husband and wife both competed in the 2003 NCAA Tournament—even if at different levels. While Sylvia and Sammy thrived as coaches, Van struggled on a team that had little leadership. In the fall of 2003, he entered the ninth grade at Cresset, liking basketball more and more. Despite Sammy's conversations with the Cresset athletic director during the previous year, the coaching situation had not improved and would become the catalyst for a major change in the Hatchell household. Veda was stable. Carroll was in great health and was helping to care for her. But this would change, too.

The UNC Lady Tar Heels' 2003–2004 season marked the ten-year anniversary of the NCAA national championship. In the intervening decade, Sylvia had begun to change the nature of women's basketball. Her 1999 desire to "fall back in love" with the game was still strong. Her continued focus on the "basics" and the desire to learn from male colleagues shaped her coaching style. The question was, "When would the payoff come?" Her Tar Heels began the year with a preseason ranking of No. 14, which did not change significantly during the season. Two strong freshmen recruits joined the team: Ivory Latta, from York (South Carolina) Comprehensive High School, was the 2001–2002 *Charlotte Observer* Player of the Year and set South Carolina state records for three-pointers and foul shots. Camille Little was an All-State player from Carver High School in Winston-Salem, North Carolina, and the daughter of Robert Little, who was called the "Dunker" when he played with the Harlem Globetrotters. For the next four years, the duo of Latta at 5'4" (as her career progressed, she "grew" to 5'6") and Little at 6'1" reigned on the court. The flashy, high-energy Latta and the quiet, shy Little were also roommates. The Tar Heels came out strong, with three wins prior to Thanksgiving.

As was their custom, Sylvia's whole family planned to spend the Thanksgiving holiday, November 27, in Gastonia. On Wednesday, Sylvia, Sammy, and Van pulled in the driveway at 504 Oliver Street, expecting a warm welcome, but Veda immediately sent them to the emergency room. A car had rammed Carroll's PT Cruiser and knocked it across the median into a tree. Carroll had a broken hip, and the PT Cruiser was totaled. Sylvia chastised herself: *If I had not bought that PT Cruiser for him, he would have been in his truck or something else that was safer.* Carroll suffered permanent nerve damage to his right foot, a condition that meant he could never drive again. After Thanksgiving, Sylvia drove back to Chapel Hill for a win against the University of Maryland, Baltimore County (UMBC), which set them on a six-game winning streak that ended when they fell to Old Dominion. During this time, Sylvia was driving to Gastonia at least one day a week. "I was just killing myself and trying to make sure someone was there to take care of Mama and to see Daddy."

The family had moved Carroll to White Oak of Kings Mountain where he began a regimen of physical therapy, but when it became apparent that he would always be dependent on a walker, the family moved him to Summit Place, an assisted-living facility. "After that, the man never spent another night at home," says Sylvia. Left at home without Carroll, Veda insisted on visiting him every day and eventually stayed at Summit Place most of the time, but they both desperately wanted to be home, so one day they went. A neighbor on Oliver Street called Ralph and said, "Your mother's car is sitting in the carport, and your mother and daddy are just sitting in the car." Ralph rushed to the house and found that Veda had driven from Summit Place, parked in the carport, gotten out of the car, and unlocked the side door of the house, but she was so frail she could not turn the door handle to go inside. Her plan was to open the door and then help Carroll inside on his walker. Instead, she went back to the car, and there they sat. "They wanted to be home that bad," says Sylvia. Ralph had no choice but to take them back to Summit Place.

The family drama competed for Sylvia's time and attention, but she stayed focused on her goals, trusting that her renewed passion for basketball and her intense study of the game would pay off. Following the loss to Old Dominion, UNC got seven more wins, most by comfortable margins, except for their 58–57 squeaker at NC State. The next challenge came from Duke—their first face-off of the season on January 11, 2004, in Cameron Indoor Stadium. Putting aside their nine-game losing streak to Duke, the Tar Heels approached the game with new expectations—and new talent in Latta and Little. Again, they played before a sold-out crowd that included the "Cameron Crazies," Duke fans who raised a thundering roar. UNC trailed by 11 at halftime but tied the game at 54 with 6:57 left. After that, they went cold, scoring only four more points, and Duke won 79–58. Duke's consecutive wins over UNC stretched to 10.

After the bitter loss to Duke, the Lady Tar Heels won five games and lost two—Wake Forest on the road and NC State at home. The Wolfpack broke UNC's 18-game winning streak in Carmichael, a major upset. NC State was unranked; UNC was No. 13 with a record of 18–4. Sylvia's team would have a five-day break to prepare for their second game against No. 4 Duke on February 14. Expecting a larger crowd than usual, and not wanting to turn away fans as they did in 2003, UNC moved the game to the Smith Center. Both teams were coming off losses. On February 4, Florida State had ended the Blue Devils' 51-game winning streak in the ACC (80–74), but Duke was still ranked No. 1 in the conference. A win for UNC would end their 10-game losing streak against Duke, and the two foes would be tied for first place. The faceoff of two, nationally-ranked ACC teams attracted 10,278 fans. It was an attendance record for a North Carolina women's basketball home game; still, it was just 98 over Carmichael's capacity and 11,472 under Smith's capacity. Early in the second half, UNC was down by 14 points and cut the deficit to seven, but at the final buzzer, the deficit was 10. They had suffered a humiliating eleventh straight loss to Duke (89–79). Sylvia's only consolation was that Latta and Little were freshmen.

Following their loss to Duke, the Lady Tar Heels won the next three games, and this momentum carried them into the tenth anniversary celebration of the 1994 NCAA Championship. Except for Sylvia Crawley, who was playing professional basketball in Japan, the entire championship team attended the two-day reunion that included a banquet on February 28, 2004 (Sylvia's birthday), and a half-time celebration at the Virginia game the next day. Even Marion Jones attended, accompanied by Tim Montgomery. Sylvia had not seen Jones since she left the UNC campus in 1997. Throughout the celebration, they were cordial to each other, but there was no close conversation or interaction.

Between 1997 and 2004, Jones's career had blossomed, despite the negative influence of Hunter. She won three gold medals and two bronze in the 2000 Olympics, in Sydney, Australia, the first woman to win five track and field medals in one Olympic competition. ESPN and the Associated Press named her Athlete of the Year. But just prior to the Games, the International Amateur Athletic Federation suspended Hunter and banned him from competition because he tested positive for the banned substance nandrolone. Hunter did not contest the decision, though he consistently denied the accusation. Because of her association with Hunter, Jones was also under investigation for banned substance use. George Kimball, with the *Irish Times*, asked in print what many people questioned privately: "Are we to assume that they maintained separate medicine cabinets? That they maintained separate training regimens—one clean and one dirty?"

At the time of the championship celebration in 2004, no formal charges had been brought against Jones, and she appeared to have shed Hunter's influence. On June 5, 2001, *Agence France Presse* had reported that Jones and Hunter were separating and she would be seeking a "divorce due to irreconcilable differences, which have made nurturing our marriage extremely difficult." Elliott Almond, with the *San Jose Mercury News*, reported that they had been separated since February 2001, so their marriage had lasted approximately two and one-half years. Her new partner, Tim Montgomery, broke the 100m world record at the International Association of Athletics Federations Grand Prix finals in 2002, and their son, Tim Montgomery, Jr., had been born on June 28, 2003. Sylvia recalls being impressed with Tim, who was from Gaffney, South Carolina, a small town 35 miles southwest of Gastonia.

The reunion celebration gave the Lady Tar Heels a boost, especially as they approached the ACC Tournament. Sylvia was pleased that her players could meet the women who had had the talent and chemistry to win an NCAA Championship. She told her team that they reminded her of the 1994 champions. The day following the reunion banquet, February 29, her team, indeed, played like champions, beating Virginia 70–64 in the final game of a 22–5 season. The Lady Tar Heels went into the ACC Tournament as the No. 2 seed, ranked No. 11 nationally. But would it be enough to wrest the ACC crown from Duke who had won the championship for four consecutive years?

In the first round on March 6, UNC defeated Virginia 64–45. Sylvia credited the win to defense and turnovers, and Nikita Bell scored 18 points—her season high. The next day, Latta scored 27 points and Little scored 24 to defeat NC State 75–64. Little had been named ACC Rookie of the Year, with Latta a close second, and the media dubbed them a "dynamic" and "determined" duo. When UNC faced Duke in the ACC Tournament championship game for the third straight year, the Greensboro Coliseum was packed with 11,466 fans, the largest crowd "to see any of the 27 title games

Martha Lawson, with Eastman Company, presents trophy to Sylvia at her induction into the Women's Basketball Hall of Fame, Knoxville, Tennessee, June 13, 2004. Courtesy Women's Basketball Hall of Fame.

in Tournament history," according to Jim Furlong.[15] But the dynamic Tar Heel duo could not get the win. Duke seniors Tillis and Beard stymied the UNC freshmen Latta and Little, holding Latta to nine points and Little to seven. Duke robbed them of the ACC Tournament title (63–47) for the fourth time in five years. The UNC score was their lowest of the season. Ned Barnett reported that Sylvia was so "frustrated" with the loss that she made her team remain on the floor during the Duke celebration. "The Tar Heels sat glumly as balloons rained down and Duke players cut down the nets.... 'I just wanted them to stay out there so they could see what happens when you win,' Hatchell said." During Duke's wild celebration, Ivory Latta sat down beside Sylvia and said, "I want to tell you something. As long as I'm here this will never happen again."[16]

Coming out of her 12th straight loss to Duke, Sylvia had less than two weeks to prepare for the NCAA Tournament. Jessica Sell recalls that after the brutal ACC Tournament loss to Duke, Sylvia banned the team from their locker room and took away all UNC gear except their shoes, hoping to shock them into attention. At the time, the players thought such action was unwarranted, if not outright crazy, but looking back on it, Sell says, "it was huge. It helped us focus on what was really important."

UNC's No. 4 seed in the East Region of the NCAA disappointed Sylvia. With a 24–6 record, she told the press she was "hoping for a No. 3." In the first round, UNC was paired with No. 13 seed Middle Tennessee State University—a team they had never played. Sylvia was also disappointed with the East Region first-round venue—the Joyce Center in South Bend, Indiana. If UNC beat Middle Tennessee, the Tar Heels would play lower-seeded Notre Dame on its home court. "That is the way it is, and we have to deal with it," Sylvia told the press. "The committee realizes this is a mistake." Another blow to the team came when Tiffany Tucker, who had become a strong reserve player, broke her left toe in practice and was sidelined for the first-round game. Sylvia told the press that her team had "the talent to advance deep into the NCAA tournament," but she questioned "whether the Heels [had] the needed focus." Without it, she said, "we know we can get our wings clipped at any time."

On March 21, 2004, the Lady Tar Heels did, indeed, get their wings clipped. They lost the round-one game to Middle Tennessee State University by five points (67–62), and their ranking dropped to No. 21. They closed out the 2003–2004 season 24–7 overall. Sylvia told Dan Fleser that after the loss, Pat Summit was one of the first people to call her: "I know you're beating yourself up over this," said Pat, "but you have a young team." "That's friendship," says Sylvia.[17] Despite the loss to Middle Tennessee, Jessica Sell believes that Sylvia's tough-love move after the Duke game had a positive impact on the team that extended to her junior and senior years. Sell also remembers an iceberg analogy that Sylvia used to motivate this team: "People see the five players on the court, but they represent merely the tip of the iceberg. What's under the water is more substantial than what is seen above the water. The hidden part of the iceberg represents the preparation and the behind-the-scenes support, practice, conditioning, and focus."

The iceberg metaphor could also have applied to Sylvia. Underneath the surface of her professional life, she and her family continued to struggle with Veda's and Carroll's health crises. She felt that she had to do something—anything. By this time, Sylvia and Sammy were building a new house on Kepley Road, which would be their fourth home. Sylvia planned the house to accommodate her parents, making the bottom floor handicap accessible, vowing to bring her parents to live with her. Some of the Rhynes' friends and even her sister Phyllis began to say, "Sylvia, this may give you peace of mind—bringing them to your house—but is this what they want?" Carroll's sisters could visit them at Summit Place, but who would visit them in Chapel Hill, where they would be away from their families, their church, their friends? Sylvia began to question her own motives: "Are they going to be happy if they can't see all these people they have known all these years? And my dad's sisters coming to see him two or three days a week, and I'm like, *Well, what do you do?*" She realized, "This is selfish." Finally, they found a helper for the Rhynes: Tony Rikard, a big, strong man who could lift and manage Carroll. Tony would put the Rhynes in the car and take them to get barbecue or to spend few hours at their Oliver Street house. He even brought Mr. Rhyne to a couple of Sylvia's basketball games. The arrangement seemed ideal, but Veda's health continued to fail.

In the summer of 2004, Veda was hospitalized, and Sylvia continued to drive to Kings Mountain every week to spend a couple of hours and then drive back to

Chapel Hill. Veda's up-and-down health crises were an undercurrent in Sylvia's life of losses and celebrations, which included her most significant recognition to date. On June 11–12, 2004, she was inducted into the Women's Basketball Hall of Fame in Knoxville, Tennessee. The festivities were "overwhelming," she told Rachel Carter: "All along, I've been, 'OK, OK.' But now that it is here, I've got flowers coming, a zillion cards, people calling."[18] In addition to Sammy and Van, many of her fans and long-time supporters attended the ceremony, including Tommy Northern, the Talbott Elementary School principal who gave her that first coaching job when she was a Carson-Newman undergraduate. UNC athletic director Dick Baddour attended. ACC commissioner John Swofford, who hired Sylvia as head UNC women's basketball coach in 1986, introduced her for the Induction Ceremony at 8:00 p.m. on Saturday, June 12, in the Knoxville Convention Center Lecture Hall. But most of all, she was proud that her parents were there. Tony Rikard and his wife Gerri drove Veda and Carroll from Gastonia to Knoxville. Both were in wheelchairs. "Oh, man. It was a job," says Sylvia. At the hotel, Carroll fell in the shower, but with Tony and Gerri's help, they made it back to Summit Place. "It absolutely wore them out," says Sylvia. "It was the last overnight trip they ever took."

8

Over the Hump

Having a caretaker for Veda and Carroll eased the pressure on Sylvia and her family. With Tony's help, her parents could take short trips, so Sylvia wanted them to attend Women's Basketball Family Day, one of the first women's basketball events held annually. She began the Family Day tradition in 1988, just two years after she arrived at UNC. It began as an early fall picnic held at The Farm (run by UNC Faculty-Staff Recreation Association) for all her women's basketball players, their families, and her extended family. Later it grew to include church services at Cresset Baptist (the Hatchells' home church) with a motivational speaker. Following the church services, everyone was invited to a luncheon at the UNC Friday Center, where players introduced their families and posed for photographs. Sylvia emphasized the "family" nature of the event and liked to include her own parents, but on Thursday before the 2004 event, Veda was readmitted to the hospital. By November, she was well enough to return to Summit Place, but she was disinterested in life. Sylvia called her parents every day and tried to motivate her mother with no success.

While Sylvia wrestled with Veda's and Carroll's situation in the fall of 2004, Sammy was also undergoing a transition. Van would be a sophomore at Cresset, where the boys' basketball team continued to rack up a dismal record. Earlier that year Sammy had made a surprising offer to the Cresset athletic director: He would leave his 16-year career at Meredith to coach the varsity boys' team. He then met with the Cresset principal, and they worked out an arrangement whereby Sammy would become the development coordinator and part-time coach at Cresset Christian Academy. His colleagues told him he was committing professional suicide, especially because his women's basketball team had earned two trips to the Division III NCAA Tournament in 2001 and 2003. Without blinking, he followed through with his "suicide move," resigning from the full-time position at Meredith to take on a Cresset boys' team that had won three games in Van's freshman year (2003–2004). The first year Sammy coached the Cresset team (2004–2005), their record was 22–4, and they won the Carolina Christian Conference. The next year their record was 23–8, and in Van's senior year 19–9. Under Sammy's leadership, the team made it to the second round of the North Carolina Independent Schools Athletic Association (NCISAA) Tournament every year.

Though Sammy's colleagues and friends thought he was crazy to leave Meredith, he never regretted his decision. He had the chance to build a boys' team, but more importantly, he had an opportunity to spend time with Van. Sylvia says, "You just can't put a price tag on that relationship." Van agrees: "I got to spend a lot of time with him. I give him credit—he and Mom made the sacrifices so he could be my coach." Sylvia acknowledges that Van profited from being the child of two coaches, and during this time he began to realize that his mother's career was "a big deal" though she excelled at keeping her family "down to earth," he says. "Despite how successful she has been, she is still home—still home—true to her Gastonia, North Carolina, and Florence, South Carolina, roots, where she started her career." Van was frequently asked, "What's it like having a mom who's always on TV?" He answered,

> What's it like having sit-down family dinners every night? It's one of those things that seems normal for you, but it's odd for the other person. So to me, it's just how it was. Growing up with twelve really tall college girls always around just seemed normal. It was a whole family to me. Our vacations centered around recruiting time or the Final Four or where Mom's team was playing at certain times of the year. That seemed normal to me.

Sylvia worked hard to keep her family "normal" and grounded amid their complex lives. For years, she and Sammy had attended an annual marriage retreat at Ridgecrest, North Carolina. In the fall of 2004, Gary Chapman and his wife Karolyn led the retreat with focus on his *New York Times* best seller *The Five Love Languages: How to Express Heartfelt Commitment to Your Mate*. Later Sylvia read *The Five Love Languages of Children* and *The Five Love Languages of Teenagers*. Chapman's first book is based on Christian principles and intended to help husbands and wives relate to each other, but Sylvia believes that Chapman's philosophy can be applied to everyone. Chapman identifies five "love languages": words of affirmation, physical touch, gifts, acts of service, and quality time. He believes that everyone has a dominant or primary love language and a secondary one.

Sylvia experimented with Chapman's technique on Sammy and Van, and once she was convinced that they worked, she started using them with her players. In 2004–2005 Ivory Latta was a returning sophomore, still honing her point-guard skills, and occasionally making foolish mistakes, as in the January 20, 2005, game against Florida State when she shot 2 of 12 from the floor and made 1 of 7 three-point attempts. During the game, Andrew Calder criticized Ivory loudly, and Sylvia could tell by the look on her face that he had made a mistake. Sylvia thought, *We have lost her, and we're not going to get her back*. She told Andrew not to scold Ivory further. Sylvia would review the game film with her. Believing that Ivory's love language was words of affirmation, she praised Ivory's quick and accurate analysis of her own mistakes: "Ivory, this is why you are the best point guard in America." The film session taught Sylvia how to communicate with her key player. Ivory needed to recognize her own mistakes, and Sylvia needed to affirm her for discerning them.

Focusing on Chapman's five love languages, Sylvia paid close attention to the players and learned to appreciate their unique personalities. From La'Tangela Atkinson's first exhibition game in 2002, Sylvia had learned that she was tender hearted and sensitive. The team had arrived and put on their uniforms. Few players were on the court when Sylvia saw La'Tangela standing at the edge, leaning on the rail, crying. Her grandmother had been ill and wasn't expected to live, so Sylvia asked, "Tangi are you all right? Is your grandmother OK?" La'Tangela said that her grandmother was doing okay; she was crying for another reason: "Coach, this is my first time in a UNC uniform; it has been my dream to attend the University of North Carolina and play basketball. I can't believe that I'm here."

During the 2004–2005 season, Sylvia used Chapman's love languages to good effect with her solid core of returning players and freshmen. Ivory Latta and Camille Little were sophomores, both having been selected to the 2004 ACC All-Freshman Team. Seniors included Nikita Bell, Kenya McBee, Leah Metcalf, and Jennifer Nelms; juniors were La'Tangela Atkinson, Jessica Sell, and Tiffany Tucker. Two promising freshmen rounded out the team—6'2" Erlana Larkins and 6'3" LaToya Pringle. UNC was ranked No. 9 in the AP preseason poll, and No. 12 in the Coaches' Poll.

On November 19, the Lady Tar Heels easily won their first game of the season over Elon (88–40), but next up was Geno Auriemma's No. 4 UConn Huskies, in the opening game of the Jimmy V [Valvano] Women's Basketball Classic at the RBC Center in Raleigh. Rachel Carter reported that the Classic—in its third year—had raised more than $100,000 for research in "cancers that primarily affect women." The Huskies had not played in the Classic since 2002, and UNC was making its first appearance.[1] Sylvia's decision to participate was not surprising, given her 2000 cancer scare and Kay Yow's diagnosis. It also meant that she knew her team was good. The buzz was all about the Lady Tar Heels' speed and fast-break offense—but UConn had won five NCAA titles. On November 21, UNC played like champions before a crowd of 6,734 in a cavernous venue that seats 19,722. Even so, the fans were loud, and the team was "on"—UNC got the win 71–65. Nolan Hayes, with the *Herald-Sun*, wrote that Erlana Larkins "looked nothing like a freshman."[2] It was UNC's first victory over a top-five team since 1994 and the first time they had defeated UConn since their 1994 Sweet-16 win that sent them to the Final Four and the NCAA Championship.

Through the fall of 2004, the team matured and developed the one characteristic that cannot be coached or taught—chemistry. Following the UConn victory, their ranking rose to No. 2, and they won five straight games before falling to Penn State 77–71. Three days later, on Wednesday, December 8, 2004, Veda would celebrate her 80th birthday. UNC held a required head coaches meeting that day, but Sylvia told Beth Miller that she would not attend: "It may be my mom's last birthday, and I am going to Kings Mountain." Sylvia and the family, Veda's friends, and Carroll's sisters were all there for the birthday party. Before Sylvia left, she begged, "Mama, now look; I want you to keep working on getting stronger." Veda said, "I'm so weak. I'm so tired; I just can't do it anymore." Though she refused to admit it, Sylvia knew that Veda was slipping away. Then came another disappointment. Her friend and mentor Kay Yow suffered a recurrence of breast cancer after 17 years of being "cancer free." Sylvia told Rachel Carter, "You feel like after that 17-year period of time, that's it. You're cancer free. But I don't know if you're ever cancer free."[3]

On December 12, the Tar Heels overpowered Coastal Carolina (94–52) and then defeated Georgia State (79–44) in the Myrtle Beach Classic. The team and staff left for the holidays, but Sylvia, Sammy, and Van spent the night and drove to Florence the next day to visit Sammy's Aunt Laura Harrell, who was in a nursing home. As they were driving through Florence around 6:00 p.m., Sylvia got the call that Veda was in the hospital and was not expected to live through the night. With 45 minutes to spare, Sylvia got a flight from Florence to Charlotte. Veda was awake when

Sylvia walked into her room; she smiled and said, "Hey, how's my 'Sylvie'?" From that moment, Sylvia did not leave her mother's side.

The family brought Carroll to Veda's hospital room. He kissed her goodbye and they took him back to Summit Place. Phyllis arrived from Florida to join the death watch in the early morning hours. All four of her children held her and told her it was okay to go. "And then she just let go," says Sylvia. "The sun was coming up, and it came right through the window just as she took her last breath. It was the hardest thing I have ever had to do." Sylvia drove to Summit Place to get Carroll. "He was sitting there eating breakfast, and when I walked in, he looked at me and said, 'She's gone, isn't she?' I said, 'Yeah, Daddy.'" Sylvia took her father back to Veda's room, and the whole family stood around the bed, holding hands: "We prayed and thanked God for her, and gave her back." For the next few days, Sylvia felt a strange peace: "I don't know if I have ever felt that way in my life. I'm thinking, *This is when I should be the most upset,* but I felt so calm and so at peace. I could just feel her. I could just feel her with me and a part of me. I was OK." Veda was buried on Christmas Eve, 2004, and as usual, they held Christmas at 504 Oliver Street in Gastonia. Everyone was there: Sylvia, Phyllis, Ronnie, Ralph, and their families. They brought Carroll home for Christmas day, but "it was rough," says Sylvia.

After the holidays, Sylvia returned to coaching a team that had slipped to No. 4. On January 9, they traveled to College Park, Maryland, for their first ACC game of the season. The Terrapins had lost seven consecutive games to the Lady Tar Heels and were ranked No. 21, so UNC was favored to win, but Maryland got the upset—92–77. The loss to Maryland was their second of the season, but it was followed by a one-point win over NC State on the Wolfpack's home court (77–75). For the first time in 30 years, Kay Yow was not on the court. She had taken a ten-day leave of absence for dietary therapy. Yow's absence was hard for Sylvia, having just lost her mother. Everyone was affected, even Sylvia's players. Leah Metcalf and Camille Little asked her if the Tar Heels could wear pink ribbons on their uniforms. Yow's players wore pink shoelaces, and their home court was decorated with signs supporting their coach. UNC got an easier win over Miami (83–52), but Florida State handed them a 79–73 defeat. In the post-game press conference, Sylvia said the matchup was "a typical road game in the ACC"; UNC "got fouled but it wasn't called." She added, "I don't know what else we can do to get more foul shots." UNC had only seven shots from the foul line as opposed to Florida State's 24. On January 23, 2005, the *Orlando Sentinel* wrote an unflattering piece about Sylvia, accusing her of "questionable sportsmanship" for "going onto the court to yell at officials as they left the floor."[4] Officiating wasn't her only problem. Following the game, Erlana Larkins spent the night in a Tallahassee hospital, suffering from severe dehydration and body cramps. She flew back to Chapel Hill a day late and missed the team shoot around on Friday, January 21—with the Duke game looming.

The loss to Florida State dropped UNC's ranking to No. 12 on the eve of their first faceoff against No. 1 Duke in 2005. The game was played in the Smith Center on January 24 and televised on ESPN2. Looking ahead to the NCAA Tournament, Sylvia was hoping that television coverage and a large, noisy crowd would help prepare her team for the spotlight. Pre-game press acknowledged UNC's pressure defense, aggressiveness, and physicality, but everyone wondered whether they had the talent and moxie to break their 12-game losing streak to the Blue Devils. Ken Tysiac wrote that Ivory Latta would have to step up her game—she was stone cold in the FSU game. Sylvia told him, "We're not afraid of them."[5] The Duke player who had laughed at Sylvia in the 2003 ACC Championship game—Iciss Tillis—had graduated, but Blue Devil Monique Currie was the top player in the ACC and an All-American candidate.

Attendance was disappointing—6,929—and the game was not pretty. Patricia Earnhardt wrote that some called it "the worst half of basketball they had ever seen, ... a highlight reel of everything bad that can happen in a basketball game. It was slow, low scoring and sloppy." These adjectives were not in Sylvia's playbook, but she was pleased with her team's rebounding and defensive play. Players for both teams were given technical fouls (Duke's Currie and UNC's McBee). Larkins had somewhat recovered from her hospital stay just four days previous, but she played only 13 minutes and scored only four points. The game may have been ugly, but the 56–51 win boosted the team's confidence. The tide had turned.

The win broke UNC's 19-game losing streak against No. 1 teams, and it knocked Duke from the No. 1 spot—Nikita Bell called it a "double victory." After all, she had played in 9 of the 12 straight losses to the Blue Devils, and she may have been remembering her 2003 comments: "Duke. Duke. Duke. That's all we hear.... We'd like people to know we're just as good as Duke." According to Nolan Hayes, Sylvia motivated her team by reading aloud media reports that Duke players "thought the Tar Heels had folded in some of the teams' previous meetings." Her locker-room tactic had worked, and she felt one step closer to her goal of making women's basketball intense, fast paced, and fun to watch.

After the Duke win, the Lady Tar Heels seemed unstoppable. Leading up to their second matchup against Duke, they won eight straight games, including an overtime squeaker against NC State (75–72). Their ranking rose to No. 4. Going into the February 27 game against the No. 2 Blue Devils, their record was 26–2 overall and 11–2 in the ACC, but they would be playing in Cameron Indoor Stadium, which had not been kind to the Tar Heels. This time the Cameron Crazies were not a factor, and the media frenzy surrounding the Duke-UNC rivalry in previous years dissolved. Monique Currie turned over the ball eight times, but rallied Duke to take the lead in the second half. Then UNC tied the game and never looked back. For once, fouls were in UNC's favor. Four Duke players had four fouls each, and point guard Wanisha Smith fouled out of the game. UNC made 27 of 31 at the foul line; Duke 6 of 12. The 88–67 win made UNC the No. 1 seed in the ACC Tournament, but Sylvia didn't gloat. "It could have gone either way," she told the press. "I'm sure we both learned a lot from this. I'm just proud of my team." Nikita Bell also played it cool: "It's just one of those humps we wanted to get over, and we did.... We can't stop here. We've got to keep it going." Given her comments from previous years, Bell probably downplayed the size of the "hump."

The ACC Tournament would be the real test for Sylvia's Tar Heels. They had many strengths—depth, speed, charisma, chemistry, and—not to be overlooked— the absence of drama surrounding individual players that had plagued Sylvia's teams in preceding years. This team gelled. Perhaps Sylvia's application of Chapman's love languages made a difference. Even so, they struggled offensively in the first round of the ACC Tournament against Miami but pulled out the win (64–57). In the second-round matchup against No. 5 seed Virginia, they again struggled. Down by 11 points at the break and by 17 in the second half, Latta led the UNC comeback, scoring a career-high 32 points to give her team the 78–72 win.

The next day, March 7—eight days after the 77–68 win in Cameron—UNC again faced Duke in the ACC Tournament title game, their fifth championship faceoff in six years. As usual, the Greensboro Coliseum was at capacity—a record 11,578 fans. Expecting a larger-than-usual crowd, the Greensboro Coliseum opened the west upper deck for the first time in ACC Tournament history. Bill Hass wrote that "Duke came into the game on fire."[6] UNC took no notice and made a 33–13 run to open the game and led by five at the half. In the second half, Duke pulled within three points but could not overcome UNC's 27–10 run and—in general—could not match UNC's athleticism and speed. Point guard Ivory Latta was playing with a cold and a sinus infection, but they did not derail her mission. She scored 26 points to give UNC the 88–67 win and was named Tournament MVP.[7] She also made good on her 2004 promise to Sylvia following the ACC Tournament championship loss to Duke: "As long as I'm here, this will never happen again."

Rachel Carter reported that after the win, Latta and Nikita Bell chanted, "We've got three. We've got three."[8] They had beaten Duke in three consecutive games and won the ACC Tournament for the first time since 1998. Moreover, they had snapped Duke's winning streak: 19-games in the Greensboro Coliseum and 17 games in the ACC Tournament. Sylvia was prepared for the victory celebration. She brought to the game the golden scissors she used to cut down the nets in the 1994 NCAA Championship victory over Louisiana Tech. She told the press that she hoped to be able to use the scissors again.

Having won the ACC Tournament, UNC got an automatic bid to the 2005 NCAA Tournament as the No. 1 seed in the Tempe Regionals, but the bracket was tough. UNC would play the first two rounds in the Smith Center—their second-home court. On March 20, they met No. 16 seed Coppin State who was making their first appearance in the NCAA Tournament. The game was a rout (97–62). Ironically, the UNC men's team was also seeded No. 1, making UNC the only school in the nation to have two No. 1 seeds going into the NCAA Tournament. Following the men's second-round victory over Iowa, in Charlotte, Roy Williams and some of his players showed up to watch the Lady Tar Heels get the win. The second-round game against No. 9 seed George Washington was a 71–47 rout. At the end of the game, Erlana Larkins—the freshman who didn't play like a freshman—left the court in a wheelchair, suffering from severe leg cramps.

The win over George Washington gave the Tar Heels a berth in the Sweet 16 for the first time since 2002. They traveled to Tempe, Arizona, for a March 26 game against No. 5 seed Arizona State—a game that was played at 9:30 p.m. Sylvia was upset. As in 2003 and 2004, the bracket was structured so that UNC had to play a lower seed on its home court. The time difference was also a factor. During the post-game press conference, Sylvia reminded the audience, "It's 20 minutes to 2 [a.m.] in North Carolina." Home-court advantage for the Sun Devils seemed insurmountable—the crowd noise was deafening—but Ivory Latta scored 20 points, La'Tangela Atkinson 14, Nikita Bell 13. Larkins had been questionable for this game, but in 26 minutes of play, she earned 18 points and got 14 rebounds. The total team effort gave UNC the 79–72 win. Sylvia's Tar Heels were going to the Elite Eight for the first time since 1998.

In the Elite Eight, the No. 1 seed UNC Tar Heels (30–3) would meet the No. 2 seed Baylor Bears (30–3) in Arizona State's Wells Fargo Arena. The Tar Heels believed they could beat Baylor, advance to the Final Four in Indianapolis, and then compete for another national championship. The teams seemed well matched. UNC was ranked No. 4; Baylor No. 5. UNC had won 16 consecutive games; Baylor 17. Both had won their conference titles; both played fast-paced, transition basketball. It was Baylor's first trip to the Elite Eight and UNC's third. The media predicted an exciting, fast-paced game in the first-ever matchup between the two schools. They were wrong. UNC took an early lead, which Baylor quickly erased. In the first half, the Tar Heels came within one point but never regained the lead. The result was a 72–63 loss. Sylvia's final comment to the press said it all: "I hate that we had to end our season like this, but tonight Baylor was better than us."

Sylvia believes that success is measured by countless yardsticks, including the quality of relationships—lasting friendships and strong connections are tallied in the "win" column, too. She did not make it to the NCAA Final Four and did not get to use the golden scissors in the 2005 NCAA Championship, but she cherished a small-stage event not long after the UNC loss to Baylor. Dal Shealy, former head coach at Carson-Newman and former CEO and President of the national Fellowship of Christian Athletes (FCA), invited Sylvia to speak at an FCA breakfast and fashion show at Carson-Newman. On the night before the event, her hosts picked her up at the hotel for dinner, and when she got into the car, a woman in the back seat handed her a photograph of the Talbott team she had coached while a student at Carson-Newman. "Coach Hatchell," she said. "I'm Sheila Turner." Sheila had been the Talbott star player in 1973–74, and there she was, 30 years later, remembering and honoring her first basketball coach—and Sylvia's first coaching job. It was a victory for Sylvia.

Another item in Sylvia's "win column" was the thriving blueberry patch on her Black Mountain property. From the beginning, the blueberry patch was an attractive feature and a selling point. It was overgrown, and Joe Kirstein had encouraged her to have it cleaned up. He told her, "All kinds of people pick berries there, and you need to charge for them." After reading about the antioxidant properties of blueberries for fighting cancer, she had another idea. She took Joe's advice and cleaned up the patch. Then she posted signs, inviting people to pick for $5.00 a gallon—on the honor system. The twist, however, was that the money would not come to her. The signs instructed pickers to mail checks to the Lineberger Cancer Center. When Sylvia learned that the checks were coming in regularly, she began to tend the patch in earnest. She installed an irrigation system for the bushes—now numbering approximately 300. Her brothers Ralph and Ronnie and her neighbor Kathy Marlowe tend to routine mowing. Other neighbors Luny and Ruby Gilliam—known locally as Mr. Luny and Miss Ruby—monitor the patch, help people pick, and visit with them. They tell Sylvia the stories of pickers who have lost loved ones to cancer and pickers who are cancer survivors. One woman wrote Sylvia a card: "I lost my husband to cancer, and when I go to the blueberry patch I feel closer to him." Another "win" for Sylvia.

In the fall of 2005, the Kepley Road house was finished. Sylvia had wanted Van to be in their new home during his high-school years, but because of construction delays, he didn't move in until he was a junior. He and Deneene moved in September. Sylvia and Sammy weren't ready until late November, when she was well into the 2005–2006 season, her 20th at UNC. She had a stable coaching staff and experienced returning players. Her assistant coaches had long tenure. Charlotte Smith was in her fourth season; Tracey Williams-Johnson her seventh. Assistant Head Coach Andrew Calder was in his

Sylvia in Black Mountain blueberry patch with donation sign for Lineberger Cancer Center. Courtesy Sheila Oliver.

20th season, having been the first person Sylvia hired upon taking the UNC job in 1986. Additionally, the Tar Heels' home court—Carmichael Auditorium—had been renovated. In the lower level, metal bleachers were replaced by cushioned chairs with cup holders, a change that reduced the seating from 10,180 to 8,010. Capacity was sacrificed to comfort.

Sylvia's team was also stable and experienced. La'Tangela Atkinson and Jessica Sell were returning seniors. Ivory Latta and Camille Little were returning juniors. Meghan Austin, Erlana Larkins, Alex Miller, and LaToya Pringle were sophomores. The Lady Tar Heels welcomed five freshmen, including Rashanda McCants, the sister of basketball star Rashad McCants, who played on the 2005 men's NCAA Championship team. (This brother-sister team would feature prominently in an off-court debacle in 2014 and 2015.)

On November 18, No. 7 ranked UNC opened the 2005–2006 season against

Davidson. The easy win (86–48) meant that all 14 players, including freshmen, entered the game. Rashanda McCants saw 21 minutes on the court—more than any other freshman—and earned her first three-pointer for the Lady Tar Heels.[9] The media emphasized UNC's speed, depth, and aggressiveness. Sylvia told Jack Daly, "Our kids love playing that way, I think we're fun to watch. It's not boring. And we play a lot of people—the bench is happier because people get tired and we have to substitute.... I just love the up-tempo game, and I think the kids love it."[10] In other words, it was what she had in mind in 1999 when she set out to fall back in love with basketball. Nolan Hayes called Sylvia's Tar Heels "the fastest team in the country."[11]

The Tar Heels' record soon stretched to 7–0. It seemed that nobody could touch them, but next up was No. 8 ranked Connecticut whom they faced for the second consecutive year in the Jimmy V Classic. In its fourth year, the Classic was moved from the RBC Center in Raleigh to the Hartford Civic Center in Connecticut and featured only two teams: UConn and UNC. ESPN made the move for financial reasons—the turnout in Raleigh had declined, ESPN wanted a higher TV profile, and No. 8 UConn would be a larger draw in Hartford than in Raleigh. Kay Yow was disappointed with the move and the two-team limit. In 2004, the Classic had featured four teams: UNC, UConn, Tennessee, and NC State. Here she was, battling cancer for the second time in her life, and her team could not compete in the fundraising event that she had launched. Sylvia wanted to defeat UConn for two reasons: UNC *and* Kay Yow.

Geno Auriemma remembered the 2004 game when UNC erased his Huskies' 10-point lead to win 71–65. He told Vicki Fulkerson that UNC was "one of the most talented teams in the country."[12] Sylvia intended to prove him right, but even she did not expect the outcome. The Hartford Center was sold out—13,527 fans came to witness the show, the largest crowd this UNC women's team had ever seen, and a hostile crowd, at that. At the break, UNC led 35–23. Jack Daly heard ESPN commentator Stacey Dales-Schuman "emphatically declare" that the Tar Heels would not be able to hold on to the lead: "UNC will shoot themselves out of it," she predicted.[13] UNC not only held on, but the lead grew. Sylvia's Tar Heels handed Auriemma the worst defeat in his UConn career—a 77–54 drubbing. In the press conference following the game, he admitted, "I'm sitting here speechless." Sylvia was anything but—she was ecstatic not only with the win but with her team. Ivory Latta was the star. When Sylvia took her out of the game with 2:22 left, the remnants of the "hostile" UConn fans applauded her. La'Tangela Atkinson was also applauded when she finally left the court. Sylvia said, "Win or lose, playing at UConn is a tremendous environment for us, ... the fans are fantastic. They are fans of women's basketball and we've always been treated first class by them when we visit.... I love it there, win or lose." ESPN commentator Doris Burke somewhat atoned for Dales-Schuman's earlier *faux pas* by saying Latta "was the best point guard in America."[14] Following the win over UConn, the undefeated Tar Heels' ranking rose to No. 6, and their winning streak continued, including an easy victory over No. 19 Vanderbilt (87–67).

The Vanderbilt game was the last before the 2005 Christmas holidays, which would be hard for Sylvia, Phyllis, Ralph, and Ronnie. They had buried their mother on Christmas Eve, 2004, and their grief was still fresh. Carroll still lived at Summit Place, so the Oliver Street house in Gastonia sat empty, except for Veda's dog Spud, who lived there—but out of doors—and Ralph went by every day to feed him. Spud was a neighborhood hero, having gained national fame in 1991 when he saved the life of Mark Pruitt, a neighbor who had a heart attack while mowing his lawn. Spud found Mr. Pruitt lying in the grass, ran to get a neighbor, and Mr. Pruitt was saved. Spud was honored as Purina Dog Chow Dog of the Year and was featured in Von Kreisler's book *The Compassion of Animals*. Thirteen years later, he was an old dog—older than Van—and needed the company of his family. There was really no question about where they would celebrate the holidays—the tradition was too strong—and Carroll was still in Gastonia. They brought him home for Christmas Day festivities, but it wasn't the same without Veda. The Gastonia family gatherings were coming to an end.

The Tar Heels began 2006 with a 102–61 win over Clemson followed by a decisive 90–57 victory over Miami—Sylvia's 699th win. NC State was next on the schedule, the team against whom she won her 500th and 600th games—a unique coincidence. Ironically, NC State was the only ACC school with a winning record over UNC (48–30). Kay Yow had been absent from the court in 2005 but was back in 2006 for this milestone game against her close friend and rival. On January 15, the Wolfpack welcomed UNC to Reynolds Coliseum with signs that said, "You're a whole Latta nothing." The signs were near-prophetic. Ivory shot 2 for 15 from the floor in 38 minutes of play. In general, Sylvia said her Tar Heels "sputtered." Fortunately, Erlana Larkins and Camille Little kept the flame going. UNC led all the way and Sylvia got her 700th win—65–53—before a truly hostile crowd.

Despite her lackluster performance, Ivory Latta was giddy and playful. Rachel Carter wrote that Wolfpack fans howled at Latta and booed every time she touched the ball: "Latta responded by pointing at them and sending an affectionate smile." La'Tangela Atkinson said, "She loves it, it's everywhere we go. Everybody's after Ivory. Everybody's trying to get Ivory out of the game, but I don't think that's possible."[15] In front of the remaining Wolfpack fans in Reynolds Coliseum, Latta donned a hat with "Coach Hatchell—700th win" across the front. Jack Daly said Latta patted the "elaborate gold lions' heads on the shoulders" of Sylvia's cream-colored suit. Daly said the "outfit was appropriate" for a coach who had "established herself as one of the queens of the women's basketball jungle."[16] It would not be the last time that Sylvia's clothing attracted media attention, but she was focused on more important things: pride in her team, gratitude for her career and for UNC, and humility upon joining the 700-win "queens" of women's basketball: Pat Summitt, Vivian Stringer, Jody Conradt, and Sue Gunter.

By January 29, when the Tar Heels faced Duke, they were still undefeated, their ranking had risen to No. 3, and they had beaten three ranked teams on the road (No. 16 Arizona State, No. 8 Connecticut, and No. 19 Vanderbilt). The pre-game press was not kind to Sylvia. Ned Barnett, with the *News & Observer*, placed Sylvia last among Triangle women's coaches. "Milestones, shmilestones," he wrote. "Yow's long, varied career is more respected. Many think Goestenkors has the most potential." But Sylvia said the real "story" was about "the two best women's teams in the country"— two undefeated teams—being "eight miles apart…. The people in this area should be ecstatic." As for herself, she said, "This is what you dream about, being in a situation like this."[17] Apparently, Triangle fans agreed with Sylvia: Duke's Cameron Indoor Stadium was, as usual, sold out. Ivory Latta told the press that she anticipated "cries of love and hate from the crowd of 9,314." The Tar Heels and the Blue Devils were the only two remaining unbeaten women's teams in the country—and Duke had just knocked off No. 1 Tennessee to claim the top spot. The game would decide the No. 1 team in the nation. It was the perfect potion to attract an ESPN2 audience of 591,000 households. The 2005 game had attracted only 65,000.

Sylvia's Tar Heels played a dismal first half of basketball. They were outrebounded, made 12 turnovers, and trailed by 13 at the half (40–27). Following Sylvia's locker-room admonition to "turn it on," they made only two turnovers in the second period and stepped up their defense to overcome a 16-point deficit, their largest of the season. With 9:00 left in the second half, Duke led by 12 points. After LaToya Pringle came off the bench and tied the game, UNC took their first lead (66–64) with 3:00 left, and they held on for a 74–70 victory that toppled unbeaten Duke from the No. 1 spot. After the game, Sylvia led an uncharacteristic celebration on Franklin Street. Jack Daly reported that the team "hooted and hollered" and toilet-papered trees.[18]

The next day, the Tar Heel women's basketball team was ranked No. 1 in the nation—their first ever top ranking. Sylvia let them enjoy their fame, but also told them, "Don't get too big for your britches." Then they went back to reviewing film and working on rebounding, hoping still to be No. 1 in April. The win and the No. 1 ranking brought recognition and respect to the Tar Heel team and to Sylvia individually. In an interview with Amy Moritz, Sylvia talked about her "run-you-down-to-death style," her desire to change the game, to ratchet up the tempo. After the January 29 win over Duke, John Calipari, then head coach of men's basketball at the University of Memphis, called Sylvia and said, "Girl, I want my team to play like North Carolina does." This call validated her mission—a path she set out on in 1999. She wanted to win games, but she had a greater purpose: "I also want to bring attention to the women's game. I want people to embrace women's basketball and talk about how much fun it is…. Our style is not for everybody but it works for us and we enjoy it."

Still on a "high" from their fourth consecutive victory over Duke, but keeping ego in check, the Tar Heels were enjoying bigger crowds in their renovated Carmichael Auditorium, and the buzz in Chapel Hill almost matched the 1994 publicity. A near-capacity crowd came out for the game against No. 6 Maryland, a matchup that was tougher and rougher than usual. Right away, Latta picked up three fouls, and Alex Miller stepped in as point guard. Both coaches protested the officiating, and Maryland Coach Brenda Frese was called for a technical. The Tar Heels led at the half 46–36, but early in the second period, Miller slammed onto the court, hit her head on the bottom of the basket support, and was carried off the court wearing a neck brace. The Tar Heels were shaken but increased their lead to 14 before Maryland tied the score at 83 and sent the game into overtime. Miller was in the emergency room; Latta and Little were both playing with four fouls; and Erlana Larkins was benched with leg cramps that had plagued her throughout the season. In overtime, Maryland outscored UNC 15–12 for a 98–95 win—UNC's first loss of the season. Sylvia told the press that the game "was too physical." Fortunately, Alex Miller was not seriously injured and did not have to be hospitalized.

UNC had enjoyed the No. 1 spot for all of one week before Maryland bumped them to No. 2 and broke the Tar Heels' 30-game winning streak at home. They were still ranked No. 2 when they met No. 1 Duke in Carmichael for the last regular game of the season. Carmichael was sold out in advance—a dream come true for Sylvia though she hated to turn people away. She began to wish she had moved the game to the Smith Center, but her seniors—La'Tangela Atkinson, Jessica Sell, and Jennifer Nelms—wanted to play their final home game in the smaller Carmichael Auditorium. They delivered the kind of game that Sylvia craved: fast-paced, transition basketball, strong on both offense and defense—for the 77–65 victory. They had beaten Duke for a fifth consecutive time. For the second time in 2006, they had bumped the Blue Devils from the No. 1 spot.

Sylvia's Tar Heels entered the ACC Tournament as conference champion and No. 1 seed in the toughest league in the nation, boasting three of the top five teams in the country: UNC, Duke, and Maryland. For the first time in seven years, the Blue Devils did not enter the Tournament as the conference champion. On March 2, Sylvia was voted ACC Coach of the Year for the second time in her career. Ivory Latta was named ACC Player of the Year. In their first game of the ACC Tournament, UNC got an easy win over unranked Virginia (82–56). In the semifinal game, they got a lopsided win (90–69) over Triangle foe NC State, the No. 5 seed. For the ACC Tournament title game, attendance (10,746) did not meet Coliseum expectations largely because Duke was not on the court. UNC would play No. 4 Maryland—not Duke—in the ACC Tournament final, but their opponent had dealt them their only loss of the season. It didn't seem to matter to the Tar Heels. The press used words like "warp-speed attack" and "firepower" to describe UNC play. As usual, Latta played the full 40 minutes and earned her second ACC Tournament MVP award. Sylvia brought the golden scissors again—just in case—and it was a good thing she did. After the 91–80 win, she used them to cut down the net. The question was whether her Tar Heels would get to use them in April.

Sylvia's team was hoping to surpass their 2005 performance in the NCAA Elite Eight. The team was playing well. In her thoughtful moments, Sylvia was grateful for the young women who had been placed under her influence. These 14 young women had arrived in Chapel Hill with little personal "baggage" of the sort that had derailed previous players and teams. Instead, the 2005–2006 Lady Tar Heels had the capacity for joy in the game, for camaraderie, for selfless play. They were the quintessential definition of a team. They fed Sylvia's passion for coaching, her desire to change women's basketball, and her belief in Chapman's love languages. The day after the ACC Tournament win, Ed Hardin wrote a thoughtful piece about Sylvia's style of play and coaching. He called her a "pioneer" who has revolutionized women's basketball. He labeled her "an equal-opportunity thief": "She's stolen and borrowed and adapted and adopted basketball theories from some of the best coaches in the country. Almost all have been men." He called her style of play the "Carolina game" and wrote, "Hatchell woke up one day ahead of her time."[19]

As ACC Tournament champion, UNC got an automatic bid to the NCAA Tournament. Immediately after the pairings were announced, furor reigned in women's basketball. Three of the top women's basketball powerhouses—Rutgers, Tennessee, and Carolina—were placed in the Cleveland Region. Carolina was the No. 1 seed, Tennessee No. 2, and Rutgers No. 3. Rutgers had a perfect 16–0 regular season in the Big East Conference. Tennessee was 11–3 and had won the SEC Tournament. UNC had a 13–1 ACC record and was both ACC Conference and Tournament champion. All three coaches might have expected No. 1 seeds in different regions, but Rutgers, in particular, deserved a higher seed. As the Cleveland bracket was stacked, Pat Summitt's Tennessee Lady Vols were on a path to face Rutgers in the Sweet 16 and then the UNC Tar Heels in the Elite Eight. Sylvia faulted the NCAA Women's Basketball Committee. "It's like the Final Four!" she told an AP reporter. "I don't know how any bracket can get tougher than our bracket.... But hey, that's just the way it is. We have to go play those games."[20] Privately she said, "Anyone who knew anything about women's basketball would have known not to put those three teams in the same bracket. It wasn't right, and it appeared to disfavor the older, successful coaches." Pat Summitt had certainly expected a No. 1 seed for her Lady Vols, and she openly expressed her outrage. She told Donna Tommelleo, "It's a slap in our program's face. I guess it's my fault for putting together the toughest schedule in the country year in and year out. But as far as I'm concerned we got no respect, and I don't understand it."[21] In *Sum It Up*, she called it the "bracket of death."[22]

North Carolina's first stop was Nashville. In round one they defeated No. 16 seed University of California, Riverside, in Vanderbilt's Memorial Gym (75–51). In pre-game press conferences, Sylvia emphasized her team's chemistry: "We've had more talented teams, but to win a championship, you've got to have chemistry.... Kids have got to put the team before themselves and they've got to like each other." Then she repeated one of her favorite

Ivory Latta celebrates UNC's victory over No. 1 Duke, February 25, 2006. Courtesy Jeffrey Allan Camarati, UNC Sports Information.

sayings: Chemistry is "like the wind: You can't really see it, but you sure can see the effects of it." Next up for round two in the Cleveland bracket was No. 8 seed Vanderbilt. Again, Sylvia was playing a lower seed on its home court, but it didn't matter. The Tar Heels outplayed Vanderbilt—on the boards, at the foul line, from the bench—for the 89–70 victory.

With the golden scissors in her suitcase, Sylvia's next stop was the Sweet 16 in Cleveland, Ohio, where they would meet No. 4 seed Purdue on March 26. Once again, the word "upset" was on everyone's mind as the Boilermakers tested the Lady Tar Heels more seriously than any team other than Maryland. It was a seesaw game. The lead changed 10 times; the score was tied five times, including the very end of the game—with 2.8 seconds left—when Ivory Latta sank a layup to give UNC the 70–68 win. In the second game of the night, No. 2 seed Tennessee beat Rutgers 76–69, which put Sylvia on a collision course with her old friend Pat Summitt in the Elite Eight.

North Carolina had not played Tennessee since March 23, 1998, when the two teams met in Vanderbilt's Memorial Gym in their first Elite-Eight matchup—and UNC lost. Would March 28, 2006, be a repeat of 1998? Going into the game UNC had the edge statistically, but Pat Summitt had been to this dance 20 times; it was Sylvia's fourth trip. Frank Litsky said the game was more like a national championship than a regional final. The 9,091 fans rooted mostly for the popular Lady Vols, but Tar Heel Ivory Latta had her own cheering section in LeBron James and the Cleveland Cavaliers. Latta and James first met as high-school seniors in 2003 at a banquet honoring McDonald's All-American teams. James was named the 2003 Boys' Player of the Year, and Latta was honored as the Morgan Wootten National Girls' High School Basketball Player of the Year. Since then, she and James had maintained a friendship, so he arrived at the Quicken Loans Arena sporting a UNC sweatshirt and accompanied by Cavalier teammates Damon Jones, Flip Murray, Donyell Marshall, Ira Newble and Drew Gooden. Latta told the press that she appreciated their "taking the time out of their busy schedule to come watch us play." During the game she flexed her bicep in his direction and said, "Mine's bigger."[23] According to Marla Ridenour, Pat Summitt called Latta "that pesky insect." Indeed, the ubiquitous Latta buzzed around the court, irritating the Lady Vols. Frank Litsky wrote, "North Carolina's speed, frenetic ball-handling and, most of all, its point guard, Ivory Latta, were so overwhelming in the first half that the game was hardly a game at all. Tennessee often looked baffled and could not take care of the ball, and it had no answers for the Tar Heels' quickness." UNC's defensive effort gave them a 43–31 lead at the break, which Tennessee whittled to five points in the second period, but it was not enough. Fouls were not an issue for the Tar Heels—they were 9 of 12 at the line. Instead, it was Summitt's turn to complain about officiating. Just five minutes into the first half, Candace Parker was called for her second foul. Summitt told the press, "I obviously wasn't happy about that foul. That's when the wheels fell off. We lost our composure and fell into panic mode." Latta said that she had been "uptight" in the Purdue game but decided that she would "go out there and leave it all on the court" against Tennessee: "Be happy, be excited and great things will happen." In this case, the "great thing" was a 75–63 win over Tennessee—the first time Sylvia had beaten Summitt. Erlana Larkins cried after the win. The team cut down the net with the golden scissors. They celebrated on the court. Litsky reported that while the party was in full swing in the locker room, Ivory Latta "walked to a section of the stands with many youngsters, whipped out a pen and signed autographs," saying, "All in the day's work." They had more basketball ahead of them, and the next day, March 29, Latta was selected for the AP All-American first team. In the post-game press conference, Sylvia admitted to savoring her first ever win over Tennessee, but she said it was an honor to be on the same court as her good friend Pat Summitt. Throughout her career, Sylvia acknowledged Pat's support and friendship, always thanking her, always saying publicly, "I would not be where I am today without her."

Unlike the 1998 Elite-Eight game, fouls were not a major issue in the 2006 UT-UNC matchup. But officiating had become a hot topic in women's basketball. During the ACC Tournament, Ed Hardin had cited a pernicious officiating weakness, especially for Sylvia's type of play: "Very few officials [are] capable of keeping up with a fast-paced game for 40 minutes."[24] Following the Elite-Eight game against Tennessee, Sally Jenkins took up the crusade. The "crew couldn't even keep track of the possession arrow on jump balls," she wrote. "Hatchell found herself imploring the refs, 'Please don't penalize us for our athleticism.'"[25] Sylvia was counting on that athleticism to carry her team beyond the Final Four, which was her next stop.

Prior to the April 2 Final Four, Jack Daly deconstructed Sylvia's recent basketball career: "The magical 3-pointer that propelled UNC to the '94 NCAA title was little more than a hazy memory that only reinforced how fast the Tar Heels had deteriorated." Daly described the 12 years between the NCAA Championship and the 2006 season as "vacillating somewhere between good and very good." Sylvia's Tar Heel team "never really regained its spot among the game's elite." But between 2004 and 2006, "something changed," he wrote. The first change was Sylvia's success in recruiting top-notch players such as Atkinson, Latta, Little, and Larkins. The second was her run-you-down-to-death offense: "She scrapped the Tar Heels' half-court game and made a commitment to running at every opportunity. This season, for instance, UNC is third in the nation in scoring offense." Daly then quoted a refrain he had heard from Sylvia "for the umpteenth time" in 2005–2006: "I want them to score a lot of points and make it exciting and fun.... I don't like low-scoring games. It's sort of like watching paint dry."[26]

The NCAA Final Four was played in Boston, on April 2, 2006. Three of the Final Four teams were from the ACC: Duke, Maryland, and UNC. (LSU from the SEC was the fourth.) Maryland lived up to its Terrapin mascot's name and slowed down the fast-paced Tar Heels, taking them out of their running game. The *Pittsburgh Post-Gazette* used the word "shellacking" to describe the defeat. Sylvia had "scrapped" UNC's half-court game only to face a Maryland team that "ran its half-court game to near perfection," according to Donna Tommelleo, "bumping feisty North Carolina point guard Ivory Latta, outmuscling the energetic, up-tempo Tar Heels and forcing a half-court game that wiped the smiles off their faces." In the first half, Latta felt that she was "pushed in the back," and she came down hard with a hyperextended knee. At the 12:24 mark, she was carried off the court to a standing ovation. The knee was examined on the sideline, and she was back in the game, missing only two minutes of play, but she was not herself. "It affected me a lot," she told reporters afterward. Maryland got the decisive 81–70 win.

In the post-game press conference, Sylvia said that after Ivory's injury, the Tar Heels never regained their energy and rhythm. "It was pretty physical out there." She and the players commented on officiating—not getting the calls they felt they should have. Near the end of the game, when Erlana Larkins got the ball inside, Sylvia anticipated a foul call that never came. "I thought it was a big turning point because that would have tied the game up. But it didn't happen." La'Tangela Atkinson, Jessica Sell, and Jennifer Nelms had played their last game in a Carolina uniform. When Latta fouled out with 0.7 seconds remaining, the 18,642 fans gave her a standing ovation. UNC ended the season at 33 wins and 2 losses, both of which belonged to Maryland. It was the Tar Heels' best record since 1993–1994. Maryland went on to beat Duke for the 2006 NCAA Championship.

On the day UNC lost to Maryland in the 2006 Final Four, the *Washington Post* ran a scathing article by Sally Jenkins (Pat Head Summitt's biographer) that agreed with Sylvia's perspective on officiating: "NCAA Leadership Isn't Matching the Talent of Its Players." Jenkins began with, "Get the biddies out of women's basketball. The game has come too far, too fast, to be held back now by a bunch of blue hairs." Jenkins argued that "the players running the floor are light years ahead of the archaic people who are running the sport." She cited "ludicrously uneven officiating" and "a selection committee that annually botches the brackets." Jenkins reported that the "top women's coaches" were so "frustrated" that they met on Friday, March 31, in a Boston hotel to vent and seek solutions. During the meeting, Sylvia was vocal, especially about officiating: "I could talk for two hours," she said. Jenkins outlined two necessary changes: "hire an entirely new set of officials" and "fire the entire women's tournament selection committee." She characterized the difference between the NCAA women's and men's selection committees as "laughable."

9

Latta-Tude vs. The Summitt

Sylvia had a good basketball team returning for the 2006–2007 season, but she was worried about Ivory Latta. The injury that Latta sustained in the April 2 Final Four game against Maryland was more serious than initially thought. Dr. Timothy Taft determined that she had torn the lateral meniscus in the left knee. On April 21, he performed arthroscopic surgery, which was deemed successful, and Latta entered a rigorous program of rehabilitation. Sylvia expected her much-lauded point guard to be fully recovered for the start of the season. Latta was named National Player of the Year by three organizations: ESPN, the U.S. Basketball Writers Association, and *Gball Online Magazine.* She also won the Lieberman Award for the U.S. top point guard. Sylvia's hopes for a 2007 national championship depended greatly on Latta's recovery and performance in her senior year.

With Latta on the road to recovery, Sylvia turned her attention to her personal life. Because she enjoyed the mountains and the blueberry patch, she wanted to spend more time there and decided to build a cabin. She chose a modular design that was fabricated off site during the fall and winter and constructed on site during the spring. By July 18, 2006, it was ready for occupancy. Sylvia arrived by 9:00 a.m. for the final walk-through and delivery of the keys. Afterward, she sat on the floor and waited for the furniture to arrive. Two young men drove up in a huge truck and began to unload. By mid-morning, Mary Lou Garnett and Jane High arrived to help. They unloaded the back of Sylvia's car, which was packed with boxes of linens and kitchen paraphernalia. Exhausted at the end of the day, Sylvia, Mary Lou, and Jane fell into the new beds. It was Sylvia's first night in her new cabin.

On Wednesday, Tony Rikard brought Carroll up for the day. He was having a fairly good summer, and Sylvia wanted him to enjoy the mountains and the cabin—she wanted him with her. He watched while the women worked. When lunchtime neared, Sylvia sent Jane to the Asheville Farmers Market for fresh vegetables. Sylvia doesn't cook, so as Jane was shucking corn, Tony offered to assist. "I can't help much with the moving," he said, "but I can help cook." Together they made a meal of butter beans, corn, fried okra, tomatoes, cornbread, and cantaloupe. By midafternoon, Carroll's energy was waning, so Tony took him back to Kings Mountain. Sylvia treasures the photographs of her father in the cabin on that day, a day she hoped to repeat, but it would be his only visit.

While Sylvia was settling into the cabin and counting her blessings, her two books were hitting the market: *The Baffled Parent's Guide to Coaching Girls' Basket-*

ball, for girls ages six to twelve, is part of the Baffled Parent's Guide series by McGraw Hill. *The Complete Guide to Coaching Girls' Basketball: Building a Great Team the Carolina Way* is for girls ages 11 to 18. Sylvia created the books with Jeff Thomas, Varsity Head Coach at Saint Gertrude High, a girls' school in Richmond, Virginia. Both books are based on Thomas's interviews with Sylvia and on her "teaching tapes"— DVD's that demonstrate tactics and techniques for her style of basketball. They are copiously illustrated with diagrams, score sheets, master plans, and photographs that feature her 2005–2006 Tar Heel team demonstrating basketball skills.

Throughout both books, Sylvia emphasizes the difference between coaching boys and girls. In *The Baffled Parent's Guide*, she devotes one whole section to five differences that "aren't based on the obvious physical contrasts." She admits that these generalizations have "plenty of exceptions." More importantly, she does not see these differences as weaknesses or flaws. Quite the contrary. "Boys think of themselves first," she says. "Girls think of themselves last." This characteristic makes girls' teams "excellent passing teams." "Boys think playing in games is the best part of the season. Girls think being part of a team is the best part."[1] This characteristic builds unity, cohesion, and the quality she cherishes most: chemistry.

Sylvia's family continued to be a priority. Her father was still living at Summit Place but was not happy about it. In Sylvia's words, "He didn't want to be there; he was so ornery all the time." After Veda died, he scribbled love letters to her on the backs of envelopes. His handwriting was poor, and the envelopes were tattered. Sylvia carried them in her purse for a while, a reminder of how much he missed Veda and how dissatisfied he was, but the letters broke her heart. Tony Rikard was invaluable to the family during this time, as they tried to keep Carroll active and engaged. Tony brought him to visit Sylvia in Chapel Hill and to Sylvia's summer basketball camp where Tanya Crevier wheeled him onto the court and spun basketballs on his upturned fingers. "We tried to do everything we could," says Sylvia, but after Veda died, he had little reason to live.

By September, Carroll suffered a deep decline, and Sylvia could hardly believe that two months prior, he had spent a day at the Black Mountain cabin. Eventually, he was placed in hospice care with a morphine drip and oxygen. On Sunday, October 29, Carroll's hospital room was filled with people: his sisters Catherine and Dorothy; his brother Tom; Jerry Falls, who sang to him; several pastors; many friends from church: "It was like a reunion—people were everywhere. They were all standing out in the hall—different ones coming in seeing Daddy. It was like a big celebration all afternoon." But as things calmed down, around 4:00 p.m., Catherine, Dorothy, and Tom went in to say their farewells: "Then we all went in," said Sylvia, "and I was holding him when he took his last breath, about 4:30."

The death of Sylvia's parents marked the end of an era. They were widely respected as salt-of-the-earth people. Jerry Thomas remembers Sylvia's mother for her devotion to the church: "She stayed there basically all the time." He remembers Sylvia's father as "an A-1 machinist." Thomas describes Sylvia's parents as typical working people. "Both of them basically worked all their lives, and the times were different. Parents didn't take off time from work to spend with their children. They worked." Jerry doesn't remember Sylvia's parents as young people who attended functions other than church or school events. He recalls that the Rhynes were like all the other parents in their 1950s and 60s neighborhood, including his own parents: "They were too busy working."

Sylvia had included Veda and Carroll in her wide circle of friends and colleagues. Dorothy Baxter knew them well and thought highly of them. Mary Lou Garnett remembers them as "sweet people: good, kind, humble, down to earth." When Sylvia's father was in a nursing home, Mary Lou accompanied Sylvia on trips to visit him and was touched "just watching Sylvia with her dad as she helped him do things." Mrs. Rhyne sent cards to Mary Lou's mother when she battled cancer. The Rhynes were strong supporters of all their children. Except for Veda's one year of college, they had no formal education, but they believed in it so strongly that all their children earned college degrees. It is even more remarkable that for 12 of the 16 years when they had children in college, they paid private-school tuition. Only Ronnie went to a public school, Western Carolina University. Phyllis and Sylvia attended Carson-Newman and Ralph went to Gardner-Webb. Two of the Rhynes' children earned master's degrees: Sylvia at the University of Tennessee and Phyllis at the University of West Florida.

Sylvia had to pivot quickly from her father's death to the 2006–2007 basketball season. The popular Latta-Little duo were seniors, so this would be their final shot at a national championship. Juniors included Alex Miller, LaToya Pringle, Erlana Larkins, and Meghan Austin. The six sophomore players (including Rashanda McCants) would create a void when they all graduated in 2009, but for the present their NCAA experience was a big plus. Two North Carolina freshmen rounded out the team: 6'3" Jessica Breland from Kelford and 5'10" Trinity Bursey from Sanford.

The No. 2 Lady Tar Heels opened the season against East Tennessee State University with a 61-point win (96–35). Their next six wins came with an average margin of 47 points, but their eighth game of the season was against No. 4 Tennessee on December 3, 2006. Carmichael was sold out. Roy Williams and UNC football coach Butch Davis were among the 8,010 in attendance. Jack Daly used words like "discombobulated," "fumbled," and "ragged" to describe the Tar Heels' play.[2] Even so, they took a 15-point lead and never looked back. For the second time in her career, Sylvia had beaten her good friend Pat (70–57). She told Dan Fleser, "We bring out the best and worst in each other."[3]

Following the victory over Tennessee, the team won five more games with an average margin of 44 points. The December 18 victory over Coastal Carolina in the Myrtle Beach Classic (82–58) was the last game before the Christmas holidays, which would be Sylvia's first Christmas without both her parents. With the death of her father in October, the tradition of an extended family Christmas at 504 Oliver Street died, too. As December 25 approached, Sylvia kept thinking that the whole family would gather in Gastonia as always: "I had been with them every Christmas of my life," she said. When her three siblings changed their holiday routine, she thought, *Well, if nobody else is going, we're not going either.* It appeared that the Hatchells would spend the holiday in Chapel Hill, but Sylvia felt unsettled about it, so at the very last minute—two days before Christmas—she decided to go to the mountains.

First, she called her Black Mountain neighbor Kathy Marlowe and asked her to turn on the heat and the lights in the cabin. She knew that Mary Lou and Bill Garnett were visiting their daughter Molly in Asheville, so she called Mary Lou to say the Hatchells were coming to Black Mountain. With no time to dawdle, Sylvia, Sammy, and Van loaded the car and headed for western North Carolina. When they came around the curve on Flat Creek Road in Fairview, they saw that Kathy had turned on the cabin lights. As they turned into the driveway, they saw Christmas lights in the front window. When they parked at the back of the house, they saw the porch decked out with Carolina blue Christmas lights. Inside the house, they found a Charlie Brown Christmas tree, a pitiful little thing with few limbs, but Mary Lou, Bill, and Kathy had decorated it, barely finishing before the Hatchells arrived. They had cut the tree on Sylvia's property behind the house and used Kathy's extra decorations, hoping to make the cabin festive and lift Sylvia's spirits on this first Christmas without her parents. Later they all attended Christmas Eve services with Kathy Marlowe's family at Nesbitt's Chapel United Methodist Church. Sylvia describes the experience as "neat—just me and Sammy and Van spent Christmas in the cabin for the first time."

When ACC Conference play began in January 2007, UNC had 15 consecutive wins, and the margins of victory against ACC teams grew. The fifth game in 2007 was in Carmichael against non-conference No. 6 UConn Huskies, whom UNC had defeated in the two previous years, but Latta struggled—Auriemma said she played "lousy." To bolster Latta, Sylvia used a strategy John Swofford had used with her back in 1991. She told Latta, "You are *my* point guard and the best point guard in the country. I believe in you." It worked. A five-point lead at the half (41–36) stretched to 15 points in the second period. Latta's hustle gave the Tar Heels the 82–76 win. Going into the game, UNC was the top scoring offense in the country. At the final buzzer, they still were, and the Tar Heels had delivered UConn its second defeat of the season, the first being at the hands of Tennessee (70–64) in December.

Over the next two weeks, Sylvia's No. 2 Tar Heels walloped Georgia Tech (78–31) and NC State (86–56), but everyone's mind was on the January 28 game at Maryland. Would the matchup be a repeat of the 2006 Final Four? The media said that Maryland was UNC's kryptonite. Comcast Center in College Park was sold out. According to *The* (Baltimore) *Sun*, it was the largest crowd for a women's game in ACC history—17,950. No. 3 Maryland had lost to No. 1 Duke on January 13 and would wage all-out war to prevent a second loss to an ACC team, but the Tar Heels were prepared. Latta was unstoppable and enjoyed every minute of her performance. The *Sun* reported that she "taunted" the crowd, "putting her finger over her lips to silence the throng or waving to the fans as they left late in the game."[4] The result was a 13-point win for UNC (84–71). Sylvia's Tar Heels were still unbeaten (23–0).

On February 1, the Lady Tar Heels got yet another lopsided win at Boston College (82–60) and then headed home for their first encounter with Duke in the 2006–2007 season. It looked to be a replay of the January 29, 2006, game—the type of contest that Sylvia dreamed about: two undefeated Triangle archenemies, No. 1 Duke vs. No. 2 UNC, and a sellout crowd in Carmichael. UNC had beaten the Blue Devils in the five previous matchups and badly wanted a sixth, but in 39 minutes of play, Latta shot 3 for 20 from the floor and was 0 for 11 three-point attempts.[5] The Tar Heels suffered their first loss of the season at the hands of their old enemy. What's more, it was a low-score game (64–53)—the sort that Sylvia hated. Deflated and defeated, she apologized afterward: "I'm sorry that we didn't protect our home court."[6]

On February 16, UNC went up against unranked NC State in Reynolds Coliseum. It was senior night, and prior to the game, the university named the Coliseum court "Kay Yow Court." Yow had missed 16 games in the 2006–2007 season because the cancer that reappeared in 2004 was advancing. There was speculation during her two-month absence that she may not return to coaching, but she was back on the court against Virginia on January 25, and since then her Wolfpack had won eight of their last nine games. Sylvia had strong loyalties to Yow, but her priority was to snatch a win from her good friend. The Tar Heels had not lost to the Wolfpack since February 8, 2004, but NC State was a determined team. Wolfpack senior Sasha Reaves told her teammates, "It's a special night, so let's go hard and give it all we have because we're playing for a special person." Her motivation worked. UNC led by two points less than one minute into the first half—and that was it. The Wolfpack ran up a 26-point lead that UNC could not overcome. Ivory Latta did not play like an All-American point guard. She was called for a technical foul, hit 5 of 21 from the floor, and was 0 of 8 from three-point range. Erlana Larkins was—again—incapacitated by leg cramps and had to be given intravenous fluids after the game. NC State's 72–65 win was an epic upset. Fans swarmed onto the court, and an emotional Kay Yow described the outcome as "incredible." "What an evening this has been," she said.[7] Her unranked Wolfpack had beaten the No. 2 team in the country, giving her the first win on Kay Yow Court.

Two days later, the Lady Tar Heels atoned somewhat for the loss to NC State when they went up against ACC newcomer Miami, who had joined the Conference in 2004. Coach Katie Meier was in her second year at Miami and was struggling. At that point, Meier's Hurricanes had won 11 games overall and only two in the ACC. Before the game against UNC in Carmichael, Meier heard a knock on the door of the locker room. Coaches and players thought it odd that someone would knock at that time. A Miami assistant coach opened the door to find Sylvia standing there. The assistant asked, "Coach Hatchell, what's wrong?" Nothing was wrong. Sylvia just wanted to encourage a young coach. She told Meier, "Everything is going to be all right." The game was another loss for Miami—the Tar Heels won 93–70—and the Hurricanes' season did not improve. They went 11–19 overall that year and 2–12 in the ACC, but forever after, Meier considered Sylvia a mentor.

The Tar Heels' ranking dropped to No. 4, but while her team was losing ACC games to Duke and NC State, Sammy and Van were flourishing. In February, Sammy was named 2007 Coach of the Year and Van was named 2007 Player of the Year for the Central Carolina Christian 1-A Conference. Van also earned honors as the Most Outstanding Player and MVP of the Tournament. The kid who did not easily warm up to basketball until 2001 had a double-digit average score for the entire season. Van also made the NCISAA 1-A boys All-State basketball team, the only boy from Cresset Christian Academy to do so. Sammy's 2004 "suicide move" had been life altering for Van.

Sylvia took inspiration from the successes of her husband and son and recommitted herself to winning. They would play Duke in their final game of the regular season. Joedy McCreary reported that for the first time in Duke history, "adventurous Duke students" put up tents outside Cameron Indoor Stadium and camped "for about a week" to assure that they got tickets for the game. The tents usually showed up for men's games only. It was the sixth sellout in the history of Duke women's basketball, and Duke senior Lindsey Harding told the media, "I wanted to come out there and give them a show"[8] The "Cameron Crazies" fed the Blue Devils' fire and stymied Ivory Latta, as they had in the February 8 win. UNC led four times and tied the game six times but could not overcome Duke's late second-half lead. With six minutes left in the game, Sylvia couldn't believe that Goestenkors switched to a zone defense. Ed Hardin couldn't believe it either because "UNC is deadly against a zone."[9] Apparently, Goestenkors saw something no one else saw. The zone interrupted the Tar Heels' rhythm and delivered them a 67–62 defeat—and Duke had made history. For the first time since 2004, the Blue Devils had won both regular season games over UNC. More importantly, they had earned their first ever unbeaten regular season, the first in the history of the ACC.

Duke was on a roll just when the Tar Heels' chemistry seemed to be waning. Jack Daly wrote that they were not the same "carefree, ebullient bunch" that they were in 2005–2006. Latta, in particular, was struggling with low scores, officials' warnings, and technical fouls. Sylvia had a solution: Following the devastating 67–62 loss to Duke on Sunday, her team spent Monday on a ropes course, designed to teach team-building through trust, communication, and confidence. Sylvia said the event had been scheduled long before the recent losses because she "thought it would delineate the break between the regular season and the tournament," but some were skeptical. Was this outing necessary to reignite the old mojo and propel the Tar Heels to a national championship? Players reported that the event was successful—and fun.[10]

Entering the ACC Tournament, four teams were ranked nationally: Duke was No. 1; the Tar Heels No. 4; Maryland No. 6; and NC State No. 24. The tournament seeds followed suit. In the quarterfinal game on March 2 against Virginia Tech, 11 Tar Heels saw time on the court, and four scored in double figures. UNC led the entire game, was up by 41 points in the second half, and got the easy win (90–60). Sylvia told the press, "We kind of rolled from the beginning." Latta still struggled, but she said she was determined get back to her "old self," and "the things that I used to do, that people enjoyed seeing me do."

It was an understatement to say that Latta needed to step it up for the ACC Tournament semifinal on March 3 against defending national champion Maryland. The Greensboro Coliseum was sold out (11,538), including the upper deck. UNC led 37–30 at the half, and though Maryland tied it twice—the second time with two minutes left in the game—they never took the lead. In the post-game press conference, Maryland coach Brenda Frese said it was "a Final Four game"—very physical, which was to UNC's advantage because they hit 16 of 20 free throws. Cliff Mehrtens called the game sloppy. Sylvia said it was ragged. Still, a ragged 78–72 win was better than a loss. Though the Terrapins wore the NCAA crown, UNC had deprived them of the ACC crown, which they had never won in 18 years.

NC State had eliminated Duke in the second semifinal of the ACC Tournament (70–65), so Sylvia would face her personal friend and basketball foe Kay Yow in the

ACC Championship game on March 4. The Wolfpack were on a roll, but Yow's cancer was taking its toll, and the entire Tournament was affected. Though Yow's chemotherapy and a blood transfusion delayed her arrival at the Tournament by one day, she was ready for the fight, and their battle on the court was intense. Running on emotion, Yow's Wolfpack led by 11 points in the first half, but UNC whittled it to three at the break (27–24). Ed Hardin captured perfectly the intensity of the Hatchell-Yow rivalry: The Wolfpack's early lead "drove Hatchell to the edge of patience. She called a timeout. She chewed out her team, a vicious lecture that forced her players to take a step back from the wild-eyed Hatchell, arms swinging and her black boots slamming against the court." Kay Yow "asked her players to give more than they had ever given before, demanded her players to play injured, to play through the pain and exhaustion, to play hurt. They all did, as she said later, except one." Yow openly "blamed her center," Gillian "GiGi" Goring, for the loss. Goring scored four points, as opposed to her 2006–2007 average of ten.[11] Sylvia, too, had issues with her star point guard—referee Dee Kantner gave Ivory Latta a warning for taunting an NC State player after a turnover. Ivory told the press that she was just trying to be her "old self" and pump up her teammates. Regardless, she had delivered a third time on her 2005 promise never to lose another ACC Tournament while she was on the team.

Hardin summarized the Tournament and the championship game with a moving tribute to Kay Yow: "For three days, N.C. State forced the pace of the ACC Women's Tournament. For three days, Yow controlled the entire event. Every other coach in the league acknowledged it, clapped for Yow and embraced her and told her how much she had inspired them." At the end of the game, she said, "'It's been overwhelming,' ... her voice almost gone, her energy almost vanquished. She was coughing at the end, barely able to express her thanks to all the people who spoke to her this week, barely able to congratulate Hatchell for her victory, barely trying to hide her anger at her center."[12] North Carolina had won its third consecutive ACC title (60–54); Sylvia and her team were jubilant. They cut down the nets, using the golden scissors, and hoped to use them again in April, but the victory was overshadowed by Yow's physical condition and what it boded for the future.

The Tar Heels' next stop was the 2007 NCAA Tournament. The bracket and pairings did not incite the same level of furor in 2007 as in 2006, but there was still controversy. For example, Duke was the No. 1 seed in the Greensboro Region—practically a home-court advantage for the Blue Devils. UNC was the No. 1 seed in the Dallas Region and would play the first and second rounds in the Peterson Events Center in Pittsburgh—and so would Tennessee, the No. 1 seed in the Dayton Region. Pittsburgh Coach Agnus Berenato told Alan Robinson, "I've never heard of two No. 1 seeds coming to the same site." Pat Summitt had never heard of such an arrangement, either. More to the point, Tennessee was in the unfortunate predicament of facing lower-seeded Pittsburgh on their home court to advance to the Sweet 16. Robinson called it a "quirky bit of scheduling": "There's almost no chance such an advantage would occur in the men's tournament," he said.[13] In 2006, Sally Jenkins had made a similar observation and recommended firing the entire women's tournament selection committee. Summitt, on the other hand, merely accepted the situation, chalked it up to growing pains in the women's division, and got ready to play NCAA basketball.

On March 18, Sylvia's Tar Heels met the Prairie View A&M Panthers and got the easy 95–38 win. The second-round victory against No. 9 seed Notre Dame on March 20 was harder. According to Jack Daly, Notre Dame's "stingy" and "junk" defensive strategies "flummoxed" the Tar Heels in the first half. In the second half, it looked as though the Fighting Irish were on the path for an upset, but LaToya Pringle helped stage the comeback. Again, Latta was not at her best. Daly reported that early in the second period, "Hatchell went down the entire length of the bench screaming at her players."[14] They got the message and the 60–51 win. She described her strategy as "Survive and advance." The Tar Heels advanced to Dallas for the regional semifinals on March 2, where they faced the No. 5 seed George Washington Colonials in Reunion Arena. For about seven minutes of the first half, the Colonials gave them a real game, keeping the score close, but UNC staged a 24–5 run and never looked back. Sylvia was happy with the 70–56 win. She had the golden scissors ready for the next game—the third straight Elite-Eight appearance for the Tar Heels—this time against No. 2 Purdue whom they had defeated in the 2006 Sweet 16.

Attendance at the Dallas regional Elite Eight was 3,311, far below crowd numbers for Triangle rivalry games and far below the 17,950 in attendance for the Maryland game. Ivory Latta preferred a big, loud crowd—even if the crowd roared for her opponent. But the Tar Heels were "on." In the first half, they shot 51.6 percent from the field, but with two minutes left in the period, Latta limped off the court. Everyone, including Sylvia, flashed back to the 2006 Final Four game against Maryland and thought *knee injury*. Spectators wondered whether UNC's chances for a second NCAA title had limped off with Latta. AP reporter Jamie Aron wrote that "Latta kept up the suspense by being the 11th of the 13 players" to emerge from the locker room for the second half. She cheerfully told the press, "It was only a cramp."

Latta displayed her old, characteristic Latta-tude, scoring 21 points, her best effort in the Tournament. Erlana Larkins hit 12 of 16 from the floor for a career-high 29 points and was named Most Outstanding Player of the Dallas regional. The 84–72 win over Purdue gave Sylvia yet another opportunity to use the golden scissors. Players and coaches snipped the net from the metal ring, and after it was cut down, Latta poked her head through it and wore it like a "necklace." Aron wrote that Latta blew kisses to the small crowd, and UNC athletic director Dick Baddour joined the celebration at center court, "dancing in a circle with three players." At a news conference, Latta grinned broadly and said she was "looking forward to visiting 'one of my best friends,' LeBron James, when UNC rolls into Cleveland this weekend." On March 29, she had cause for another celebration: She was named an All-American for the second consecutive year.

The Tar Heels headed off to Cleveland, Ohio, for a second straight Final Four against none other than Tennessee. Sylvia's career record against Summitt was 2–6. Going into the game, Latta appeared to be her old, jubilant self who had fun on the court. Joedy McCreary wrote that Latta made a layup to give "North Carolina a big lead, ... drew a foul and celebrated by flexing her biceps." He noted that the "flashy Latta-tude," her "trademark," was back.[15] At the end of the first half, the Tar Heels were down by only one point (21–22), but Sylvia was dismayed by the low score and her players' performance. Neither team could hit from the floor. With 90 seconds

Sylvia coaches courtside during the Final Four, Cleveland, Ohio, April 1, 2007. Left to right: Sylvia Hatchell, Rashanda McCants, Ivory Latta, Camille Little, Erlana Larkins, and Alex Miller. Courtesy Jeffrey Allan Camarati, UNC Sports Information.

remaining, Latta missed two three-point attempts, the second of which would have tied the game at 56, but the real story was officiating—Sylvia's old anathema. With eight minutes left in the second half, the Tar Heels took a 48–36 lead—and blew it when Tennessee went on an 18-point run that was fueled at the foul line. Tennessee had an 18 foul-shot advantage. Sylvia told the press, "They got on the foul line. We didn't." She said her players "needed to be more aggressive in attacking the basket." Whatever the reason, Pat Summitt's Lady Vols defeated Sylvia's Tar Heels 56–50 and ended their chances for a national championship. Two days later, Tennessee defeated Rutgers 59–46 to win a seventh national NCAA title. After the game, Sylvia was more riled up than usual about foul calls: "Anybody who knows the sport would tell you that there were some really bad calls in that game." Two in particular were the worst she had seen in 32 years of coaching. Others agreed.

A Final-Four loss to Tennessee at the foul line was not the way she wanted Camille Little and Ivory Latta to end their college careers. The two seniors shed tears during the post-game press conference. They had led the Tar Heels to a 122–17 record between 2003 and 2007. In addition to her other achievements and honors, Latta was the top scorer in UNC women's basketball history with 2,285 points. On April 4, both players entered the WNBA draft. Ivory Latta was the No. 11 first-round pick by the Detroit Shock. Little was the No. 17 second-round pick by the San Antonio Silver Stars. Many of Sylvia's players would make it to the professional leagues, beginning with Pearl Moore in 1979, but none of them would achieve the stardom or salaries that the NBA affords men. The day after UNC's Final-Four loss to Tennessee, the

Greensboro News & Record published a telling article by Jim Schlosser. It begins, "If she were only a man, though she loves being a woman.... Had she been a he and as valuable to the North Carolina men's basketball team as she is to the women's, senior Ivory Latta would soon be pulling down millions." Schlosser wrote that Latta and her fellow 2007 draft picks would be lucky to make $60,000 a year in the WNBA, but she and other U.S. star women athletes can earn six figures in Europe, so many of them play there in the off season and return stateside to play in the WNBA regular season. Latta and Little and all the other 2007 WNBA draft picks had to accept the situation: "I don't think about it that much," Latta told Schlosser.

Sylvia had used the golden scissors twice in 2007 but not for the NCAA Championship game that she coveted. They would go back in the drawer. In the interim, she had a family to nurture and a program to run. In June of 2007, Van finished high school at Cresset Christian Academy. At the same time, Sylvia's long-time administrative assistant Joan Nipper announced her retirement. Searching for a replacement, Sylvia discovered that Van's Cresset kindergarten teacher, Jane High, was contemplating a career change, so she asked Jane, "Would you be interested in the job?" Sylvia and Jane had developed a strong friendship after Van's kindergarten year. Jane worked in Sylvia's summer camps and sold merchandise at the women's games. Jane knew the entire basketball family—players, staff, coaches. She also had previous experience in banking and accounting, which—combined with her teaching experience and love of basketball—made her the ideal candidate for the job, so she was hired. The only downside to the arrangement was that, come August of 2007, Van could no longer call his kindergarten teacher "Mama High." She was a UNC employee and Coach Hatchell's assistant.

Sylvia went about her usual summer routine of recruiting and speaking and running her summer camps, and in August as she was getting ready for the fall term, her friend and colleague Pat Summitt was in the news for something other than basketball: On August 15, 2007, just eight days shy of her 27th wedding anniversary, Pat Summitt filed for an absolute divorce from her husband Ross B. Summitt, II, on grounds of irreconcilable differences. R.B. and Pat were high-profile members of the Knoxville community and the basketball world. He was president of Sevier County Bank. She was the NCAA winningest coach, with 880 victories, and her seven NCAA titles were second only to John Wooden's 10. The University of Tennessee, Knoxville, and the University of Tennessee at Martin had named campus streets in her honor: Pat Head Summitt Drive. In Knoxville, the court inside Thompson-Boling Arena was named The Summitt; in Martin, the court inside Elam Center was named Pat Head Summitt Court. So she would keep the name "Summitt." The bitter divorce would stretch into 2008.

10

Hurdles and Hitches

When Roy Williams returned to Chapel Hill as the men's basketball coach in 2003 and led UNC to a national championship in 2005, Van became obsessed with Carolina men's basketball. Sylvia and Sammy knew that he could have been a starter at a smaller Division I university or a school with a different basketball history, but that was not his dream. UNC had been his top choice since he was 12, so in August 2007, he enrolled as a freshman business major. Van could also have lived at home, but he opted to live on campus in Craig Dorm, ignoring Sylvia's suggestion that he had a "perfectly good room at home."

In his freshman year, Van was a walk-on for the UNC JV squad. As a 6'3" guard, he was one of 14 selected from approximately 60 who tried out. Following his success in high school, he felt that he was a pretty good basketball player, but he quickly learned otherwise. He told Ryan Davis of the *Daily Tar Heel*, "My freshman year [at UNC] … was the first time in my life I'd ever been the worst player on a team…. That year I realized that, if this was a goal I had, I really needed to start working on it." In a 2012 interview, he confessed, "I made the JV team by the skin of my teeth, and I was the last sub off the bench—I was probably lucky to be even that." When Van made the JV team, he shared a private goal with Sylvia. He wanted to make the UNC varsity team: "Mom, I got it figured out. When I'm a senior, the senior game will be against Duke in the Dean Smith Center. The seniors always start. That's my goal. When I'm a senior, I am going to start against Duke in the Dean Smith Center." Sylvia encouraged him: "If that's what you want, then you have to work for it." Privately she thought, *OK. It's a long shot, but it's a good goal.*

Van's moving out of the Kepley Road house and going to college were not the only changes in the Hatchell household. Deneene, who had been with the Hatchells since Van was a baby, was preparing to move out. She had worked alongside them as a live-in nanny, a household manager, basketball-camp administrator, and a friend. Sylvia says, "I couldn't have done it without her." And then there was Spud, Veda's dog, who had been part of the Hatchell household since Veda died in 2004. By 2007 he was at least 17 years old, deaf, and blind. He liked to lie under warm cars, a habit that ended his life when a driver unwittingly backed a car over him. As the whole family gathered and grieved in the vet's office, Sylvia thought, *This dog has a greater legacy than most human beings. He saved a man's life.* "The fact that he was my mama's dog made it even worse. He was a smart dog."

And then there was Marion Jones—again. Hers was a long and ugly story. In

2000, Jones' husband C.J. Hunter had tested positive for nandrolone and was suspended from Olympic competition in 2001. The couple separated that same year, and she sued for divorce in 2002. In 2004, Hunter reported that he himself injected Jones with banned substances and that he saw her inject herself. She denied these allegations but remained under a cloud of suspicion. In the meantime, her relationship with sprinter Tim Montgomery also disintegrated. Sylvia had met Montgomery in 2004 when he accompanied Jones to the ten-year anniversary celebration of the NCAA Championship. She was disappointed when she learned that Montgomery was also banned from Olympic competition in 2005 for doping. In 2006, Marion tested positive for the banned hormone EPO, but a second sample tested negative. Throughout the allegations, Jones insisted she did not knowingly take steroids but had been told she was taking flaxseed oil. Eventually, she pleaded guilty to lying under oath and impeding the investigation of steroid use.

In February 2007, Jones married Obadele Thompson, a sprinter from Barbados, and their first child Ahmir was born in July. On October 5, 2007, she admitted to using performance-enhancing drugs prior to the 2000 Olympics, and all of her results since 2000 were voided, including her five Olympic medals. Edward Robinson with the *News & Observer* wrote that the admission "officially" ended "her career as a role model and athletic superstar." In an emotional interview with the media, Jones said, "I have let my country down, and I have let myself down. It is with a great amount of shame that I stand before you and tell you I have betrayed your trust."[1] Throughout all of this, Sylvia held firm in her support, telling the media that Marion had "trusted her coaches and the people around her, and she was hurt by the bad decisions they made.... She has learned from those mistakes and ... will be a much better person for it. We love her. We care about her. We support her, and we will do whatever we can do to help."

The news about Marion reminded Sylvia that her job as the head coach of a sports program was to help players cultivate their best selves. The next few seasons would test that belief and hone her philosophy that "Success is not just determined by the wins and losses. It's by the outcome." Sylvia defines "outcome" as "getting the most out of the talent or the potential that you have." True, she had lost major talent when Ivory Latta and Camille Little moved on to the WNBA, but her returning players had experience and—she thought—untapped potential. She turned to senior Erlana Larkins for leadership but emphasized that she wanted "a whole team effort." In addition to her seasoned players, such as LaToya Pringle, and Rashanda McCants, she had Sophomore Jessica Breland and three promising freshmen: Cetera DeGraffenreid from Sylva, North Carolina; Rebecca Gray from Georgetown, Kentucky; and Italee Lucas, from Las Vegas, Nevada. This 2007–2008 freshmen recruiting class was ranked between the top fifth and seventh in the nation. Sylvia believed they would live up to their ranking, and she started the season with *three* point guards: freshmen Cetera DeGraffenreid and Italee Lucas plus senior Alex Miller. Rachel Carter called the strategy a "three-headed monster that the team can ride into national title contention."[2] Sylvia described DeGraffenreid and Lucas as "fast and quick and athletic," telling the media, "They can flat out go." Speed would be necessary because the Lady Tar Heels would be tested against four non-conference teams, three of which were ranked nationally: No. 1 Tennessee, No. 2 Connecticut, unranked Purdue, and No. 12 Arizona State. The media questioned whether No. 7 UNC could compete with the top teams in the country.

On November 11, 2007, the Lady Tar Heels faced their first real test against No. 12 ranked Arizona State in the State Farm Tipoff Classic. Sylvia downplayed the 26 turnovers in the first half: "At times we were a little out of sync, but I told them, 'Just don't slow down.' We'll make those corrections going 100 miles per hour." UNC got the 75–60 win in Carmichael Auditorium before a big crowd—7,519. Always pushing for increased attendance, Sylvia was pleased.

Defeating a top 25 team boosted the Lady Tar Heels' confidence, and they won the next seven games with an average margin of 34 points, but Sylvia did not let up. She was embarrassed when Coppin State outrebounded her Tar Heels 20–17 on November 16, though UNC won (92–63). Their national ranking rose to No. 4, and on December 2, they felt ready to face No. 1 Tennessee, eight months after the Lady Vols nixed their chance for the 2007 NCAA Championship. Sylvia had not taken her Tar Heels to Knoxville in 20 years, and this time she would play on a basketball court named for her nemesis-friend: The Summitt in Thompson-Bowling Arena. The media said the two teams put on a "show" for the 16,845 fans. The score was tied three times and the lead changed five times. Tennessee led by 13 with 6:28 left, but Sylvia's Tar Heels staged a 17–5 run that brought them within one point—79–78. Rebecca Gray was fouled on a three-point attempt with five seconds left. She hit the first free throw, missed the second, and intentionally missed the third, giving UNC a chance at the rebound. The strategy didn't work—UNC lost 83–79. Sylvia told the press, it was a "national-championship game." Pat Summitt said it was a "game of runs."

The Tar Heels won the next eight games—again with a hefty average margin of 27 points—and their national ranking rose to No. 3. During this eight-win run, the only team to give Sylvia's Tar Heels a challenge was unranked NC State. Jessica Breland took the game personally. This would be her second time to play in "hostile" Reynolds Coliseum, and she did not want a repeat of the 2007 loss to the Wolfpack. She said the "atmosphere" on Kay Yow Court was worse than the pandemonium in Duke's Cameron Indoor Stadium. Kay Yow was back coaching her team and sparring with cancer—everyone acknowledged her strength and dedication.

Sylvia told Aaron Beard, "I think whatever you're here for, your purpose in life, you've got to keep doing it as long as you can. Without a doubt, Kay knows her purpose."[3] The Tar Heels battled not only the Wolfpack basketball team but also their emotional commitment to win for their coach. Larkins and Pringle took charge, but Jessica Breland was "really fired up"—it was she who sparked the team. She came off the bench to score 10 points in 24 minutes. UNC led all the way and got the 79–70 win. Breland was proving her worth, living up to Sylvia's expectations.

Her former star point guard, however, was back in the news—and the news was not good. On January 11, U.S. District Judge Kenneth Karas sentenced Marion Jones to six months in prison (with two years' probation) and 800 hours of community service. The track world was brutal in its response,[4] but Sylvia held firm in support of her former player and mother of two children. In a UNC statement, Sylvia said, "We have been steadfast in our support of Marion throughout this ordeal and we will continue to support her in any way we can.... She is still a member of the Carolina basketball family and I am confident that she will come out of this situation a better person."[5]

After a lopsided win over Boston College (87–59), the Tar Heels faced "a brutal four-game stretch": Connecticut, Maryland, Wake Forest, and Duke.[6] On January 21, they traveled to Storrs, Connecticut, to face the unbeaten No. 1 Huskies. Both teams had strong, high-scoring offenses, but Connecticut was "spurred on by an electric sellout crowd."[7] The 10,167 fans expected—and got—an electrifying game. UNC led by 11 (44–33) at the half. In the second period, UConn not only erased the 11-point lead but outscored the Tar Heels 49–27. The Huskies got 33 points off turnovers, and they beat UNC on the boards. The final score (82–71) meant that the Tar Heels had lost twice in the same season to two different No. 1 ranked teams. UConn remained unbeaten. UNC was 17–2 overall but still unbeaten in the ACC.

Following the loss to UConn, the No. 3 Tar Heels faced No. 4 Maryland—their kryptonite. Maryland was the preseason pick to win the ACC title and had won 12 consecutive games. In 2007, UNC beat Maryland twice, but in 2008, both teams had undergone changes: Sylvia did not have the Latta-Little duo, and Maryland coach Brenda Frese was absent from the court because she was scheduled to deliver twins in February. Acting head coach Darren Clark took her place. Carmichael attendance was 7,914, just 96 seats under capacity—Sylvia couldn't have asked for a better atmosphere. But there were concerns. Pringle told the press—and Sylvia agreed—that playing smart at the end of a game had "been a problem" for the Tar Heels. This night, Pringle did not intend to let that happen. It was a see-saw game, tied 12 times with six lead changes. At the buzzer, the score was tied at 79. Both teams scored eight points in the first overtime period to send the game into double overtime, tied at 87. In the second overtime, two Terrapins fouled out, and the Larkins-Pringle duo took advantage of their absence to outscore Maryland 18–7 for the 97–86 double-overtime win. Pringle suffered a cut lip and a cut to the face, but she wiped away the blood and kept going. After the game Sylvia told the press, "They're our warriors. These two: I just don't want to let them graduate."

The third matchup in the four-game "brutal" stretch was not brutal at all. On January 31, UNC trounced Wake Forest 76–55 and moved on to face No. 11 Duke—bitter rival and worse-than-kryptonite for the Tar Heels. In Sylvia's 50 games against the Blue Devils, the series was split 25–25. In 2007, Duke had delivered UNC two of their three ACC losses, but in 2008, the Blue Devils had a new coach. When Gail Goestenkors departed for Texas, Joanne Palumbo-McCallie was hired as her replacement. Sylvia told the media that the Blue Devils had "recently turned to a more transition-oriented offense that makes them dangerous." Transition and speed were Sylvia's game! She relished the competition and a match-up against a team that was borrowing from her playbook: "The competition doesn't get any better than what we're going to face Monday night."[8] But it did not go well for the Blue Devils. UNC outrebounded and outscored Duke. McCallie said that DeGraffenreid "was an X-factor,"[9] but she was not alone—five players scored double digits in a game of milestones. UNC scored the most points in Cameron Indoor Stadium since 1997 and won by the biggest margin in Cameron since 1993. Sylvia earned her 499th win at UNC. Sylvia told the press, "We're unorthodox.... We have a lot of ways to get the milk in the jug. I like how we play." She also liked the 17-point margin of victory (93–76). On the way home, she and the players toilet-papered the trees on Franklin Street in celebration, but their enthusiasm was curbed when police gave Sylvia a warning ticket for littering. The *News & Observer* noted that "when the men win, the police tolerate and even abet public celebrations that include littering and worse."[10] Sylvia ignored this controversy and kept her focus on the team, which earned yet another lopsided victory on February 7, this time against Clemson in Carmichael (79–47). The win was No. 500 for Sylvia in her 22 seasons as head women's basketball coach at the University of North Carolina at Chapel Hill. Her UNC record was 500–194, but she was marching toward win No. 800 overall. Three days later, Sylvia and her Tar Heels were back on the court for a decisive win over Georgia Tech (75–61) followed by Virginia (90–82), Florida State (97–77) and Miami (79–61). Their ranking rose to No. 2.

On February 25, Sylvia's Tar Heels met Kay Yow's unranked Wolfpack for the second faceoff in 2008, this time in Carmichael. A quiet undercurrent was Yow's extended battle with breast cancer. Mike Potter wrote that she received a "warm round of cheers when she was introduced before the game." The Wolfpack gave the game—and Yow—their all. The score was tied twice, and the lead changed five times. They outrebounded the Tar Heels 46–38. Sylvia told the press that the only other team to outrebound the Tar Heels at that level was Connecticut. UNC was abysmal at the free-throw line, making only 20 of 41. Sylvia concluded that with such poor rebounding and missed foul shots, the 85–79 win against "a really good team like N.C. State" meant that her Tar Heels were "pretty good" after all,[11] but next up was Duke. They had six days to prepare.

On March 2, Joanne McCallie brought her No. 12 Blue Devils to Chapel Hill for their second matchup of the season and the last game in regular play before the ACC Tournament. Ed Hardin wrote that McCallie "walked into an ambush"—senior night in a sold-out, steamy-hot Carmichael Auditorium that was like a "sauna." The Tar Heels delivered Duke an even worse shellacking than on February 4, prompting Hardin to describe the old Duke-UNC hostility as a "rivalry gone cold."[12] Aaron Beard wrote that UNC "turned the rivalry into a rout." Though Duke managed to tie the game twice, UNC led all the way and handed the Blue Devils their worst loss in 15 years—82–51. According to Beard, "The Tar Heels entered this season wondering whether it could keep rolling after losing Ivory Latta and Camille Little, who led them to three straight ACC Tournament titles and consecutive Final Fours. Instead, North Carolina—with freshman DeGraffenreid at the point, seniors Larkins and LaToya Pringle controlling the inside, and Rashanda McCants roaming all over the court—managed to accomplish something even its graduated stars couldn't do by going unscathed through the league schedule."[13] UNC was unbeaten in the ACC. Given the strength of the Conference, Sylvia felt that this was a remarkable accomplishment—the only UNC women's basketball team ever to reach this plateau and only the eighth team in ACC history. In celebration, Sylvia and her players rolled Carmichael with toilet paper—she may have been afraid to celebrate on Franklin Street after the February 4 warning. It was the last game in Carmichael before a multimillion-dollar renovation and the last regular-season game for seniors Erlana Larkins and LaToya Pringle.

Four Tar Heels earned accolades for their unpredicted, stellar season. On March 6, Sylvia was honored as ACC Coach of the Year for the third consecutive year. Sophomore Jessica Breland was named ACC Sixth Player. Cetera DeGraffenreid was an All-ACC Freshman. LaToya Pringle was named to the All-ACC first team and earned honors as ACC Defensive Player of the Year. Erlana Larkins joined the All-ACC first team for the third straight season and was runner-up for ACC Player of the Year. But they put these aside because they had a mere five days to prepare for the ACC Tournament.

The Tar Heels were the No. 1 seed in the 2008 ACC Tournament. Maryland was No. 2, Duke No. 3, and all three were ranked nationally. Virginia was also ranked— No. 25. With four of the top 25 teams in the ACC, Sylvia's opinion that the ACC was the toughest conference in the country was validated. Even so, Ed Hardin wrote that the 11,132 fans "saw some abysmal basketball, and not until the Tar Heels took the court for the first time did we see what ACC basketball really is. North Carolina plays a game different from any other team."[14] In the quarterfinals, the Tar Heels' defeated Clemson 97–77. (On this same date—March 7, 2008—Marion Jones entered Carswell Federal Prison in Fort Worth to serve her six-month sentence.) The Lady Tar Heels then met No. 25 Virginia in the ACC semifinals. The media used words like "steamrolled" to describe the UNC performance. Aaron Beard wrote that Rashanda McCants was a force, roaming the court, refusing to be denied, earning 23 points and 10 rebounds, despite spraining her ankle about seven minutes into the first half. She was sidelined for six minutes, while trainers taped her ankle and administered Tylenol. She went back on the court and played a total 29 minutes. Virginia coach Debbie Ryan called her the UNC "X-factor," and Sylvia called her a "warrior."[15] UNC got the 80–65 win and a shot at another ACC Championship on the following day against their perennial opponent, Duke. Tension had built all year as both teams anticipated this rematch of Triangle rivals who had traded the ACC crown back and forth for six years. According to Hardin, Sylvia "stood at mid-court Sunday, awaiting a pregame handshake from the new Duke coach that never came."[16]

UNC had won 8 of 10 recent UNC-Duke face-offs and wanted to make it 9 of 11. The entire team stepped up, demonstrating the Lady Tar Heels' depth, and gave UNC the 86–73 win. Sylvia praised their unselfishness: "They don't care who scores as long as we win. And that is what makes them a championship team." When Duke's Abby Waner was given a technical foul, Sylvia chose Larkins, who shot only 58 percent from the foul line, to make the shots. She told the press, "[S]he's my leader, she's my senior, … I know what this game means to her…. So I put her on the line to make those foul shots, and she did exactly what we needed her to do." In her four years at UNC, Erlana Larkins had never lost an ACC Championship game—and she was named MVP of the Tournament.

The Lady Tar Heels savored the win—the balloons, the confetti, the trophy presentation, the ceremonial cutting down the net with Sylvia's golden scissors—but their focus shifted immediately to the 2008 NCAA Tournament. When the bracket and pairings were announced on March 17, disbelief and ire erupted—even more vehemently than in 2005. Sylvia was hoping for a No. 1 seed in the Greensboro Regional. After all, in 2007, Duke had gone undefeated in the ACC and was given the

No. 1 Greensboro slot. Sylvia expected the same consideration, but she was denied—and the pairings pleased few. The No. 1 Greensboro seed went to Connecticut with Rutgers as No. 2. Geno Auriemma called the bracket "ironic" and added that if he were Vivian Stringer, he would "be questioning a little bit what's going on." Doug Feinberg wrote that Stringer "stared at the television in disbelief," saying "I didn't think there was any way on God's earth that this would happen…. This is a mindblower…. If I were a betting woman I would have lost all my money today."[17] As it was, the Scarlet Knights would have to face Connecticut to advance to the Final Four. Sylvia was steaming. As the No. 1 seed in the New Orleans regional, her Tar Heels would play the first two rounds in Norfolk but were on a path to face the No. 2 seed LSU in New Orleans to get to the Final Four in Tampa Bay. Feinberg pointed out, "If that happens, it would be the fourth time in six years North Carolina has had to face a lower-seeded team playing close to home." But Sylvia kept mum: "I don't really have any thoughts…. We're just ready to play…. I'm going to wait until after the tournament's over to say anything."[18]

Holding her tongue, trying not to let her furor affect the team, she headed for Norfolk, Virginia, and a first-round game on March 23 against Bucknell. It was a blowout—85–50—but the media described UNC's play as sloppy. The second-round game was against the No. 8 seed Georgia, coached by Andy Landers, who had beaten out Sylvia for the Roane State coaching job in 1975. Starting in 1986, her Tar Heels had lost four consecutive games to Georgia, most recently in the 2000 NCAA West Regionals Sweet 16, when Al Myatt wrote that UNC "amounted to little more than a bug on Georgia's windshield."[19] Eight years later, Sylvia intended to be a more formidable foe, but her team sputtered early on. Edward Robinson said the 2008 Tar Heels were "[m]ired in a funk" and speculated that the 10:00 p.m. start time had affected their play. Larkins said they "had to shake the cobwebs off" before they woke up and went on a 20–0 run that the Lady Bulldogs could not match.[20] Sylvia got her first victory (80–66) over Landers' UGA Bulldogs.

The win against Georgia sent the Lady Tar Heels (ranked No. 2 nationally) to the Sweet 16 in New Orleans to face No. 4 seed Louisville (ranked No. 23) who was making a first-time appearance in the NCAA women's third round. UNC was on a 15-game winning streak and had a 32–2 record, neither of which mattered to Louisville. The media described the first half as "bumbling," but the Tar Heels dug themselves out of a deep pit to tie the game at 53 in the second half and went on a 20–6 run to get the 78–74 win—overcoming 25 turnovers and an 18-point deficit. They knew they had to play better in the Elite-Eight game against LSU on March 31.

UNC and LSU had not faced off since Sylvia's first year at UNC—a game LSU won 79–63. Though both schools had made multiple NCAA appearances, their paths had never crossed in the tournament. Sylvia and her team wished they were playing in Greensboro instead of New Orleans, a scant 80 miles from the LSU campus. They would have to execute Carolina basketball to perfection in enemy territory—but they didn't. The Lady Tigers took away their signature fast break, and Sylvia's worst nightmare—a slow-paced, low-scoring game—materialized. Pringle acknowledged, "We just couldn't get it going. We tried and we fought, but we just couldn't get it going." The final 56–50 score sent the Lady Tigers to the Final Four for the fifth straight year, and it was hard not to blame the skewed bracket for UNC's loss. The Tar Heels ended the season ranked No. 5. Seniors LaToya Pringle and Erlana Larkins would never wear the Carolina blue uniform again, but on April 9, they would join the growing number of UNC players in the WNBA, being selected in the first round of the draft. Pringle was the No. 13 pick by the Phoenix Mercury and Larkins was the No. 14 pick by the NY Liberty.

The loss to LSU was devastating, but there was more embarrassment to come when the media took an odd detour into the world of women's courtside attire. Sylvia's jackets had been gossip fodder for a long time, but after the loss to LSU, social media picked up a "thread" from 2006 and wove an ugly tapestry. For her 700th win on January 15, 2006, against NC State, Sylvia wore a cream-colored suit that caught the eye of Jack Daly, or rather, its

Sylvia uses the golden scissors to cut down the net after defeating Duke to win the ACC Championship, March 9, 2008. Courtesy Jeffrey Allan Camarati, UNC Sports Information.

"'elaborate gold lions' heads on the shoulders" caught his eye, and he wrote that the "outfit was appropriate" for a coach who had "established herself as one of the queens of the women's basketball jungle."[21] On April 20, 2006, the jacket made news again, this time at the Sports Excellence Tribute Gala, sponsored by the Raleigh Sports Club, to honor the three Triangle head coaches: Gail Goestenkors, Kay Yow, and Sylvia Hatchell. More than 500 people turned out for the fundraiser at the RBC Center. Each coach donated her share of the proceeds to a select charity—Sylvia's share went, of course, to the UNC Lineberger Comprehensive Cancer Center. Rachel Carter described the event for the *News & Observer* as an evening of barbs and embarrassing moments in the coaches' lives. Stephanie Lawrence Yelton remembered a "roaring" Sylvia in the locker room, "wearing her infamous white suit with, coincidentally, two lions on it." And Lin Dunn, then assistant coach with the Indiana Fever, chimed in: "Only one of these coaches has the exclusive right to wear jackets worn by

Elvis."[22] Sylvia enjoyed the roast; she would gladly suffer humiliation for the benefit of the Lineberger Cancer Center.

For the 2008 Elite-Eight game against LSU, Sylvia had worn the suit again. Perhaps she thought it would bring good luck—after all, she got her 700th win while wearing it—but the charm turned vicious when footage of her court-side interview hit YouTube with the title "The Sylvia Hatchell Jacket Saga." It was posted on March 31, 2008, immediately following the UNC Elite-Eight loss to LSU (56–50). The video loop zooms in on a downcast Sylvia and the gold lions' heads. Sylvia's commentary is muted, but the background music is Barbra Streisand's rendition of "Second Hand Rose." The site has attracted 2,265 hits with comments such as, "I couldn't hardly watch the game and Big Syl for that jacket! LMAO." Another comment was even worse: "That is one filthy jacket to end the season in." Sylvia ignored the personal attack.

The next week, on April 25, she was again in the news but for a reason more fitting her status than jackets: The position of head women's basketball coach at the University of South Carolina became vacant on April 14 when USC coach Susan Walvius resigned. In her 11 years at USC, Walvius had a losing record in the SEC (51–103) but had taken the Gamecocks to the NCAA Tournament twice. After a 16–16 overall record in 2007–2008, there was "pressure," according to the press, for her to leave. Reports spread quickly that USC officials had met with Sylvia on April 24 at the Hatchells' North Myrtle Beach house. Sylvia, Sammy, and UNC athletic director Dick Baddour all declined to comment, as did USC athletic officials.

Some felt that Sylvia would be a perfect fit for USC. Her ties to South Carolina ran deep because of her 11 successful years at Francis Marion, success that guaranteed her excellent recruiting opportunities. If she left North Carolina, the women's basketball program would suffer. With Sylvia at the helm, the Tar Heels had one NCAA Championship, eight ACC Titles, six Elite-Eight appearances, and three trips to the Final Four. Sylvia's desire to "fall back in love with basketball," combined with her desire to change the nature of women's basketball, had paid off. In four consecutive years, between 2005 and 2008, UNC entered the NCAA Tournament as a number one seed. More importantly, she had put her stamp on Carolina women's basketball and forever changed the game. Between 2003 and 2008, the Tar Heels were 130–13 overall. Sylvia had won 512 games at UNC and was just 16 games shy of her 800th career win (784–275). With such a strong record, the obvious question was "Why would she consider leaving?" The obvious answer was "salary"—a salary that fell far below her colleagues' compensation packages.

Sylvia's interest in the USC job was eventually confirmed by her agent, John Meadows, who told Edward Robinson that her salary ranked below "the salaries of the top 20 highest-paid coaches in NCAA Division I women's basketball." Then he asked, "Is 24th where she belongs?"[23] Meadows' question resonated with her fans and UNC administrators. Sylvia's salary was $260,000 plus incentives. Tennessee's Pat Summitt earned $1.3 million; Texas' Gail Goestenkors $1 million. In the ACC, Maryland's Brenda Frese reportedly earned $300,000, and Joanne McCallie's first-year salary at Duke reportedly exceeded $500,000. Dick Baddour told Robinson, Sylvia has "built this program.... It's got her mark on it, she's led it for over 20 years. It has enjoyed a tremendous amount of success as a result of her hard work and dedication. I very much want her to continue to be here." He added that UNC "would be working on her contract" at the end of the 2008 season.[24] And, so, she stayed. On May 1, 2008, the AP announced that Sylvia had withdrawn her name from consideration.[25] On May 5, Dawn Staley was hired as the USC head women's basketball coach at an annual salary of $650,000, making her the third highest-paid women's basketball coach in the SEC. Only Pat Summitt at Tennessee and Van Chancellor at LSU earned more. Two months later, on July 25, the AP reported that UNC had extended Sylvia's contract through 2015 at an "average" salary of $330,000 plus supplements. Sylvia never acknowledged the discrepancies.[26]

Following a disappointing end to Sylvia's 2007–2008 season, the Hatchell family returned to its usual summer routine. Vowing to realize his dream of making the UNC varsity team, Van worked out in the men's basketball weight room, getting there in the early morning hours and leaving before the varsity players arrived. "Mom and Dad taught me how to work really hard and emphasized that if you lose, it should not be because you worked the least." As was their usual practice, Sylvia and Sammy worked in the UNC women's basketball camp. One day in July, Sammy said he wasn't feeling well and luckily got an appointment for a stress test. He was sent immediately to the hospital for a heart catheterization and stent. Sylvia and he downplayed the incident: "They kept him overnight," says Sylvia, "dismissed him the next morning, and he came back to camp and worked all day." It was a mere blip in the hard-work ethos of the Hatchell family.

11

Black Clouds on the Horizon—Again

In the fall of 2008, Van moved from Craig Dorm into Mrs. D's House—a Carolina institution. The house is named for a Mrs. Delancey who began renting rooms to UNC male students after the death of her husband. When she died, the house was sold, but the tradition continued, and Van was eager to be part of it. Sylvia was not impressed. "You've got this really, really nice room at home with a bathroom!" she told Van. Sammy was appalled: "Are *you* going to *let* him **live** there? Live in a place like that?" he asked Sylvia. "You throw a match in there, and it will go up like that!" Sylvia's and Sammy's objections went unheeded. Van liked Mrs. D's House so well that he stayed there for the next three years, moving to larger rooms as he gained seniority.

With Van fully committed to living outside the Kepley Road house, and Sassafras, Scooter, and Spud gone, Sylvia wanted another dog and found a golden retriever sired by Coach, ranked No. 1 in the Canine Chronicle Breed Point System. Matilda Faye (named for Sylvia's grandmother and Sammy's mother) was born on September 4, 2008, and Sylvia brought her home in mid–November. Van says that "Maddie" was his "replacement": "When Maddie gets to ride in the front seat of the car and I have to ride in the back, I understand where I rank in the world."

The big question, however, was not where Van ranked but where Sylvia's Lady Tar Heels ranked. The 2007–2008 season had exceeded expectations, and even though Larkins and Pringle were gone, the Tar Heels' prospects looked good. Their No. 4 preseason ranking was higher than in 2007. The media continued to emphasize Sylvia's brand of Carolina basketball—high scores and fast pace. The freshman recruits were promising, and Sylvia had five returning seniors, including Alex Miller and Rashanda McCants. Miller was recovering from knee surgery but was expected to perform well. McCants had averaged 15.8 points in the previous season, but her final game against LSU in the NCAA Final Four had been a disaster. She told the press that the loss felt like "failure.... I feel like I didn't do my job as a teammate." McCants would have one more year to atone, and Sylvia looked to her for maturity and stability, along with sophomore Italee Lucas. Finally, there was Jessica Breland, a junior who had averaged double-digit scores and was named the 2008 ACC Sixth Player. Sylvia expected a stellar performance from her, but she was having difficulty breathing and began the 2008–2009 season on a regimen of allergy shots.

The Lady Tar Heels quickly racked up 17 straight victories, including a November 23 squeaker against No. 2 Oklahoma to win the preseason WNIT (80–79). If

Jessica Breland had any health issues, they were not apparent. She scored a career-high 31 points and hit two critical shots in the last two minutes, a performance that earned her the Tournament MVP honor. UNC's ranking rose to No. 2. When the UNC Lady Tar Heels went up against the No. 18 Ohio State Buckeyes on December 3 in the ACC/Big Ten Challenge, Breland scored 29 points, but Sylvia was concerned with her team's six-minute scoreless stretch: "That's the way we play," she acknowledged. "At times we were really ragged."

The first three ACC games went in the win column, but the Lady Tar Heels struggled against Clemson, blowing a 12-point lead. Fortunately, they recovered for an 83–74 victory. Sylvia was aghast. She told the media that during the game she was thinking, "This ain't my team. Where'd this team

Sylvia and Maddie in the Black Mountain blueberry patch. Courtesy Sheila Oliver.

come from?" Even so, McCants, Shegog, Lucas, and Breland gave Sylvia her 799th career win. Next up was NC State—who else? No one needed a reminder that NC State games had marked major milestones in Sylvia life. The rivalry with her mentor was perhaps "karmic." Van was born on an NC State game day, and she got her 500th, 600th, and 700th wins against the Wolfpack, but in 2009, the rivalry and Sylvia's win-loss record were secondary to Kay Yow's 22-year fight with cancer, a fight she was losing. On January 6, after 38 years of coaching the Wolfpack—the only coach to lead the NC State women's basketball program—Yow took her final medical leave of absence. Edward Robinson wrote, "Basketball season is over for Kay Yow."[1] Luke Decock, with the *Charlotte Observer* reported that Sylvia "expressed surprise at her news conference Friday when the first question was about win No. 799, not about Yow." An hour before the January 11 game, coaches, staff, and players from both universities stood at center court in the Dean Smith Center, "arms interlocked in an unbroken circle of love." Yow's chair sat empty on the NC State bench, but her "presence was felt as much as her absence."

The Lady Wolfpack were playing for a dying Yow. The Lady Tar Heels were playing for Sylvia's 800th victory. Under the leadership of interim coach Stephanie Glance, the unranked Wolfpack gave No. 2 UNC a fight, including a 1–3-1 zone defense that held the Tar Heels to 32.8 percent from the field. Breland, UNC's top scorer, sprained an ankle and had to leave the game after 16 minutes, but Chay Shegog and Cetera DeGraffenreid fought for a two-point lead with barely two minutes left in regulation. NC State closed the gap to tie the game at 59 and send it into overtime—a fitting end. The Lady Tar Heels came out strong in overtime with a 10–0 run and handed Sylvia her 800th win (75–66). She joined three other 800-win women's coaches: Jody Conradt, Vivian Stringer, and Pat Summitt. A celebration followed. UNC Athletics Director Dick Baddour and Chancellor Holden Thorp gave Sylvia a UNC jersey with "No. 800" on the front. A video highlighted her career and brought good wishes from former players and colleagues—including Ivory Latta, Pat Summitt, and Roy Williams—but it was hard for Sylvia to celebrate while her friend and mentor was dying.

Five days later, the Tar Heels trounced No. 12 Virginia (103–74) for their 17th straight win. Breland played 25 minutes, but she was still having difficulty breathing, and doctors were stymied as to the cause. This win gave them confidence for the January 19 game against No. 1 Connecticut, a match-up of the two top women's teams—both with 17–0 records. The game was played before 12,722 fans in the Smith Center and broadcast on ESPN2. Sylvia was thrilled with the record turnout for the Big East-ACC matchup between two teams who liked to run. She told the media, "I love to play them because they play like we do.... They get up and down the floor. They score points. They are fun to watch." Huskies coach Geno Auriemma agreed: "When two teams play an up-tempo style it's really fun to watch.... It's great for women's basketball." The anticipated close game never materialized. Instead, it turned into a rout for Connecticut, who served up the Lady Tar Heels an embarrassing 88–58 loss. UNC was outmatched everywhere: on the perimeter, on the boards, at the foul line. In the press conference, a downcast Sylvia said, "They came into our house and showed us how to play basketball. I wish we could have given them a better game." The sting of the embarrassing loss was compounded by her quiet acknowledgment to a small group in the media room that Kay Yow was near death.

On Wednesday, January 21, Sylvia took time away from her team to pay a final visit to Yow. The two said their goodbyes privately, each affirming what the other had meant as friend and coach and mentor. Tim Crothers, with the *ACC Journal*, featured Sylvia's public comments about their private time together:

> It was a very special time.... Kay was pretty weak. She could only say a few words. I held her hand and ... told her how much she meant to me and to my coaching career and how there were some tough times when I would stop and ask myself, "How would Kay handle this? What would Kay do here?" And Kay smiled and that's when tears started streaming down her face and she said, "Thank you. I love you."

The next day, UNC blew a 15-point lead in the second half to give Georgia Tech their first win over the Tar Heels on their home court (66–62) since 2000. Turnovers, poor ball handling, and 38.5 percent shooting from the floor flummoxed Sylvia. In the press room she did not hide her frustration and speculated that perhaps she needed to start five new players.

Kay Yow died two days later—Saturday, January 24, 2009, at age 66—and the day afterward, Sylvia's team traveled to No. 12 Maryland, who handed them their third straight loss (77–71). Breland sprained an ankle—again. McCants fouled out. Sylvia was called for a technical foul. Maryland played rough, and UNC paid the price—the Terrapins attempted 28 foul shots; the Tar Heels 9. Sylvia told the media, "I've been coaching 34 years and I don't know if I've ever seen a game like tonight." UNC had not lost three consecutive games in seven years. Following this loss, their ranking dropped to No. 10, the biggest one-week drop from No. 2 in NCAA history.

Yow's memorial service was held on January 30 at Colonial Baptist Church in Cary, North Carolina. More than 1,400 mourners attended, including Geno Auriemma, Pat Summitt, Vivian Stringer, Gail Goestenkors, Joanne McCallie, Sylvia Hatchell, and Debbie Antonelli, one of Yow's former players who had become a successful TV sports analyst. Though dozens could have delivered eulogies, no one spoke except two ministers and Kay Yow. She had planned the service, and she herself delivered a 25-minute message that she video-recorded in 2004 when the cancer recurred. She told the crowd not to question or "fret" over her passing because "God knows what he's doing. He doesn't make mistakes." She emphasized her strong faith, ending with "And now I say farewell.... [I]t's been a wonderful journey, especially since the time I accepted Jesus as my lord and savior." Pat Summitt said, "I have never known of a service like this. And it would be just like Kay to be the absolute first."[2]

Following the loss to Georgia Tech, Sylvia had implemented a new training regimen: running and practice at 6:00 a.m. The players hated it but seemed to benefit. UNC won the next three games against Wake Forest, North Carolina Central, and Virginia Tech. Before the Wake Forest win, Jessica Breland said she was "ready to win" because she didn't like 6:00 a.m. practices. Against Wake Forest, Breland earned a double-double in her 32 minutes on the court, but Alex Miller was out for the season—and for the rest of her college career. Her knee injury would not heal, despite surgery and extensive rehabilitation. When UNC defeated Virginia Tech (93–77) on February 5, their ranking rose to No. 9. Indeed, the Lady Tar Heels seemed ready to win—to have gained a new appreciation for work and commitment and focus. But Sylvia continued to puzzle over Breland. She felt that Jessica "had greatness in her" but was not "willing to commit." She frequently had to take her out of games because she was lagging on the court, and the various diagnoses for her lack of stamina were piling up: allergies, pneumonia, asthma, bronchitis, flu.

On February 9, the Tar Heels went up against their old Triangle foe No. 4 Duke in the Smith Center. In the past 11 matchups against Duke, UNC had won 9, and attendance was high for the popular showdown—7,080—which was broadcast on ESPN2. As usual, UNC started slowly. Aaron Beard wrote that the Tar Heels "looked as bad as [they] possibly could," but Sylvia's resolute players came through.[3] McCants was credited with sparking the comeback that gave the Tar Heels the 75–60 win, and their prospects looked good as they neared the end of the regular season, but consistency and momentum still escaped them. Sylvia was baffled, especially when they suffered an embarrassing loss to No. 14 Florida State (77–70) and dropped to 6–3 in the

ACC. Then they miraculously won the next four games with an average margin of 20 points, including a February 23 win over NC State (74–57) when McCants scored her 1,500th career point.

On February 26—Senior Night—UNC took on Miami for an easy win (90–76), and Jessica Breland earned her 1,000th career point. The Tar Heels were 25–4 overall and 10–3 in the ACC, but their last regular-season game was against Duke—in Cameron. Duke was 24–4 overall, so the teams were evenly matched. Since the February 9 meeting of the two Triangle foes, the Blue Devils had slipped from No. 4 to No. 10; UNC was No. 9. The buzz and excitement of the old rivalry had waned after UNC's four-year losing streak to Duke ended. The tents disappeared, but the Cameron Crazies and large crowds still fueled the competition. Sylvia told the media, "We love playing over at Cameron, great environment.... The students are funny and I really think that relaxes us. We've actually played pretty well over there." On March 1, the Lady Tar Heels did not play well before the capacity crowd that witnessed the Tar Heels' overtime loss 81–79. Sylvia said her team would use the game as "motivation," which they certainly needed. Their national ranking dropped to No. 11, but they were seeded No. 4 in the ACC Tournament and still considered a contender for the title. They had played in every ACC Championship game since 2002, and they hoped to take home the title for a fifth straight year.

In the quarterfinal game against Clemson on March 6, attendance in the Greensboro Coliseum reached a new ACC Women's Tournament high—13,599. As usual, UNC was slow out of the gate but gained momentum throughout the game and earned a season-high rebounding advantage—59 to Clemson's 33—for the 74–55 win. Sylvia was encouraged as they went into the semifinal game against No. 4 Maryland, the top Tournament seed who had beaten UNC on January 25. The Terrapin-Tar Heel rivalry was not as intense as the Blue Devil-Tar Heel rivalry, but it came close. UNC desperately wanted and needed a win. Again, the Tar Heels began slowly, falling behind 44–38 in the first half, and though they eventually took a two-point lead, the effort was not enough. The Lady Tar Heels would not compete for the ACC Championship—Maryland went on to win the 2009 title.

Disappointment hung like a black cloud over the team, but Sylvia still thought her Tar Heels could succeed, and she was trying something new that year. Sylvia says that some coaches don't like change: "I am not like that. I like change, but it's got to be change for a purpose, a reason." Her reason was the dormant two-week stretch between the end of the ACC Tournament and the first round of the NCAA Tournament—long enough to get rusty. Hoping to keep her team sharp, Sylvia scheduled an interim game. She told Andy Gardiner, with *USA Today*, that during the regular season, teams "don't take two weeks off.... I can guarantee you, if it works for us, everybody will be doing it next year." (Only one other team in the country was trying out the same strategy—Saint Mary's men's team.) So, on March 15, UNC played unranked Division II South Dakota. In 2008, the Coyotes nearly won the Division II national championship, getting knocked out in the title game. In 2009, they came to Chapel Hill to win—and nearly did. The Coyotes led 41–32 at halftime and stretched the lead to 15 points in the second half. UNC eventually got the 75–69 win, but the game should not have been that close and did not bode well for the upcoming NCAA

Tournament. Breland admitted that the team had been "sagging off" and had to step up its defense. Sylvia put a good spin on the outcome: "This was exactly what we needed."[4] Privately, she and the team were concerned. Another worry was Breland's night sweats and chest pains and ongoing sore throats.

The next day, March 16, the NCAA brackets were announced. Brackets had been Sylvia's bugaboo for years, but in 2009 she did not complain, and neither did other coaches. Doug Feinberg reported that "the field went back to 16 first and second round sites for the first time since 2004." Jacki Silar, chair of the Women's Basketball Committee, said it was business as usual,[5] but the Committee appeared to have heard the coaches screaming about brackets. Having won the ACC Tournament, Maryland was the No. 1 seed in the Raleigh Regional; Duke the No. 1 seed in the Berkeley Regional; Connecticut the No. 1 seed in the Trenton Regional. For the first time in four years, UNC was not a No. 1 seed but took the No. 3 spot in the Oklahoma City Regional behind No. 1 Oklahoma and would play rounds one and two in Chattanooga, Tennessee.

On March 21, No. 14 seed Central Florida nearly ended the Lady Tar Heels' season in the first round. UNC led for most of the game, but Teresa Walker said they "nearly squandered a 14-point lead in the final 30 seconds." Like the game against South Dakota, this one did not indicate that UNC had the steam to make it to the Final Four. Still touting the success of her experiment with the interim game against South Dakota, Sylvia speculated that they might have lost to Central Florida had they not played the Coyotes.[6] With a first-round win in her pocket, Sylvia faced the No. 6 seed Purdue, who had knocked off UNC Charlotte in the first round. Since 1994, the Tar Heels and Boilermakers had met four times in the NCAA Tournament, and UNC had the edge, three wins to one. UNC went into this game as the top scoring team in the country with an average of 83.1 points per game, but they struggled against the Boilermakers—hitting 29 of 79 shots. Fouls were not in their favor—Purdue hit 24 of 27 free throws; UNC 9 of 11. The game was intense and physical—tied 30 all at halftime. The score seesawed. Purdue was playing with five seniors. UNC was playing with four seniors who did not have the experience of Purdue's three, fifth-year players. Walker reported that Rashanda McCants "had written a reminder to herself on her shoe that it could be her last game."[7] It was. She scored a mere six points, a miserable end to her college basketball career. UNC lost the game 85–70. For the first time in five years, Sylvia would not advance to the Sweet 16.

Both UNC and UNC Charlotte had lost to Purdue in the NCAA Tournament, prompting Sylvia to tell her long-time friend Judy Rose, the UNC Charlotte athletic director, "I'll tell you what—this losing just stinks." The Tar Heels slid to No. 17 and ended the season with their worst record since 2004–27–7 overall; 10–4 in the ACC. What had gone wrong? Sylvia knew the team had talent, but injuries, slow starts, turnovers, and poor performance at the foul line had been problems all season. The team's best player, Jessica Breland, had played in all 35 games and started 27. Except for point guard Cetera DeGraffenreid, Breland spent more time on the court than any other player. She scored 493 points and had 298 rebounds, the highest for the team. Despite Breland's success on the court, Sylvia labeled her effort as merely "decent." She expected more than Breland gave—she had tried "to make her a great player" but failed. "Breland couldn't stay on the court more than a few minutes," says Sylvia. "She couldn't run up and down the court. She couldn't breathe. She was fatigued all the time. I just thought that she wasn't making a commitment, wasn't getting her rest and eating right." In the final meetings of the year, Sylvia "ripped" into her: "I said, 'Jessica, you could be so good, but you have got to make a commitment. You're not in shape. If you were in shape and could run up and down the floor, we could keep you in the game longer. Your numbers would be unbelievable. You would be an All-American. But you're not making a commitment.'" The season ended on this frustrating note for player and coach.

Two Lady Tar Heels—Cetera DeGraffenreid and Jessica Breland—were among 29 players invited to the U.S. Olympic Training Center in Colorado Springs to try out for 12 spots on the USA women's team for the World University Games. Just before the players were scheduled to leave, Breland came to Sylvia and said, "Coach I can't breathe. I can't go to these tryouts. I can't do it." Sylvia describes Breland as "a real homebody. She loved Chapel Hill and had lots of friends—maybe too many. I just thought she didn't want to go!" A frustrated Sylvia sent her to the student health clinic, even though she had been there "a zillion times that year and they had treated her for everything under the sun." The student clinic staff "checked her out and sent her back" with no diagnosis.

The following day, Breland came to Sylvia's office again, this time in tears, and said, "Coach Hatchell, I *cannot* breathe." Exasperated, Sylvia made one last attempt to help her struggling player: She called Dr. Harold Pillsbury, with UNC Otolaryngology, who had previously treated Breland for pneumonia. Dr. Pillsbury examined her that night and sent her for additional tests the next day. After a season of complaints, doctors' appointments, and wrong diagnoses, Breland had a definitive diagnosis within 24 hours: Hodgkin's lymphoma. On May 9, 2009, while Sylvia was delivering the commencement address and being awarded an honorary Doctor of Humanities degree during the Francis Marion graduation ceremony, Dr. Pillsbury was delivering the dreadful news to her team. "I wasn't there!" says Sylvia. Breland's teammates were devastated, and Sylvia was stunned: She thought, *cancer*? "I've gone through everything with players, from drugs to depression to death and bad influences, but never cancer." She deeply regretted her attitude toward Breland's 2009 performance and her suspicion that Breland wasn't making a commitment: "But I just wanted her to succeed."

During this time, emotions ran high. Sylvia had lost Kay Yow barely three months earlier, and now she and her team were processing the news that Breland had cancer. Accepting the honorary doctorate at Francis Marion seemed incongruous—perhaps more emotional that it would have been otherwise. In her commencement speech, Sylvia expressed her deep gratitude: "I wouldn't be where I am now if it weren't for all those folks. [Francis Marion] was a great place to start out." She "had tears in her eyes ... as she marched in for the school's graduation ceremony, her team's championship banners fluttering above. 'They were my foundation,' Hatchell said humbly."[8] Right away, Breland started chemotherapy, which continued through November. "I tell you, it was rough," says Sylvia. The team was unprepared to face what was to come. She characterized the players' initial response as somewhat cavalier: "'OK, put a Band-Aid on it—fix it. Let's move on.' But it just doesn't happen like that." On Thursday mornings, Breland took chemotherapy, and by Friday she began to suffer the effects. She was still living in the dorm, trying to stay in school so she would have health insurance. Breland's stepfather was there for every treatment, and Dr. Jan Boxill, academic counselor for the women's basketball team, was with her much of the time. The players tried to help. They brought her food, most of which she couldn't keep down. She lost her sense of taste and had no appetite. Her hands changed color. She began to lose her hair. With the assistance of tutors and a reduced academic load, Jessica made it through the semester. According to Sylvia, Boxill often sat by Jessica's bed and typed assignments as she dictated: "Everyone wanted to be there for her. We felt responsible for her and were trying to take care of her, and we couldn't escape it. We were depressed and scared. After all, she was one of the team, one of us! We knew that any one of us could have been in her shoes. But we made it through."

12

Holding the Rope

In the fall of 2009, Van began his junior year at UNC, hanging on to his dream of playing for Roy Williams. Having used up his JV eligibility, he let the coaches know he aspired to a varsity walk-on spot and went to the men's JV practices with all the other varsity hopefuls. When he didn't make the cut, he was devastated. Sylvia was matter of fact: "Van, you weren't good enough. You're not going to make that team just because you're my son. You're going to have to work hard and earn it." Around Christmas he confided to Sylvia that he wanted one last shot at the UNC men's varsity team: "Mama, I want to make a commitment and work at it." He started running every day, and Sylvia hired a personal trainer with whom he lifted weights at least three days a week. He also worked on shooting and ball handling. Van was dedicated: "It wasn't going to be said that I was cut the next year because I didn't try hard enough. It was the most determined thing I ever did in my life." Sylvia needed that same level of determination and hard work from her Tar Heels. She was trying to "walk the walk," to practice her coaching principles and philosophy. Despite her previous teams' inability to advance beyond the NCAA early rounds, she believed in her primary purpose: to coax quality performance out of players who had potential and talent, to help them become their best selves. But she needed an equal commitment from her team, a team that faced serious obstacles.

Jessica Breland had talent, but her potential was momentarily staunched. Preseason 2009 "watch lists" included her as a candidate for the Wade Trophy and the Wooden Award. She should have been a returning senior and a team leader. Instead, she had a medical redshirt for the season while she recovered from treatments for Hodgkin Lymphoma. Her absence meant that returning starters Cetera DeGraffenreid and Italee Lucas would have to take leadership roles. Sophomores She'la White and Chay Shegog had played in all 35 games, making strong contributions from the bench. Finally, the team had six freshmen, dubbed the second-best recruiting class in the nation, including Waltiea Rolle, from Nassau, Bahamas, who attended Westbury Christian School in Houston, Texas. When Sylvia and Charlotte Smith went to Texas to scout her talent, Charlotte said, "Oooh, wow! She's green." Sylvia countered: "She is 6'6", has long arms, and can run the floor. This kid has major potential. She's green right now, but if she wants to learn, she can be really good." Another freshman, Tierra Ruffin-Pratt, was named preseason ACC Rookie of the Year and showed considerable promise.

The Lady Tar Heels began strong, ranked No. 4 and selected to finish first in the

ACC. Between November 13 and January 6, they won 13 games and lost only one to No. 22 Michigan State in the ACC/Big Ten Challenge. After this loss, their ranking dropped to No. 11, but a win over unranked South Carolina (93–85) kicked it back up to No. 7. This was Sylvia's first game against Coach Dawn Staley who took the job Sylvia had considered in 2008. This was also the last game before Christmas, so the whole Hatchell-Rhyne clan headed for the Black Mountain cabin to enjoy the holidays. They had barely settled in when a monster Nor'easter hit the entire east coast, dumping 24" of snow and a coating of ice on western North Carolina. Sylvia's family was safe in the cabin, but as the ice broke trees and limbs, the sound echoed like gunshot through the woods. The cabin lost electricity, and they were marooned with no power and no water. They could run the generator for short periods only and had to melt snow in the gas fireplace to flush toilets. The world seemed out of kilter, a feeling that would persist into spring basketball season.

After Christmas, the Lady Tar Heels got a boost. They had played 26 home games in the Smith Center while Carmichael Auditorium was being renovated, and they were ecstatic when they saw the result. Italee Lucas said she was "speechless" when the team first toured the building: "It's just amazing!" Their first game in the updated arena was on December 29 against Kennesaw State whom they handily defeated 89–44. On January 6, 2010, the Lady Tar Heels beat No. 20 Georgia Tech, but for the rest of the season, they won only six games. They were embarrassed nationally when CBS broadcast their 88–47 loss to No. 1 Connecticut on the Huskies' home court. They suffered another nationally-televised humiliation when they lost to No. 8 Duke 79–51. The next day, their ranking slipped to No. 20 in the Coaches' Poll; thereafter, they dropped out of the top 25. In their second faceoff against Duke on February 28, they fought hard for a 64–54 victory, but it was rough. Rolle and Chay Shegog fouled out, and freshman Cierra Robertson-Warren was ejected for hitting a Duke player. Sylvia was nevertheless happy with the win, which gave her Tar Heels confidence going into the ACC Tournament. She also hoped the win would boost their slim chances for an NCAA slot.

The Tar Heels were the No. 8 seed in the ACC Tournament—a long way from their predicted No. 1 spot, which went to Duke. In the first-round game against Maryland, UNC trailed for the whole game. Though they clawed their way back to a two-point deficit with seconds left, they could not overcome the Terrapins. The 83–77 loss marked the first time in 13 years that the Lady Tar Heels were knocked out in the first round of the ACC Tournament. Duke won the championship, and Joanne McCallie was named ACC Coach of the Year. Fate appeared to be rubbing salt in Sylvia's wounds.

For a second time in UNC women's basketball history, Sylvia scheduled a game between ACC and NCAA Tournaments. On March 14, the Tar Heels defeated North Carolina Central 88–66, a score that did not match their usual margins of victory against this Triangle team. UNC was undoubtedly a bubble team, and Sylvia admitted to lobbying the NCAA for an at-large bid. She succeeded. Despite having lost eight of their last ten games, the Tar Heels were named the No. 10 seed in the Sacramento Regionals—their lowest NCAA Tournament seed since 1991. On March 20, they traveled to Seattle, Washington, to face No. 7 Gonzaga in the first round.

Sylvia on sideline in Carmichael, UNC vs. Duke, February 28, 2010. Left to right: Tracey Williams-Johnson, Charlotte Smith, Greg Law, Sylvia Hatchell, Nyree Williams, Chay Shegog, and Martina Wood. Courtesy Sheila Oliver.

The teams seemed evenly matched, but the Zags were in charge from the tipoff and were motivated by an old grudge. Two Gonzaga seniors were freshmen in 2006 when UNC humiliated them with a 101–63 rout. This time, the Zags got the "signature win," according to Gonzaga Coach Kelly Graves, who described UNC as "the standard by which a lot of college basketball programs are judged. This is a great day for our institution."[1] The loss to Gonzaga was anything but a "great" day for UNC who finished the season 19–12 overall, 6–8 in the ACC, and unranked.

Like Sylvia's team, her son Van was still chasing a goal. When school started in the fall of 2010, Van "was possessed," says Sylvia. "All he could think about was making the UNC men's varsity team in his senior year." After practicing with the JV team and other hopeful walk-ons, he was finally invited "up" to try out with the varsity. Van was "pumped" but anxious because this was "going up to another level in college basketball," he says. "It's a lot faster. The players are big and strong. I was really nervous." He practiced for four days with the varsity team and felt he had done well, but when Coach Williams identified five picks who would join the varsity team, Van was not included. The next week was fall break, and as Sylvia headed out for the cabin, she felt powerless. Her son was devastated, but there was little she could do or say other than, "Life is full of disappointments. You have to move on."

After fall break, Van received a text message asking him to meet with Roy Williams following varsity practice on a Thursday. He assumed that the meeting was a courtesy to his mother. Instead, Williams explained that after he cut Van, he reconsidered because Van was a good shooter, and they needed another shooter on the practice squad. He asked Van to consider the offer and give him an answer by the end of the next day. Van's answer was never in question—a resounding "Yes!" Sylvia told Van, "You need to learn some lessons from this. You need to bust your behind—be the first one there and the last one to leave. Show them how bad you want to be on that team." That afternoon Van practiced with the UNC men's varsity basketball team as a *bona fide* member. When Van appeared for practice, Coach C.B. McGrath asked him, "How does it feel to be back from the dead?" Van, indeed, felt raised from the dead—and his basketball jersey was No. 13.

Jessica Breland also felt raised from the dead, though she struggled with the residual complications from chemotherapy. She had been cleared to return to practice in late February 2010, but "it was not like flipping the light on and saying, 'I'm back!'" says Sylvia. "It was a gradual process." Though Breland worked one-on-one with Charlotte Smith, picking up her basketball skills where she left them in May of 2009 was a slow process. Through it all, Sylvia continued to support Jessica and the fight against cancer. On Saturday, November 6, 2010, Sylvia, her players, and staff hosted the Rebounds and Rhinestones fundraiser to launch the Jessica Breland Comeback Kids Fund for pediatric oncology at the Lineberger Comprehensive Cancer Center. Sylvia gave a formal welcome and introduced the keynote speaker, Robin Roberts, host of ABC's *Good Morning America*. Herself a breast cancer survivor, Roberts emphasized overcoming adversity: "Make your Mess your Message." In addition to this fundraiser, Hatchell donated $50,000 to the Pediatric Oncology Endowment Fund to sponsor one of two oncology classrooms in the UNC Hospital School, which was created so that children under treatment for cancer will not fall behind academically.

As the 2010 season was gearing up, Marion Jones reentered Sylvia's world after a long absence. Jones accepted an invitation to speak at the 30th anniversary of the UNC Black Alumni Reunion on October 28, 2010. Her appearance launched a book tour to promote *On the Right Track*. The book tells the story of Jones's Olympic success, which was negated by her confession to lying and doping and her prison stint. Marion's agent called the Women's Basketball Office to say that Marion wanted to visit Sylvia while she was on the UNC campus. The two had not seen each other since the 10th anniversary celebration of the 1994 national championship, and their relationship had been strained since 1995, but Sylvia did not hesitate. She told the players and coaches, "Marion Jones is coming to speak at UNC. We're going to go hear Marion. We're going to sit on the front row, and we're going to support her." Sylvia asked Marion to talk with the team before their 3:00 p.m. practice, and Marion consented.

Though they had not had a real conversation in more than a decade, coach and player still respected each other. "There was not going to be any finger-pointing," says Sylvia. "There would not be any 'I told you so' comments or anything like that." Around midday on October 28, Marion appeared in a big, black SUV outside Carmichael. Sylvia slipped out a side door for a private, emotional reunion: "Marion got out of the car, and she wrapped her arms around me and hugged me, and she said, 'I am so sorry. I am so sorry.' She held on to me for like two minutes, crying—just sobbing." They walked to the Carolina Club for a quiet lunch, then back to Carmichael for a tour of the renovated arena and a press conference, after which Marion spoke privately to the team about what it means to wear the Carolina blue—both opportunities and responsibilities. That evening, in the George Watts Hill Alumni Center, Marion told a compelling tale of success and humiliation and recovery. Steve Wiseman wrote that Sylvia led the standing ovation when Jones entered the room. He added, "The trip back to Chapel Hill wasn't easy, as Jones broke down a few minutes into her speech."[2] A book signing followed, and Jones gave each player and coach a signed copy of *On the Right Track.*

Sylvia hoped that the time with Marion would inspire her team and motivate them to forget their 2009–2010 season. DeGraffenreid said she wanted to put it out of her mind: "I don't think I've ever had a season like that ever." Sylvia argued, "We're better than what people think we're going to be." Tierra Ruffin-Pratt said, "It's a fresh start." True, it was a fresh start, but a black cloud still hovered in blue heaven. Two of the 2009–2010 top-ranked freshman class had transferred—Cierra Robertson-Warren and Nyree Williams. Waltiea Rolle, now a sophomore, had started 15 games and played in all 30, but she was still inexperienced. Sylvia had three returning seniors who had scored over 1,000 career points: Cetera DeGraffenreid, Italee Lucas, and Jessica Breland, who was struggling to regain muscle memory, footwork, and lung capacity.

When the 2010–2011 season opened, the Lady Tar Heels were back among the nationally ranked teams at No. 14. In November and December, they won 14 straight games, including a 79–67 victory over No. 18 Iowa in the ACC/Big 10 Challenge, but their ACC opener against Georgia Tech was a disappointing one-point loss (71–70) that caused the media to question the strength of UNC's nonconference schedule. Edward Robinson wrote, "It's a schedule that has drawn sharp criticism from many observers of women's college basketball." ESPN analyst Debbie Antonelli agreed with him: "I don't see any pressure teams on there that prepared them for Georgia Tech." Antonelli speculated that the Tar Heels' "soft" schedule had also not prepared them to face No. 2 Connecticut in Carmichael on January 17.[3] For whatever reason, the Huskies delivered the Tar Heels another nationally-televised, humiliating blowout—83–57. Following this loss, Sylvia's team racked up six wins, including a close victory over Duke in Carmichael (62–60), and five losses. Among the losses was a lopsided thrashing by No. 15 Maryland and a bitter wounding at the hands of No. 9 Duke. On February 28, Sylvia's 59th birthday, her Tar Heels' ranking—which had been as high as No. 8—dropped to No. 19 in the AP Poll. The loss to Duke was a blow, and no one expected the Tar Heels to advance in the ACC Tournament. They had lost four consecutive games, and their sixth-place conference finish did not merit a bye.

As Sylvia prepared her team for the ACC Tournament, she dug deep into her "tournament box" for a good motivational tool. Then, out of the blue, one appeared— from Brenda Paul, women's basketball coach at Young Harris. In 1983, Paul had been the coach at Berry College—the coach whom Sylvia took out on the town the night before the two competed for a chance at the NAIA National Tournament. Paul never forgot Sylvia's collegiality, and the two had remained friends. In 2011, Paul sent "Hold the Rope" to Sylvia and other coaching friends whose teams were entering conference play. She had borrowed the concept from Clemson Coach Jim Davis—the same Jim

Davis who refused to shake Sylvia's hand in 2003. It had made the rounds for years in coaching circles, but it was new to Sylvia, and it appealed to her Christian faith. "Hold the Rope" is attributed to 18th-century British missionaries William Carey and Andrew Fuller, who told their Baptist colleagues, "I will go down [to India], if you will hold the rope."[4] Applied to basketball, the concept is simple: On a winning team, players "hold the rope" for each other. Sylvia used metaphor: "Imagine that you are falling off a 200-foot cliff, and the only thing keeping you from dropping to your death is a rope. You're holding one end, and you must have a person on the other end who won't let go, no matter what. No matter how much their hands bleed, no matter how much it hurts, they are not going to let go, because if they do, they know you are going to die." Then she produced a knotted piece of rope and challenged the players to hold the rope for each other in the ACC Tournament. "If you do, you're going to be really good. If you don't, your season will die."

The Lady Tar Heels headed off to Greensboro as the No. 6 seed in the ACC Tournament, knowing they would have to win four games on four consecutive days to stay alive and believing that they could if they held the rope. They had "bought into" the concept, says Sylvia. In the first round, they knocked off unranked Clemson 78–64. The quarterfinal game against the No. 3 seed Florida State was exactly what Sylvia relished: fast, transition basketball that gave UNC a 78–65 win. The Tar Heels then faced No. 2 seed Miami in the semifinal game. Jessica Breland scored 28 points and nabbed 11 rebounds for the decisive 83–57 victory and a chance to play for the title. Everyone was surprised that UNC was in the ACC Championship game. No one was surprised that they would be matched up against their old enemy Duke—for the eighth time in Sylvia's UNC career. Cetera DeGraffenreid told the press, "We don't like them." Sophomore Krista Gross said, "It's Carolina-Duke. Even if you didn't originally hate Duke, as soon as you put on this jersey, you have to. It's just something that comes to you. After beating them at home and losing to them there, it's like we want to beat them even more now. Especially in the championship game, it would be the sweetest revenge." Despite their teamwork and holding the rope and players such as Breland who "dug deep," there was no sweet revenge for UNC. Duke won the title game 81–66.

Being the runner-up in the ACC Tournament, UNC was named the No. 5 seed in the Spokane Region of the NCAA Tournament. The team had the talent to advance: Edward Robinson wrote, "It's Breland who truly makes the Heels' frontcourt formidable." She was the main cog in the UNC offense.[5] Another factor was their height, with Rolle defending the basket at 6'6". Rolle had ended the ACC season with 78 blocked shots, which earned her All-ACC Defensive Team honors. These gifted players were holding the rope for each other and doing their homework. They watched old film featuring the teams who went to the Final Four in 2006 and 2007, a trip they wanted badly. As the NCAA Tournament neared, Sylvia noticed a change in Waltiea Rolle in practices—a subtle difference. Though she wondered, *What is going on with Waltiea?* she said nothing. Her tallest player was performing well, so she would let it ride. In the meantime, Sylvia had scheduled a game between the ACC and NCAA Tournaments for the third consecutive year, this time against Kennesaw State—a game they won decisively (98–52). She would not try this strategy again. It had been an experiment—something new—but the tactic did not seem to improve their play in the NCAA.

NCAA rounds one and two were played in The Pit in Albuquerque, New Mexico, where UNC defeated No. 12 seed Fresno State (82–68) and No. 4 seed Kentucky (86–74) for a trip to the Sweet 16 in Spokane, Washington—their first in three years. Prior to their game against top seed Stanford, Waltiea told Sylvia that they needed to talk. Sylvia said, "Sure. Come on in and we'll talk." But Waltiea changed her mind: "No, I'll wait till the season is over." The thought crossed Sylvia's mind that Waltiea wanted to transfer, but she put that thought aside and focused on Stanford. The Tar Heels had met the Cardinal only once before in the 1995 Los Angeles Sweet 16. Stanford won that game, and Sylvia never forgot it. She told the media, "I've had a lot of flashbacks the last week or so.... I have that game in my mind very well." The Tar Heels fought to the finish. Italee Lucas tied the score at 59 at the 5:15 mark and hit two free throws to tie it again at 65 with 2:56 left, but the Tar Heels went cold and lost the game 72–65, ending the season ranked No. 14. They were disappointed not to advance in the Tournament, but they had exceeded all expectations in the postseason, and the numbers—28–9 overall, 8–6 in the ACC—did not tell the whole story. The numbers did not show that they had held the rope for each other.

Jessica Breland had envisioned a different ending to her college career, especially before her battle against cancer when she was a potential No. 1 draft pick in the WNBA. In 2011, she was the 13th pick by the Minnesota Lynx. Her teammate Italee Lucas was the 21st pick by the Tulsa Shock. Waltiea Rolle had envisioned a different ending to her sophomore year as well. After the season was over, she went to Sylvia for the talk she had proposed before the Stanford game. She did not want to transfer, as Sylvia feared. She was pregnant. Some thought an abortion was the answer, but Sylvia asked Waltiea, "What do *you* want to do?" "Finally," says Sylvia, "she came in and she looked at me and she had tears in her eyes and she said, 'Coach Hatchell, I cannot take the life of this child.' I said, 'Then your decision is made, and I will support you.' I said, 'Let's do a game plan here.'" The plan was for Waltiea to sit out the fall 2011 semester, return to Nassau, have the baby, and resume play after Christmas break. Other players, such as Jessica Breland, had overcome adversity. So could Waltiea Rolle, who had stolen Sylvia's heart: "I mean, I loved Waltiea. I try not to play favorites, but I really liked the kid, and she grew up through that process. I really enjoyed having her on the team and having her around. I didn't mind doing things for her because she was a really good kid."

Jessica Breland and Waltiea Rolle embodied qualities that Sylvia wanted to instill in her players: the determination to overcome adversity and disappointment. She had tried to instill the same qualities in her son. Though his achievement paled in comparison with cancer and pregnancy, he had, nevertheless, realized his dream. During the 2010–2011 season, he played in 11 UNC men's varsity games and was named to the National Association of Basketball Coaches' 2010–2011 Honors Court, which recognizes the top student-athletes with a GPA of 3.2 or higher. But the most gratifying part was that as a senior, he got to start in the last home game against Duke. He graduated with honors from UNC on Sunday, May 8, 2011, with a BS in Business Administration. On the prior Saturday evening, the young men from Mrs. D's house and their families celebrated at the Hatchell home with Gillis' barbecue. The little boy who celebrated the 1994 national championship with a cast on his arm had grown up.

In June of 2011, Charlotte Smith decided to pursue a coaching career at Elon after nine years as Sylvia's assistant. Smith had become a much-revered assistant coach and a friend to Sylvia, so it would be hard to replace her. Sylvia likes having a former player as an assistant coach—someone who knows her brand of Carolina basketball inside and out. Ivory Latta would have made the perfect replacement, but Ivory was under contract with the WNBA Tulsa Shock and had already signed a contract to play offseason basketball overseas. Another possibility was Sammy Hatchell, who resigned his coaching job at Cresset on August 1. There would have been complications because Sylvia's husband could not report directly to her, but she cited the NC State arrangement whereby Kellie Harper's husband Jon worked as an unpaid assistant because of the state's nepotism law.

Sylvia never had to navigate the complications because she got an unexpected phone call in August from Trisha Stafford-Odom, assistant coach to Duke's Joanne McCallie. Stafford-Odom had helped McCallie sign the 2009–2010 No. 1 recruiting class in the nation. Sylvia couldn't believe that she would want to leave the Blue Devils after that degree of success. Tricia said she thought UNC might be a better fit and asked Sylvia to consider her for the job. Stafford-Odom had joined Duke on June 1, 2009, so she assisted McCallie only two seasons, and some, such as ESPN analyst Debbi Antonelli, thought the move was odd: "I think on the men's side you see it happen somewhat more often.... On the women's side, particularly these two schools, wow. It's a little surprising." Having played basketball under Kay Yow at NC State, Antonelli understood Triangle basketball better than most—"the rivalry, the bitter hatred between those two programs in basketball."[6] Sylvia dismissed these concerns and focused on what she saw as Stafford-Odom's primary strengths—recruiting and "talking the kid's language nowadays with email and Facebook and Twitter. Kids communicate differently today—Trish was good with all that stuff." Tracey Williams-Johnson was still in charge of recruiting, but Stafford-Odom would bring a different set of skills.

Though Sylvia's team did not advance beyond the Sweet 16 in 2011, she believed that she was nevertheless fulfilling her mission. Her hold-the-rope strategy had motivated players to maximize their potential, an achievement more important than winning. In the meanwhile, she saw clouds on the horizon that could portend dark days for her women's basketball program, but at this stage, she never imagined that the clouds would become an all-out tempest. In short, an academic fraud scandal had been brewing on the UNC campus for 20 years. The core infraction was fake or "paper" courses. The charge was that some faculty and academic counselors had directed athletes to register for these classes to boost GPAs and maintain athletes' eligibility, but there were additional complications that forced the firing of football coach Butch Davis on July 27, 2011. The next day, athletic director Dick Baddour announced that he would step down as soon as a new AD could be hired. On November 14, Bubba Cunningham took the reins, the third AD for whom Sylvia had worked. John Swofford and Dick Baddour had held the rope for her; she expected Cunningham to do the same.

Sylvia was gearing up for the fall semester, looking forward to another year of coaching, remembering her high-school and college days when there were few people holding the rope for young women who wanted to play sports, Pat Summitt chief among them. Soon Pat would need her friends to hold the rope for her. On August 23, 2011, she made public her diagnosis of Alzheimer's disease. As early as 2008, Sylvia had suspected that something was wrong when Pat asked her if she was "taking anything" for her memory. Sylvia thought the conversation on that occasion was "weird." In 2010, Sylvia, Judy Rose, and Susan Phillips were planning their annual graduate-school reunion, but Pat never returned their calls. Eventually, Sylvia saw Pat on a recruiting trip and asked why they had not heard from her. Pat said, "Y'all are calling the wrong number." Sylvia asked, "Have you changed your cell number?" Pat turned to her assistant, Mickie DeMoss, and echoed the question, "Have I changed my cell number?" Mickie explained that, yes, the staff had changed Pat's cell number because it was too widely known. Pat said, "Well they changed my cell number, and I didn't even know it." Sylvia was aghast—stunned. She told Judy and Susan, "Something is very wrong with Pat." Though not a total surprise, Pat's announcement was a shock. Sylvia had lost Kay Yow in 2009; just two years later, she was losing her friend of 37 years to Alzheimer's.

In September, Sylvia had to switch her focus back to her team. She and Tracey Williams-Johnson flew to Nassau to visit Waltiea Rolle. She wanted Waltiea to know that her coach was holding the rope for her, but at the preseason press conference on October 18, 2011, Sylvia did not mince words: "Waltiea won't be with us until Christmas. She is going to have a baby in November, but then she will be back." Having learned a lesson about media gossip with Nikki Teasley's leave of absence, Sylvia opted for the blunt, honest approach. She admitted that her team faced "uncertainties" and that "those young kids have just got to have some time. But ... we're going to be better than people think." At the start of the season, the Tar Heels were ranked No. 19 and were predicted to place sixth in the ACC. Miami was picked to win its first ACC Championship. At the ACC Women's Hoops Kick-Off in Greensboro, Sylvia was asked about being the ACC coach with the longest tenure. She said, "I miss my buddies.... There was a time when I was a rookie, and they all looked after me." No doubt, she was also thinking of her SEC buddy Pat Summitt.

From the get-go, UNC was beset by injuries in 2011–2012. Sylvia told the press, "I've never had injuries like we've had this year.... It just seems like as soon as we get one or two back out there, something else happens." Edward Robinson catalogued the list: Sophomore Latifah Coleman and freshman Megan Buckland were out for the season with surgery for torn ACLs. Freshman Whitney Adams injured her shoulder in preseason practice and missed three games. Senior She'la White missed two games with a sprained ankle. Senior Laura Broomfield suffered a "stress reaction" in her foot and an eye injury. Junior Tierra Ruffin-Pratt, a key starter, missed 13 games from shoulder surgery.[7] Senior Waltiea Rolle gave birth to a baby girl, Carlisa, on November 8. Rolle returned to play after Christmas, but—like Breland's return in 2010—the comeback was slow. When Sylvia first saw her on the court, she thought, *Oh, dear God! Waltiea is not moving like she had been*. Sylvia heard a TV analyst say, "Boy, what a maternity leave. Having a baby and coming back to play basketball in a month is not exactly a maternity leave." Rolle had to lose 20 pounds and get back in shape. She told the press that leaving her daughter Carlisa to come back to the basketball court "was tough. I miss her, but I need to finish what I started [with basketball]."

The effect of Tar Heels' injuries was apparent when they lost by 19 points to No. 16 Penn State on November 30 in the ACC/Big Ten Challenge. Unranked South Carolina embarrassed them 78–49 on December 18 in the Myrtle Beach Crescent Bank Holiday Invitational, Dawn Staley's first victory over Sylvia. Pete Iacobelli dubbed the game a "street fight." Sylvia concurred: "[Their] nickname around the country is 'street fighters.' And that's the way they play." Sylvia said, "One time I had four freshmen out there. They're not ready for anything like this."[8] After this loss, the Tar Heels won five straight games, including a double overtime win at Virginia (78–73), which gave Sylvia her 600th UNC victory. Former UNC athletic director Dick Baddour handed out white T-shirts with "600 Wins @ Carolina" lettered across the front, but the celebration was subdued, and the Tar Heels' winning streak ended on January 16 in Storrs, Connecticut. The No. 3 Huskies dished up a bitter loss on national television for the fifth consecutive year—their worst loss ever (86–35). UNC has not played Connecticut since.

After the humiliating 51-point loss, team chemistry deteriorated, and Sylvia wondered whether social media was the gremlin. She'la White posted unfortunate comments saying she did not want to deal with some of her teammates—she wished the season were over. White was a senior and should have been a leader, but Sylvia had to reprimand her. The damage was irreversible. Still hanging on at No. 23, UNC enjoyed another five-game winning streak that was snapped on February 6, when No. 5 Duke beat them by 40 points in Cameron—televised on ESPN before a crowd of 8,595. The fans had turned out for the game, but it was lackluster. The media yearned for the days when the rivalry was hot and fueled the drama on and off the court. ESPN announcer Beth Mowins said the former "marquee matchup" had recently "taken a bit of a dip." Sylvia reminded the press that the rivalry still meant a great deal to the teams.[9]

For the rest of the season, UNC would win only three games. Their second loss to Duke on February 26 was a three-point heartbreaker. Two days later, on February 28, 2012, Sylvia turned 60, and various neighbors and friends helped her celebrate. She had five birthday parties, but her best present, albeit belated, came the next day: a 90–51 win over Clemson in the first round of the ACC Tournament. This win was erased by a loss to No. 15 Georgia Tech in the quarterfinal game (54–53). UNC finished the season 20–11 overall and 9–7 in the ACC—in fifth place. For the first time in a decade, Sylvia's Tar Heels did not get a bid to the NCAA Tournament. During spring break, Waltiea Rolle went back to Nassau to see her daughter for the first time since December. Sylvia had weathered a tough year: Rolle's pregnancy; unprecedented injuries; players' comments on social media. Her team did not advance in the ACC, much less get a bid to the NCAA. Topping everything else was Pat Summitt's failing health. On April 19, 2012, Summitt handed the reins over to Holly Warlick, her former All-American player and assistant coach for 27 years.

Having little to celebrate in her own right, Sylvia enjoyed the success of her husband. In January of 2012, Sammy had joined Shaw University in Raleigh as Associate Head Coach for Women's Basketball. Sammy describes the 2011–2012 Shaw women's basketball season as a "storybook year." On March 23, his Shaw Bears defeated Ashland 88–82 in San Antonio, Texas, to win the NCAA Division II national championship. Van called Sammy that night to congratulate him: "Now Mama is not the only Hatchell in the family with a national championship ring."

Then the Lady Tar Heels' future got brighter. On Saturday, May 4, 2012, UNC women's basketball celebrated its best recruiting day in the history of the program when four top-tier, high-school players verbally committed to UNC. Diamond Deshields, Allisha Gray, Stephanie Mavunga, and Jessica Washington had played USA basketball together, and when they realized that the University of North Carolina was among their individual top five schools, they made a pact to come to UNC. Sylvia gave credit to her new assistant coach for this windfall and felt that Stafford-Odom used social media to good advantage, keeping up with Facebook posts and Tweets from current and potential players, such as DeShields. It was what Stafford-Odom had been hired to do. Unfortunately, these top recruits would not join the Tar Heels until fall 2013.

In May of 2012, academic fraud was again front-page news when UNC released an internal report that Chancellor Holden Thorp could not ignore, and the scandal spread like wind-driven fire when the *Washington Post* published an exposé.[10] Between 1993 and 2011, approximately 3,100 UNC students had enrolled in fake courses in the Department of African and Afro-American Studies. Thorp resigned amid an unrelated controversy, and news of yet another investigation—called for by the UNC Board of Governors and led by former North Carolina Governor Jim Martin—kindled the blaze. Watching all this unfold, the beloved and respected W.C. Friday—who championed academic excellence and athletic integrity—told the *Post*, "The University of North Carolina has suffered a humiliation unlike anything it ever had before."[11] Six days later, he died at the age of 92. Sylvia remembered him from her childhood when as a young man he dropped by the Rhynes' home in Dallas on Sunday afternoons. She, too, was appalled but never imagined that she and her Lady Tar Heels would be tainted by the humiliation.

While the scandal eroded the integrity of "the Carolina way," the Lady Tar Heels opened the 2012–2013 season unranked—a low that matched the dreadful 2000–2001 season. The team was inexperienced and young. Sylvia had only three seniors—Krista Gross, Waltiea Rolle, and Tierra Ruffin-Pratt—and no juniors. Four other sophomores had seen limited playing time, and the team was overloaded with six freshmen, including Xylina McDaniel. Standing at 6'2", she was rated the No. 6 forward and the No. 25 overall player by ESPN HoopGurlz.

The first test was the Preseason WNIT. The Lady Tar Heels defeated Davidson, Duquesne, No. 25 Georgetown, and Iowa to win the Tournament and claim the No. 25 spot. Ruffin-Pratt was named Tournament MVP and freshman Xylina McDaniel was named to the All-Tournament team. Their winning streak continued with a 57–54 victory over No. 15 Ohio State in the ACC/Big Ten Challenge. On December 2, the Lady Tar Heels traveled to Knoxville to face the No. 16 Lady Vols for the first time since Pat Summitt's retirement. Warlick's Lady Vols gave them a good old-fashioned whipping, forcing 30 turnovers on The Summitt in Thompson-Bowling Arena for a 102–57 win, another nationally-televised humiliation.

The Tar Heels regained their equilibrium and racked up 11 straight wins, including a 60–57 victory over No. 8 Maryland, who returned the favor on January 24 with an 85–59 drubbing. By February 2, 2013, Sylvia's record was 899 wins, 316 losses. Her 500th, 600th, 700th, and 800th career wins had been against NC State. She could perhaps get her 900th win in Carmichael on February 3 against her other Triangle foe, Duke. Sylvia said, "Never mind getting my 900th win! I just wanted to beat Duke!" It was not to be. Duke came into Carmichael and robbed Sylvia of her moment with another whipping—84–63.

Four days later, The Lady Tar Heels traveled to Boston College, which was unranked. When Sylvia walked onto the Eagles' court during pre-game warm ups, she was surprised to see her husband and son sitting in the stands. Expecting the Tar Heels to give Sylvia her 900th win, Beth Miller, UNC Associate Director of Athletics, had flown Sammy and Van to Boston for the game. As expected, Sylvia's team gave her the 80–52 win—another milestone. Krista Gross told the press that it was "a great honor" to "learn from such a great coach." Sylvia's 900th win put her ahead of all other active coaches. Two retired coaches had reached the milestone: Jody Conradt and Pat Summitt, who stood at 1,095. UNC assistant coaches proudly handed around "900 Wins" caps. Even the Boston College athletic department was prepared for the victory. Coach Erik Johnson and his staff brought out a cake and flowers. Sylvia thought the gesture was especially poignant: "Though we had just beaten the Boston College team, their contribution to our celebration speaks volumes about the tight-knit fraternity of coaches in our profession. We always want to beat each other on the court, but when the game is over, we are colleagues who work together to improve the game of women's basketball—even to the point of providing cake and flowers to applaud a rival for her milestone." Pat Summitt released a statement calling Sylvia "one of the great ambassadors of the women's game." Jimmy Golen observed that Andrew Calder "leaned over to give Hatchell a peck on the cheek," a rare demonstration of affection from her usually reserved assistant of 27 years. The milestone was celebrated again in Carmichael when the Lady Tar Heels beat Wake Forest 76–56 on Valentine's day; then Sylvia moved on. She was fixated on her team's erratic performance. She told the press, "They get a lead, they relax. That's what I don't like. Get me one of those cow-pokers, [and] if [freshman Xylina McDaniel is] not hustling down the floor, I can utilize it. I can give her a little electric shock or something." Lauren Brownlow said Sylvia grinned when she made the comment, but she was scarcely joking. She wanted her players to achieve their potential—and her seniors had only four regular-season games left.

A week after her 900th win, Sylvia finished a workout with her personal trainer and went to the grocery store to pick up a salad, which she intended to eat at her desk. While she was sitting in the Harris Teeter parking lot, her phone rang. She did not recognize the number, but "something" told her to answer it. It was John Doleva on the line—President and CEO of the Naismith Memorial Basketball Hall of Fame. She heard him say, "It is my pleasure to inform you that you have been nominated for enshrinement in the Naismith Memorial Basketball Hall of Fame." Though she had dreamed of that moment, when it actually happened, she was numb: "I couldn't move. I hope I had the good manners to say 'Thank you' to John, but after the call I just sat there. For several minutes, I didn't trust myself to drive and considered calling Jane High to drive me back to campus." The Women's Basketball Committee had nominated Sylvia Hatchell and Dawn Staley. Ten men were nominated. When her nomination was announced, she was caught up in a media whirl with the spotlight on her previous achievements: She had won eight ACC Championships and taken the Tar Heels to three Final Fours. She was named ACC Coach of the Year three times and National Coach of the Year three times. Remarkably, she was the only coach to have won national championships in three different associations (AIAW, NAIA, and NCAA). The nomination was but the first step. Then the wait began—the wait to see whether she would be voted in. Sylvia was a first-time nominee and needed 18 of 24 Naismith Honors Committee votes to be inducted—but she had to focus on basketball, not votes.

Their last regular game of the season was against Duke, but the day before, Sylvia and her staff flew to Atlanta to watch Diamond DeShields lead her Norcross team to a 62–16 win in the Georgia State 6-A High-School Tournament semifinal game. Sylvia said DeShields reminded her of Michael Jordan. DeShields—who had just won the Naismith Award for the nation's top high-school senior—said, "I already feel part of the North Carolina Family." The next day, when the Tar Heels faced the No. 5 Blue Devils in Cameron, they did everything right—defense, rebounding, guarding the perimeter, forcing turnovers—except shooting. They shot 29.7 percent from the floor. Waltiea Rolle fouled out with 5:30 left. Without her, the Blue Devils finished off the Tar Heels 65–58.

The loss to Duke—combined with Sylvia's 900 wins and Naismith nomination—seemed to motivate the team, and they began to play up to their potential in the ACC Tournament as the No. 3 seed. On March 8, they beat Boston College 62–57 and advanced to the semifinal game against No. 10 Maryland, the No. 2 seed. Playing before 8,754 fans, Sylvia's Tar Heels overcame the second biggest deficit in ACC history. Down 48–24 in the first half, and shooting 31.3 percent from the floor, they clawed their way back to a 72–65 win. It was a total-team effort, but Latifah Coleman, the smallest player on the team, was the catalyst. When Tierra Ruffin-Pratt left the game with nausea, Sylvia told Coleman that she had to be the leader, and she caught fire. During her 18 minutes on the court, she scored 19 points, hitting 5 of 6 two-pointers, 1 three-pointer, and 6 of 8 free throws. TV analysts said they had never seen a performance like hers in the ACC Tournament and wondered where she came from. Sylvia said she "shipped her in from Mars this morning."[12]

The 2013 ACC Championship game told a familiar story—Tar Heels vs. Blue Devils—for the ninth time. ESPN2 analysts chatted about how much the two teams hated each other. Despite the rivalry, attendance at the Greensboro Coliseum was way down—8,166. Duke was the best three-point shooting team in the nation and probably had the edge. Joedy McCreary wrote, "No. 15 North Carolina keeps going cold at the wrong times against its fiercest rival." In the second half, UNC went cold for seven minutes, and Duke took advantage for an 18 to 4 run. During one stretch, the Lady Tar Heels missed 25 of 28 shots. Duke won 92–73. McCreary called it the "most lopsided ACC title game since North Carolina beat Duke by 21 in 2005."[13]

As the ACC runner-up, UNC was named the No. 3 seed in the NCAA Bridgeport

Region and played the first two rounds in Newark, Delaware, beating No. 14 seed Albany in round one 59–54. In round two, the ugly bracket monster, which had lain quiet for a few seasons, resurfaced. Sylvia was—again—in the unenviable position of playing a lower seed on its home court, No. 6 seed Delaware. David Ginsburg called the packed house a "biased throng," which included Vice President Joe Biden, cheering for his home-state team. Officiating was questionable: UNC was called for 24 fouls; Delaware 13. Rolle and Ruffin-Pratt got in early foul trouble. Sylvia was irate: "I wish Delaware good luck when they get on a neutral court." (Having played the first two rounds on their home court, Delaware then faced No. 2 seed Kentucky in Connecticut and lost 69–62.) At the end, Sylvia told her team the same thing she told her son Van: "This is a great lesson. Life isn't always fair." They had made an excellent showing—far better than predictions: 29–7 overall; 14–4 in the ACC. Seniors Tierra Ruffin-Pratt and Waltiea Rolle entered the WNBA: Ruffin-Pratt joined the Washington Mystics, and Rolle was drafted by the Minnesota Lynx—the first WNBA player from the Bahamas. Not being one to sidestep tough decisions, Rolle deferred her professional career to complete her BS in Sports Administration at the University of North Carolina before entering the WNBA. Her forthright approach to life was evident in public interviews; she never dodged questions about her pregnancy and the birth of her daughter Carlisa: "She's a good kid, a sweetheart. I'm not married, though, waiting for the right one."

At the end of the season, Sylvia was still waiting to hear whether she would join the Naismith Hall of Fame. On April 3, 2013, the suspense ended: She was notified that she was voted in on her first nomination. Then the accolades began. On July 25, the town of Gastonia turned out *en masse* for "A Tribute to Our Hometown Hero— Sylvia Hatchell" at the Gastonia Conference Center. According to Phillip Gardner, Sylvia was feted and roasted by friends and colleagues, including Judy Rose and her son Van, who spoke about her lack of skill in the kitchen: "You taught us that the expiration date on food actually is more of a suggestion." The *Gastonia Gazette* called her "a true hometown girl who hasn't forgotten her Gastonia roots as she's reached elite status in the coaching world." There was a toast, a proclamation, a key to the city, and a presentation of the Order of the Long Leaf Pine, the state's highest civilian service award. Sylvia could add this to the Order of the Palmetto, the top civilian honor in South Carolina, which Governor Richard Riley had presented her twice—in 1982 and 1986. The most ironic gesture of the evening came from Former Hunter Huss athletic director Don Saine when he announced the retirement of a No. 7 jersey—which Sylvia had never worn because Hunter Huss did not offer basketball for girls in the 1960s.[14]

To show her appreciation to the people who helped her succeed, Sylvia embarked on a 900 Wins Thank-You Tour. First, she toured northeast Tennessee, and paid a visit to Carson-Newman President Dr. Randall O'Brien in Jefferson City. She visited Tommy Northern, now deceased, who gave her that first coaching job at Talbott Elementary School, and her Carson-Newman teammate Gracie Woolwine Stroup. Her last Tennessee stop was in Knoxville at the home of Pat Summitt. They sat on Pat's deck overlooking Fort Loudon Lake on the Tennessee River enjoying a quiet, pleasant afternoon, but their animated conversation of former days was absent. In June, Sylvia

Sylvia and Pat Summitt in Pat's kitchen, Knoxville, Tennessee, April 24, 2013. Courtesy Sheila Oliver.

traveled to the South Carolina home of founding Francis Marion President Dr. Doug Smith, now deceased, and spent time with Kim Slawson Hawkins, who was a senior on the 1986 NAIA national championship team. In May, she thanked ACC commissioner John Swofford, who helped her win her dream job in 1986.

Amid the celebrations and accolades, Sylvia had to come down to earth and deal with staffing changes. On June 13, 2013, Tricia Stafford-Odom announced that she would be leaving UNC to become head women's basketball coach at Concordia-Irvine in California. Stafford-Odom had been an assistant coach at UNC for two seasons. Sylvia was accustomed to having assistants with longer tenures: Andrew Calder 27 years; Tracey Williams-Johnson 14 years; Charlotte Smith 9 years. When Stafford-Odom was hired at UNC, Ivory Latta was not free to take the job. In July 2013, her circumstances had changed, and she was Sylvia's only candidate for the position. Like Charlotte Smith, Latta would continue to play professional basketball with the Washington Mystics while she assisted the Tar Heels. And, like Charlotte Smith, Ivory held a special place in Sylvia's heart from the moment she saw her in UNC summer basketball camp: "I just fell in love with her, and she fell in love with us—and Carolina."

Stafford-Odom's departure was not without consequence. During the summer of 2013, she had responded to two tweets from recruits, which was considered a secondary-level NCAA violation. UNC reported the incident to the NCAA. There were no consequences at that level, but after Stafford-Odom departed for California, UNC athletic director Bubba Cunningham told Sylvia that she would have to bear the punishment—suspension from the first UNC game of the 2013–2014 season. Later, he adjusted the punishment to sitting out the first two exhibition games against Carson-Newman and Wingate. Sylvia had no choice but to comply, though she believes that she is the only Division I coach ever to be suspended for a secondary NCAA violation.

The only other dark cloud in Sylvia's blue heaven was the ongoing investigation of academic fraud that gained momentum after December 19, 2012, when former North Carolina Governor Jim Martin released the report commissioned by the UNC Board of Governors. The report examined data back to the 1990s and found egregious violations of academic integrity—classes that never met, dozens of unsupervised independent studies, and fraudulent grade changes.[15] By 2013, the academic scandal had become a full-blown athletic scandal that implicated Jan Boxill, the women's basketball academic counselor who had tutored Jessica Breland during her chemotherapy. In the coming months, the scandal would continue to taint North Carolina's flagship university, and Sylvia would be embroiled in an ugly legal battle. For the interim, she focused on her talented players from whom she could coach quality performance—young women whose lives she could affect positively, young women for whom she could hold the rope.

13

Riding the Highs and
Weathering the Lows

The 2013–2014 season began with the annual women's basketball Family Day at Cresset Baptist Church on Sunday, August 18. Over the years, Sylvia had invited notable speakers such as Anne Graham Lotz, Governor Beverly Perdue, and former players Charlotte Smith and Sylvia Crawley. In 2013, she chose Marion Jones. Sylvia was exuberant—flying high and anticipating her best season since 2006. It was her 28th year at UNC and her 39th as a head coach. Ivory Latta had joined the Tar Heels as an assistant coach, and the team was picked to finish fourth in the ACC. Sylvia had the top recruiting class in the country: Diamond DeShields, Allisha Gray, Stephanie Mavunga, and Jessica Washington. On February 7, she had earned her 900th win, and she was about to be inducted into the Naismith Memorial Basketball Hall of Fame on September 8. As she put it, "I had a great staff—everything was good—life was good." She joked with Sammy, "Everything is going so well, something bad is bound to happen." She woke up one August morning and said, "'Sammy, I had the weirdest dream last night. I dreamed that I was sitting in the stands watching my team play. I thought, *Why would I be sitting in the stands watching my team play?*' It was bizarre, and I had no clue about what was coming."

On Thursday, August 29, Sylvia had her yearly physical: "Went be-bopping in—I was feeling great." Melinda Everett, the physician's assistant, said, "Insurance has changed, and you don't have to get a blood test." Remembering her ovarian cancer scare in 2000, Sylvia insisted on blood tests, whether her insurance covered them or not. Afterward she drove to North Myrtle Beach for Labor Day weekend, which is important for Sylvia and Sammy: "Those few days give Sammy and me a little time together before basketball season gets underway." The next morning, Friday, August 30, she got a phone call from Everett's office saying that everything looked good except a low white blood count that could signal a viral infection or an autoimmune condition. The nurse said, "We want you to see a hematologist today." Being in North Myrtle Beach, Sylvia had to opt for an appointment the next Tuesday. Until then, she was told to stay away from people who may be sick, not to shake hands, not to eat raw fruits or vegetables, and to stay away from salad bars. Sylvia was stunned: "I'm like, 'WHAT!?'"

The centerpiece of her weekend was the Forrest Gump Labor Day Shrimp Bunch, held annually on the Saturday before Labor Day. Sylvia initiated the event in 2009 for approximately 50 long-time friends. Sylvia and Sammy provided the steamed shrimp—about 20 pounds of it from Berry's Seafood Market—and the guests brought casseroles, coleslaw, fried cornbread, and desserts. Another feature of the weekend was Shagging: "Sammy and I love to go to Shag clubs and dance, so we drop in at Fat Harold's and Ocean Drive Pavilion and the Spanish Galleon." On this occasion, when Sylvia and Sammy took to the dance floor at Fat Harold's, she heard comments from a group of onlookers. One said, "There's Sylvia Hatchell. The Carolina women's coach." Another said, "Man, she can Shag." A third joined in with "I bet Roy can't do that." As they left the dance floor, Sylvia passed by the group and said, "You're right. Roy can't do that." Throughout the weekend, it was impossible for her to comply with Everett's instructions, but she was careful and did not share her concerns with anyone—not even Sammy.

On Tuesday morning, she saw the hematologist, who called the next day with the report. Again, he "ruled out" anything serious. Sylvia heard "viral infection" or "some autoimmune thing." He suggested that she wait a couple of weeks and be retested. In the interim, he reiterated, she should not shake hands or be around sick people. She said, "Look, tomorrow I'm flying to Springfield, Massachusetts, to be inducted into the Naismith Hall of Fame. I'm going to be shaking thousands of hands in the next few days." He cautioned her to "be careful and wear a mask on the airplane." She thought, *Come on now! I'm getting ready to go have one of the best weekends of my life; don't be ruining it for me!*

On Thursday, September 5, she flew to Springfield, Massachusetts, for the Naismith Memorial Hall of Fame Festivities, which she describes as "an incredible time. Unbelievable." On Friday evening, inductees were presented their Hall-of-Fame rings at the Induction Celebration. Sylvia's fellow inductees included one other woman, Dawn Staley, head women's basketball coach at the University of South Carolina, who was inducted as a player, not a coach. Saturday's events included the Enshrinement Class Press Conference followed by the Reunion Reception Dinner where they received their Hall of Fame blazers. Sylvia loved mixing with "all the greats and legends of basketball." This was her kind of event—and she did not wear a mask.

On Sunday, September 8, UNC Athletics sponsored the GALA VIP Reception prior to the Enshrinement Ceremony. Sylvia saw rows of plaques honoring former inductees. Publicly she said, "This is the next best thing to heaven.... And as I look up and see all the pictures of all these people in the Basketball Hall of Fame, I say they're all basketball angels, because to me, they are. They're people I've looked up to all my life and my coaching career." Prior to the 2:00 p.m. ceremony, Sylvia and her guests walked the red carpet to this televised, live event. She was formally presented by Nancy Lieberman, whom she had coached in the 1979 Hanes All-American Basketball Classic, and Hubie Brown, from whom she had sought advice in 1999 as she fell back in love with basketball. The after-party ran late into the night. Sylvia forgot about her immune system and enjoyed this pinnacle achievement—recognition for 38 years of hard work. "It was a dream come true—one of the most special weekends of my life." The only flaw was the absence of Pat Summitt, who was scheduled to present Sylvia but was unable to attend.

She flew back to Chapel Hill on Monday morning but had no "down time": "I

Sylvia at the Naismith Hall of Fame Induction Ceremony, Springfield, Massachusetts, September 8, 2013. Courtesy Naismith Memorial Basketball Hall of Fame.

came home, got something to eat, changed clothes, and went right back to the air-port" for a recruiting visit with the number one player in the country, A'Ja Wilson, in Hopkins, South Carolina. Then she went to Springdale, Maryland, for a visit with De'Janae Boykin. During the presentation in Boykin's home, she noticed a slight sore throat, which became worse on the trip home. On Thursday, she was scheduled for two visits in Atlanta, including one with Te'a Cooper, who had verbally committed to UNC but was waffling. Before she left for Atlanta, Sylvia checked in with Dr. Harold Pillsbury, who prescribed steroids, so she could "stay on the road." She immediately felt better and continued this grueling recruitment schedule for the next three weeks, but not without a second round of steroids. When practice began in early October, Sylvia told Jane High, "I'm just really tired. I don't feel great." Again, she consulted Dr. Pillsbury, who sent her back to the Division of Infectious Diseases at the UNC School of Medicine for a third blood test. The results were unchanged: Sylvia heard—again— "You've probably got a viral infection or an autoimmune thing going on." Her white blood count was still low, but she had no diagnosis. It was time to act. At the urging of her friend Dianne Glover, Sylvia called the Lineberger Comprehensive Cancer Center to ask for a bone marrow biopsy. On Friday morning, October 11, Dianne drove her to the Center for the biopsy and took her home afterward. Sammy was at a coaching clinic at East Carolina University, so Dianne went back after work to sit with her, not wanting her to be alone when the call came with the results.

It was late when Dr. Voorhees called. Sylvia took the call in private; then she announced to Dianne, "I have leukemia." "I thought my heart would stop. It was a surreal moment," says Dianne. The preliminary diagnosis was acute myeloid leukemia (AML), one of the most pernicious types. Dr. Voorhees was reassuring: It was treatable—curable—but he needed to see her immediately. She asked, "Like when?" He answered, "Tomorrow." She retorted, "Tomorrow!? Tomorrow is Saturday!" He said, "Tomorrow, Coach. This is serious." Sylvia had a long list of reasons why she couldn't enter the hospital the next day: Fall break was coming up. On October 21, she was scheduled to attend an event at Carson-Newman honoring bluegrass legend Ricky Skaggs for endowing a scholarship. She had already planned her fall visit to Black Mountain and was scheduled to ride horses with friends at Biltmore House in Asheville. But Dr. Voorhees wouldn't budge; he emphasized the gravity of her diagnosis.

Her response was typical Sylvia: shift into take-charge mode. She didn't want anyone to know about the diagnosis, not even Sammy, but she reluctantly asked him to return home on Saturday and take her to the hospital for blood tests. She called her staff and asked them to drop by the house at 10:00 on Saturday morning. She called Van and asked him to drop by around noon. She packed a suitcase with gym shorts, warm up pants, several Dry-Fit T-shirts, tennis shoes, bedroom slippers (her fluffy "ram shoes"), her Bible, and a nightgown. Except for the latter two, everything carried UNC athletic logos. In the hospital, she would be a walking advertisement for UNC athletics. Because Sylvia was alone, Dianne stayed the night. "I don't know what time I went to bed," says Sylvia, "but I did sleep a little bit."

At 9:00 a.m. on Saturday, Sylvia met with her tax adviser to settle loose ends for her 2012 IRS return, for which she had been granted an extension. At 10:00, she delivered the news to Andrew, Jane, and Tracey. Her newest staff member, Ivory, was out of town. Says Sylvia, "There were tears. I said, 'I'm going to fight this. I'm going to beat this, but I need you to be strong. You are going to have to run things for me until I can get back out there. I don't know how long it's going to take.'" Andrew, who had been with her at UNC from the beginning, would be at the helm in her absence.

Later that day, Sammy and Van took her to the hospital, and the tests began immediately, so she sent them home. That night, alone in her hospital room, she thought, *This is crazy. I'm OK. I got all these great things going on. We have recruited a great team. The season is getting ready to start. I have just been inducted into the Naismith Hall of Fame. What am I doing here in the hospital? This is a bad dream:* "It was hard for me not to just get up and walk out of there and go home. I'm a control freak, so I thought, *I can control this.*" Alone with thoughts such as these, she suffered. She naively asked Dr. Voorhees, "Don't you have a pill or something you can give me?" Saturday night was "the hardest." "I have to admit, I cried myself to sleep." When Dianne learned that Sylvia spent her first night in the hospital alone, she vowed that it would not happen again, so she developed a schedule of friends and family who would be with Sylvia 24–7 for as long as she needed them. The first was Jackie Koss, who drove 500 miles through the night from Manchester, Tennessee, and arrived on Sunday morning even before Dianne developed the schedule. Being a Women's Health Nurse Practitioner at Vanderbilt Medical Center, Jackie's background in oncology was vital for Sylvia at that early stage.

On Sunday afternoon, October 13, 2013, Sylvia met with her team—in the hospital instead of Carmichael Arena where they would normally be having Sunday afternoon practice. The staff brought the knotted rope that was an important metaphor for team strength and unity in 2011. Now, the team would need to hold the rope for her, for Andrew Calder, and for each other. Wearing a mask, she delivered the news: She had leukemia and would not be coaching for a while. At that time, she did not know that "a while" would stretch into an entire season: "The girls were crying," she says. "It was rough." The meeting was short, and by 5:00 p.m., she was in her room, receiving chemotherapy through a double port.

On Monday, October 14, 2013, UNC issued a press release: "Sylvia Hatchell is temporarily stepping away from her on-the-court coaching responsibilities due to a recent diagnosis of leukemia." Athletic director Bubba Cunningham pledged "complete support." Roy Williams said he was "heartbroken": "But she's tough," he said, "and she will fight this with everything she has. All of us at Carolina and all of her friends in the coaching community will support her 100 percent in this fight."[1] As word spread, the basketball community reached out to Sylvia. John Swofford was one of the first, followed by Larry Fedora, Mike Krzyzewski, Charlotte Smith, Pat Summitt, Nora Lynn Finch, and a host of others. And then there was her good friend and right hand—Associate Head Coach Andrew Calder. She had been at his bedside in 1998; now he would be her proxy on the court. Calder told the press that Sylvia annually "evaluates the talent that she has coming in and, with her philosophy, puts together a master game plan for that year. We're just implementing that game plan. When she returns we will be on schedule. What we lose," he said, is "her experience and knowledge," but he pledged to "coach the game through her eyes." Aaron Beard wrote that Calder "fought back tears" as he described the Saturday meeting when the coaches learned the news. Andrew said that the players were "hit" hard but also "motivated to work hard" for their coach.[2]

The wider community began to send text messages and e-mails. Sylvia heard from Michael Jordan, Howard White with Nike, former North Carolina Governor Bev Purdue, and Robin Roberts with *Good Morning America*, who had just undergone a bone marrow transplant. "I got messages from everybody except President Obama!" says Sylvia. The daughter of Billy Graham, Anne Graham Lotz, told her, "We'll get people all around the world praying for you." Sylvia believes in prayer: "Word went out. I *did* have people all over the world praying for me, including Billy Graham! Trust me, I don't know how much you believe in the power of prayer, but let me tell you what, here's one, right here, who believes!" Sylvia's on-campus Bible study group, the Lamb's Club, made a calendar, and every minute of every day one of them was praying for her. "I know I'm a miracle," says Sylvia. "I could feel the strength when I needed it. It was there."

Sylvia felt the strength of her friends and family, who watched over her, holding her welfare uppermost. She and her sister Phyllis were scheduled to attend the McCall Family Reunion in Balsam Grove over the weekend of October 18, and Phyllis had already purchased a plane ticket. When she learned of Sylvia's predicament, she used the ticket to spend the time in Chapel Hill, sitting with Sylvia in the hospital during the day and taking care of the home and Sammy in the evening.

For 25 days, Sylvia Hatchell was an inpatient at Lineberger, undergoing a 3+7 protocol for induction chemotherapy. To show their support, her players borrowed one of her own motivational techniques. After every game, the Tar Heel coaches and staff evaluate the game film for more than 20 categories of achievement, such as blockouts, deflections, and steals. Sylvia awards a stuffed-animal trophy to the top player in each category. For dives on the floor, the trophy is a huge stuffed fish. For the most assists, a giraffe. For rebounds, a kangaroo or a frog. For steals, a monkey. For deflections, an octopus. The overall top player gets a big lion for being king of the jungle. When Sylvia began to lose her hair, the players brought her a big stuffed lion symbolizing her king-of-the-jungle courage.

True to form, Sylvia courageously staged a Shave-Coach-Hatchell's-Head party and used the event to promote her team. She called her hair dresser, Wanda Guthrie: "Come over here and bring your shears!" Wanda obliged. At 5:00 p.m. on Tuesday, October 29, Wanda spread a white sheet on the floor and began shaving while nurses and visitors looked on. When Sylvia's head was bald, Wanda painted "GO HEELS" across the crown of her head and added a big blue-and-white foot with the black "tar heel" stretching down to the nape of her neck. On this same day, October 29, Dr. Vorhees walked into her room with the best news she had had since October 11: The chemotherapy was working. She was in remission. She still had a long, hard fight ahead, but this news was a solid first step. Fearing that she may need a bone marrow transplant, Sylvia had earlier begun a Be-the-Match campaign (run by the National Marrow Donor Program). Because the first round of chemotherapy brought the cancer into remission so quickly, the doctors ruled out a transplant in favor of consolidation chemotherapy.

Sylvia hoped that her good news and painted "Tar-Heel head" would motivate her team for their exhibition game against Carson-Newman the next night. When Bubba Cunningham suspended her for the first two exhibition games of 2013–2014, as well as the first regular season game, no one knew that she would be sidelined for a much more serious reason—a cancer diagnosis. Assistant coach Billy Lee took the suspensions for her, and Andrew Calder coached the first game *sans* one assistant coach. Word about Sylvia's leukemia diagnosis and treatment spread to her alma mater, so the Carson-Newman women's basketball team appeared in Carmichael on October 30 wearing orange "Hoops 4 Hatchell" warm-up T-Shirts. Calder and her UNC Lady Tar Heels won 111–50. Sophomore Xylina McDaniel said the team won for Sylvia.

Sylvia left the hospital for the first time on November 7, eager to be home and eager to see the usually rambunctious Maddie, who was surprisingly subdued and gentle when Sammy helped Sylvia out of the car. Maddie knew. The next day Jane High took Sylvia to get a wig, and that night—for the first time in her career—she was not on the court for the first regular game of the season. Andrew Calder coached UNC to an 87–26 win over Air Force. Three days later, Sylvia had another biopsy, and that night her UNC team suffered a nationally-televised loss to No. 4 Tennessee 81–65. On November 13, she was back in the hospital for consolidation chemotherapy.

This routine would be repeated over the next five months—going in and out of the hospital for chemotherapy, biopsies, and transfusions of platelets and blood; bottoming out; fearing that she would die; praying to live; being sustained by the people who loved her. Sylvia endured the side effects—skin rash, sore throat, nausea, physical pain, chills, fever, weakness, loss of hair—while trying to "be there" for the team. She watched practices and game film on her tablet, often with Calder by her side, and when possible, she watched games on television and the Internet. When her medical team thought she was strong enough, they allowed her to visit campus for coaches meetings and team practices.

The hype about the 2013–2014 UNC women's basketball team focused almost exclusively on the four top freshman recruits. The team had no seniors and only two returning starters: Sophomore Xylina McDaniel and junior Brittany Roundtree. Andrew Calder depended on these two for leadership and experience, along with junior Latifah Coleman. Calder led the inexperienced Lady Tar Heels to a strong start with 2 losses and 12 wins. The losses were to No. 4 Tennessee (81–65) and to unranked Arizona State in overtime (94–81). On November 15, the team took its first road trip, and Sylvia was frustrated to be stuck in a hospital room. She was concerned for the freshmen, so before the team boarded a plane for Los Angeles, she called them from the hospital:

> We are heading into territory where we've never been. This is your first road trip as college students. For me, this is my first season of not being in full control. Be patient and let the game come to you. I'm having to learn that too—to be patient and follow the game plan developed by my medical team. I expect you to go into the game against UCLA with a warrior mentality but go in as a team. Show strength and unity but be warriors. I'll be a warrior too!

Her challenge was effective. UNC beat unranked UCLA 78–68. Freshman Allisha Gray scored 30 points and was named ACC Rookie of the Week. Their next significant win was against undefeated No. 10 South Carolina 74–66.

Thanksgiving ushered in the 2013 holidays, the most difficult for Sylvia since the deaths of her parents. Phyllis arrived on Monday before Thanksgiving to stay the week. She prepared turkey and all the fixings for Sylvia, Sammy, and Van, but the extended family stayed away because of Sylvia's compromised immune system. Shortly after Thanksgiving, Sylvia's hairdresser Wanda Guthrie and a coworker Wendy Elliott decorated Sylvia's house for Christmas—she needed a boost. Her white cell count had hit bottom, her energy was depleted, and her immune system was so compromised that she could not take the second consolidation treatment before Christmas as she had hoped. She was at her lowest when Phyllis and Bobby drove from Pensacola for the Christmas holidays, arriving at Kepley Road on December 21 while carolers were congregating in the front yard—75 girlfriends, church friends, neighbors, staff, family, and Lamb's Club members singing Christmas carols. She could not mingle or invite them inside, so she stood on the porch wearing a mask while they sang. The finale was an Elvis impersonator—Keith Henderson—who regaled her with "White Christmas," "Blue Christmas," and traditional hymns. Sylvia was elated. On Christmas Day, she had enough energy to exchange gifts with the family and enjoy the Christmas dinner that Phyllis prepared. Sylvia later wrote, "Though my recovery was not going as I had hoped, the little things were bringing me joy."[3]

In early 2014, the Lady Tar Heels were ranked No. 14, and their first ACC conference game was on January 5 against No. 8 Maryland, a team that ranked right up there with Duke as a spoiler, having robbed the Tar Heels of the chance to play for a national championship in 2006. Sylvia's doctors allowed her to attend this game. Wearing a mask, she sat isolated behind the bleachers on a platform built for television cameras. UNC erased Maryland's 18-point lead but lost 78–72. This loss was followed by five straight wins. On January 16, Sylvia entered the hospital for her second consolidation chemotherapy treatment and was released from the hospital five days later, too weak to attend games. By January 30, UNC's record stood at 16–3, and they were ranked No. 6. Then they lost three straight games to unranked teams that they should have beaten—Syracuse, Miami, and Georgia Tech. By the time they came up against No. 3 Duke in Cameron on February 10, the Tar Heels were tired of losing, or so Diamond DeShields said. She must have meant it because they got the 89–78 win, their first in Cameron since 2008. It snapped a seven-game losing streak to Duke. On March 2, they defeated Duke for the second time (64–60). It had been six years since UNC had won both regular-season games against the Blue Devils.

On March 3, Sylvia attended a public event, regardless of its health risk to her—a ceremony at Lineberger Comprehensive Cancer Center for the presentation of a $1 million grant from the Kay Yow Cancer Fund and the V Foundation for Cancer Research (named for the beloved NC State men's basketball coach Jim Valvano). The grant would fund research into the effect of physical activity on breast cancer survivors.[4] Among other factors—such as excellent medical care, prayer, and the love of her friends and family—Sylvia credits her good physical condition for her ability to withstand chemotherapy: "For the prior six years, I had worked out with a trainer. I had muscles!" She also credits the mental toughness that comes with 38 years of coaching. AML statistics are not good for patients over 60, so Sylvia's age—61—was not in her favor, but she told her doctors, "Don't lump me in there with all those other people because I'm not your average patient. I'm healthier than most 35- to 40-year-olds who get AML." Booklets and pamphlets about the disease appeared in her hospital room, but she refused to read them: "I was not going to be another statistic. I was going to be my own person and do my own thing. I was going to beat this thing." Despite her resolve, Sylvia was often lower than she had been at any other point in her 61 years:

> There were days when I felt pretty decent, and there were other days I felt like a Mack truck had run over me. I had nothing left to give except my willpower, my faith, my inner strength. In my soul—my inner being—I knew that I had to be strong. I wanted so much to get back to coaching. You don't realize how much something is a part of you until it's taken away. There were nights when I went to bed, I was so weak I just hoped I would wake up in the morning.

No matter how bad she felt, she exercised every day. Dr. Claudio Battaglini, UNC professor of exercise and sport science, told her that every day in the bed takes seven days to recover the lost physical mobility and strength. So she walked: "Seventeen times around the [hospital] halls was a mile. Every day that I worked out, I felt better. It helped me physically as well as mentally to exercise. I never wore a hospital gown or pajamas during the day, and the only time I was in the bed was to sleep at night or to take a nap." Sylvia thought about the legacies of Yow and Valvano, two NC State coaches who died from cancer. She briefly wondered what her own legacy would be—then quickly shifted focus to the value of physical activity. She was confident that physical conditioning and exercise were her allies.

Sylvia was readmitted to Lineberger Cancer Center on March 6 for her third and final consolidation treatment—the same day that her Tar Heels entered the ACC Tournament in the Greensboro Coliseum as the No. 6 seed. On that day, they defeated Wake Forest (69–65); then Maryland in the quarterfinal (73–70). Sylvia desperately wanted to attend the semifinal game against Duke on March 8, but her doctors refused. Greensboro was an hour away, and mingling with a crowd was too risky. Powerless and dejected in her hospital room, she watched the game on ESPNU.

Watching her Tar Heels play in a semifinal game could have given her a boost—but not this game. It was close. With 8:08 left, Diamond DeShields got a technical foul for taunting Duke forward Haley Peters—DeShields' third technical of the season. Aaron Beard wrote that this was "one of a series of small mistakes that proved costly" for UNC.[5] With 18 seconds left, Duke was up by two points, but Xylina McDaniel and Latifah Coleman committed fouls, and both DeShields and Coleman missed three-point shots, giving Duke the 66–61 win. Duke would go on to lose to Notre Dame in the title game.

Three days later, Sylvia left the hospital. In just 12 days, her team would enter the NCAA Tournament as the No. 4 seed in the Stanford Region, and all she could do was wait and watch from home. UNC hosted the first two rounds in Carmichael, and they needed whatever advantage their home court could give when they faced the No. 13 seed UT Martin—Pat Summitt's alma mater. On the morning of the game, March 23, Sylvia was enjoying a hearty breakfast when Sammy came downstairs with bad news: Phyllis had suffered a heart attack. On the previous day, Phyllis had ridden her

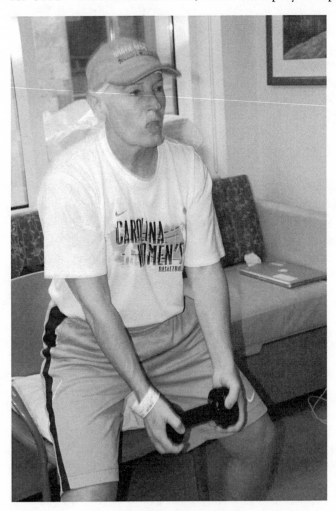

Sylvia exercising in Lineberger Cancer Center during chemotherapy, 2013. Courtesy Sheila Oliver.

bike 10 miles. The previous week, she had won a senior biking competition. After stents to correct arterial blockage, she was doing fine, but this news was a blow to Sylvia who thinks of her older sister as invincible.

There was more disappointment to come. Sylvia was scheduled to attend the UT-Martin game and give a halftime interview with ESPN, but Dr. Voorhees nixed this plan as too risky. She was confined to her living room, and the game did nothing to lift her spirits. DeShields spent the first five minutes on the bench because UNC's team policy prohibits a player who commits a technical foul from starting the next game. DeShields later told the press that she was unfazed by the episode, but Aaron Dodson noted that once she entered the game, "things were a little off." At halftime, Sylvia stood up from the sofa and said, "Somebody needs to fire this team up!" She picked up the gas-log remote, pointed it at the fireplace, and when the logs ignited, she said, "maybe this will do it." Then she retreated upstairs to her bedroom, covered her head with a blanket, and listened to the second half. She could not bear to watch. With 8:59 left in the game, the Skyhawks were ahead 50–37. DeShields fouled out of the game, but the Tar Heels clawed their way back to a two-point victory (60–58). Xylina McDaniel made the shot of the game while sitting on the floor under the basket. It was a win, but it was ugly. Sylvia said later, "I was curled in a ball, just trembling. Not hot, not cold, but trembling."

In round two, the Tar Heels faced the No. 5 seed Michigan State. Before the game, Sylvia called the team, urging them to be assertive and aggressive but cautioning against technical fouls. On a scale of 1–10, she told them, their effort against UT Martin was a 4. They would need better effort to beat Michigan state—8, 9, or 10. She reminded them that they were playing on their home court before fans who loved them. She reminded them that *she* loved them. Finally, she cautioned them against selfishness. They needed to work as a team and to score team points, not "their" individual points. Her effort to fire up the team worked. Aaron Beard wrote that DeShields "put on a dominating show," atoning somewhat for her "lackluster" showing against UT Martin.[6] This time, Sylvia did not retreat to her bedroom. UNC took a second-half lead and never looked back, eliminating the Spartans 62–53. Andrew Calder would be taking her Tar Heels to the Sweet 16 in Stanford, California.

The UNC women's team had not been to the Sweet 16 since 2011, and none of the current players had ever advanced that far in the NCAA Tournament. This time they would be up against South Carolina, the No. 1 seed in the Stanford Region. It was impossible for Sylvia to fly across the country for this game, but she met with the players in the Carmichael conference room and surprised them when she pulled out the golden scissors that she had used to cut down the net at every championship win since 1994—three ACC Championships and two Regional Championships. She then handed the scissors to assistant coach Ivory Latta, who said, "Good feeling!" Latta had used the scissors in 2005, 2006, and 2007. On Sunday, March 30, Sylvia coached from her living room, yelling at Andrew Calder, a continent away, to put Danielle Butts or Brittany Roundtree in the game: "Brittany won't miss foul shots!" The Gamecocks came within one point (43–42) with 8:43 left in the game, but UNC held the lead. Janie McCauley wrote that Diamond DeShields gave "everything" to stave off the

Gamecocks' comeback, despite getting banged up on the court in a physical game. UNC got the 65–58 win and a trip to the Elite Eight, their first since 2008.

Sylvia was elated—proud of her team and proud of Andrew Calder. Her doctors told her that she could travel to Nashville if her team made it to the Final Four. Her Lady Tar Heels had defeated the No. 1 seed and were ready to take on No. 2 Stanford. Diamond DeShields was bruised and sore, playing with an injured ankle and knee—remnants of the hard-fought game against South Carolina. The Tar Heels got off to a 22–9 start against the Cardinal and led 36–30 at the half. And then the fire went out. Fouls forced UNC to back off from their aggressive play of the first half, and the Cardinal took advantage, winning the game 74–65. There would be no trip to the Final Four for the team or for Sylvia. Andrew was distraught. Grace Raynor wrote, "The tears trickled down his face, the gut-wrenching emotion evident in his quavering voice as he spoke between gasps of air." Between sobs he thanked Sylvia for "the respect she gave me…. For trusting me with her team." He blamed himself for the loss: "We had the talent to get us to the Final Four, and I didn't get us there…. For that I'm sorry." Xylina McDaniel responded, "We love you, coach Calder."[7] Sylvia and Andrew believed that this team could advance even further in 2014–2015. They had no graduating seniors and expected only one freshman to join the team in the fall of 2014—Jamie Cherry. Their star freshman class was now seasoned, and Diamond DeShields racked up national honors, including ACC Rookie of the Year. She was also named National Freshman of the Year by Full Court, espnW, and U.S. Basketball Writers Association (USBWA).

When Sylvia was "riding high" in August of 2013—when she was enshrined in the Naismith Basketball Hall of Fame on September 8—she could never have imagined how low she would go during the 2013–2014 season or how high she would rise again. The first 3+7 chemotherapy protocol and three rounds of consolidation chemotherapy lasted six months. On April 25, 2014, Dr. Vorhees reported that her recent bone marrow tests showed no cancer. She had been in remission since the first chemotherapy treatment, and the consolidation therapy had worked. She would continue to have monthly blood tests, and if there was any indication that the cancer had returned, she would need a bone marrow transplant. Be-the-Match outreach had identified a donor who matched 9 of 10 Human Leukocyte Antigens (HLA), so Sylvia had a good match should she need it. That day has yet to come, but the match campaign developed a life of its own and ultimately saved a nine-year-old girl and a fourteen-year-old boy. The eight-month ordeal filled Sylvia with gratitude: "I promise you, I will never, ever take anything for granted again. Every day is a blessing. Every day when I open my eyes I tell God, 'Just put the opportunities in front of me and I promise You, I will utilize them.'"

Gradually, she gained the strength to re-engage with her life—her activities and routines. On May 2, 2014, she returned to the cabin for the first time in 10 months to host the annual blueberry-patch workday, an event Sylvia promotes to keep the blueberries in production and to keep donations flowing to the Lineberger Cancer Center. On this occasion, approximately 50 neighbors, family, and friends showed up to help, including Jackie Koss—all the way from Manchester, Tennessee. These friends had nursed her back to health; now they were cultivating her blueberry patch for the benefit of other Lineberger cancer patients. This annual event typically has a party atmosphere with hotdogs and sandwiches and good fellowship. In 2014, Sylvia's effort was limited, but she borrowed her brother Ralph's truck and drove to the Asheville Farmers Market to pick up additional blueberry plants, which Lonnie Israel donates. Sylvia was grateful for the plants and grateful to be back in the mountains, still connected to nature and to her friends. She felt blessed.

Her resolve to view every day as a blessing and to "utilize" the "opportunities" that God put in front of her was tested immediately. In her book *Fight! Fight!*, Sylvia writes that when she returned to coaching in May 2014, one of her first actions was to meet with Diamond DeShields and her mother: "To be honest, even though my numbers were starting to rise, I probably shouldn't have gone. I was still extremely weak. But part of me still hoped that my presence and power of persuasion might be able to change her mind.... But the die had already been cast. She was leaving."[8] Sylvia was dumbfounded and hurt as the news of DeShields' departure for the Tennessee Lady Vols spread through the basketball world. On top of DeShields' departure, Te'a Cooper—who had verbally committed to UNC as an eighth-grader—announced that she, too, would sign with the Lady Vols. When Sylvia visited Te'a in September 2013, she knew that Cooper was still considering UNC though she had reopened her recruitment to include 10 other schools.

DeShields denied that there was any complicity between her and Cooper. To this day, Sylvia says she never fully understood why DeShields left UNC for Tennessee. In June 2014, DeShields said "that she didn't want to talk anymore about why she left North Carolina."[9] In 2015, she said that she loved Coach Hatchell, "and I'm proud of her for bouncing back the way she has leading that team.... I texted her earlier in the year, just checking on her. She and I have no bad blood."[10] For her part, Sylvia keeps mum. Losing DeShields after one season was devastating for UNC women's basketball, but this setback was soon compounded by the academic fraud scandal that would not die. In June 2014, Rashad McCants, a starter on the 2005 UNC men's NCAA Championship basketball team, told Steve Delsohn that he was "steered" toward the "no-show classes," that "tutors wrote papers for him," and that these practices were widely known among players and others in the athletic department. At this point, women's basketball had not been directly implicated, but the fallout was widespread, and having Jan Boxill's name at the forefront of the story did not bode well for Sylvia's program.

Sylvia kept out of the fray and focused on her team. She had 12 of 13 players returning, including four starters: senior point guard Latifah Coleman, junior Xylina McDaniel, and sophomores Allisha Gray and Stephanie Mavunga, the tallest player at 6'3". With only one freshman, Jamie Cherry, Sylvia was confident in the experience and talent of her Lady Tar Heels. The team and the fans were as excited for her to be back on the court as she was. Daniel Wilco reported that she attended Friday Late Night with Roy in the Smith Center on October 3 and was "brought to tears by the standing ovation and cheers that rivaled that of a Duke game." She told the crowd that she "might get a technical every single game" because she was so "fired up" about her team.[11]

This upbeat beginning to the 2014–2015 basketball season was sullied on

October 16, 2014, when former FBI general counsel Kenneth Wainstein released a 131-page report showing that 47.4 percent of UNC students enrolled in the fake classes were athletes and 6.5 percent of the athletes were women's basketball players—12.2 percent were men's basketball players and 50.9 percent football players. The report also said that Jan Boxill told an administrator "the grades that the players should receive." For the first time, the investigation directly implicated women's basketball. Sylvia told Chip Alexander that she was "aware many of her players took AFAM [African and Afro-American Studies] courses but did not know they did not require attendance or that the grades were assigned by [an] administrator." She said she "relied" on Jan Boxill—the women's basketball academic counselor—to "coordinate the classes" and insisted that "Boxill never told her about any irregularities with the classes." The Wainstein report suggested that Sylvia had trusted Boxill "too much." True to her nature, Sylvia defended Boxill publicly and said she believed in Boxill's "academic integrity." Boxill became a target as supporters and detractors launched barbs. Sylvia remained steadfast in her belief that Boxill's intentions were above reproach. Against this backdrop of accusation and innuendo, Sylvia flung herself into coaching, determined to win at basketball and rise above the scandal.

Notre Dame was the preseason favorite to win the ACC; UNC was ranked fourth. Sylvia's first return to the court was—ironically—for the exhibition game against Carson-Newman exactly one year after Andrew Calder coached the 2013 game in her stead. It was her first opportunity to coach Gray, Mavunga, and Washington; Xylina McDaniel said it was "like having our mother back." UNC won the game 88–27. Between November 14 and January 4, they lost only one game to No. 16 Oregon State—a lopsided 70–55—but they got strong wins over ranked teams. In 2014, no one could call the Tar Heels' preseason schedule "soft." First, they defeated No. 19 Oklahoma State (79–77), largely on the performance of Gray and Mavunga. Sylvia said, "we call it Vegas because they're money." They walloped No. 5 Stanford 70–54 in a sweet-revenge rematch of the 2013 NCAA Elite Eight. They beat No. 18 Rutgers in double overtime (96–93). Xylina McDaniel—who started the first 12 games—injured her leg in the December 21 game against Elon and was out for the season after having surgery. Despite the loss of a strong starter, the team won its first ACC game against unranked NC State by a hefty margin—72–56. By January 5, the Lady Tar Heels were ranked No. 6.

Their five-game winning streak ended on January 8 when unranked Pittsburgh embarrassed the Lady Tar Heels 84–59. Sylvia credited the loss to poor rebounding and the absence of McDaniel, but the academic scandal was still roiling. On January 6, 2015, two former UNC athletes—Devon Ramsay and Rashanda McCants—filed a class-action lawsuit against the NCAA and the university, charging UNC and the NCAA with negligence—*McCants v. UNC*. Ramsay played football for UNC between 2007 and 2012. McCants was Sylvia's starting forward between 2005 and 2009. The lawsuit charged that UNC and the NCAA "breached their duties to student-athletes in spectacular fashion" and failed "to provide a meaningful education to scholarship athletes." In February, two additional former Lady Tar Heels, Kenya McBee and Leah Metcalf, both of whom played from 2002 to 2005, joined two other lawsuits against North Carolina. Having these former players enter the public arena of the

Sylvia with Dorothy Baxter at dedication ceremony for the Sylvia Rhyne Hatchell Court, Hunter Huss High School, January 16, 2015. Courtesy Sheila Oliver.

scandal surely affected the team, but—as with the Marion Jones–C. J. Hunter debacle in 1996—it was impossible to gauge the impact. After January 8, the Lady Tar Heels could not gain momentum. They got a strong win against No. 7 Florida State but lost to other ranked teams, such as Notre Dame, Syracuse, and Louisville. Sylvia continued to acknowledge the absence of McDaniel, especially after the January 15 loss to Notre Dame. Her Lady Tar Heels lost both regular-season games to No. 15 Duke, the second by one point, and finished sixth in the ACC—two places below the preseason prediction.

One of the highlights of the spring season was the January 16, 2015, naming of the Hunter Huss basketball court the "Sylvia Rhyne Hatchell Court." Sylvia's entire family turned out—Van, brothers, sisters, in-laws, nephews, nieces—everyone except Sammy, who was coaching that night. The Hunter Huss school sign read, "Welcome Sylvia Hatchell," and the *Gastonia Gazette* reported that fans held "Sylvia" signs while the pep band played. The girls' and boys' basketball teams were both playing in the Hunter Huss gym that night. The dinner and program were held in the cafeteria during the girls' game because NCAA recruitment rules prohibited Sylvia from watching it. The naming ceremony was held on the court before the boys' game. The formerly-retired No. 7 Hatchell jersey from 2013 made an appearance, as did Sylvia's high-school PE teacher Dorothy Baxter, who said Sylvia "was then like she is today." Sylvia told the crowd, "This is special because it's my hometown and it's people that have known me since the day I was born." When asked about her energy level, she said "If you saw me after that referee" during the Notre Dame game, "you wouldn't

UNC bench, UNC vs. Clemson, January 18, 2015. Left to right: Tracey Williams-Johnson, Billy Lee, Sylvia Hatchell, Andrew Calder, and Latifah Coleman. Courtesy Russell Oliver.

question my energy."[12] She was referring to the previous day's 89–79 loss to Notre Dame. According to Aaron Beard, Sylvia "nearly drew a technical" for a "screaming tirade" at officials. When her staff pulled her off the court, she "ripped off her jacket and threw it down on the bench."[13] Sylvia stayed in Gastonia on Friday and joined her team on Saturday at the I-85 Cracker Barrel on their way to play unranked Clemson on Sunday, January 18. They won the game 78–56.

UNC entered the ACC Tournament as the No. 6 seed; Duke was No. 4. After the one-point loss to Duke in the regular season, Sylvia said that her practices would include boxing lessons. John McCann with the *Herald Sun* reported that she said it with a straight face.[14] Allisha Gray said the loss was a definite motivator—a "booster"—for the ACC Tournament. Sylvia acknowledged that she herself was a little low on energy, despite her January comments to the Hunter Huss audience. "My reserve tank isn't quite what it used to be," she told the media. If it was low, it wasn't obvious when she was honored with the ninth annual Bob Bradley Spirit and Courage Award given by the Atlantic Coast Sports Media Association. Her energy level seemed high during the Tournament as the Lady Tar Heels dispensed with Georgia Tech in the second round (84–64). The next day, they faced No. 3 seed Louisville—a newcomer to the ACC—in the quarterfinal game. Freshman Jamie Cherry's free throw with 25 seconds on the clock sent the game into overtime, tied at 66. Washington missed a three-point shot; Mavunga fouled out; and UNC went down 77–75. There would be no ACC title game for the Tar Heels.

Between the ACC and NCAA Tournaments, another scathing exposé of the

UNC scandal hit the newsstands, and this one included comments from Sylvia. On March 16, 2015, *Sports Illustrated* featured a lengthy article by Scott L. Price who wrote that Sylvia "had trusted [Jan] Boxill." Speaking of the "114 enrollments in paper classes," Sylvia argued, "When you look at the whole big picture, this was a small, small, small fraction.... And I'm not making light of it. But when you compare that with everything else? Carolina still has the It factor. We are elite. We are the school. It's still the Carolina Way. It's still extremely prestigious to go to school here, to play here."

For the umpteenth time in her career, Sylvia had to "put on her big girl britches" and believe her own words. Her Tar Heels were the No. 4 seed in the NCAA Greensboro Region and would play the first two rounds in Carmichael. Sylvia had no complaints about this bracket, unlike years past. First up was No. 13 seed Liberty. Attendance was low—2,098—and Liberty athletics director estimated that Liberty fans accounted for 600–700 of that number. Stephanie Mavunga said she was startled when she saw so much red "walking in." Mavunga and her teammates got the 71–65 win for their "mama bear." Mavunga told the press that Sylvia "really takes care" of her players: "If I get hit [in the post] ... Coach Hatchell's not having it. She's like, 'Hey, my player's getting killed in there!' ... It's different when your mom's coming out there saying, 'Yo, watch it, they're hitting my kid!' She's not going for that." Mama Bear then led her team to a win in the second-round against No. 5 seed Ohio State. Freshman Jamie Cherry worked her magic for the second time in two weeks. With .6 seconds left, she sank a two-pointer to give UNC the 86–84 win and a trip to the Sweet 16 for the second consecutive year.

Sylvia at courtside (with Megan Buckland, seated) in Carmichael, NCAA first-round game, UNC vs. Liberty, March 24, 2015. Courtesy Sheila Oliver.

Sylvia thrived on the energy and momentum of her team. They had filled her tank! When she was fighting her way through chemotherapy in 2013 and 2014, her team was a beacon of hope. *This* was why she fought so hard. She and the Lady Tar Heels packed their bags—and the golden scissors—but had to travel only a short distance to the Greensboro Coliseum, where the team now felt comfortable and where they would face the No. 1 seed South Carolina. The press made much of Sylvia's connections to the state. Dawn Staley told the press that UNC "got every high-profile player" in South Carolina before she took over as head coach. David Caraviello wrote that Sylvia thinks of the state line as "only a suggestion," but Staley's appearance made recruiting "more of a challenge." The Sweet-16 game on March 27 was also a challenge—and a repeat of the 2014 Sweet-16 game. The Tar Heels found themselves in familiar territory—down two points with 3.5 seconds left. Jamie Cherry's last-ditch effort hit the rim and did not fall through the net. But the fault lay with the whole team, not just Cherry—turnovers, missed shots, and fouls gave South Carolina the 67–65 win.

The Lady Tar Heels finished the season 26–9 overall and 10–6 in the ACC, a record that matched the previous season when Diamond DeShields was Sylvia's star point guard. Had the impact of DeShields' departure been overestimated? Sylvia began to feel confident that she had a strong, experienced team returning for 2015–2016—then her Lady Tar Heels fell apart. In May of 2015, Jessica Washington announced via Twitter that she would join the Kansas Jayhawks, saying she wanted more playing time. Washington had played in all 35 UNC games in her sophomore year, averaging 7.3 points and 2.4 rebounds. Then the other shoe dropped: On June 5, 2015, Sylvia returned from a 10-day Nike coaches event in Hawaii and was immediately summoned to UNC for a 2:00 p.m. called meeting with UNC attorney Rick Evrard and UNC Vice Chancellor for Communications and Public Affairs Joel Curran. In this meeting, Sylvia and the players heard for the first time that allegations against women's basketball could result in NCAA sanctions, probation, and vacated wins. The Lady Tar Heels could be prohibited from postseason play.

The players were rattled—stunned. Right away, they and their parents blitzed Sylvia with questions and phone calls. Soon after, Allisha Gray's father told Sylvia, "She's out of here," and Gray announced her departure for South Carolina, openly citing the NCAA academic scandal as the primary reason. Then, Stephanie Mavunga announced that she was transferring to Ohio State. The Tar Heels' much-touted, top recruiting class of 2013 was gone, and Te'a Cooper, whom Sylvia had expected to join the Tar Heels in fall 2015, signed with Tennessee. She would play alongside Diamond DeShields on The Summitt. There was no way to compensate for the departure of Washington and starters Mavunga and Gray two months before the opening of the fall semester. Sylvia had lost two additional starters to graduation—Latifah Coleman and Brittany Roundtree. Her team was decimated.

UNC was not the only program in the country whose players opted to transfer. Jim Fuller called it the "newest trend in women's college basketball" and pointed out that Geno Auriemma lost his entire 2003 recruiting class. Auriemma downplayed the "trend" as "a reflection of the society that we live in." Others blamed the NCAA scandal for Sylvia's dilemma: Bret McCormick said he was "sure" the players would not have left UNC "without the threat of NCAA punishment." He speculated that the NCAA would place UNC on probation and that "they won't be able to go to the postseason."[15] Jeremy Vernon wrote that "several pundits" blamed the NCAA investigation as the "main culprits" for the players' defection. He quoted Brian Barbour, who said the threat of NCAA punishment was "massive" and the "effects on the program's future recruiting classes could be alarming." Barbour wrote that 2017 and 2018 recruiting classes "are pretty well toast."[16]

With the threat of NCAA sanctions looming, Sylvia never imagined that the situation could worsen. She was wrong. On June 11, the news broke that UNC's academic accrediting body—the Southern Association of Colleges and Schools (SACS)—had placed UNC on 12 months' probation "for failing to meet seven accreditation standards, including academic integrity and control of athletics." Belle Wheelan, SACS president, said, "It's the most serious sanction we have."[17] When a university's accreditation standing is compromised, students fear that their degrees will be worthless. Top level employers and graduate schools do not recognize degrees from nonaccredited academic institutions. Sylvia's players now had yet another concern: would their degrees be worthless? A *News & Observer* editorial captured the nation's sentiment: "People within the university, either by intent, neglect or incompetence, traded the university's honor for hollow victories."[18]

14

The End of an Era

The 2015–2016 Lady Tar Heel season began with a change in assistant coaches: Ivory Latta returned to the professional ranks and was replaced by Sylvia Crawley. This was Crawley's second stint with the Tar Heels, having served as assistant from 2000 to 2002. Sylvia knew she could rely on Crawley, and she needed a strong staff to guide her untested team. She had only six scholarship players, including one returning starter, junior Xylina McDaniel. Sophomore Jamie Cherry had seen substantial time on the court, and she had freshmen Stephanie Watts and Destinee Walker, both of whom were high-school All Americans. This inexperienced team never gelled. After a preseason ranking of No. 20, the Lady Tar Heels dropped out of the top 25 and struggled through a miserable season—14–18 overall and 4–12 in the ACC. It was Sylvia's worst record since the black-cloud years between 1987 and 1991. Bonitta Best observed, "For the first time since 1988, none of the Triangle ACC teams made the NCAA Tournament,"[1] but this was hardly a consolation for Sylvia. She was frustrated.

Her frustration reached a peak during an away game against Duke on January 24. According to Andrew Carter, "she was upset with a no-call" and "made contact with an official," which resulted in a technical foul.[2] Brandon Chase was more specific in his description: "Hatchell launched into a fit of rage that found her at least 10 steps onto the court," and she "collided with referee Bruce Morris." Sylvia later said, "It was worth it." The Tar Heels lost 71–55, and UNC athletic director Bubba Cunningham suspended her for the next game, which was at NC State and resulted in another embarrassing loss for the Tar Heels (78–49). Cunningham then suspended her a second time, along with Tracey Williams-Johnson, for a secondary, Level III, NCAA rules violation that occurred during Late Night with Roy. The *Daily Tar Heel* reported that the infraction involved "activities that simulate game day introductions of prospects during an official visit." Sylvia publicly accepted responsibility for both suspensions and said the rules violation was unintentional: "a mistake we will not make again."[3] She and Williams-Johnson sat out the game at Boston College on February 7, 2016, which the Lady Tar Heels won 86–78. Sylvia continued to believe that she was unique. Had any other Division I coach ever been suspended for such minor violations?

The ongoing academic-athletic scandal at UNC fed Sylvia's frustration and eroded her ability to coach and recruit. Day by day, the evidence increasingly focused on Jan Boxill and women's basketball. According to the *News & Observer*, Athletic Director Bubba Cunningham said there was yet "more evidence … that a few more former women basketball players had received improper academic help." Men's basketball and football would suffer no consequences, even though "UNC's football and men's basketball teams were the two highest in terms of enrollments in the fake classes within the African studies department."[4] The seeming inequity in the treatment of men's and women's sports incited public reaction. Andrew Carter and Dan Kane wrote, "UNC officials aren't explaining why two top-flight coaches [Hatchell and Williams] would be treated differently."[5] A side issue was contracts for both coaches, which ran through 2018. During this time, Roy Williams was given a contract extension to 2020. Sylvia was not. Even the *Daily Tar Heel*, weighed in:

> The focus on women's basketball, an easier, less popular target than men's basketball, is troubling. The team ... seems no more complicit in wrongdoing than others mentioned in the Wainstein report.... It's up to UNC to prove these suspicions wrong by treating Hatchell with consistency. Hatchell is a hall-of-fame coach, same as Williams. If she says she needs a contract extension to do her job properly, that request does not seem unreasonable.[6]

Carter and Kane wrote that because of the perceived inequities, "the university has attracted questions about whether it is sacrificing Hatchell and her program to spare the men's basketball program from harsh NCAA sanctions. Neither coach has been accused of doing anything wrong."[7]

Supporters of UNC women's basketball—male and female—began to use words such as "sacrificial lamb" and "scapegoat" to explain the perceived unfairness. Albert Long, described by the *Herald-Sun* as "one of the finest all-around athletes UNC ever produced," said he was "thoroughly disgusted with the way the athletics department has treated Coach Hatchell.... They are throwing her under the bus." Former player Tonya Sampson, a senior on the 1994 NCAA Championship team, defended Sylvia, as did Meghan Austin, who agreed with Long: "UNC is sacrificing Hatchell and her program to the NCAA to spare men's basketball and football."[8] In an editorial published in the *News & Observer*, Austin wrote, "I am proud to be a member of the UNC women's basketball program, but I cannot say I am proud to [be] represented by an administration that will throw a legendary coach to the wolves to protect men's athletic teams."[9] As for Sylvia, she stuck by Jan Boxill, refusing to throw *her* under the bus. She told John McCann, "Jan's my friend, and she'll always be my friend. I don't turn my back on people."[10] The pressure on Boxill was insurmountable; she had resigned in February 2016.

On May 22, 2016, Sylvia met with UNC attorney Rick Evrard and Bubba Cunningham to discuss allegations against UNC and possible NCAA sanctions. There were no charges against the women's basketball program, the coaches, or the staff, but Jan Boxill continued to be *the* problem. Cunningham and Evrard argued that Boxill's relationship to the women's program put it in jeopardy. Sylvia argued that Boxill had been assigned to the program long before she arrived and that Boxill worked with many UNC athletes, not just women's basketball—Sylvia did not hire her, supervise her, or evaluate her. Sylvia was told that if the NCAA ruled against Boxill—if there was a finding of academic misconduct—the women's basketball program might be forced to "vacate wins." She was worried about recruiting: "Kids we were used to getting would not even visit because they thought we were going to get the death penalty from the NCAA."

Sylvia needed events to turn in her favor—she needed good news. Instead, she learned that her colleague and friend of 42 years—Pat Summitt—died on June 28, 2016, at age 64. On June 29, Summitt's family held a private service in her hometown, Clarksville, Tennessee, which was followed by a public celebration of Summitt's life on July 14 on The Summitt in Thompson-Boling Arena. Notable coaches, politicians, athletes, and friends honored her legacy: 1,098 wins, eight NCAA Championships, and 16 SEC Tournament titles. Speakers included Holly Warlick, Mickie DeMoss, Pat's son Tyler, and Peyton Manning. Robin Roberts from *Good Morning America* was master of ceremonies. Tributes from Pat's close friends flooded the media. Sylvia recalled their first meeting at UT in 1974 and repeated two of her frequent statements about Summitt: "No one has done more for women's basketball than Pat Summitt" and "I wouldn't be at North Carolina today without her." Sylvia also shared that during her 2013–2014 battle against leukemia, Pat called her often: "What a friend. What a lady." She told Andrew Carter, "I don't know in my lifetime if I have ever known or been around a more assertive, aggressive, dominating female than Pat Summitt." In her grief, Sylvia remembered Kay Yow: "I thought 'Well, Pat and Kay are up in heaven doing a coaching clinic.' ... I can just see them both sitting there right now, X'ing and O'ing."[11] In his tribute to Summitt, Ed Hardin aptly described Sylvia's and Pat's legacies: "Just a couple of college kids from Tennessee helped blaze a trail for women's basketball in America. One of them died Tuesday. And one of them promises to fight on in her memory."[12]

While Sylvia mourned the loss of her friend of 42 years, she fought for her career, for women's basketball, and for her Tar Heels against the backdrop of persistent conflicts at UNC—the university she loved, the place where she found her dream job in 1986. In September 2016, her contract was renewed through the 2019–2020 season with a base salary of $366,000 that would increase to $400,000 in the final year. This good news was sullied by ongoing reports about the NCAA allegations. She and other UNC representatives were expected to testify before the NCAA Committee on Infractions in September or October, but the "back-and-forth" between UNC and the NCAA delayed the process. Aaron Beard characterized the long, tedious process as "oft-delayed" and "filled with starts, stops and twice-rewritten charges." He wrote, "After sanctioning the football program in March 2012 in the original case, the NCAA reopened an investigation in summer 2014, filed charges in May 2015, revised them in April 2016 and again in December."[13] Sylvia began to express public dismay about the impact on her program. She told the press that it was "'hard not to say' that women's basketball had become a scapegoat during the NCAA investigation.... I'm real happy for the other sports—for football and men's basketball, that they've sort of been taken out of this.... But I must admit that I'm heartbroken that this has happened to women's basketball." Her team was gutted. With the pall of NCAA sanctions hanging over her program, she could not recruit. The unranked Lady Tar Heels had three returning starters, Jamie Cherry, Destinee Walker, and Stephanie Watts; eight freshmen, including Jocelyn Jones; and Paris Kea, who was a redshirt sophomore transfer from Vanderbilt the previous season.

During this time, Sylvia thanked God for her blessings—continuing good health and her family. Sammy retired from Shaw University in 2016, and Van was thriving.

After his graduation from UNC in 2011, he became marketing director of Extraordinary Ventures, a nonprofit organization that created small businesses to employ developmentally challenged adults. Their enterprises included cleaning the interiors of the Chapel Hill transit bus fleet, a laundry service for UNC fraternities, and an online, small-gifts business. Van loved the work because it gave him "four wins: I can be learning a lot, I can be getting paid to do what I'm totally into, I can be making a huge impact on other people's lives, and I am making connections in the area where my future hangs." His future included admission to the Darden School of Business at the University of Virginia, so he moved to Charlottesville.

Van's future also included a serious relationship with a woman—for the first time in his life. While he watched his college roommates suffer through romantic entanglements, Van was levelheaded about dating. Sylvia always encouraged him to develop many friends rather than date one girl exclusively. When he was choosing between his relationship with a girl and his desire to play on the UNC men's varsity basketball team, she cautioned him, "Now Van, you only go through this life once; don't make decisions that you will regret. Don't get so wrapped up in a girl that you ignore opportunities and your own goals." He listened—until he met Lucy Ireland at a wedding reception. They announced their engagement at Christmas in North Myrtle Beach, where the Hatchells had begun to celebrate the holidays.

Sylvia's team struggled through a dismal 2016–2017 season: 15–16 overall and 3–13 in the ACC. They finished 14th in the ACC and did not get a bid to the NCAA. Having little to celebrate in her own right, she savored the success of her former player and assistant coach Charlotte Smith. After joining Elon as the head women's basketball coach in 2011, Smith gradually built a winning team. In 2016–2017, her Phoenix women won the Colonial Athletic Association championship and got a bid to the NCAA Tournament for the first time in the history of the school. Sylvia traveled the 40 miles from Chapel Hill to attend the selection party as the Phoenix awaited their NCAA pairing: the No. 11 seed in the Bridgeport Region paired with No. 6 seed West Virginia. Sylvia told the press that she would not want to play the Phoenix in round one of the NCAA Tournament—her Tar Heels barely escaped their December 4 matchup in Carmichael (78–73), and on December 8, Elon had given Duke a fight (68–61). Sylvia said, "I'm proud of Elon, how they've treated her and embraced her and embraced women's basketball." Though Elon lost the NCAA first-round game to West Virginia 75–62, Sylvia was proud of her friend, the woman who changed her life in 1994 with that miracle shot.

As Sylvia was gearing up for the 2017–2018 basketball season, a date was finally set for hearings before the NCAA Committee on Infractions. On August 16–17, 2017, a six-member panel conducted closed hearings in a guarded conference room at the Gaylord Opryland Resort and Convention Center in Nashville. Sylvia and various UNC personnel attended, including Roy Williams, Bubba Cunningham, Chancellor Carol Folt, and 11 attorneys representing UNC's interests.[14] Sylvia's personal attorney Wade Smith was by her side. Because the hearings were closed, the media observed goings and comings from the outside and speculated. Steve Kirschner, a university spokesman, sent a text message saying, "Can't talk about the hearing and can't talk about the facts of the case."[15] UNC had long argued that the alleged infractions were academic in nature and did not fall under the purview of the NCAA; the press could only guess that that argument was still a strong thread inside the hearings. Later, Sylvia said she was asked only one general question about the quality of academic support at UNC. Jan Boxill, on the other hand, was on the "hot seat" during the inquisition. Sylvia was impressed with Boxill's testimony and believes that UNC would have suffered major penalties had she not told her story: "She cleared up a lot of misconceptions."

The first day lasted from 8:30 a.m. to 6:15 p.m. The second day from 8:30 a.m. to 1:00 p.m. Witnesses and panel members emerged tired and silent from the closed, guarded room. Then the wait for the NCAA ruling began. Sylvia went back to coaching a team that was more experienced than the previous season's—she had five returning starters—but the bench was not deep.

Eight weeks later, the committee published its findings. On October 13, 2017, word came down that UNC would face no penalties or sanctions, but the panel did not absolve North Carolina's flagship university. SEC commissioner Greg Sankey, the chief hearing officer, said, "what happened was troubling…. But the panel applied the membership's bylaws to the fact." In short, UNC won its argument: The NCAA could not impose sanctions for an academic misdeed because it is not an academic accreditation agency. Bubba Cunningham told the media, "We're not proud of the behavior but we didn't think it violated the [NCAA] bylaw, and today the Committee on Infractions revealed to us that they came to that same conclusion." Chancellor Carol Folt said, "This isn't a time of celebration."[16]

Indeed, there was little to celebrate. The UNC women's basketball program had escaped the "death penalty"—they would not have to vacate wins and would be eligible for postseason play—but the damage was irreparable. Brian Barbour's 2015 observation that the threat of NCAA punishment was "massive" and his prediction that the effects on "recruiting classes could be alarming" were accurate. When he wrote that 2017 and 2018 recruiting classes "are pretty well toast," he was spot on.[17]

The threat of sanctions was lifted, but Sylvia's team was indeed "toast." She had been unable to attract top talent because the ruling came too late for the 2017 and 2018 recruiting cycles. Rebuilding her Tar Heels would take longer than she had imagined, and the team continued to struggle throughout the season. After six straight losses to Duke, UNC pulled out a win in overtime on January 2, 2018 (92–86), but lost the second matchup in Cameron on February 25 (70–54). They lost nine straight games at the end of the regular season, finishing 15–16 overall and 4–12 in the ACC. For the third consecutive year, they were at the bottom of the Conference; five years previous, they were a contender for the ACC Championship. The scandal that decimated the team had disappeared from the public mind, but it lingered in the locker room, on the court, and in Sylvia's consciousness.

Amid this unsettled environment—aftermath of the NCAA ruling and continued failure of her team to perform—Sylvia celebrated a major milestone in her career, a pinnacle of achievement ranking alongside induction into the Naismith Hall of Fame. The 79–63 victory against nonconference Grambling State on December 19, 2017, was her 1,000th career win. Minutes later, Geno Auriemma won his 1,000th game to become the only male coach to achieve this milestone in women's basketball. He,

Sylvia celebrates her 1,000th career win against Grambling State with Juanita Floyd, longtime fan of UNC Women's Basketball, Myrtle Beach, South Carolina, December 19, 2017. Courtesy Sheila Oliver.

Sylvia, Pat Summitt, Barbara Stevens, Vivian Stringer, and Tara VanDerveer made an elite group. Auriemma was having greater success than Sylvia—he had won 100 of his last 101 games—but he acknowledged publicly the obstacles that impeded her journey to this moment, her "challenges, personal and professional." He praised her determination: "You would see her during the summer and nothing changed. The look on her face was like: 'What, me? Worried? I don't worry about anything.' She kept going and going and here she is. She hasn't changed one iota from when I first met her 30-something years ago. I'm happy for her."[18] To say "thank you" to the people who helped her achieve 1,000 wins, Sylvia gave bags containing 1,000 one-dollar bills to 17 individuals, primarily her assistant coaches and staff, but she also included the team's physician Dr. Harry Stafford and Jan Boxill. Jan no longer worked for UNC, but Sylvia continued to be loyal.

In April 2018, Tracey Williams-Johnson retired from UNC, after assisting Sylvia for 19 years. They had traveled the country together, looking for talent, including the trip on that fateful day in 2001 when terrorists struck the World Trade Center. Sylvia says, "I was in her wedding. We had been through a lot together, and I care about her a lot." She hired Bett Shelby to replace Tracey as an assistant coach and recruiting coordinator. Shelby had recruited top players for Maryland, where she worked from 2016 to 2018. Sylvia needed her to do the same for the Tar Heels—she urgently needed effective recruiting to rebuild a team. She was 66 years old and struggling through the same difficulties she faced 30 years prior at UNC—but she was relieved that she was out from under the threat of NCAA sanctions. She had every reason to believe that strong recruits would again choose UNC. With seasoned assistants Andrew Calder and Sylvia Crawley at her side, Sylvia had continuity, and Bett Shelby brought new blood—a winning combination.

Sylvia's family gifted her with another winning combination, one in which she found joy—her son's wedding in Charlottesville over Memorial Day weekend: a gala at The Lodge at Mount Ida Farm for 210 guests. The elegant ceremony on Saturday, May 26, was a wedding-planner's dream, complete with custom-designed stationery and a personal watercolor crest. The wedding party was large. The Lodge was an explosion of flowers and crystal and silver. The food represented tastes of the bridal couple—sushi for Lucy and tacos for Van; Italian for Lucy's heritage and Southern for Van's. Custom sugar cookies represented their dogs: chocolate lab Larry and yellow lab Colonel Mustard. The festivities ended with a colossal fireworks display. Sylvia was a stylish mother of the groom—in a Carolina blue dress—and was silently thankful that she lived to enjoy this day.[19] During chemotherapy in 2013, she feared that she would never be part of her son's future.

Then it was basketball time. Sylvia had four returning starters, including Paris Kea, a redshirt senior, and Janelle Bailey, both of whom were named to the preseason All-ACC Team. The 2018–2019 Lady Tar Heels were predicted to finish seventh out of 14 ACC teams, and their mixed start matched the prediction—eight wins and five losses to unranked teams they should have beaten, such as Kentucky, Ohio State, and Maine. On December 14, her team defeated UNC Greensboro to make her the all-time winningest coach in the ACC with 740 wins. This was followed by a UNC announcement that Roy Williams was awarded a contract extension through 2027 with a final base salary of $800,000 and $2.15 million in supplemental income. On top of this, his Nike package was $340,000. Williams was one of 11 UNC head coaches whose contracts were extended—Sylvia was not among them. Her contract would expire in 2020.

Sylvia looked askance at the proverbial handwriting on the wall and turned toward the holidays in North Myrtle Beach. She was eager to see Van and Lucy—she and Sammy had not seen much of the new couple since their May wedding. Their Christmas gift was the best she had ever received: a sonogram showing that Lucy was pregnant with a due date of July 24, 2019—a reminder that life goes on—the circle turns. She was buoyed up—encouraged that her troubled times at UNC were past, that she could rebuild her team, reclaim her position in women's basketball, and begin a new phase of life as a grandmother. Her optimism would be short lived.

Immediately after Christmas, Sylvia's team was back on the court for a game on December 28, 2018, against Howard University in Carmichael. Her Tar Heels got a solid win (85–63), but they did not play well. Howard was the last non-conference game of the season—ACC conference play began with Louisville on January 3, 2019. Several Lady Tar Heels had never played in an ACC game, and Sylvia wanted to prepare them: "After the Howard game, I went into the locker room with only the players and coaches. I gave them a passionate two- to three-minute speech about the competition level in ACC, the best women's conference in the country, and a level of competition that was the highest." Sylvia pointed out that playing on the home court of the team ranked No. 2 in the nation would be tough: "I wanted to emphasize the brutality of play they should expect. The crowd would be large and noisy; Louisville would play with reckless abandon. I said, 'Louisville will want to string you up and hang you out to dry. There will be nails in the coffin. Get yourself ready.'" Two days later, on Sunday, December 30, Sylvia was notified that a parent had complained about her locker-room comments. She had "said something about a hanging." She was aghast that her motivational speech had been misinterpreted.

At the next practice, Sylvia addressed the issue with the team. "If any of you have a problem with anything I ever say to you, talk to me about it. I would never do anything or say anything to hurt you guys. If there is something we need to talk about, let's do it. Is there anything we need to talk about?" One player said "yes," there was something they needed to discuss. She was upset about Sylvia's language after the Howard game. Again, Sylvia apologized: "I said, 'That's not how I meant it. You know me. You know my heart. I was just trying to get you to understand the brutal mentality of the ACC. I am sorry that you took it that way. I would never say anything to hurt you guys. Are we OK now?'" The player said that she did not accept Sylvia's apology. She felt that Sylvia apologized for how the team interpreted the words, not for the words themselves. Again, Sylvia, apologized: "It was a poor choice of words, and I apologize." Then the team got down to the routine business of film work and the scouting report in preparation for their first ACC conference game in Louisville.

When Sylvia went home, she had residual concerns about the exchange with one of her star players, so she called Paris Kea, the team captain and only senior. She said, "It breaks my heart that you guys would even think I meant it like it was taken. That is not what I meant." Paris suggested that she apologize again—and Sylvia did just that. Before the Louisville game, she told the team that she had spoken with Paris: "Once again, I want to apologize for what I said. It was a poor choice of words. Are we OK?" No one said anything. Because they were playing Louisville in Kentucky, Sylvia decided to use the Kentucky Derby and thoroughbred horses as a motivational metaphor. She told the players, "You are thoroughbreds. You are quick, fast, and athletic!" No one said anything. Later, an assistant coach told her not to compare the players with horses—not to compare them with animals. Sylvia was horrorstricken: "I was trying to motivate them and make them realize how special they are, not compare them to animals. I had no idea I was offending anyone." Her Tar Heels lost the game to Louisville 73–66. Nothing was said for the remainder of the season regarding Sylvia's comments, so she thought the issue was dead.

But another issue had arisen during the spring semester that would prove catastrophic for Sylvia. In the February 17 game against Virginia, Stephanie Watts injured her knee. The team physician Dr. Harry Stafford said she would be out for 10 days to two weeks, and she began a rehab protocol. Before the ACC Tournament, she was cleared for limited practice, and during a session she reinjured the knee. The Tar Heels won the round-one game against Georgia Tech (80–73), but in round two they were up against No. 4 Notre Dame, whom they had beaten earlier in the season. Without Watts, they lost this critical matchup (95–77). In press conferences, Sylvia remained hopeful about her star player's condition as the NCAA Tournament neared.

By NCAA Tournament time, the Tar Heels were unranked with an 18–14 overall record and 8–8 in the ACC—they were climbing back. True, the climb was slow, but Sylvia could see progress. This would be their first appearance in the NCAA Tournament since 2015—her team needed to perform well. A quiet Watts was present for the pairings party on March 18 at the Rizzo Center where they learned they were the No. 9 seed in the Greensboro Region. If the Tar Heels advanced through the first and second rounds, they would practically have home-court advantage for the Sweet 16, but they would have to play without Watts. She was out for the season. On March 23, they traveled to Waco, Texas, for the first-round matchup against No. 8 seed California, which they lost by 20 points. In the post-game press conference, Sylvia said she was "excited" about the next season when her returning players would be "healthy" and new recruits would boost Tar Heel play to "another level."

Sylvia's next problem was a series of defections—three graduating seniors and a walk-on: On March 12, Destinee Walker entered her name in the NCAA transfer portal. On March 25, two more players entered their names: Stephanie Watts and Kennedy Boyd. On March 27, Jocelyn Jones became the fourth Tar Heel to defect. On this same day, an assistant coach received a call that one parent was trying to arrange a meeting of other parents with Bubba Cunningham. Shortly afterward, Cunningham came to Sylvia's office and asked if she knew what was going on. Parents had asked to meet with him. Sylvia assured him that "not one parent" had contacted her, and that night, she spoke with Robbi Pickeral Evans, UNC associate athletic director, about the rumored meeting between Cunningham and parents. Evans had no knowledge, so Sylvia put it aside.

The next day, Thursday, March 28, 2019, Sylvia drove to her North Myrtle Beach house. Within 24 hours, she received a call from her attorney, Wade Smith, who had been contacted by UNC attorney Mark Merritt about Cunningham's meeting with parents. There were three areas of concern: racial, medical, and general. Sylvia wondered why she was hearing this news from attorneys, not from Cunningham. She returned from the beach to meet with Wade Smith late on Sunday afternoon, March 31. Andrew Calder went with her. Smith suggested that UNC might ask Sylvia to "take a few days off" while the university probed the matter. Sylvia said, "I will do whatever is necessary, Wade."

On April 1, Sylvia was summoned to a noon meeting in the Carmichael conference room with Cunningham, Robbi Pickeral Evans, Felicia Washington (Vice-Chancellor in charge of Title IX), Wade Smith, and Joyce Fitzpatrick of Fitzpatrick Communications, who was assisting Smith. Cunningham informed Sylvia about his meeting with parents. Their "serious" concerns had prompted him to hire the Charlotte law firm Parker Poe Adams & Bernstein to conduct an internal investigation. A news release would go out at 2:00 p.m. Sylvia and her assistant coaches were placed on administrative leave and were prohibited from being on campus or talking with players, staff, and coaches. Her UNC email account was deactivated. Uppermost in her mind was recruiting. She said, "I have recruits who will hear this on the news or social media, and if I can't talk with them, we could lose them. I need time to talk to them and explain this situation." Cunningham refused. She asked Wade Smith to intervene. He tried but failed. Cunningham then met with Andrew Calder, who emerged from the conference distraught and in tears: He said to Sylvia, "You don't deserve this." Then he was gone—as were Crawley and Shelby. At 2:00 p.m., Cunningham met with the team and told them they were not allowed to communicate with their coach. They would be part of the investigation. "We were all stunned," says Sylvia. She had to leave campus immediately, and as she was pulling out of the Carmichael parking lot, she saw a group of her players standing on the corner: "I could tell they were in shock. I just waved at them because I couldn't talk with them. It was the last time I saw them."

At 2:16, UNC issued a press release: "The North Carolina women's basketball coaching staff has been placed on paid administrative leave pending an internal investigation into 'issues raised by student-athletes and others.'" The statement promised that the investigation would be "thorough and prompt." Sylvia issued a statement simultaneously:

> I've had the privilege of coaching more than 200 young women during my 44 years in basketball. My goal has always been to help them become the very best people they can be, on the basketball court and in life. I love each and every one of the players I've coached and would do anything to encourage and support them. They are like family to me. I love them all. Of course, I will cooperate fully in this review. I look forward to a prompt conclusion of this matter and the continuation of our very successful women's basketball program.[20]

Then came the media barrage. The suspension of a Division I Hall-of-Fame coach was a hot topic for every news source in the country—major and minor. On April 4, the *Washington Post* published a long article by Will Hobson, who characterized Sylvia's program as "marked by mediocre records and high-profile players transferring, some of which Hatchell has blamed publicly on the 2015 academic scandal in which a long-time academic advisor to the women's basketball team [Jan Boxill] played a pivotal role."[21] Sylvia was prohibited from making public comments, but parents were free to talk. Hobson interviewed seven individuals, "including six parents of current players," who spoke with the guarantee of anonymity, except Michael Jones, father of Jocelyn Jones. He reportedly told Cunningham, "Bubba, you know me; you mean to tell me my daughter has to go through, in 2019, what I went through in 1985." When Hobson contacted him by phone, "Jones did not dispute making this remark, and declined further comment." Parents reported to Hobson that Stephanie Watts's father had "submitted a written statement" and that he was "angered" by the way his daughter's diagnosis was managed.[22] In a later article, on April 19, Hobson implicated Andrew Calder. Parents said he blamed "their daughter for the team missing the tournament."[23]

According to Hobson, the allegations were disturbing. First, Sylvia was said to have used racially inappropriate language: She allegedly told her players that "they would get 'hanged from trees with nooses' ... if their performance didn't improve." In another instance, she reportedly urged "her players to engage in a 'war chant' to 'honor' the Native American ancestry" of then-assistant-coach Tracey Williams-Johnson, who was "visibly uncomfortable" during the incident—according to parents. Sylvia was also accused of saying "she should have known she couldn't win championships with 'a bunch of old mules.'" A second accusation was that she "pressured" three players "to compete through serious injuries." According to Hobson, "Parents differed on whether the blame for these situations belonged to Hatchell or the team physician, Dr. Harry Stafford," who declined comment.[24]

In Hobson's article, Wade Smith characterized the accusations as "incorrect and misconstrued." He echoed Sylvia's explanation: "She said, 'They're going to take a rope and string us up, and hang us out to dry.'" She would never use the word "noose." Smith told Hobson that "Hatchell didn't recall the allegations about pressuring injured players to return to play, but said she never would have tried to convince anyone to play whom the medical staff had not cleared." Smith said that Sylvia did not recall making any reference to "old mules." What the players interpreted as a "war chant" was probably an imitation of the "tomahawk chop" prior to a game against Florida State. Smith told Alan Blinder and Marc Tracy with the *New York Times*, "I believe this is a case in which things are not what they seem."[25] But the damage was done—there was no way to put this cat back in the bag.

On April 4, the *Charlotte Observer* joined the *Post* with a scathing editorial, "Stop Tolerating Abusive College Coaches," which cited a number of offensive coaches and incidents, including Michigan State's Tom Izzo and Georgia State's MaChelle Joseph. The editorial concluded, "Other women's basketball programs ... have fired coaches in recent years for mistreating players. If UNC finds abuse from any coach—men's or women's—it should do the same." Geno Auriemma told Mechelle Voepel,

> Everybody's got to coach to their personality.... It's harder today than it's ever been to motivate players. I mean, I get we have to keep an eye on things. We don't want people to abuse the system. I get that. I'm all in favor of that. I just find it a little bit disconcerting that more and more coaches are being told, "This is inappropriate; you're not acting the right way." What is the right way, and who is going to decide what the right way is? I don't know what the answer to that is.[26]

Sylvia agreed with both perspectives: Coaches should not abuse players, but the line between perceived abuse and intense, emotional coaching and motivation is blurry. Notre Dame coach Muffet McGraw acknowledged that players are "demanding to be treated better," and rightly so, but "kids are going to get yelled at. They need to be able to take a little bit of that."[27]

While Sylvia's predicament was aired in the national press, she attended the Women's Final Four in Tampa Bay on April 5. Fearing that she would be accosted by the press, Joyce Fitzpatrick went with her. According to Fitzpatrick, there was no media onslaught; instead, Sylvia was treated like a queen. She "was met by hundreds of coaches, players, and parents who were eager to tell her how much she meant to them and how they admired her." One veteran Hall-of-Fame coach said, "I don't know how you are going to survive this." Sylvia recalls that "at least 10 coaches" told her they were in similar situations, and many of them did not have the resources to fight. At the Final Four, Sylvia participated on a panel of 1,000-win coaches that included Geno Auriemma, Barbara Stevens and high-school coach Andy Zihlman. That night, they were honored on the court after the first quarter of the Oregon-Baylor semifinal. A ceremony (sponsored by the Kay Yow Cancer Fund) also honored coaches and staff members who had survived cancer. Sylvia had two reasons to be on the court. On Sunday, April 7, Sylvia and Sammy attended a 7:30 worship service, and Charlotte Smith joined them in the front row, repaying Sylvia's loyalty of more than 30 years. Sylvia had told Charlotte, "Stay out of this; make no statements." She feared repercussions for the thriving Elon coach, but Charlotte was steadfast. Later, at the Kay Yow breakfast in the banquet room, Charlotte joined her again. Following these events, Sylvia and Sammy flew home—they did not stay for the NCAA Championship game to watch Baylor defeat Notre Dame by one point.

On this same day, the UNC *Daily Tar Heel* published an editorial titled "Coaches Like Sylvia Hatchell Don't Belong at UNC": "Behavior that may have been acceptable decades ago is not to be tolerated now. And that has nothing to do with the basketball players, and their allegations toward Hatchell certainly don't make them too 'sensitive' or 'weak.' The lack of empathy toward both the players and their injuries is jarring, no matter the time period." The *News & Observer* gave a more balanced view in "Parents, Players Offer Contrasting Accounts of UNC Women's Basketball Coach Hatchell." Author Andrew Carter did not sidestep the serious accusations that were published widely, but he interviewed current and former players who held different opinions about Hatchell: "[S]everal parents of players who either transferred or dealt with injuries during their time at UNC said they had no problem with the way Hatchell and her staff treated their daughters." Another parent said that Hatchell is "just from another era" and "hasn't 'kept up' with advancements in medical treatment of sports injuries." One father said he had "written a letter of complaint to Hatchell and Bubba Cunningham ... detailing 'experiences over [five] years that were not acceptable to us.'" This parent, however, "declined to share a copy of the letter and he refused to detail its contents." Former player Rashanda McCants told Carter that use of the word "nooses ... is not [Hatchell's] character.... I don't believe it, not from my experience with Sylvia and her coaching staff.... She doesn't even like for you to use profanity." Ivory Latta agreed: "She's an amazing person.... She changed my life. Went to college as a little girl, came out as a grown woman. She taught me a lot of principles. Not only about basketball but about life, period."[28]

Deborah Morgan with WRAL-TV in Raleigh also interviewed Ivory Latta, along with Erlana Larkins, both All Americans. Latta cited Sylvia's "honesty": "Whether you had ups and downs with her, you knew that, when you left there, you were a better person." She added that Sylvia was "like my second mom." Larkins was sensitive to the current players' concerns and said she did not "want to take away from whatever it is the girls may or may not have experienced." However, she joined Latta in saying she "never heard racially insensitive remarks" from her coach. According to Morgan, "The idea prompted [both women] to laugh." Latta said, "When it first came out and I saw it, I was like, 'What? A racist! This lady out of all people?' I'm from South Carolina, and to be honest, I've encountered a lot of racism.... Coach Hatchell? Seriously? That's the hurtful part." As for medical injuries, Latta and Larkins both said "they played through pain because of a desire to contribute to the team, not because of any pressure from the coach." Latta said, "Our jerseys aren't hanging up in Carmichael Arena because we said, 'Oh coach, we can't play today. We have a little soreness.' ... When you get in the real world, nobody is going to be holding your hand. So you learn these lessons in college so when you get to the real world, you're good." Larkins expressed concern that Sylvia's legacy could "be possibly tarnished" but ended with, "Her legacy—it lives forever." Nikki Teasley told Morgan, "Coach created a culture and atmosphere at Carolina that allowed me and all my teammates to become the best women we can become in life."[29]

Sylvia's trip to the Final Four had been a nice "cease fire" for her, but the battle that raged while she was in Tampa continued when she returned to Chapel Hill. On April 10, she met with two Parker-Poe attorneys—from 1:00 to 5:00 p.m. Several players were interviewed, but others refused to participate in what they characterized as a "witch hunt." On April 11, she enjoyed another respite when she drove to Black Mountain for the annual blueberry patch cleanup day. The crowd was larger than in any previous year—60–70 people turned out, including the UNC Asheville women's basketball team and two players from the Montreat College men's team. On Sunday, April 14, she drove back to Chapel Hill to face the final chapter of her career as head women's basketball coach at the University of North Carolina at Chapel Hill.

On Monday she heard nothing. On Tuesday, Wade Smith asked for a Wednesday morning conference call, which she took at her kitchen table. Smith gave her the news: The report from Parker Poe was complete. It recommended termination of Sylvia Hatchell for cause. She had until five o'clock to resign or be fired. The threat of making the report public was a deciding factor—a report that was described as highly damaging, a report she has yet to see. UNC agreed to resume negotiations the next day, but all parties were at an impasse. On Thursday, April 18, UNC emailed a separation agreement to Sylvia's home, which she had to accept by midnight or submit to termination. Shortly after 11:00 p.m., Wade Smith, Joyce Fitzpatrick, and Andrew Calder came to her house to review the document, and the message she inferred from her attorney was, *You do not have to sign the agreement, but we recommend that you do rather than be fired.* Against her better judgment, she signed. Then, she and Fitzpatrick composed a statement, which they sent to UNC for inclusion in the official UNC press release.

Sylvia signed the agreement at 11:57 p.m. on April 18, and on April 19 at 12:02 a.m., UNC issued a press release, including her prepared statement.[30] The press release said Parker Poe Adams & Bernstein interviewed 28 individuals and found "widespread support for three overarching themes." First was the accusation of "racially insensitive" comments, which she did not address "in a timely or appropriate manner. The report concluded that Hatchell is not viewed as a racist," but that "she lacked awareness and appreciation for the effect her remarks had on those who heard them." Second were medical issues: "Players and medical staff" reported that Hatchell exercised "undue influence ... regarding medical issues and pressure to play." Third was "a breakdown of connectivity between the players and Hatchell." Sylvia's 400-word statement followed. She thanked John Swofford for her "dream job" at Carolina. She thanked her assistant coaches and staff for their "loyalty and support." She cited her faith:

> While this is a bittersweet day, my faith remains strong. After the fight of my life with leukemia, I count every day as a blessing. I am grateful that God granted me more days on this earth to continue my calling as a coach. I have always believed that we are blessed so we can bless others. My goal has been to plant enough seeds to reap a good harvest. Today, I can truly say that my harvest has been abundant.

She ended with, "I will forever love the University of North Carolina. I am Sylvia Hatchell, and I am a Tar Heel."[31]

On Wednesday, April 24, Sylvia Hatchell left her office for the final time. She,

Sammy, and several friends packed boxes, loaded two trucks, and drove back and forth from campus to her home to clear out the remains of 33 years at UNC. Sylvia says, "The barn is full, the garage is full, upstairs in the house, the camp office is full." She admits, "I was mad." She did not feel relief or sadness: "I just wanted to get my stuff and get out of there." The next day, UNC sent a staff member to retrieve her university car, telephone, iPad, computer, and keys to her Carmichael office.

On April 30, UNC hired Courtney Banghart from Princeton as the head UNC women's basketball coach—the first new Lady Tar Heel head coach in 33 years and only the fourth in the program's 47-year history. Jonathan Alexander reported that Banghart's initial salary would be $650,000; her contract would run through 2023–2024. Among other comments, Banghart told the press that she would be visiting the UNC campus "to meet the players who remain with the program.... That will include the players that have chosen North Carolina and are standing by it, and that will also include the people who have chosen North Carolina, and there was a gap in what they were hoping for.... So I look forward to meeting both kind of sets of people, and know that I want—after I listen, is to know what I want moving forward is people excited about our journey, because I am [sic]."

When the dust began to settle, Mechelle Voepel with ESPN asked the question that was on everyone's mind: "Is North Carolina really committed to returning women's basketball to the top?" Being careful not to disparage Banghart or the Ivy League, Voepel wondered why UNC selected a coach who has "won once in an NCAA tournament game" and comes from a conference that has "a 2–28 all-time record in the NCAA tournament." She asked further, "Was this the very best résumé UNC saw? Did the Tar Heels pursue successful coaches from any major conference? Or were they not willing to pay top dollar for a coach with a more extensive track record?" And the question that loomed perhaps larger than any other: "How much consideration was given to Elon's Charlotte Smith?" The answer was "none." Voepel also questioned the wisdom of forgoing a press conference to reignite support for women's basketball on the UNC campus:

> Where was the on-campus announcement with fellow Tar Heels head coaches, returning players (not everybody is transferring), school officials, boosters, cheerleaders, Rameses the mascot, some Carolina blue and white balloons, and all the local TV stations' cameras? The school said Banghart might meet with some local media Wednesday and likely would have a gathering for fans/boosters in "the near future." Well, OK.[32]

Though the *News & Observer* called for the release of the Parker-Poe report in an April 25 editorial, it was never made public.[33] The basketball world may never know the details that ended the career of a Hall-of-Fame coach who affected the lives of hundreds of young woman.

Sylvia's 1950s Gastonia culture, the milieu of her early coaching career at Francis Marion, the reverence of 1980s and 1990s players for their coaches—these are gone. Sylvia was snagged on the ragged edge of change. Her high profile as a Division I coach made her an unwitting agent in a revolutionary shift of power. Cat Ariail wrote that her "actions reflect an outmoded imitation of what a coach has been imagined to be—the absolute authority who is empowered to treat players harshly in order to teach them the 'hard truths' needed to win titles." Ariail believes that athletics in

this country has aided the "settler colonialism of white Americans," that UNC wom-
en's basketball players "are demonstrating the determined and disruptive attitudes
needed to succeed in the contemporary late-capitalist economy." But Sylvia doesn't
theorize about capitalism and shifts in power. In many ways, she is still that little girl
who just wanted to play sports, a Tar Heel from Gastonia who values relationships
above all—above success and winning and power. Sylvia may have been a catalyst in
the shift of power, but her values mirror William Faulkner's old verities: "love and
honor and pity and pride and compassion and sacrifice." Built on these truths, her legacy will endure—while the pendulum of change arcs across time.

List of Accomplishments

Coaching Positions

1974—Head Coach Francis Marion College in Florence, South Carolina

1979—Assistant Coach for the East All-Star Team in the Hanes Underalls All-American Basketball Classic

1982—Head Coach National Sports Festival IV–South Team

1983—Assistant Coach World University Games in Edmonton, Canada

1984—Court Coach United States Olympic tryouts

1984—Events staff U.S. Olympic games

1985—Assistant Coach World Championship Games in Kobe, Japan

1986—Assistant Coach FIBA World Championships for Women in Moscow

1986—Assistant Coach Goodwill Games in Moscow

1986—Head Coach University of North Carolina-Chapel Hill

1988—Assistant Coach United States Olympic Team in Seoul, South Korea

1992—Court Coach U.S. Olympics basketball tryouts

1994—Head Coach for the R. Williams Jones Cup in Taipei, Taiwan

1995—Head Coach Goodwill Games in Fukoka, Japan

2003—Head Coach WBCA All-Star Challenge "STARS" in Atlanta, Georgia

Championships

1982—AIAW Division II Women's Basketball Tournament Championship

1986—NAIA National Tournament Championship

1994—ACC Women's Basketball Tournament Championship

1994—NCAA Championship

1995—ACC Women's Basketball Tournament Championship

1997—ACC Regular Season Champion

1997—ACC Women's Basketball Tournament Championship

1998—ACC Women's Basketball Tournament Championship

2005—ACC Regular Season Champion—Tie

2005—ACC Women's Basketball Tournament Championship

2006—ACC Regular Season Champion

2006—ACC Women's Basketball Tournament Championship

2007—ACC Women's Basketball Tournament Championship

2008—ACC Regular Season Champion and undefeated in ACC regular season

2008—ACC Women's Basketball Tournament Championship

Coach-of-the-Year Awards

1980—South Carolina (state) Coach of the Year

1986—AMF Voit Championship Coach Award

1986—Converse NAIA Coach of the Year

1986—NAIA District Six Coach of the Year

1986—NAIA Russell Athletic/WBCA National Coach of the Year

1986—South Carolina (state) Coach of the Year

1994—*College Sports Magazine* National Coach of the Year

1994—*USA Today* National Coach of the Year

1995—Athletes International Ministries Coach of the Year

1995—Converse NAIA Regional Coach of the Year

1997—ACC Coach of the Year

2006—AP Coach of the Year

2006—CAA Russell Athletic/WBCA National Coach of the Year

2006—Naismith College Coach of the Year

2006—ACC Coach of the Year

2006—U.S. Basketball Writers Association Coach of the Year

2008—ACC Coach of the Year

Halls of Fame

1993—Francis Marion University Athletic Hall of Fame

1999—Carson-Newman Athletic Hall of Fame

2004—Women's Basketball Hall of Fame in Knoxville, Tennessee

2005—Gaston County Sports Hall of Fame

2009—North Carolina Sports Hall of Fame

2009—South Carolina Athletic Hall of Fame

2013—Naismith Memorial Basketball Hall of Fame

Honors and Awards

1982—Order of the Palmetto

1986—Order of the Palmetto

1994—Carson-Newman Distinguished Alumnus of the Year

2009—Honorary Doctor of Humanities–Francis Marion University

2013—"A Tribute to Our Hometown Hero" by city of Gastonia, North Carolina

2013—Order of Long Leaf Pine

2014—Kay Yow Champion Award

2015—"Sylvia Rhyne Hatchell Court," Hunter Huss High School

2015—Bob Bradley Spirit and Courage Award

Milestones

2017—1000th career win

2018—740th ACC Victory with most wins of any ACC women's basketball coach

2019—Fifty-two total victories in ACC Tournament play. Sylvia Hatchell has the most ACC tournament wins.

2019—With a record of 45–21, Hatchell's UNC teams won more NCAA post-season games than any other ACC school.

2019—Career record 1,023–405

Interviews

All interviews were by Sheila Oliver unless otherwise stated

Baxter, Dorothy. November 16, 2009; October 25, 2011; April 28, 2012.

Bell, Joyce M. June 3, 2012; March 16, 2013.

Bilbrey, Sharron Perkins. May 18, 21, 25, 2012; June 3, 2012; February 26, 2013; April 23, 2018.

Birmingham, Peggy W. December 28, 2011; May 1, 2018.

Blanc, Linda Gay. May 2, 2012.

Braddock, Phyllis Alred. February 8, 2009.

Buck, Maureen Walling. July 30, 2012.

Burns, Eleanor Rogers. June 19, 2012.

Cooley, Phyllis Rhyne. March 19, 2008; October 11, 13, 2011; January 8, 2012; June 3, 2012; October 2, 2012; March 19, 20, 2013; April 23, 2013; December 3, 2013.

Cronan, Joan C. May 11, 2012.

Dalton, Nancy Blanc. May 15, 2012.

Dixon, Roger H. December 15, 2012.

Garnett, Mary Lou. January 24, 2008; March 15, 17, 2018.

Gilliam, Luny. March 28, 2018.

Gilliam, Ruby. March 28, 2018.

Grimes, Cecilia Budd. June 16, 2012; June 14, 2018.

Hatchell, Carl D. (Sammy). March 29, 2012; July 21, 2012; July 9, 14, 17, 2017.

Hatchell, Sylvia Rhyne. June 18, 2009; March 4, 7, 8, 2012; March 29, 2012; May 8, 2012; May 18, 2012; June 8, 2012; July 16, 17, 2012; September 23, 2012; March 16, 2013; August 26, 2017; November 17, 2013; February 8, 2018; February 13, 2018; March 7, 2018; April 5, 2018; October 20, 2018; March 14, 2019; May 8, 2019; June 23, 27, 30, 2019.

Hatchell, Sylvia Rhyne, interview by Sheila Oliver and Carolyn Allen. July 19, 2007.

Hatchell, Sylvia Rhyne, interviews by Sheila Oliver and Roberta Herrin. June 26, 2010; October 6, 2011; March 7, 2012; May 6, 7, 2019.

Hatchell, Van Davis. July 3, 6, 2012.

Hawkins, Kim Slawson. April 25, 2012.

Hawkins, Michael G. April 24, 2012.

High, Jane C. May 10, 2012; June 8, 2012; March 17, 2018; June 27, 2019.

Hovis, Dorothy Rhyne. May 17, 2012.

Humphries, Sarah. January 27, 2012.

Johnson, Niesa. November 15, 2017.

Jones-Thompson, Marion, interview by Sheila Oliver and Roberta Herrin. August 18, 2013.

Koss, Jackie. June 6, 2012.

Magher, Ruth R. October 26, 2009.

Markland, Regina S. April 14, 2012.

Marlowe, Kathy R. March 15, 17, 2018.

McGlade, Bernadette V. March 26, 2018.

Meier, Katie. February 23, 2012.

Moore, Pearl. January 25, 2010; February 3, 2012.

Northern, Thomas E. May 16, 2012.

Paul, Brenda. April 27, 2012; April 2, 2019.

Reid, Tracy. May 9, 2014.

Rhyne, Karen L. January 8, 2012.

Rhyne, Ralph V. May 9, 2009.

Rhyne, Ronnie Lamar. August 22, 2010.

Rikard, Tony. March 23, 2018.

Rose, Judy. June 3, 2009.

Saine, Don. December 28, 2011.

Sell, Jessica L. June 3, 2009; June 13, 2012.

Simpson, Debbie Morrow. September 25, 2011.

Smith, Charlotte. May 12, 2009.

Snodderly, Michael E. January 23, 2012; February 14, 2012; February 27, 2012; April 3, 4, 2012; March 27, 2012; February 13, 2013; September 28, 2017.

Stanley, Marianne C. September 28, 2017.

Stroud, Judy. April 19, 2009.

Stroup, Gracie Woolwine. April 4, 2012.

Strunk, Rick. January 11, 2012; April 30, 2012.

Swofford, John D. January 26, 2010.

Thomas, Jerry Dean. April 18, 2009.

Tribble, Annie. May 1, 2012.

Wilson, Martha B. April 10, 2012.

Wilson, Nancy R. E-mail to Sheila Oliver. July 11, 2011.

Wodrich, Bitha Creighton. May 15, 2012; January 27, 2013.

Yelton, Stephanie Lawrence. November 5, 2017.

Young, Tracey Tillman. February 19, 2012.

Yow, Susan. September 20, 2017.

Chapter Notes

Preface

1. Arthur Daley, "A Remarkable Woman" in *Sports of the* Times*: The Arthur Daley Years.* Edited by James Tuite (New York: Quadrangle, 1975) 148.

2. United States Department of Justice. "Overview of Title IX of the Civil Rights Act of 1964." https://www.justice.gov/crt/fcs/TitleVI-Overview.

3. Jenny McCoy, "13 Times Women in Sports Fought for Equality." *Glamour.* April 1, 2020. https://www.glamour.com/story/13-times-women-in-sports-fought-for-equality.

4. *Daily Press,* "Duke Students Seek Remorse from Packer." March 5, 2000.

5. Rudy Martzke, "CBS' Packer Issues Apology for Words to Duke Students." *USA Today* (Arlington, VA), March 8, 2000.

6. Benjamin Hoffman, "Newton Draws Rebukes for Mocking a Female Reporter." *New York Times* (NY), October 5, 2017.

7. *Ibid.*

8. Norah O'Donnell, "Notre Dame Head Coach Muffet McGraw Drew Attention for Her Powerful Words About Gender Equality." *CBS This Morning,* April 17, 2019. https://www.cbs.com/shows/cbs_this_morning.

Chapter 1

1. Sylvia Hatchell, "Sylvia Hatchell: An Interview" in *The Secret to Their Success: How 33 Women Made Their Dreams Come True.* Edited by Emily A. Colin (Wilmington, NC: Coastal Carolina Press, 2000), 250.

2. Early women's basketball play was variously described as "three-on-three," "six-on-six" and "half-court."

3. Tim Stevens, "N. C. Code Prohibited Tournaments for Girls Before 1972." *News & Observer* (Raleigh, NC), March 7, 2012.

4. Robert Allison Ragan, *History of Gastonia and Gaston County, North Carolina* (Charlotte, NC: Loftin & Company, 2010), 449.

Chapter 2

1. *Gastonia Gazette* (NC), "Hope Plastics Team Captures 9–5 Victory." August 17, 1974.

Chapter 3

1. Fran Ellis, "Another 'First' Initiated at FMC: Intra-mural Football—For Girls!" *Florence Morning News* (SC), November 9, 1975.

2. *Florence Morning News,* "Men's Summer League Basketball Results." July 17, 1977.

Chapter 4

1. MaryEllen Williams, *TRIUMPH: Inspired by the True Life Story of Legendary Coach Kay Yow* (LuLu.com: MaryEllen Williams, 2012) 120.

2. *New York Times,* "Judgment Call on a Good Deed." November 12, 1986.

3. Associated Press, "U. S. Olympic Official Concerned About Yow's Bible Smuggling." *Sports News,* November 11, 1986.

4. Francis Marion College, "FM Hosts Public Farewell Reception for Sylvia Rhyne Hatchell." News Release, August 14, 1986.

5. Associated Press, "U.S. Olympic Official Concerned."

6. United Press International, "U.S. Olympic Coach Criticized for Smuggling Bibles." November 11, 1986.

7. *New York Times,* "Judgment Call on a Good Deed." November 12, 1986.

8. *The State,* "Hatchells Land First Recruit: It's a Boy." January 26, 1989.

9. Jim Furlong, "Black Cloud in Blue Heaven." *Herald-Sun* (Durham, NC), January 29, 1991.

10. Marjo Rankin Bliss, "UNC Guard Adjusts to Redefined Role." *Charlotte Observer* (NC), April 3, 1994.

11. Celeste E. Whittaker, "Chapil [*sic*] Hill N. C. Tar Heel Women's Team Nets Hoopla." *Atlanta Journal-Constitution* (GA), March 22, 1994.

12. *Daily Press,* "Brawl-Marred Game Goes to UNC Women: Old Dominion's Season Ends 63–52." March 21, 1994.

13. Jeff Drew, "Heels Survive, but Forward Smith Ejected." *News & Observer* (Raleigh, NC), March 21, 1994.

14. Milton Kent, "North Carolina Gains Final Four Trip, 81–69." *The Sun* (Baltimore, MD), March 27, 1994.

15. *Louisiana Tech vs. North Carolina: 1994 NCAA Division I Women's Basketball National*

Championship. Ann Meyers and Tim Ryan, Announcers. DVD. NCAA on Demand Production, 2010.

16. *Ibid.*

17. Richard Walker, "Afterglow." *Charlotte Observer* (NC), April 8, 1994.

18. *Louisiana Tech vs. North Carolina: 1994 NCAA Division I Women's Basketball National Championship.*

19. Vic Dorr, "Alabama Players Won't Forget Coach." *Richmond Times-Dispatch* (VA), March 31, 1994.

20. White House Briefing, "President Clinton Meets with University of North Carolina NCAA Women's Basketball Team." Federal News Service, July 27, 1994.

21. Whittaker, "Clinton Gets Strategy Tips from NCAA Champions." *Atlanta Journal-Constitution*, July 30, 1994.

22. People.com, "Star Tracks." August 15, 1994. https://people.com/archive/star-tracks-vol-42-no-7/.

23. Wendy Parker, Women's Notebook, *Atlanta Journal-Constitution* (GA), October 8, 1994.

Chapter 5

1. Mechelle Voepel, "UNC Has Potential to Repeat." *Daily Press* (Newport News, VA), December 02, 1994.

2. Norman Arey, "Lady Heels Trample Duke 95–70 in Final." *Atlanta Journal-Constitution*, March 6, 1995.

3. *New York Times*, "A Problem for Seton Hall: Just Too Many Tar Heels." March 19, 1995.

4. *Herald-Sun*, "UNC's Ready for Tall Test," March 23, 1995.

5. Dave Trimmer, "Stanford Women Dethrone North Carolina." *Orange County Register* (CA), March 24, 1995.

6. Melissa Murphy, "Sports News." Associated Press, April 1, 1995.

7. Murphy, "WBCA Coaches to Meet with Congress at Title IX Hearings May 9." Associated Press, May 3, 1995.

8. Marion Jones with Kate Sekules, *Life in the Fast Lane: An Illustrated Autobiography* (New York: Warner, 2004) 61.

9. Furlong, "Jones Decides to Go for Gold: UNC Basketball Star Sets Priority on Track." *Herald-Sun* (Durham, NC), September 13, 1995.

10. Marion Jones with Kate Sekules. *Life in the Fast Lane* (New York: Warner, 2004) 65.

11. *Orlando Sentinel*, "If You Aim at Batter, Be Sure to Hit Him." July 31, 1996.

12. Whittaker, "UNC Signs Top Recruits to Ease Loss of Jones." *Atlanta Journal-Constitution*, November 9, 1997.

13. Associated Press, "No. 11 North Carolina 67, No. 8 North Carolina State 64." January 22, 1998.

14. Furlong, "From Her Younger Days in Gastonia, to College and at UNC, Sylvia Hatchell's Life Has Proven She Was ... Born to Coach." *Herald-Sun* (Durham, NC), January 31, 1998.

15. Furlong, "Ordeal: UNC's Calder Showed Heart to Survive Illness." *Herald-Sun* (Durham, NC), April 10, 1998.

16. *Ibid.*

17. Al Myatt, "A Special Coach for UNC Women." *News & Observer*, March 3, 1998.

18. Furlong, "Coach Facing Surgery Gets Look at Title Trophy." *Herald-Sun* (Durham, NC), March 2, 1998.

19. Furlong, "Ordeal: UNC's Calder Showed Heart to Survive Illness."

20. Aaron Beard, "Calder Returns to Carmichael: Seniors Leave Legacy." *Daily Tar Heel* (University of North Carolina, Chapel Hill, NC), March 18, 1998.

21. Associated Press, "Friends Reid, Holdsclaw Finally Foes Tonight." *Herald-Sun* (Durham, NC), March 23, 1998.

22. Kent, "Down 12, Lady Vols Prevail—37–0." *The Sun* (Baltimore, MD), March 24, 1998.

23. Marcia C. Smith, "Tennessee Women Narrowly Advance: North Carolina Led for Much of the Second Half." *Philadelphia Inquirer* (PA), March 24, 1998.

24. Associated Press, "No. 11 Duke 93, No. 7 North Carolina 71." January 23, 1999.

Chapter 6

1. John Altavilla, "Tar Heels Could Be on the Outside Looking In." *Hartford Courant* (CT), March 5, 2000.

2. Myatt, "Balanced Bulldogs Send Tar Heels Packing." *News & Observer* (Raleigh, NC), March 26, 2000.

3. University of North Carolina, "Sylvia Hatchell Heads Toward Season with New Outlook." News Release, July 19, 2000.

4. William Elliott Warnock, "Tar Heels Take Classic Against Wolfpack." *News & Observer* (Raleigh, NC), January 17, 2001.

5. *Herald-Sun*, "UNC Falls Short of Attendance Mark." January 15, 2001.

6. Warnock, "UNC Rides Bubble into Tournament." *News & Observer* (Raleigh, NC), February 28, 2001.

Chapter 7

1. Gregg Doyel, "Teasley Says Depression, Anxiety Led to Exit from UNC." *Charlotte Observer* (NC), December 17, 2001.

2. *Ibid.*

3. Furlong, "Point Well-Taken: Teasley Returns to 'Natural Position,' Leads UNC Past Virginia." *Herald-Sun* (Durham, NC), January 28, 2002.

4. Furlong, "Back to Work: Heels Come Off Break Looking Sluggish in Easy Win Over Charles-

ton Southern." *Herald-Sun* (Durham, NC), December 30, 2002.

5. Warnock, "UNC Getting an Earful About Duke." *News & Observer* (Raleigh, NC), January 8, 2003.

6. Furlong, "Clemson Coach Apologizes." *Herald-Sun* (Durham, NC), January 18, 2003.

7. Doyel, "Blue Devils Dominate After Replay Decision: TV Exposure Helps UNC Lose Chance at Late Regulation Foul Shot." *Charlotte Observer* (NC), January 21, 2003.

8. Parker, "Rising Tar Heels Strong Enough to Take on Duke." *Atlanta Journal-Constitution* (GA), February 16, 2003.

9. Doyel, "Duke Plasters Its Point Across UNC: No. 2 Blue Devils Back up 'Lucky' Win with Rout of No. 6 Tar Heels." *Charlotte Observer* (NC), February 21, 2003.

10. *Ibid.*

11. Jenna Fryer, "No. 2 Duke 77, No. 11 North Carolina 59." Associated Press, March 11, 2003.

12. Ed Hardin, "Another Sour Loss for Hatchell." *Greensboro News & Record* (NC), March 11, 2003.

13. *Atlanta Journal-Constitution*, "Mideast Women." March 17, 2003.

14. Furlong, "Tar Heels Survive Scare: Bell Ignites UNC with Key Buckets Down Stretch." *Herald-Sun* (Durham, NC), March 23, 2003.

15. Furlong, "Devils Beat Heels for Third Straight Year." *Herald-Sun* (Durham, NC), March 9, 2004.

16. Ned Barnett, "Future Is Not Now for Runner-up UNC." *News & Observer* (Raleigh, NC), March 9, 2004.

17. Dan Fleser, "Hatchell Proud of ET Upbringing." *Knoxville News Sentinel* (TN), June 11, 2004.

18. Rachel Carter, "Women's Hall Gains Hatchell." *News & Observer* (Raleigh, NC), June 12, 2004.

Chapter 8

1. Rachel Carter, "Auriemma, Huskies to Face Heels in Jimmy V." *News & Observer* (Raleigh, NC), August 04, 2004.

2. Nolan Hayes, "Big Win Just the Beginning for Tar Heels." *Herald-Sun* (Durham, NC), November 23, 2004.

3. Rachel Carter, "Yow Stricken with Cancer Again." *News & Observer* (Raleigh, NC), January 11, 2005.

4. *Orlando Sentinel*, "NASCAR Boss Isn't Jumping to NFL." January 23, 2005.

5. Ken Tysiac, "Duke-UNC Rivalry Lopsided Lately: Devils Take 12-Game Win Streak Against Heels to Chapel Hill Tonight." *Charlotte Observer* (NC), January 24, 2005.

6. Bill Hass, "Show Stoppers: Tar Heels Halt Duke's Dominance at Coliseum." *Greensboro News & Record* (NC), March 8, 2005.

7. *Ibid.*

8. Rachel Carter, "Tar Heels Seal the Deal." *News & Observer* (Raleigh, NC), March 8, 2005.

9. Warnock, "Carolina Dismantles Davidson in Opener." *News & Observer* (Raleigh, NC), November 20, 2005.

10. Jack Daly, "Tar Heels Shackle Liberty in 1st Half: Tar Heels Force 24 Turnovers in First Period for Big Win." *Herald-Sun* (Durham, NC), November 22, 2005.

11. Hayes, "UNC's Full Speed Even Faster." *Herald-Sun* (Durham, NC), November 18, 2005.

12. Vickie Fulkerson, "Huskies Want New Memories: Would Like to Forget Last Year's Collapse vs. UNC." *The Day* (New London, CT), December 05, 2005.

13. Daly, "R-E-S-P-E-C-T? Hatchell Hopes UNC's Win at UConn Attracts Attention." *Herald-Sun* (Durham, NC), December 7, 2005.

14. *Ibid.*

15. Rachel Carter, "Latta Love, a Lot of Points Ignite UNC." *News & Observer* (Raleigh, NC), January 29, 2006.

16. Daly, "Hatchell Earns Win No. 700: UNC Coach Reaches Milestone with Win Over Rival N.C. State." *Herald-Sun* (Durham, NC), January 16, 2006.

17. Barnett, "More on Line Than Ranking for Hatchell." *News & Observer* (Raleigh, NC), January 29, 2006.

18. Daly, "Celebration: North Carolina Climbs to No. 1 but Still Has N.C. State, Maryland and Duke Coming." *Herald-Sun* (Durham, NC), January 31, 2006.

19. Hardin, "Hatchell's Ideas Revolutionizing Women's Game." *Greensboro News & Record* (NC), March 6, 2006.

20. Associated Press, LSU, UNC Among Top Seeds: Duke and Ohio State Also Are No. 1s." *Orlando Sentinel* (FL), March 14, 2006.

21. Donna Tommelleo, "Tar Heels Awarded Top Seed." *Augusta Chronicle* (GA), March 14, 2006.

22. Pat Summitt with Sally Jenkins, *Sum It Up* (New York: Crown, 2013) 314.

23. Frank Litsky, "Tar Heels and Latta Keep Vols Under Foot." *New York Times*, March 29, 2006.

24. Hardin, "Hatchell's Ideas Revolutionizing Women's Game."

25. Sally Jenkins, "NCAA Leadership Isn't Matching the Talent of Its Players." *Washington Post* (DC), April 2, 2006.

26. Daly, "Recruiting and Defense Helped Heels Get Back." *Herald-Sun* (Durham, NC), April 02, 2006.

Chapter 9

1. Hatchell with Jeff Thomas, *The Baffled Parent's Guide to Coaching Girls' Basketball* (Camden, ME: McGraw-Hill, 2006) 7–8.

2. Daly, "Sloppy, but UNC Gets Win—Larkins' Second-Half Spark Helps the Heels." *Herald-Sun* (Durham, NC), December 4, 2006.

3. Fleser, "Singing Carolina Blues—North Carolina 70, Tennessee 57." *Knoxville News-Sentinel* (TN), December 4, 2006.

4. Kent, "Heels Quiet Crowd, UM—Terps Women Fall to Second ACC Power Before 17,950." *The Sun* (Baltimore, MD), January 29, 2007.

5. Tysiac, "In Battle of Unbeatens, Duke Stays Atop the Hill." *Charlotte Observer* (NC), February 9, 2007.

6. Joedy McCreary, "No. 1 Duke Earns First Post-Beard Victory Over No. 2 North Carolina." Associated Press, February 9, 2007.

7. Associated Press, "N.C. State Hangs on to Upset No. 2 UNC." February 17, 2007.

8. McCreary, "Duke Wraps Up 1st Perfect Regular Season in ACC History." Associated Press, February 26, 2007.

9. Hardin, "Tune in Next Week to See What Duke's Win Means." *Greensboro News & Record* (NC), February 26, 2007.

10. Daly, "Heels Take Time to Learn the Ropes." *Herald-Sun* (Durham, NC), March 2, 2007.

11. Hardin, "A Hard Day Ends with a Hug," *Greensboro News & Record* (NC), March 05, 2007.

12. *Ibid.*

13. Alan Robinson, "Mysteries of Pittsburgh: UT, UNC There." Associated Press, March 18, 2007.

14. Daly, "Hard to Hang On—UNC Survives a Scare from Irish." *Herald-Sun* (Durham, NC), March 21, 2007.

15. McCreary, "Tar Heels' Year Ends Again in Final Four." Associated Press, April 2, 2007.

Chapter 10

1. Edward G. Robinson, "Jones Acknowledges Lying About Steroid Use." *News & Observer* (Raleigh, NC), October 6, 2007.

2. Rachel Carter, "Heels' Trio to Replace Latta at Point." *News & Observer* (Raleigh, NC), October 30, 2007.

3. Aaron Beard and Joedy McCreary, "N.C. State's Yow Continues to Inspire in Her Fight with Cancer." Associated Press, November 1, 2007.

4. Mike Harris, "'Good for the Judge': Response to Jones' Plight Is Icy Among Area Track Devotees." *Richmond Times-Dispatch* (VA), January 12, 2008.

5. *Ibid.*

6. Daly, "VERY SATISFIED—Heels Run Past Terps for 2OT Win." *Herald-Sun* (Durham, NC), January 27, 2008.

7. Jim Fuller, "Counterpunch: Huskies Charge Past Heels in Second Half." *New Haven Register* (CT), January 22, 2008.

8. Robinson, "Devils Rout Hokies, Gear up for Heels." *News & Observer* (Raleigh, NC), February 2, 2008.

9. Megan Crotty, "Tar Heels Women Top Blue Devils." *Courier-Tribune* (Asheboro, NC), February 4, 2008.

10. *News & Observer,* "Double Standard on Celebrations?" February 17, 2008.

11. Mike Potter, "Larkins Powers Heels by Wolfpack." *Herald-Sun* (Durham, NC), February 26, 2008.

12. Hardin, "Carolina Ready to Call Greensboro Its Home." *Greensboro News & Record* (NC), March 3, 2008.

13. Beard, "DeGraffenreid, No. 2 North Carolina Beat No. 12 Duke 82–51." Associated Press, March 3, 2008.

14. Hardin, "After Tragic Week Back Home, Heels Can Smile." *Greensboro News & Record* (NC), March 10, 2008.

15. Beard, "Steamrolling No. 2 Tar Heels Wins 12th Straight, Rolls Past Virginia 80–65 in Women's ACC Semifinals." *Daily Dispatch* (Henderson, NC), March 9, 2008.

16. Hardin, "After Tragic Week Back Home, Heels Can Smile."

17. Doug Feinberg, "Connecticut, North Carolina, Tennessee, Maryland No. 1 Seeds NCAA Tournament." *Monitor* (McAllen, TX), March 17, 2008.

18. *Ibid.*

19. Myatt, "Balanced Bulldogs Send Tar Heels Packing."

20. Robinson, "Heels Fend Off Upset Bid." *News & Observer* (Raleigh, NC), March 26, 2008.

21. Daly, "Hatchell Earns Win No. 700: UNC Coach Reaches Milestone with Win Over Rival N.C. State." *Herald-Sun* (Durham, NC), January 16, 2006.

22. Rachel Carter, "Roast Honors Basketball Trio." *News & Observer* (Raleigh, NC), April 21, 2006.

23. Robinson, "South Carolina Courts Hatchell as Head Coach." *News & Observer* (Raleigh, NC), April 29, 2008.

24. *Ibid.*

25. Associated Press, "North Carolina's Hatchell Opts to Stay with the Tar Heels." May 1, 2008.

26. Associated Press, "UNC Extends Hatchell's Contract Through 2015." July 25, 2008.

Chapter 11

1. Robinson, "Basketball Season Is Over for Kay Yow." *News & Observer* (Raleigh, NC), January 7, 2009.

2. Beard, "In Funeral Video, NC State's Kay Yow Affirms Faith." Associated Press, January 31, 2009.

3. Beard, "No. 8 Tar Heels Rally Past No. 4 Blue Devils 75–60." Associated Press, February 10, 2009.

4. Andy Gardiner, "Schools Seek Extra Credit: Games Added to Pass Time, Gain NCAA Favor." *USA Today* (Arlington, VA), March 13, 2009.

5. Feinberg, "Unbeaten UCONN Earns No.1 Overall Seed for NCAAs." Associated Press, March 17, 2009.

6. Teresa Walker, "North Carolina Opens with 85–80 Win Over UCF." Associated Press, March 21, 2009.

7. *Ibid.*

8. Pete Iacobelli, "Hatchell Among Inductee Class for S.C. Hall of Fame." *Herald* (Rock Hill, SC), May 19, 2009.

Chapter 12

1. Trimmer. "Zags Sign Up—GU Reaches New Level with Win Over Heels." *Spokesman-Review* (Spokane, WA), March 21, 2010.

2. Steve Wiseman, "Marion Jones Kept an Eye on the Guards." *Herald-Sun* (Durham, NC), October 28, 2010.

3. Robinson, "No. 2 Connecticut at No. 11 N. Carolina, 7 p.m. (ESPN2): Tar Heels, Schedule to Be Put to UConn Test." *Charlotte Observer* (NC), January 17, 2011.

4. John Piper, *Andrew Fuller: Holy Faith, Worthy Gospel, World Mission* (Wheaton, IL: Crossway, 2016) 21.

5. Robinson, "Breland Powers Tar Heel Women." *News & Observer* (Raleigh, NC), March 6, 2011.

6. Robinson, "UNC Lures Duke Aide: Stafford-Odom Joins Rival Women's Team, a Rare Move in College Basketball." *News & Observer* (Raleigh, NC), August 25, 2011.

7. Robinson, "Injuries Take Toll on UNC Women." *News & Observer* (Raleigh, NC), January 16, 2012.

8. Iacobelli, "Crushing Carolina—South Carolina 79, No. 18 North Carolina 48." *The State* (Columbia, SC), December 19, 2011.

9. Robinson, "For Younger Players, Devils-Heels Rivalry Has Meaning." *News & Observer* (Raleigh, NC), February 6, 2012.

10. Liz Clarke, "Knight Commission Cofounder William Friday Laments State of College Athletics. *Washington Post.* October 6, 2012.

11. *Ibid.*

12. Potter, "UNC Women Beat Maryland 72–65 Setting up ACC Final with Duke." *News & Observer* (Raleigh, NC), March 9, 2013.

13. McCreary, "No. 15 UNC Falls to No. 6 Duke in ACC Title Game." *Herald-Sun* (Durham, NC), March 10, 2013.

14. Phillip Gardner, "Hometown Girl: Gastonia Pays Tribute to Hall of Fame Coach Hatchell." *Gastonia Gazette* (NC), July 26, 2013.

15. University of North Carolina, *Report of Findings: Academic Anomalies Review.* James G. Martin with Baker Tilly. December 19, 2012. https://carolinacommitment.unc.edu/files/2013/01/UNC-Governor-Martin-Final-Report-and-Addendum-1.pdf.

Chapter 13

1. University of North Carolina, "Hatchell Temporarily Stepping Away for Health Reasons."

News Release, October 14, 2013. http://www.goheels.com/.

2. Beard, "UNC's Calder Steps in as Hatchell Fights Leukemia." Associated Press, October 15, 2013.

3. Sylvia Hatchell with Stephen Copeland. *Fight! Fight!: Discovering Your Inner Strength When Blindsided by Life* (Indian Trail, NC: The Core Media Group, 2016) 104.

4. Jason deBruyn, "UNC Cancer Center Nabs $1M Grant from Kay Yow Fund." *Triangle Business Journal* (Raleigh, NC), March 4, 2014.

5. Beard, "No. 10 Duke Women Edge No. 13 UNC 66–61." Associated Press, March 9, 2014.

6. Beard, "UNC Women Beat Michigan State 62–53 in NCAAs." Associated Press, March 26, 2014.

7. Grace Raynor, "Cardinal Crushes UNC Women's Basketball Title Dreams." *Daily Tar Heel* (University of North Carolina, Chapel Hill, NC), April 1, 2014.

8. Hatchell, *Fight! Fight!,* p. 127.

9. Fleser, "Diamond DeShields: 'I Always Wanted to Play for Tennessee, Period.'" *Knoxville News Sentinel* (TN), June 12, 2014.

10. Kayla Johnson, "The Real Diamond DeShields." *ESPN Total Access,* February 23, 2015. http://www.espn.com/womens-college-basketball/story/_/id/12369231/the-real-diamond-deshields.

11. Daniel Wilco, "Sylvia Hatchell and Kennedy Meeks Stole the Show at Late Night with Roy." *Daily Tar Heel* (University of North Carolina, Chapel Hill, NC), October 6, 2014.

12. Gardner, "Hunter Huss Honors a Legend with 'Sylvia Rhyne Hatchell Court.'" *Gaston Gazette* (Gastonia, NC), Jan 18, 2015.

13. Beard, "No. 7 Notre Dame Women Beat No. 12 North Carolina, 89–79." Associated Press, January 16, 2015.

14. John McCann, "Hatchell Vows to Toughen Tar Heels for Tourney." *Herald-Sun* (Durham, NC), March 1, 2015.

15. Fuller, "Transferring Is Newest Trend in Women's College Basketball." *New Haven Register* (CT), July 4, 2015.

16. Jeremy Vernon, "Questions Abound for the North Carolina Women's Basketball Team." *Daily Tar Heel* (University of North Carolina, Chapel Hill, NC), June 25, 2015.

17. Dan Kane and Jane Stancill, "Review Agency Hits UNC-Chapel Hill with Probation." *News & Observer* (Raleigh, NC), June 11, 2015.

18. *News & Observer,* "Probation Is Sad Verdict for UNC-CH." Editorial. June 11, 2015.

Chapter 14

1. Bonitta Best, "The Media Are Letting Down Women's Basketball." *News & Observer* (Raleigh, NC), November 9, 2016.

2. Andrew Carter, "UNC Women's Basketball

Coach Sylvia Hatchell Suspended for 2 Games." *News & Observer* (Raleigh, NC), January 29, 2016.

3. *Daily Tar Heel*, "Sylvia Hatchell Suspended for Two Games." January 29, 2016.

4. Andrew Carter and Dan Kane, "UNC Academic Scandal—It's a Tale of Two UNC Coaches" *News & Observer* (Raleigh, NC), August 15, 2015.

5. *Ibid.*

6. *Daily Tar Heel*, "UNC Should Stand by Employees in a Consistent Manner." Editorial, August 20, 2015.

7. Andrew Carter and Dan Kane, "UNC Academic Scandal—It's a Tale of Two UNC Coaches" *News & Observer* (Raleigh, NC), August 15, 2015.

8. McCann, "Lack of New Deal for UNC's Hatchell Angers Supporters." *Herald-Sun* (Durham, NC), July 2, 2015.

9. Meghan Austin, "UNC Sacrificing Hatchell to Protect Men's Teams in Scandal." *News & Observer* (Raleigh, NC), July 20, 2015.

10. McCann, "Lack of New Deal for UNC's Hatchell Angers Supporters."

11. Andrew Carter, "UNC's Sylvia Hatchell Mourns Death of Longtime Friend Pat Summitt." *News & Observer* (Raleigh, NC), June 28, 2016.

12. Hardin, "UNC's Hatchell: 'We Have to Keep the Legacy Alive.'" *Greensboro News & Record* (NC), June 29, 2016.

13. Beard, "UNC Academic Case Finally Reaches NCAA Infractions Hearing." Associated Press, August 16, 2017.

14. Carter, "NCAA Investigation: What to Expect Behind Those Closed Doors at UNC's Hearing in Nashville." *Charlotte Observer* (NC), August 15, 2017.

15. Carter, "After Nearly 10 Hours, First Day of UNC's Infractions Hearing Comes to a Close." *News & Observer* (Raleigh, NC), August 16, 2017.

16. Beard, "UNC Set to Move Past Academic Probe, Not Celebrating Ruling." Associated Press, October 13, 2017.

17. Vernon, "Questions Abound for the North Carolina Women's Basketball Team."

18. Feinberg, "UNC's Hatchell, UConn's Auriemma Reach 1,000 Victories." Associated Press, December 20, 2017.

19. Mikkel Paige, Hatchell-Ireland Wedding. July 13, 2018. https://www.mikkelpaige.

com/lodge-mount-ida-farm-wedding-photos-charlottesville/.

20. University of North Carolina, "Sylvia Hatchell Steps Down as Women's Basketball Head Coach." News release, April 19, 2019. https://www.goheels.com/.

21. Will Hobson, "Sylvia Hatchell Accused of Racially Insensitive Remarks, Forcing UNC Players to Play Hurt." *Washington Post* (DC), April 4, 2019.

22. *Ibid.*

23. Hobson, "UNC Women's Hoops Coach Sylvia Hatchell Resigns Amid Allegations of Berating Players, Racial Remarks." *Washington Post* (DC), April 19, 2019.

24. Hobson, "Sylvia Hatchell Accused of Racially Insensitive Remarks, Forcing UNC Players to Play Hurt."

25. *Ibid.*

26. Voepel, "Auriemma: Most Coaches 'Afraid' of Their Players." espnW.com. April 4, 2019. https://www.espn.com/womens-college-basketball/story/.

27. Feinberg, "Coaches Are Changing the Way They Communicate with Players." Associated Press, April 3, 2019.

28. Carter, "Parents, Players Offer Contrasting Accounts of UNC Women's Basketball Coach Hatchell." *News & Observer* (Raleigh, NC), April 7, 2019. https://www.newsobserver.com/sports/article228904519.html.

29. Deborah Morgan, "Former Players: UNC's Hatchell 'like My Second Mom.'" WRAL. April 8, 2019. https://www.wralsportsfan.com/former-players-unc-s-hatchell-like-my-second-mom./.

30. University of North Carolina, "Sylvia Hatchell Steps Down as Women's Basketball Head Coach." News release, April 19, 2019. https://www.goheels.com/.

31. *Ibid.*

32. Voepel, "Is North Carolina Really Committed to Returning Women's Basketball to the Top?" espnW.com. May 1, 2019. https://www.espn.com/womens-college-basketball/story/.

33. *News & Observer*, "UNC Should Reveal Report That Led to Hatchell's Resignation." Editorial, April 26, 2019.

Bibliography

Adamec, Carl. "Hungry Like Wolff: Point Guard Making up for Time Lost to Injury." *Journal Inquirer* (Manchester, CT), November 22, 2004.

———. "Triple Olympic Champion Jones to Seek Divorce." Journal Inquirer (Manchester, CT), June 5, 2001.

Aiken Standard. "Francis Marion Is No. 1; Lady Pats Take NAIA Title." March 19, 1996.

Alexander, Chip. "Paper Classes Spanned Many Teams: 30 Percent Bogus Enrollments from Olympic, Other Sports." *News & Observer* (Raleigh, NC), October 23, 2014.

Alexander, Jonathan M. "UNC Hires Princeton's Banghart as Women's Basketball Coach." *News & Observer* (Raleigh, NC), April 30, 2019. https://www.newsobserver.com/sports/article229838434.html.

Alfonso, Robert, Jr. "Heels Seek to Rebound: Fresh Start Begins with Preseason WNIT Tonight." *News & Observer* (Raleigh, NC), November 9, 2001.

Almond, Elliott. "Track Star Jones Splits from Hunter [sic] She Seeks to End Marriage to Shot-Putter After 2½ Years." *San Jose Mercury News* (CA), June 6, 2001.

Altavilla, John. "Hatchell Loves UConn Fans and Wants to Keep Playing." *Hartford Courant* (CT), January 7, 2010.

———. "Tar Heels Could Be on the Outside Looking In." *Hartford Courant* (CT), March 5, 2000.

Anderson, Kelli. "Beat the Clock." *Sports Illustrated* 80, no. 14 (1994): 30.

Arey, Norman. "Lady Heels Trample Duke 95–70 in Final." *Atlanta Journal-Constitution*, March 6, 1995.

Ariail, Cat. "UNC Women's Basketball Players Are Entitled—and That's a Good Thing." Swishappeal.com, April 24, 2019. https://www.swishappeal.com/2019/4/24/18511601/ncaa-north-carolina-tar-heels-sylvia-hatchell-resignation.

Aron, Jaime. "Unfinished Business for Latta, Tar Heels." Associated Press, March 30, 2007.

Associated Press. "Duke, North Carolina Land Home-Court Advantage for Early Rounds." March 7, 1999.

———. "Folkl Leads Stanford into Regional Final: Cardinal Faces Purdue for Spot in Final Four." *St. Louis Post-Dispatch* (MO), March 25, 1995.

———. "Friends Reid, Holdsclaw Finally Foes Tonight." *Herald-Sun* (Durham, NC), March 23, 1998.

———. "Hatchell Leaves Meredith." *News & Observer* (Raleigh, NC), May 4, 2004.

———. "Hornbuckle, Tennessee Hold off North Carolina." *Journal Inquirer* (Manchester, CT), December 3, 2007.

———. "LSU, UNC Among Top Seeds: Duke and Ohio State also Are No. 1s." *Orlando Sentinel* (FL), March 14, 2006.

———. "N.C. State Hangs on to Upset No. 2 UNC." February 17, 2007.

———. "No. 1 Vols Remain Perfect: Tennessee Women Edge 4th-Ranked North Carolina." *Seattle Times* (WA), December 3, 2007.

———. "No. 11 Duke 93, No. 7 North Carolina 71." January 23, 1999.

———. "No. 11 North Carolina 67, No. 8 North Carolina State 64." January 22, 1998.

———. "No. 14 North Carolina 64, Northeastern 55." March 12, 1999.

———. "No. 15 Virginia 105, No. 7 North Carolina 100, 3OT." January 15, 1998.

———. "No. 19 North Carolina 93, Florida St. 81." January 3, 2002.

———. "No. 19 UNC Halts 4-Game Slide by Beating Clemson." March 4, 2011.

———. "North Carolina St. 87, No. 6 North Carolina 70." January 8, 1999.

———. "North Carolina's Hatchell Opts to Stay with the Tar Heels." May 1, 2008.

———. "Summitt Files for Divorce After 27 Years of Marriage." *ESPN.com*, August 16, 2007. http://www.espn.com/womens-college-basketball/story?id=2977117/.

———. "Tar Heels Cruise Behind Reid's 16." *New York Times* (NY), January 30, 1998.

———. "Tara VanDerveer Chosen to Coach 1996 Olympics." April 13, 1995.

———. "Three Former UNC Athletes Join McAdoo in Lawsuit Against School." *USA Today* (Arlington, VA), February 24, 2015.

———. "Top Seeds Announced in Women's N.C.A.A. Basketball Tournament." *New York Times* (NY), March 13, 2006.

_____. "UNC Extends Hatchell's Contract Through 2015." July 25, 2008.

_____. "UNC Suspends Teasley: Capel Out for UConn Game." *Charlotte Observer* (NC), January 19, 2002.

_____. "UNC's Hatchell Gets Vote as ACC's Best: Gastonia Native Led Team to First No. 1 Rank." *Charlotte Observer* (NC), March 03, 2006.

_____. "U.S. Olympic Official Concerned About Yow's Bible Smuggling." Sports News, November 11, 1986.

_____. "Wolfpack Loses Its Top Scorer and Rebounder: Ankle Sprain to Bench Moody at Least 3 Weeks." *Charlotte Observer* (NC), January 9, 2002.

Atlanta Journal-Constitution (GA). "Tara Van-Derveer's Selection as 1996 Olympic Coach." April 21, 1995.

_____. "Mideast Women." March 17, 2003.

_____. "UNC Signs Top Recruits to Ease Loss of Jones." College Basketball, November 9, 1997.

Austin, Meghan. "UNC Sacrificing Hatchell to Protect Men's Teams in Scandal." *News & Observer* (Raleigh, NC), July 20, 2015.

Baden, Ben. "UNC Preps for Work on Carmichael: Closing Shifts Teams to Smith Center." *The Daily Tar Heel* (University of North Carolina, Chapel Hill, NC), April 17, 2008.

Banks, Margaret Moffett. "Teasley, Tar Heels Get by Minnesota." *Greensboro News & Record* (NC), March 19, 2002.

Barnes, Nate. "No. 8 North Carolina Women Lose 84–59 at Pittsburgh." Associated Press, January 9, 2015.

Barnett, Ned. "Future Is Not Now for Runner-up UNC." *News & Observer* (Raleigh, NC), March 9, 2004.

_____. "More on Line Than Ranking for Hatchell." *News & Observer* (Raleigh, NC), January 29, 2006.

Bartolucci, Noah. "Girls' Basketball Camps Take off After UNC Wins Title." *News & Observer* (Raleigh, NC), July 9, 1994.

Baum, Bob. "North Carolina 79, Arizona St. 72." Associated Press, March 27, 2005.

Beard, Aaron. "Balanced Offense Helps No. 2 North Carolina Beat No. 12 Duke 86–73 to Win ACC Tournament." Associated Press, March 9, 2008.

_____. "Calder Returns to Carmichael: Seniors Leave Legacy." *Daily Tar Heel* (University of North Carolina, Chapel Hill, NC), March 18, 1998.

_____. "DeGraffenreid, No. 2 North Carolina Beat No. 12 Duke 82–51." Associated Press, March 3, 2008.

_____. "Hatchell Gets 800th Win as UNC Tops N.C. State." Associated Press, January 11, 2009.

_____. "In Funeral Video, NC State's Kay Yow Affirms Faith." Associated Press, January 31, 2009.

_____. "N.C. State's Yow Continues to Inspire in Her Fight with Cancer." Associated Press, November 1, 2007.

_____. "No. 4 Duke 89, No. 15 North Carolina 79." Associated Press, February 15, 2004.

_____. "No. 4 North Carolina 88, No. 5 Duke 67." Associated Press, March 8, 2005.

_____. "No. 7 Notre Dame Women Beat No. 12 North Carolina, 89–79." Associated Press, January 16, 2015.

_____. "No. 8 Tar Heels Rally Past No. 4 Blue Devils 75–60." Associated Press, February 10, 2009.

_____. "No. 9 North Carolina Beats NC State 74–57." Associated Press, February 24, 2009.

_____. "No. 10 Duke Women Edge No. 13 UNC 66–61." Associated Press, March 9, 2014.

_____. "No. 10 North Carolina 64, Virginia 45." Associated Press, March 06, 2004.

_____. "No. 11 North Carolina Beats South Dakota 75–69." March 15, 2009.

_____. "North Carolina 71, George Washington 47." Associated Press, March 23, 2005.

_____. "Steamrolling No. 2 Tar Heels Wins 12th Straight, Rolls Past Virginia 80–65 in Women's ACC Semifinals." *Daily Dispatch* (Henderson, NC), March 9, 2008.

_____. "Tar Heels' Hatchell Goes for Career Win No. 800." Associated Press, January 9, 2009.

_____. "UNC Academic Case Finally Reaches NCAA Infractions Hearing." Associated Press, August 16, 2017.

_____. "UNC Set to Move Past Academic Probe, Not Celebrating Ruling." Associated Press, October 13, 2017.

_____. "UNC Women Beat Michigan State 62–53 in NCAAs." Associated Press, March 26, 2014.

_____. "UNC's Calder Steps in as Hatchell Fights Leukemia." Associated Press, October 15, 2013.

_____. "UNC's Hatchell Named ACC's Top Coach." *Daily Journal Messenger* (Seneca, SC), March 6, 2008.

Beard, Aaron, and Emery P. Dalesio. "Probe: UNC Academic Fraud Was 'Shadow Curriculum.'" *Associated Press*, October 22, 2014.

Beard, Aaron, with Joedy McCreary. "N.C. State's Yow Continues to Inspire in Her Fight with Cancer." Associated Press. November 3, 2007.

Beaton, Gregory. "UNC Wins Battle of Unbeatens: No.1 Duke Falls." *The Chronicle* (Duke University, Durham, NC), January 30, 2006.

Becker, Debbie. "Pan American's Next Test: Louisiana Tech." Women's Notes, *USA Today* (Arlington, VA), January 26, 1989.

Bedore, Gary. "Aycock to Play in Italy." *Lawrence Journal-World* (KS), August 17, 1995.

Belshe, Ethan. "'I Was Really Proud of These Kids': UNC Women's Basketball First-Years Step up in ACC Tournament Loss to Syracuse." *Daily Tar Heel* (University of North Carolina, Chapel Hill, NC), March 3, 2017.

_____. "Three Takeaways from UNC Women's Basketball Media Day." *Daily Tar Heel* (University of North Carolina, Chapel Hill, NC), October 28, 2016.

Berlet, Bruce. "Wolters Finds Word Has Traveled." *Hartford Courant* (CT), September 10, 1995.

Best, Bonitta. "Hillside Football Standouts Get Awards: Women's Basketball Coaches Talk of Raising Profile." *News & Observer* (Raleigh, NC), October 15, 2013.

_____. "The Media Are Letting Down Women's Basketball." *News & Observer* (Raleigh, NC), November 9, 2016.

Blais, Michael. "Breland's Road to WNBA Serves as an Inspiration." *New Haven Register* (CT), July 31, 2011.

Blinder, Alan, and Marc Tracy. "North Carolina Women's Basketball Coach Faces Complaints of Racially Insensitive Comments." *New York Times* (NY), April 4, 2019.

Bliss, Marjo Rankin. "UNC Guard Adjusts to Redefined Role." *Charlotte Observer* (NC), April 3, 1994.

_____. "Wolfpack Gets ERB Back for NCAAS: N.C. State One of 5 ACC Teams Invited." *Charlotte Observer* (NC), March 13, 2000.

Bodenhamer, David J., Robert G. Barrows, and David G. Vanderstel. *Encyclopedia of Indianapolis.* Bloomington: Indiana UP, 1994.

Bonner, Lynn. "ACC Women Drawing Fans." *News & Observer* (Raleigh, NC), March 02, 2006.

Brown, Sarah. "Former Tar Heel Ivory Latta Returns for Coaching Job." *Daily Tar Heel* (University of North Carolina, Chapel Hill, NC), July 17, 2013.

Brownlow, Lauren. "Heels Go Wire-to-Wire for Hatchell's 902nd Win." *Herald-Sun* (Durham, NC), February 15, 2013.

Brownsville Herald (TX). "College Women's Basketball: No. 17 Texas Knocks off Miami 76–65." December 29, 2009.

The Capital (Annapolis, MD). "NCAA Women: Pringle Powers North Carolina to Comeback Win Over Louisville." March 30, 2008.

Caraviello, David. "In Women's Basketball, Battle of Carolinas Bigger Than One Game." *Post and Courier* (Charleston, SC), March 25, 2015.

Carlton, Jeff. "Freshmen Lead UNC into Tourney: The Tar Heels' Ivory Latta and Camille Little Combine Style and Substance into a Winning Formula." *Greensboro News & Record* (NC), March 5, 2004.

_____. "Heels Play at Dome, Not Home: The Women's Teams Take Center Stage at the Smith Center When No. 1 Duke Takes on North Carolina." *Greensboro News & Record* (NC), January 24, 2005.

_____. "Ivory Towers." *Greensboro News & Record* (NC), March 06, 2006.

_____. "Storied Carmichael Hosts Round 2." *Greensboro News & Record* (NC), February 25, 2006.

Carr, A. J. "Heels Escape Pack." *News & Observer* (Raleigh, NC), January 9, 2004.

Carroll, Charlotte. "UNC Coach Roy Williams Signs Eight-Year Contract Extension Through 2028." *Sports Illustrated Online,* December 19, 2018. https://www.si.com/college-basketball/2018/12/19/roy-williams-unc-basketball-contract-extension?.

Carson-Newman University. "About C-N athletics." *CNEagles.com.* http://www.cneagles.com/information/about/index.

Cart, Julie. "A Night of Milestones for Cheryl Miller." *Los Angeles Times* (CA), December 14, 1985.

Carter, Andrew. "After Nearly 10 Hours, First Day of UNC's Infractions Hearing Comes to a Close." *News & Observer* (Raleigh, NC), August 16, 2017.

_____. "Hatchell Among UNC Coaches Receiving New Contracts." *News & Observer* (Raleigh, NC), September 23, 2016.

_____. "Heels Shock UConn at Women's Jimmy V." *Rocky Mount Telegram* (NC), November 22, 2004.

_____. "NCAA Investigation: What to Expect Behind Those Closed Doors at UNC's Hearing in Nashville." *Charlotte Observer* (NC), August 15, 2017.

_____. "Parents, Players Offer Contrasting Accounts of UNC Women's Basketball Coach Hatchell." *News & Observer* (Raleigh, NC), April 7, 2019. https://www.newsobserver.com/sports/article228904519.html.

_____. "UNC Women's Basketball Coach Sylvia Hatchell Suspended for 2 Games." *News & Observer* (Raleigh, NC), January 29, 2016.

_____. "UNC's NCAA Committee on Infractions Hearing Ends After Nearly 15 Hours of Deliberation." *News & Observer* (Raleigh, NC), August 17, 2017.

_____. "UNC's Sylvia Hatchell Mourns Death of Longtime Friend Pat Summitt." *News & Observer* (Raleigh, NC), June 28, 2016.

Carter, Andrew, and Dan Kane. "UNC Academic Scandal—It's a Tale of Two UNC Coaches." *News & Observer* (Raleigh, NC), August 15, 2015.

Carter, Rachel. "ACC Party in Boston." *News & Observer* (Raleigh, NC), March 29, 2006.

_____. "Auriemma, Huskies to Face Heels in Jimmy V." *News & Observer* (Raleigh, NC), August 04, 2004.

_____. "Dewitt Won't Play for UNC This Season." *News & Observer* (Raleigh, NC), October 30, 2007.

_____. "Heels Smaller, Quicker, Resolved." *News & Observer* (Raleigh, NC), November 21, 2004.

_____. "Heels' Trio to Replace Latta at Point." *News & Observer* (Raleigh, NC), October 30, 2007.

_____. "Latta Love, a Lot of Points Ignite UNC." *News & Observer* (Raleigh, NC), January 29, 2006.

_____. "North Carolina vs. 16. Coppin State 7 P.M." *News & Observer* (Raleigh, NC), March 14, 2005.

_____. "Roast Honors Basketball Trio." *News & Observer* (Raleigh, NC), April 21, 2006.

_____. "Tar Heels Seal the Deal." *News & Observer* (Raleigh, NC), March 8, 2005.

_____. "Terps Foul up UNC Women's Run for

Perfection." *News & Observer* (Raleigh, NC), February 10, 2006.

_____. "UNC, Duke Fall Short." *News & Observer* (Raleigh, NC), March 29, 2005.

_____. "Women Take Center Court." *News & Observer* (Raleigh, NC), January 21, 2003.

_____. "Women's Hall Gains Hatchell." *News & Observer* (Raleigh, NC), June 12, 2004.

_____. "Yow Stricken with Cancer Again." *News & Observer* (Raleigh, NC), January 11, 2005.

Cary, Kevin. "Passion Lost for the Game: Scholarship Forsaken After Sport Becomes a Chore." *Charlotte Observer* (NC), March 27, 2005.

CBS17 WNCN (Raleigh-Durham, NC). "UNC, NCAA Set to Meet in Nashville Over Infractions." August 15, 2017. https://www.cbs17.com/news/unc-ncaa-set-to-meet-in-nashville-over-infractions.

Chapman, Gary D. *The Five Love Languages: How to Express Heartfelt Commitment to Your Mate.* Chicago: Northfield, 1995.

_____. *The Five Love Languages of Teenagers.* Chicago: Northfield, 2000.

Chapman, Gary D., and Ross Campbell. *The Five Love Languages of Children.* Chicago: Moody Press, 1997.

Charlotte Observer (NC). "Stop Tolerating Abusive College Coaches." Editorial. April 4, 2019.

Chase, Brandon. "Hatchell Erupts in UNC Women's Basketball Loss to Duke." *Daily Tar Heel* (University of North Carolina, Chapel Hill, NC), January 24, 2016.

Clarke, Liz. "Knight Commission Co-founder William Friday Laments State of College Athletics." *Washington Post*, October 6, 2012.

Cohen, Marilyn. *No Girls in the Clubhouse: The Exclusion of Women from Baseball.* Jefferson, North Carolina: McFarland, 2009.

Cole, Bob. "They Never Quit: Hard Work Paid off for Hatchell, UNC." *The State* (Columbia, SC), April 5, 1994.

Colorado Springs Gazette (CO). Briefing, July 20, 1995.

Conner, Josh. "Sylvia Hatchell Joins the Prestigious 1,000-Win Club." *Daily Tar Heel* (University of North Carolina, Chapel Hill, NC), December 20, 2017.

Courier-Tribune (Asheboro, NC). "Hatchell Honored by ACSMA." March 5, 2015.

Coyne, Tom. "North Carolina Coach Worried About Team's Focus." Associated Press, March 20, 2004.

Crothers, Tim. "Hatchell Shares Her Yow Memories." *ACC Journal* (January 29, 2009): 113.

Crotty, Megan. "Tar Heels Women Top Blue Devils." *Courier-Tribune* (Asheboro, NC), February 4, 2014.

Curtright, Guy. "UNC Coach Likens Deshields to Famous Ex-Tar Heel." *Gwinnett Daily Post* (Lawrenceville, GA), March 2, 2013.

Daily Herald (Columbia, TN). "Consensus National 'Freshman of Year' Joins Lady Vols." June 13, 2014.

Daily Press (Newport News, VA). "Brawl-Marred Game Goes to UNC Women: Old Dominion's Season Ends 63–52." March 21, 1994.

_____. "Duke Students Seek Remorse from Packer." March 5, 2000.

Daily Tar Heel (University of North Carolina, Chapel Hill, NC). "Coaches Like Sylvia Hatchell Don't Belong at UNC." Editorial. April 7, 2019.

_____. "Sylvia Hatchell Suspended for Two Games." January 29, 2016.

_____. "UNC Should Stand by Employees in a Consistent Manner." Editorial, August 20, 2015.

Dalesio, Emery P. "Probe Finds UNC Academic Fraud Started Earlier." Associated Press, December 20, 2012.

Daley, Arthur. "A Remarkable Woman" in *Sports of the Times: The Arthur Daley Years.* Edited by James Tuite. New York: Quadrangle, 1975: 147–149.

Daly, Jack. "Celebration: North Carolina Climbs to No. 1 but Still Has N.C. State, Maryland and Duke Coming." *Herald-Sun* (Durham, NC), January 31, 2006.

_____. "Currie, Latta On Top of All-ACC Team: Duke, UNC Stars Were the Only Unanimous Picks." *Herald-Sun* (Durham, NC), February 28, 2006.

_____. "Hard to Hang on—UNC Survives a Scare from Irish." *Herald-Sun* (Durham, NC), March 21, 2007.

_____. "Hatchell Earns Win No. 700: UNC Coach Reaches Milestone with Win Over Rival N.C. State." *Herald-Sun* (Durham, NC), January 16, 2006.

_____. "Heels Take Time to Learn the Ropes." *Herald-Sun* (Durham, NC), March 2, 2007.

_____. "Hurricane Creates Health Concerns for No. 7 Tar Heels: UNC in Cancun." *Herald-Sun* (Durham, NC), November 24, 2005.

_____. "Recruiting and Defense Helped Heels Get Back." *Herald-Sun* (Durham, NC), April 02, 2006.

_____. "R-E-S-P-E-C-T? Hatchell Hopes UNC's Win at UConn Attracts Attention." *Herald-Sun* (Durham, NC), December 7, 2005.

_____. "Sloppy, but UNC Gets Win—Larkins' Second-Half Spark Helps the Heels." *Herald-Sun* (Durham, NC), December 4, 2006.

_____. "Tar Heels Shackle Liberty in 1st Half: Tar Heels Force 24 Turnovers in First Period for Big Win." *Herald-Sun* (Durham, NC), November 22, 2005.

_____. "UNC Has High Hopes Despite Key Losses: Tar Heels Feel They Can Replace Holes Left by Latta, Little." *Herald-Sun* (Durham, NC), October 24, 2007.

_____. "UNC Runs Wild on Lady Vols." *Herald-Sun* (Durham, NC), March 29, 2006.

_____. "USC Reportedly Meets with Hatchell." *Herald-Sun* (Durham, NC), April 25, 2008.

_____. "VERY SATISFIED—Heels Run Past Terps for 2OT Win." *Herald-Sun* (Durham, NC), January 27, 2008.

Daniels, Rob. "Three Coaches Provide Living History of ACC." *Greensboro News & Record* (NC), November 5, 2001.

Davis, Elizabeth A. "Enshrined Near Roots as a Coach: Hatchell Enters Women's Basketball Hall Near the Small Tenn. Town Where Coaching Career Began." *Herald-Sun* (Durham, NC), June 12, 2004.

Davis, Ryan. "Van Hatchell Living His Dream with UNC Men's Basketball." *Daily Tar Heel* (University of North Carolina, Chapel Hill, NC), May 29, 2012.

deBruyn, Jason. "UNC Cancer Center Nabs $1M Grant from Kay Yow Fund." *Triangle Business Journal* (Raleigh, NC), March 4, 2014.

Decock, Luke. "Rivalry Takes Back Seat to Love for Yow." *Charlotte Observer* (NC), January 12, 2009.

Delsohn, Steve. "UNC's McCants: 'Just Show up, Play.'" *ESPN Outside the Lines*, June 5, 2014. http://www.espn.com/espn/otl/story/_/id/11036924/former-north-carolina-basketball-star-rashad-mccants-says-took-sham-classes.

Dodson, Aaron. "DeShields Benched for Start of Matchup with Tennessee Martin but Finishes Strong." *Daily Tar Heel* (University of North Carolina, Chapel Hill, NC), March 23, 2014.

Dodson, Aaron, and Daniel Wilco. "Sylvia Hatchell coaches UNC from Afar." *Daily Tar Heel* (University of North Carolina, Chapel Hill, NC), April 1, 2014.

Dorr, Vic, Jr. "Alabama Players Won't Forget Coach." *Richmond Times-Dispatch* (VA), March 31, 1994.

_____. "Heels Spoil Cavaliers' Party: U.Va.'s Tourney Bid in Doubt." *Richmond Times-Dispatch* (VA), February 22, 2002.

Doyel, Gregg. "Blue Devils Dominate after Replay Decision: TV Exposure Helps UNC Lose Chance at Late Regulation Foul Shot." *Charlotte Observer* (NC), January 21, 2003.

_____. "Duke Plasters Its Point Across UNC: No. 2 Blue Devils Back up 'Lucky' Win with Rout of No. 6 Tar Heels." *Charlotte Observer* (NC), February 21, 2003.

_____. "Teasley Says Depression, Anxiety Led to Exit from UNC." *Charlotte Observer* (NC), December 17, 2001.

Drew, Jeff. "Gillingham Struggles to Stay Motivated." *News & Observer* (Raleigh, NC), March 24, 1994.

_____. "Heels Survive, but Forward Smith Ejected." *News & Observer* (Raleigh, NC), March 21, 1994.

_____. "Miami Star Flips for the Heels." *News & Observer* (Raleigh, NC), May 15, 1994.

Droschak, David. "No. 1 Duke 78, No. 9 North Carolina 67, OT." Associated Press, January 20, 2003.

Drum, Keith. "Olympic Personality Spotlight: Cheryl Miller and 1988 Olympic Team." United Press International, June 20, 1988.

Duncan, Chris. "North Carolina 70, Alabama 56." Associated Press, March 14, 1999.

DuPree, Jimmy. "Coach Relishes in UNC Victory." *Herald-Sun* (Durham, NC), March 10, 2008.

_____. "No Thriller Here: Tar Heels Fail to 'Show Up,' Making for a Yawner." *Herald-Sun* (Durham, NC), February 21, 2003.

Earnhardt, Patricia. "Carolina Women End 12-Game Skid vs. Duke." *Daily Dispatch* (Henderson, NC), January 25, 2005.

Ehrlich, Mike. "Tar Heels Get Lift from Bench." *Daily Tar Heel* (University of North Carolina, Chapel Hill, NC), January 14, 2008.

Ellis, Fran. "Another 'First' Initiated at FMC: Intra-mural Football—For Girls!" *Florence Morning News* (SC), November 9, 1975.

_____. "Francis Marion Wives Club Welcomes 13 New Members." *Florence Morning News* (SC), October 5, 1975.

Evans, Jayda. "Storm 2014 Exit Interviews: Waltiea Rolle Made Use of Short WNBA Stay." *Seattle Times* (WA), August 29, 2014.

Evans, Murray. "Breland's 31 Lifts N. Carolina Past Oklahoma 80–79." Associated Press, November 23, 2008.

Evansville Courier & Press (IN). "Tar Heels Show UE the Door in WNIT." November 12, 2001.

Faulkner, William. "William Faulkner's Nobel Prize Acceptance Speech." *Southern Cultures* 12, no. 1 (2006): 71. https://muse.jhu.edu/.

Feeney-Gardner, L. J. "Hatchell's Basketball Camp Builds Confidence in Young Girls." *News & Observer* (Raleigh, NC), July 22, 2001.

Feinberg, Doug. "Coaches Are Changing the Way They Communicate with Players." Associated Press, April 3, 2019.

_____. "Connecticut, North Carolina, Tennessee, Maryland No. 1 Seeds NCAA Tournament." *Monitor* (McAllen, TX), March 17, 2008.

_____. "UConn Routs UNC 88–58 in Matchup of Nation's Top Two Teams." *Evening Sun* (Norwich, NY), January 20, 2009.

_____. "Unbeaten UCONN Earns No.1 Overall Seed for NCAAs." Associated Press, March 17, 2009.

_____. "UNC's Hatchell, UConn's Auriemma Reach 1,000 Victories." Associated Press, December 20, 2017.

Firestone News. "All the Way to the Top." October 1965.

Fleser, Dan. "Diamond DeShields: 'I Always Wanted to Play for Tennessee, Period.'" *Knoxville News Sentinel* (TN), June 12, 2014.

_____. "Hatchell Proud of ET Upbringing." *Knoxville News Sentinel* (TN), June 11, 2004.

_____. "Singing Carolina Blues—North Carolina 70, Tennessee 57." *Knoxville News-Sentinel* (TN), December 4, 2006.

Florence Morning News (SC). "Hatchell, Leo C." February 11, 1993.

_____. "Men's Summer League Basketball Results." July 17, 1977.

_____. "Mrs. Hatchell." September 11, 1981.

Foreman, Tom, Jr. "Late Three-Pointer Dooms Bama in OT: North Carolina Ousts Tide with

Tough 74–73 Win in Mideast Regional." *Press-Register* (Mobile, AL), March 22, 1993.

Francis Marion College (Florence, SC). "FM Hosts Public Farewell Reception for Sylvia Rhyne Hatchell." News Release, August 14, 1986.

_____. "Lady Pats to Serve as Marshals at Balloon Classic." *Campus Crier*, April 21, 1986.

Friedman, Vicki L. "Another One Gets Away." *Virginian-Pilot* (Norfolk, VA), December 30, 2005.

Friend, Tom. "She Just Might Be the World's Greatest Athlete. To Prove It, Marion Jones Wants to Win Five Golds." *Chicago Sun-Times* (IL), March 5, 2000.

Fryer, Jenna. "No. 2 Duke 77, No. 11 North Carolina 59." Associated Press, March 11, 2003.

_____. "No. 11 North Carolina 88, Virginia 78." Associated Press, March 10, 2003.

Fulkerson, Vickie. "Huskies Want New Memories: Would Like to Forget Last Year's Collapse vs. UNC." *The Day* (New London, CT), December 5, 2005.

_____. "Women's Game Must Find Room for Best Game in Town (UConn-Tennessee)." *The Day* (New London, CT), March 20, 2010.

Fuller, Jim. "Counterpunch: Huskies Charge Past Heels in Second Half." *New Haven Register* (CT), January 22, 2008.

_____. "Matchup Revisits Pivotal Moment in UConn's Rise." *New Haven Register* (CT), November 15, 2001.

_____. "Transferring Is Newest Trend in Women's College Basketball." *New Haven Register* (CT), July 4, 2015.

Furlong, Jim. "Back to Work: Heels Come off Break Looking Sluggish in Easy Win Over Charleston Southern." *Herald-Sun* (Durham, NC), December 30, 2002.

_____. "Black Cloud in Blue Heaven." *Herald-Sun* (Durham, NC), January 29, 1991.

_____. "Blue Devils Bounce Back to Practice: UNC Women's Hoops Hires Charlotte Smith as Assistant." *Herald-Sun* (Durham, NC), October 16, 2002.

_____. "Clemson Coach Apologizes." *Herald-Sun* (Durham, NC), January 18, 2003.

_____. "Coach Facing Surgery Gets Look at Title Trophy." *Herald-Sun* (Durham, NC), March 2, 1998.

_____. "Devils Beat Heels for Third Straight Year." *Herald-Sun* (Durham, NC), March 9, 2004.

_____. "Duke Picked to Win ACC Again." *Herald-Sun* (Durham, NC), November 5, 2001.

_____. "Duke, UNC Women Open the Show: Tar Heels Head Down Familiar Tournament Trail." *Herald-Sun* (Durham, NC) March 16, 1995.

_____. "Duke Women Roll, Extend UNC's Slump." *Herald-Sun* (Durham, NC), January 25, 2002.

_____. "Elevation: Can the Return of Nikki Teasley Restore the Tar Heels to Contender Status?" *Herald-Sun* (Durham, NC), November 9, 2001.

_____. "Freshmen Pace Tar Heels." *Herald-Sun*

(Durham, NC), March 8, 2004.

_____. "Friendship Survives; One Advances: UNC's Atkinson, Prep Teammate Set to Square." *Herald-Sun* (Durham, NC), March 19, 2004.

_____. "From Her Younger Days in Gastonia, to College and at UNC, Sylvia Hatchell's Life Has Proven She Was ... Born to Coach." *Herald-Sun* (Durham, NC), January 31, 1998.

_____. "Going the Extra Miles to Support Tar Heels." *Herald-Sun* (Durham, NC), March 24, 2002.

_____. "Hatchell, UNC Seniors Reflect: Missing the Final Four Took Toll on 1994 NCAA Champ." *Herald-Sun* (Durham, NC) March 30, 1995.

_____. "Hatchell's Heels Young." *Herald-Sun* (Durham, NC). October 24, 1995.

_____. "Jones Decides to Go for Gold: UNC Basketball Star Sets Priority on Track." *Herald-Sun* (Durham, NC), September 13, 1995.

_____. "Later Is Better as UNC Women Prepare to Go West." *Herald-Sun* (Durham, NC), March 14, 2000.

_____. "Ordeal: UNC's Calder Showed Heart to Survive Illness." *Herald-Sun* (Durham, NC), April 10, 1998.

_____. "Point Well-Taken: Teasley Returns to 'Natural Position,' Leads UNC Past Virginia." *Herald-Sun* (Durham, NC), January 28, 2002.

_____. "Reunion a Chance to Reflect: Former UNC Players Look Back on '94 NCAA Title." *Herald-Sun* (Durham, NC), March 1, 2004.

_____. "Smoking Jackets: Georgia Tech Completely Dominates the Befuddled Tar Heels." *Herald-Sun* (Durham, NC), January 18, 2002.

_____. "Tar Heels Survive Scare: Bell Ignites UNC with Key Buckets Down Stretch." *Herald-Sun* (Durham, NC), March 23, 2003.

_____. "Teasley Sits Out Loss." *Herald-Sun* (Durham, NC), November 2, 2001.

_____. "Transition: From Hardwood to the Track." *Herald-Sun* (Durham, NC), March 30, 1995.

_____. "UNC Runs Away: Tar Heels Shake off Slow Start, Blast Terrapins." *Herald-Sun* (Durham, NC), December 31, 2001.

_____. "What Does It Take? All UNC Has to Do Is Beat Top-Ranked, Unbeaten Duke." *Herald-Sun* (Durham, NC), January 20, 2003.

Garber, Mary. "Women's Sweet 16 Has Strong ACC, SEC Flavor." *Winston-Salem Journal* (NC), March 25, 2000.

Gardiner, Andy. "Schools Seek Extra Credit: Games Added to Pass Time, Gain NCAA Favor." *USA Today* (Arlington, VA), March 13, 2009.

Gardner, Phillip. "Hometown Girl: Gastonia Pays Tribute to Hall of Fame Coach Hatchell." *Gastonia Gazette* (NC), July 26, 2013.

_____. "Hunter Huss Honors a Legend with 'Sylvia Rhyne Hatchell Court.'" *Gaston Gazette* (Gastonia, NC), Jan 18, 2015.

Gargan, Henry. "UNC Women's Basketball Loses to Duke." *Daily Tar Heel* (University of North Carolina, Chapel Hill, NC), March 3, 2013.

Gastonia Gazette (NC). "Big Step Taken with

Dignity and Aplomb." Editorial, September 22, 1965.

_____. "Hope Plastics Team Captures 9–5 Victory." August 17, 1974.

_____. "Tennessee Graduate." September 25, 1975.

_____. "Winners in Contest Get Prizes." December 22, 1961.

Gentry, James K., and Raquel Meyer Alexander. "Pay for Women's Basketball Coaches Lags Far Behind That of Men's Coaches." *New York Times* (NY), April 2, 2012. https://www.nytimes.com/2012/04/03/sports/ncaabasketball/pay-for-womens-basketball-coaches-lags-far-behind-mens-coaches.html.

Giglio, J. P. "Heels Edge Tigers." *News & Observer* (Raleigh, NC), February 17, 2003.

_____. "Sloppy Heels Bury Phoenix." *News & Observer* (Raleigh, NC), December 18, 2002.

_____. "Teasley Has Heels Feeling Confident." *News & Observer* (Raleigh, NC), March 17, 2000.

_____. "UNC Wants Respect." *News & Observer* (Raleigh, NC), February 20, 2003.

Gilfillan, Chris. "Title Sweep for Eagles: Cresset Boys, Girls Triumph in TAC 2-A." *Herald-Sun* (Durham, NC), February 16, 2003.

Gillespie, Bob. "Marion's Donnelly Driven by Hatred of Losing." *The State* (Columbia, SC), November 23, 2008.

Ginsburg, David. "No. 12 Maryland Tops No. 2 Carolina 77–71." Associated Press, January 26, 2009.

_____. "North Carolina Women Lose to Delaware 78–69." Associated Press, March 27, 2013.

Glier, Ray. "The NCAA Women's Basketball Tournament Regional Finals Represented the End of an Era and the Start of Something New." *USA Today* (Arlington, VA), March 27, 1994.

Golen, Jimmy. "No. 16 UNC Women Beat BC for Hatchell's 900th Win." Associated Press, February 8, 2013.

Gordon, Jean. "UNC Coach's Recovery from Leukemia Incudes Blueberry Patch." Associated Press, April 26, 2015.

Gorman, Briana. "Hatchell Gives 50K to Cancer Fund." *Herald-Sun* (Durham, NC), June 26, 2010.

_____. "Her Time to Shine: McCants Leads the Tar Heels into the NCAA Women's Tournament." *Herald-Sun* (Durham, NC) March 21, 2008.

_____. "Tar Heels Spread It Around." *Herald-Sun* (Durham, NC), March 8, 2008.

Gorman, Chrissie. "Interior Collapse Brings Down Duke's Dynasty." *The Chronicle* (Duke University, Durham, NC), February 28, 2005.

Greensboro Daily News (NC). "Shop Talk ... Women's Basketball Variety." April 1, 1979.

Gullan, Scott. "Not-So-Nice Finish: Sprint Queen Comes Clean on Steroid Use." *Herald Sun* (Melbourne, Australia), October 6, 2007.

Gutmann, Harold. "Hatchell Says She Was Unaware of Academic Fraud." *Herald-Sun* (Durham, NC), November 1, 2014.

_____. "UNC Will Still Play 'Sylvia Hatchell Basketball.'" *Herald-Sun* (Durham, NC), October 24, 2013.

Hardin, Ed. "After Tragic Week Back Home, Heels Can Smile." *Greensboro News & Record* (NC), March 10, 2008.

_____. "Another Sour Loss for Hatchell." *Greensboro News & Record* (NC), March 11, 2003.

_____. "Carolina Ready to Call Greensboro Its Home." *Greensboro News & Record* (NC), March 3, 2008.

_____. "A Hard Day Ends with a Hug." *Greensboro News & Record* (NC), March 05, 2007.

_____. "Hatchell Inks Six-Year Extension." *Herald-Sun* (Durham, NC), February 19, 2003.

_____. "Hatchell's Ideas Revolutionizing Women's Game." *Greensboro News & Record* (NC), March 6, 2006.

_____. "Tune In Next Week to See What Duke's Win Means." *Greensboro News & Record* (NC), February 26, 2007.

_____. "UNC's Hatchell: 'We Have to Keep the Legacy Alive.'" *Greensboro News & Record* (NC), June 29, 2016.

Harris, Mike. "'Good for the Judge': Response to Jones' Plight Is Icy Among Area Track Devotees." *Richmond Times-Dispatch* (VA), January 12, 2008.

_____. "NCAA Exposes a Sisters' Act: Death of Father Has Saddened Season for Gillinghams." *Richmond Times-Dispatch* (VA), March 23, 1994.

Hartford Courant (CT). "U.S. Women Lose Final: Allen Has 21 for Men." September 2, 1995.

Hass, Bill. "Dynasty Built on Defense: Blue Devils Capture Record Fifth Straight Tournament Crown." *Greensboro News & Record* (NC), March 9, 2004.

_____. "Show Stoppers: Tar Heels Halt Duke's Dominance at Coliseum." *Greensboro News & Record* (NC), March 8, 2005.

Hatchell, Sylvia. "Sylvia Hatchell: An Interview" in *The Secret to Their Success: How 33 Women Made Their Dreams Come True.* Edited by Emily A. Colin. Wilmington, NC: Coastal Carolina Press, 2000: 240–252.

_____. "An Unbreakable Bond" in *Leader of the Pack: The Legacy of Legendary Coach Kay Yow,* by Stephanie Zonars. Kearney, NE: Cross Training, 2009.

Hatchell, Sylvia, with Jeff Thomas. *The Baffled Parent's Guide to Coaching Girls' Basketball,* Camden, ME: McGraw-Hill, 2006.

_____. *The Complete Guide to Coaching Girls' Basketball: Building A Great Team The Carolina Way.* Camden, ME: McGraw-Hill, 2006.

Hatchell, Sylvia, with Stephen Copeland. *Fight! Fight! Discovering Your Inner Strength When Blindsided by Life,* Indian Trail, NC: The Core Media Group, 2016.

Hayes, Nolan. "Big Win Just the Beginning for Tar Heels." *Herald-Sun* (Durham, NC), November 23, 2004.

_____. "Blue (Berry) Heaven: Coach's Patch Raises

Funds, Spirits for UNC Cancer Fight." *Herald-Sun* (Durham, NC), August 22, 2005.

_____. "Heels Played Out of Tourney by Baylor." *Herald-Sun* (Durham, NC), March 29, 2005.

_____. "UNC's Full Speed Even Faster." *Herald-Sun* (Durham, NC), November 18, 2005.

Henry, George. "Montgomery Leads Ga. Tech to Upset of No. 2 UNC." Associated Press, January 23, 2009.

Herald-Sun (Durham, NC). "ACC Women's Hoops Kick Off in Greensboro." October 19, 2011.

_____. "Cresset Christian Eagles." June 26, 2005.

_____. "Douglas Wins Tatum Award." November 26, 2003.

_____. "Ga. State Center Dies After Accident." November 1, 2001.

_____. "Hatchell Is Finalist for Naismith Hall of Fame." February 16, 2013.

_____. "Heels on the Road ... Again." March 15, 2004.

_____. "Jones Suffers Setback in Training for Olympics." January 10, 1996.

_____. "NCCU to Host Event for New Mascot." July 20, 2005.

_____. "No. 600 Nice Belated Birthday Gift for Hatchell." March 4, 2002.

_____. "Painful Win for Carolina Women: Hillside Product Alex Miller Suffers Knee Injury and Will Likely Miss Rest of Season." November 17, 2007.

_____. "Stakes High in Regular-Season Finale." March 2, 2008.

_____. "Tar Heels Extra." October 16, 2002.

_____. "Tar Heels Sign Two Players from In-State." November 10, 2005.

_____. "UNC Falls Short of Attendance Mark." January 15, 2001.

_____. "UNC's Ready for Tall Test: Cardinal May Have Edge Inside." March 23, 1995.

_____. "Wildcats Can't Stay with UNC." November 23, 2002.

History, Art, and Archives, U.S. House of Representatives, "Green, Edith Starrett" (January 16, 2013). https://history.house.gov/People/Listing/G/GREEN,-Edith-Starrett-(G000407)/.

Hobson, Will. "Sylvia Hatchell Accused of Racially Insensitive Remarks, Forcing UNC Players to Play Hurt." *Washington Post* (DC), April 4, 2019.

_____. "UNC Women's Hoops Coach Sylvia Hatchell Resigns Amid Allegations of Berating Players, Racial Remarks." *Washington Post* (DC), April 19, 2019.

Hoffman, Benjamin. "Newton Draws Rebukes for Mocking a Female Reporter." *New York Times* (NY), October 5, 2017.

Honeycutt, Brett. "Duke Surge Buries Tar Heels: Top-Ranked Blue Devils Use 25–3 Run to Close Game Against Rival." *Charlotte Observer* (NC), January 12, 2004.

Hopkins, C. Howard. *History of the Y.M.C.A. in North America.* New York: Association Press, 1951.

Hurst, Matt. "UNC Women Roll to Matchup with Bulldogs: UNC Has No Trouble with Rice in the NCAA West Regional." *Greensboro News & Record* (NC), March 22, 2000.

Iacobelli, Pete. "Crushing Carolina—South Carolina 79, No. 18 North Carolina 48." *The State* (Columbia, SC), December 19, 2011.

_____. "Hatchell Among Inductee Class for S.C. Hall of Fame." *Herald* (Rock Hill, SC), May 19, 2009.

_____. "McCants, No. 2 Tar Heels Survive Against Clemson." Associated Press, January 9, 2009.

_____. "South Carolina 79, No. 18 North Carolina 48: South Carolina Women Top No. 18 Tar Heels." *The Herald* (Rock Hill, SC), December 19, 2011.

_____. "Tar Heels Hold Off South Carolina." *Herald-Sun* (Durham, NC), December 21, 2002.

Jacobs, Jeff. "Women's Bracket a Vision with Poor Site Lines." *Hartford Courant* (CT), March 27, 2003.

James, Pat. "Hatchell Makes Emotional Return to the Court." *Daily Tar Heel* (University of North Carolina, Chapel Hill, NC), November 6, 2014.

_____. "North Carolina Women's Basketball Beats Oklahoma State Thanks to Mavunga, Gray." *Daily Tar Heel* (University of North Carolina, Chapel Hill, NC), November 20, 2014.

James, Wallace. "College and Community Honor Lady Patriots," *Campus Crier* (Francis Marion College, Florence, SC), April 21, 1986.

Jameson, Norman. "Faith Permeates Hatchell's Winning Program." *Biblical Recorder: Baptist Life,* August 11, 2006.

Jeansonne, John. "Marion Jones Has Found Love, Fortune and Success, Now She's Looking for ... A Storybook Finish." *Newsday* (Long Island, NY) September 14, 2000.

Jeffreys, Nick. "Yow Pleased with Wolfpack Women's Hoops Tempo Despite Loss." *Technician* (North Carolina State University, Raleigh, NC), February 26, 2008.

Jenkins, Sally. "Get Rid of the Biddies." *Los Angeles Times* (CA), April 01, 2006.

_____. "NCAA Leadership Isn't Matching the Talent of Its Players." *Washington Post* (DC), April 2, 2006.

_____. "999 Victories and Still Rising: Pat Summitt Is Speeding Toward a Milestone Untouched by Any Coach." *Pittsburgh Post-Gazette* (PA), January 31, 2009.

_____. "Rising to Her Own Level." *Los Angeles Times* (CA), January 28, 2009.

Johnson, Austin, and Andrew Tanker. "Chones, Wolfpack Roll Over Tar Heels." *Technician* (North Carolina State University, Raleigh, NC), February 09, 2004.

Johnson, Kayla. "The Real Diamond DeShields." *ESPN Total Access,* February 23, 2015. http://www.espn.com/womens-college-basketball/story/_/id/12369231/the-real-diamond-deshields.

Jones, John Christopher. *It Gets Foggy at Mossy*

Creek: *The Origin and Development of Intercollegiate Athletics at Carson-Newman College.* Jefferson City, TN: Standard Press, 1974.

Jones, Marion, with Kate Sekules. *Life in the Fast Lane: An Illustrated Autobiography.* New York: Warner, 2004.

Kane, Dan. "Report Finds Academic Fraud Evidence in UNC Department—No-Show Professors, Unauthorized Grade Changes Affect More Than 50 Classes." *News & Observer* (Raleigh, NC), May 4, 2012.

Kane, Dan, and Jane Stancill. "Review Agency Hits UNC-Chapel Hill with Probation." *News & Observer* (Raleigh, NC), June 11, 2015.

Kee, Lorraine. "Women's Game Shows Signs of Looming Lunacy." *St. Louis Post-Dispatch* (MO), April 1, 1994.

Kelly, Dave. "Lady Patriots Defend Ranking in Tournament." *The State* (Columbia, SC), February 25, 1986.

Kent, Milton. "Down 12, Lady Vols Prevail—37–0." *The Sun* (Baltimore, MD), March 24, 1998.

_____. "Heels Quiet Crowd, UM—Terps Women Fall to Second ACC Power Before 17,950." *The Sun* (Baltimore, MD), January 29, 2007.

_____. "North Carolina Gains Final Four Trip, 81–69." *The Sun* (Baltimore, MD), March 27, 1994.

Kimball, George. "America Adopts a Smug Silence." *Irish Times,* October 5, 2000.

Krest, Shawn. "Without Hatchell, Heels Open with Win." *Herald-Sun* (Durham, NC), October 31, 2013, B1.

Kurz, Hank, Jr. "Women's Basketball Roundup: No. 24 Tar Heels Give Coach 600th Win at UNC." *Charlotte Observer* (NC), January 20, 2012.

Lananna, Michael. "Coming Clean Is a First Step." *News & Observer* (Raleigh, NC), October 7, 2007.

_____. "Rolle and Ruffin-Pratt Continue to Improve." *Daily Tar Heel* (University of North Carolina, Chapel Hill, NC), February 19, 2012.

_____. "Roy Joins an Elite Circle." *News & Observer* (Raleigh, NC), September 9, 2007.

Lang, Chris. "Hatchell Thrilled to Be Back on the Bench." *News & Advance* (Lynchburg, VA), March 21, 2015.

Lannin, Joanne. *A History of Basketball for Girls and Women: From Bloomers to Big Leagues.* Minneapolis: Learner, 2000.

Layden, Tim. "Back on the Ball." *Sports Illustrated* 95, no. 20 (2001): 134.

Laye, Leonard. "Girl Cagers Haven't Played Here Since 1947: Intramurals Only Avenue for 4-A Girls" *Gastonia Gazette* (NC), December 15, 1972.

Lazenby, Del. "First Negro Students in White High Schools Treated Well." *Gastonia Gazette* (NC), February 23, 1964.

The Ledger (Lakeland, FL). "No.2 Tar Heels Slam No. 12 Cavaliers." January 16, 2009.

Lee, Victor. "UNC Coach Hatchell Builds Character—and Championships." *Sports Spectrum Magazine* 11, no. 3 (1997): 5.

Lewis, Michael. "ACC Champs: Tigers Rally to Topple North Carolina." *Morning Star* (Wilmington, NC), March 2, 1999.

Lipper, Bob. "Three Weeks Later, Smith Savoring Shot." *Richmond Times-Dispatch* (VA), April 24, 1994.

Litsky, Frank. "Tar Heels and Latta Keep Vols Under Foot." *New York Times,* March 29, 2006.

Loomis, David. "The Nike Contract with UNC-Chapel Hill: The Power of Money Here at Home." Unpublished paper written for International Studies 92, University of North Carolina, Chapel Hill, April 30, 1998.

Louisiana Tech vs. North Carolina: 1994 NCAA Division I Women's Basketball National Championship. Ann Meyers and Tim Ryan, Announcers. DVD. NCAA on Demand Production, 2010.

Lucas, Adam. *Carolina Basketball: A Century of Excellence.* Chapel Hill: University of North Carolina Press, 2010.

Maier, Daniel, ed. *YMCA in America, 1851–2001: A History of Accomplishment Over 150 Years.* Chicago: National Council of Young Men's Christian Associations of America, 2000.

Marslan, Paul. "Lobo Heads Huskies at Basketball Trials." *New Haven Register* (CT), May 20, 1995.

Martel, Brett. "Don't Be Confused, Louisville-North Carolina Is a Women's Showdown, Too." *AP Archive,* March 28, 2008.

Martzke, Rudy. "CBS' Packer Issues Apology for Words to Duke Students." *USA Today* (Arlington, VA), March 8, 2000.

Masuda, Nick. "Rice up in Arms Over Win: Lady Owls Try to Double Their Pleasure Tonight." *Houston Chronicle* (TX), March 20, 2000.

Mayer, Mercedes. "Big 12 Women's Tournament Notes: Baylor Women's Team Thrilled with the Not-So Bear Necessities." *Fort Worth Star-Telegram* (TX), March 13, 2005.

_____. "UNC, Baylor Keep It Upbeat." *Fort Worth Star-Telegram* (TX), March 28, 2005.

McCann, John. "Hatchell Vows to Toughen Tar Heels for Tourney." *Herald-Sun* (Durham, NC), March 1, 2015.

_____. "Lack of New Deal for UNC's Hatchell Angers Supporters." *Herald-Sun* (Durham, NC), July 2, 2015.

_____. "700 UNC Wins in 30 Years for Hatchell." *Herald-Sun* (Durham, NC), January 6, 2016.

McCann, Michael, and Jon Wertheim. "Rashanda McCants, Devon Ramsay File Suit Against UNC, NCAA." *Sports Illustrated Online,* January 6, 2015. https://www.si.com/college-basketball/2015/01/06/rashanda-mccants-unc-paper-classes-lawsuit.

McCauley, Janie. "South Carolina's Year Ends Against North Carolina." Associated Press, March 31, 2014.

McCoy, Jenny. "13 Times Women in Sports Fought for Equality." *Glamour.* April 1, 2020. https://www.glamour.com/

story/13-times-women-in-sports-fought-for-equality.

McCray, Pam. "2013 Basketball Hall of Fame Inductee Sylvia Hatchell Tells Hall of Fame Crowd to Follow Their Passion." *The Republican* (Springfield, MA), July 9, 2013.

McCreary, Joedy. "Duke Wraps Up 1st Perfect Regular Season in ACC History." Associated Press, February 26, 2007.

_____. "Larkins, McCants Lead North Carolina Past Arizona State, 75–60." Associated Press, November 11, 2007.

_____. "Miami Picked to Win 1st ACC Women's Hoops Title." Associated Press. October 18, 2011.

_____. "No. 1 Duke Earns First Post-Beard Victory Over No. 2 North Carolina." Associated Press, February 9, 2007.

_____. "No. 15 UNC Falls to No. 6 Duke in ACC Title Game." *Herald-Sun* (Durham, NC), March 10, 2013.

_____. "No. 2 UNC Claims Share of ACC Title by Beating N.C. State 85–79." Associated Press, February 26, 2008.

_____. "Pringle Leads No. 3 Tar Heels Past No. 11 Duke 93–76." Associated Press, February 5, 2008.

_____. "Tar Heels to Rely on Larkins in First Season of Post-Latta Era." Associated Press, November 3, 2007.

_____. "Tar Heels, Terrapins Top Seeds: Frese Returns in ACC Women's Tournament." *Daily Dispatch* (Henderson, NC), March 6, 2008.

_____. "Tar Heels' Year Ends Again in Final Four." Associated Press, April 2, 2007.

_____. "UNC Women Hold off Liberty 71–65 in NCAA 1st Round." Associated Press, March 21, 2015.

_____. "UNC's Breland Ready to Return After Cancer Fight." Associated Press, October 19, 2010.

McDonald, G. Mark. "U.S. Women's Basketball Team Halts Soviet Dominance, 83–60." *Dallas Morning News* (TX), July 11, 1986.

Megargee, Steve. "No. 16 Lady Vols Rip No. 22 North Carolina 102–57." Associated Press, December 2, 2012.

_____. "Pat Summitt Remembered for Achievements on, off Court." Associated Press, July 15, 2016.

Mehrtens, Cliff. "Tar Heels Tough One Out." *News & Observer* (Raleigh, NC), March 4, 2007.

Melick, Ray. "Tar Heel's Women's Team All Grown Up." Scripps Howard News Service, March 22, 1997.

Miami Herald (FL). "Reid Named Nation's Top Player." March 23, 1994.

Moody, Walt. "Lady Lions Dominate Rebounding Battle in Second Half to Upset No. 2 North Carolina." *Centre Daily Times* (State College, PA), December 06, 2004.

Moore, Randy. *Hoop Tales: Tennessee Lady Volunteers*. Guilford, CT: Globe Pequot, 2005.

Morgan, Deborah. "Former Players: UNC's Hatchell 'Like My Second Mom.'" WRAL. April 8, 2019. https://www.wralsportsfan.com/former-players-unc-s-hatchell-like-my-second-mom/.

Moritz, Amy. "Foes Drawn from Summitt's Buddy List." *Buffalo News* (NY), March 28, 2006.

Mossman, John. "Colorado 86, North Carolina 67." Associated Press, March 25, 2003.

Murphy, Melissa. "Sports News." Associated Press, April 1, 1995.

_____. "WBCA Coaches to Meet with Congress at Title IX Hearings May 9." Associated Press, May 3, 1995.

Myatt, Al. "Balanced Bulldogs Send Tar Heels packing." News & Observer (Raleigh, NC), March 26, 2000.

_____. "Playing Against the Best Is Nothing New for Barksdale." *News & Observer* (Raleigh, NC), March 24, 2000.

_____. "A Special Coach for UNC Women." *News & Observer* (Raleigh, NC), March 3, 1998.

Nadel, John. "Tar Heels Overpower Rice, 83–50." *Dallas Morning News* (TX), March 22, 2000.

New Pittsburgh Courier (PA). "UNC Welcomes Back Sylvia Crawley as Assistant Coach." July 15, 2015.

New York Times (NY). "Judgment Call on a Good Deed." November 12, 1986.

_____ "A Problem for Seton Hall: Just Too Many Tar Heels." March 19, 1995.

_____. "Results Plus." January 25, 1989.

_____. "Stars Defeat Cornets for W.B.L. Crown." April 9, 1980.

Newman, Jerrie. "The Changing Schools: At Hunter Huss Emphasis Is on Good Citizens." *Gastonia Gazette* (NC), July 5, 1969.

Newman, Samantha. "Tar Heels to Face LSU in Big Easy." *The Daily Tar Heel* (University of North Carolina, Chapel Hill, NC), March 31, 2008.

Newport News Daily Press (VA). "Ruling Puts Dream on 'Dream Team.'" July 22, 1995.

News & Observer (Raleigh, NC). "A 'Berry' Nice Opportunity." August 17, 2005.

_____. "A Double Standard at UNC-CH Over Contracts for Williams And Hatchell." Editorial. August 17, 2015.

_____. "Double Standard on Celebrations?" February 17, 2008.

_____. "Meredith Falls in NCAA Opener." March 6, 2003.

_____. Names & Notes. April 10, 2002.

_____. Names & Notes. November 22, 2001.

_____. "Probation Is Sad Verdict for UNC-CH." Editorial. June 11, 2015.

_____. "Timeline of the UNC Investigation." April 25, 2016.

_____. "UNC Should Reveal Report That Led to Hatchell's Resignation." Editorial, April 26, 2019.

_____. "UNC's Hatchell to Lead University Games Team." January 27, 1995.

O'Donnell, Norah. "Notre Dame Head Coach

Muffet McGraw Drew Attention for Her Powerful Words About Gender Equality." *CBS This Morning,* April 17, 2019. https://www.cbs.com/shows/cbs_this_morning.

The Orange and Blue (Carson-Newman College, Jefferson, TN). "Callies Tromp Hyps." November 10, 1972.

Orlando Sentinel (FL). "If You Aim at Batter, Be Sure to Hit Him." July 31, 1996.

_____. "NASCAR Boss Isn't Jumping to NFL." January 23, 2005.

Paige, Mikkel. Hatchell-Ireland Wedding. July 13, 2018. https://www.mikkelpaige.com/lodge-mount-ida-farm-wedding-photos-charlottesville/.

Parker, Wendy. "Rising Tar Heels Strong Enough to Take on Duke." *Atlanta Journal-Constitution* (GA), February 16, 2003.

_____. Women's Notebook, *Atlanta Journal-Constitution* (GA), October 8, 1994.

Parsons, Keith. "No. 8 North Carolina 77, No. 2 Duke 68." Associated Press, February 28, 2005.

Patrick, Dick. "Jones Keeps Heels Clicking in Excitement." *USA Today* (Arlington, VA), June 1, 1994.

_____. "New U.S. Olympic Coach Can Launch Era for Women." *USA Today* (Arlington, VA), March 24, 1995.

_____. "UNC, Tennessee Move On." *USA Today* (Arlington, VA), March 27, 2006.

Patterson, Lezlie. "Hatchell-ing a Little Heel: Pregnancy Hasn't Slowed UNC Coach." *The State* (Columbia, NC), January 6, 1989.

Peeler, Tim. "Hatchell Devoted to Increasing Awareness." *Greensboro News & Record* (NC), July 20, 2000.

People.com. "Star Tracks." August 15, 1994. https://people.com/archive/star-tracks-vol-42-no-7/.

Person, Joseph. "Staley Accepting the Challenge." *The State* (Columbia, SC), May 11, 2008.

_____. "USC Chases Top Names for Coaching Spot: UNC's Hatchell and Temple's Staley Among the Names on the Search List." *The State* (Columbia, SC), April 26, 2008.

Philadelphia Inquirer (PA). "Connecticut Rallies to Remain Unbeaten." January 22, 2008.

Phillips, Mike. "Reid Going to Olympic Festival." *Miami Herald* (FL), January 25, 1994.

_____. "Reid Picks N. Carolina." *Miami Herald* (FL), May 3, 1994.

Piper, John. *Andrew Fuller: Holy Faith, Worthy Gospel, World Mission.* Wheaton, IL: Crossway, 2016.

Politi, Steve. "Effect of Buzzer-Beater Sinks in at Chapel Hill." *Greensboro News & Record* (NC), April 5, 1994.

Potter, Mike. "Big Rivalry Welcomes Blue Devils' McCallie." *Herald-Sun* (Durham, NC), February 4, 2008.

_____. "Duke, UNC Hit Road in Women's Bracket: Devils Receive Top Seed in Berkeley Regional." *Herald-Sun* (Durham, NC), March 17, 2009.

_____. "Larkins Powers Heels by Wolfpack." *Herald-Sun* (Durham, NC), February 26, 2008.

_____. "UNC Cruises in Rolle's Return: Heels Set Defensive Mark in New Mother's First Game Since Giving Birth." *News & Observer* (Raleigh, NC), December 30, 2011.

_____. "UNC Women Beat Maryland 72–65 Setting up ACC Final with Duke." *News & Observer* (Raleigh, NC), March 9, 2013.

_____. "Wolfpack Hosts No. 3 Tar Heels." *Herald-Sun* (Durham, NC), January 13, 2008.

Price, Scott L. "How Did Carolina Lose Its Way?" *Sports Illustrated* 122, no. 11 (2015): 64–71.

Pryor, Brooke. "Cherry on Top." *Herald-Sun* (Durham, NC), March 23, 2015.

Pugh, Mitch. "Illinois Women Face Quick, Athletic Foe." *State Journal-Register* (Springfield, IL), March 21, 1998.

Ragan, Robert Allison. *History of Gastonia and Gaston County, North Carolina.* Charlotte, NC: Loftin & Company, 2010.

Raynor, Grace. "Cardinal Crushes UNC Women's Basketball Title Dreams." *Daily Tar Heel* (University of North Carolina, Chapel Hill, NC), April 1, 2014.

_____. "Women's Basketball Downs Eagles." *Daily Tar Heel* (University of North Carolina, Chapel Hill, NC), October 30, 2013.

Reed, Steve. "UNC Comes Back from 18 Down to Top UT Martin 60–58." Associated Press, March 23, 2014.

Ridenour, Marla. "Tar Heels Swat Away Vols with Pesky Defense." *Akron Beacon Journal* (OH), March 29, 2006.

Riley, Lori. "Teasley's Timeout." *Hartford Courant* (CT), November 15, 2001.

_____. "Yow, N.C. State Get Lost in Classic TV Shuffle." *Hartford Courant* (CT), December 04, 2005.

Riley, Lori, and Bruce Berlet. "No Way to Keep Her Down: Tireless Hatchell Turns Heels Around." *Hartford Courant* (CT), December 1, 1995.

Robinson, Alan. "Mysteries of Pittsburgh: UT, UNC There." Associated Press, March 18, 2007.

Robinson, Edward G., III. "Basketball Season Is Over for Kay Yow." *News & Observer* (Raleigh, NC), January 7, 2009.

_____. "Breland Powers Tar Heel Women." *News & Observer* (Raleigh, NC), March 6, 2011.

_____. "Coaching Coaches is [Debbie] Yow's Passion." *News & Observer* (Raleigh, NC), July 4, 2010.

_____. "Devils Rout Hokies, Gear up for Heels." *News & Observer* (Raleigh, NC), February 2, 2008.

_____. "Duke Goes Inside, Beats UNC: Blue Devils Win ACC Regular Season Outright; No. 7 Duke 69, North Carolina 63." *News & Observer* (Raleigh, NC), February 27, 2012.

_____. "Duke Women Defeat North Carolina 96–56." *News & Observer* (Raleigh, NC), February 6, 2012.

_____. "For Younger Players, Devils-Heels Rivalry Has Meaning: Despite Less National Attention, Game Is Paramount." *News & Observer* (Raleigh, NC), February 6, 2012.

_____. "Heels Fend Off Upset Bid." *News & Observer* (Raleigh, NC), March 26, 2008.

_____. "Heels Oust Noles in Women's ACC Tournament." *News & Observer* (Raleigh, NC), March 5, 2011.

_____. "Heels Take Charge." *News & Observer* (Raleigh, NC), March 3, 2008.

_____. "Heels Taking Their Cue from Senior Trio." *News & Observer* (Raleigh, NC), November 11, 2010.

_____. "Injuries Take Toll on UNC Women." *News & Observer* (Raleigh, NC), January 16, 2012.

_____. "Jackets Bounce Tar Heels in Women's Tourney." *News & Observer* (Raleigh, NC), March 3, 2012.

_____. "Jones Acknowledges Lying About Steroid Use." *News & Observer* (Raleigh, NC), October 6, 2007.

_____. "McCants Arrives." *News & Observer* (Raleigh, NC), November 12, 2007.

_____. "McCants Ready to Lead the Tar Heels." *News & Observer* (Raleigh, NC), November 16, 2008.

_____. "New Cast Ready for ACC Starring Roles." *News & Observer* (Raleigh, NC), November 10, 2009.

_____. "No. 2 Connecticut at No. 11 N. Carolina, 7 p.m. (ESPN2): Tar Heels, Schedule to Be Put to UConn Test." *Charlotte Observer* (NC), January 17, 2011.

_____. "North Carolina Women's Basketball Team Looks for Fresh Start." *News & Observer* (Raleigh, NC), Oct. 19, 2010.

_____. "South Carolina Courts Hatchell as Head Coach." *News & Observer* (Raleigh, NC), April 29, 2008.

_____. "Terps End Tar Heels' Streak." *News & Observer* (Raleigh, NC), March 8, 2009.

_____. "Thomas, Rolle Named to All-ACC Defensive Team." *News & Observer* (Raleigh, NC), March 2, 2011.

_____. "Top 2 Teams Face off Tonight: Hatchell Says UConn's High-Pace, High-Scoring Tactics Will Put the Tar Heels' Defense to Test." *Charlotte Observer* (NC), January 19, 2009.

_____. "UNC Lures Duke Aide: Stafford-Odom Joins Rival Women's Team, a Rare Move in College Basketball." *News & Observer* (Raleigh, NC), August 25, 2011.

Rocky Mount Telegram (NC). "Tar Heels Women Withstand Albany's Upset Bid." March 24, 2013.

Roe, Jon. "Carolina Kicks up Its Heels: Smith's Shot Beats Buzzer, La. Tech," *Star Tribune* (Minneapolis), April 4, 1994.

Rogers, Carroll. "Coaches Remain Civil as Heels Defeat Tigers," *Atlanta Journal-Constitution* (GA), March 09, 2003.

San Jose Mercury News (CA). "UNC Wakes up, Wins: Rutgers Cruises, Irish Pound Iona." November 30, 2005.

Sarni, Jim. "U.S. Women Rout Soviets: Miller's 18 Lead Way to 83–60 Romp." *Sun-Sentinel* (Fort Lauderdale, FL), July 11, 1986.

Schlosser, Jim. "Curtain-Raiser: UNC Women's Title Win Watched by Record Crowd." *Greensboro News & Record* (NC), March 8, 2005.

Schoffner, Chuck. "No. 2 Tennessee 74, No. 17 North Carolina 54." Associated Press, March 25, 1993.

_____. "Purdue 82, North Carolina 59." Associated Press, March 20, 1999.

Schramm, Stephen. "It Takes Two Overtimes as Tar Heels Top Maryland Women." *Times-News* (Burlington, NC), January 27, 2008.

Schwartz, Valarie. "Community Offers a Choice for Service Groups." *News & Observer* (Raleigh, NC), August 18, 2002.

Seattle Times (WA). "Women Heels' Rout Creates Hard Feelings." College Basketball. March 2, 1998.

Seitz, Denny. "York's Latta Named National Player of Year: S. C. Star Joins Ohio's James with Top Honors." *Charlotte Observer* (NC), March 27, 2003.

Sewell, Dan. "UNC Gives Hoops Coach Roy Williams 8-year Contract Extension." Associated Press, December 19, 2018.

Shelby Daily Star (NC). "One Killed, Ten Hurt in Auto Accidents in County Over Week-End." May 10, 1937.

Shelton, Chris. "BYU First Foe for Buff Women: Austin Peay, Tar Heels Also Coming to Boulder." *Daily Camera* (Boulder, CO), March 17, 2003.

_____. "UNC'S Bell Given Oxygen After Win." *Boulder Daily Camera* (CO), March 24, 2003.

Skaine, Rosemarie. *Women College Basketball Coaches.* Jefferson, NC: McFarland, 2001.

Smith, Marcia C. "North Carolina's Plan Includes Prayer: The Tar Heels' Women Have Had Little Success Against No. 1 Tennessee, Losing 11 of 12 Meetings." *Philadelphia Inquirer* (PA), March 23, 1998.

_____. "Tennessee Women Narrowly Advance: North Carolina Led for Much of the Second Half." *Philadelphia Inquirer* (PA), March 24, 1998.

Sneed, Mitch. "Lawrence and Heels: Perfect Fit; Former Morrow Player Now Starring at UNC." *Atlanta Journal-Constitution* (GA), February 16, 1995.

Solomon, Jon. "ACC Cracks Down on Coaches, Officials." Scripps Howard News Service, January 22, 2003.

_____. "Ex–North Carolina Athletes Sue NCAA, UNC Over Academic Scandal. *CBS Sports Online.* January 22, 2015. https://www.cbssports.com/college-football/news/ex-north-carolina-athletes-sue-ncaa-unc-over-academic-scandal/.

Stancill, Jane. "Jan Boxill, Implicated in UNC Scandal, Resigns." *News & Observer* (Raleigh, NC), March 5, 2015.

The State (Columbia, SC). "Hatchells Land First Recruit: It's a Boy." January 26, 1989.

_____. Sports Briefs. August 15, 1995.

Stevens, Tim. *The News and Observer* "N. C. Code Prohibited Tournaments for Girls Before 1972." *News & Observer* (Raleigh, NC), March 7, 2012.

Strickland, Bryan. "Hatchell: 'Too Much Politics' Involved with Women's Basketball Tournament." *Herald-Sun* (Durham, NC), April 2, 2008.

_____. "UNC Faces Tough Task of LSU in New Orleans." *Herald-Sun* (Durham, NC), March 31, 2008.

Suggs, Welch. "Poll Finds Strong Public Backing for Gender Equity in College Athletics." *Chronicle of Higher Education* (Washington, D.C.), July 7, 2000.

Summitt, Pat, with Sally Jenkins. *Raise the Roof.* New York: Broadway, 1999.

_____. *Sum It Up.* New York: Crown, 2013.

Sutton, Bob. "The North Carolina Women's Basketball Team Will Have Plenty of Time for Campaigning." *Times-News* (Burlington, NC) March 5, 2010.

_____. "Peers, Players Bid Farewell to Kay Yow: 'We Lost a Part of Us.'" *Times-News* (Burlington, NC), January 31, 2009.

_____. "Playing for Something Different: Top Teams Might Be Out of First-Place Mix." *Times-News* (Burlington, NC), March 1, 2009.

_____. "Tar Heels Coach Hatchell Joins Elon Celebration in Honor of Charlotte Smith." *Times-News* (Burlington, NC), March 14, 2017.

Svriuga, Susan. "Grade Point: Lawsuit Filed Against NCAA, University of North Carolina in 'Paper Class' Athletics Scandal." *Washington Post* (DC), January 22, 2015.

Technician (North Carolina State University, Durham, NC). "Jimmy V Classic Special to Yow." November 19, 2004.

Thomas, Jim. "Hatchell Feels U. S. Is the Team to Beat." *Florence Morning News* (SC), August 19, 1988.

Tolbert, Keith. "No Question, Hatchell's Back." *Greensboro News & Record* (NC), March 4, 2015.

Tolchin, Susan J. *Women in Congress, 1917–1976.* Washington, DC: Government Printing Office, 1976.

Tommelleo, Donna. "No. 7 North Carolina 77, No. 8 Connecticut 54." Associated Press, December 06, 2005.

_____. "Shellacking: Maryland Terrapins Surprise North Carolina, Advance to National Championship Game with 81–70 Triumph." *Pittsburgh Post-Gazette* (PA), April 03, 2006.

_____. "Tar Heels Awarded Top Seed." *Augusta Chronicle* (GA), March 14, 2006.

Tracy, Marc, and Alan Blinder. "U. N. C. Women's Coach Is Out After Claims of Mistreatment." *New York Times* (NY), April 20, 2019.

Trekell, Marianna, and Rosalie M. Gershon. "Title IX, AIAW, and Beyond: A Time for Celebration!" in *A Century of Women's Basketball: From Frailty to Final Four.* Eds. Joan S. Hult and Marianna Trekell, Reston, VA: National Association for Girls and Women in Sport, 1991 (424).

Trimmer, Dave. "The Cardinal Sets up Regional Final Matchup Against Purdue on Saturday." Basketball. *Aiken Standard* (SC), March 19, 1986.

_____. "Stanford Women Dethrone North Carolina." *Orange County Register* (CA), March 24, 1995.

_____. "Zags Sign Up—GU Reaches New Level with Win Over Heels." *Spokesman-Review* (Spokane, WA), March 21, 2010.

Tysiac, Ken. "Duke-UNC Rivalry Lopsided Lately: Devils Take 12-Game Win Streak Against Heels to Chapel Hill Tonight." *Charlotte Observer* (NC), January 24, 2005.

_____. "In Battle of Unbeatens, Duke Stays Atop the Hill." *Charlotte Observer* (NC), February 9, 2007.

_____. "Krapohl Comes Up Big for Duke" *Charlotte Observer* (NC), February 15, 2004.

_____. "UNC to Host Duke, Crowd: Top 25 Matchup Is Set for Smith Center." *Charlotte Observer* (NC), February 14, 2004.

United Press International. "U. S. Olympic Coach Criticized for Smuggling Bibles." November 11, 1986.

United States Department of Justice. "Overview of Title IX of the Civil Rights Act of 1964." https://www.justice.gov/crt/fcs/TitleVI-Overview.

University of North Carolina. "Andrew Calder." Goheels.com. https://www.goheels.com/.

_____. *Carolina Basketball 2011–12 Fact & Records Book.* http://grfx.cstv.com/photos/schools/unc/sports/m-baskbl/.

_____. "Carolina, Nike Extend Agreement for Eight Years." News Release, October 16, 2001. http://www.goheels.com/.

_____. "Hatchell Temporarily Stepping Away for Health Reasons." News Release, October 14, 2013. http://www.goheels.com/.

_____. "Post Game Quotes." Goheels.com, April 2, 2006. http://www. goheels.com/.

_____. *Report of Findings: Academic Anomalies Review.* James G. Martin with Baker Tilly. December 19, 2012. https://carolinacommitment.unc.edu/files/2013/01/UNC-Governor-Martin-Final-Report-and-Addendum-1.pdf.

_____. "Sylvia Hatchell Heads Toward Season with New Outlook." News Release, July 19, 2000.

_____. "Sylvia Hatchell Steps Down as Women's Basketball Head Coach." News release, April 19, 2019. https://www.goheels.com/.

_____. "Tracy Reid Named ACC Basketball Legend." News Release, January 27, 2015. https://www.goheels.com/.

University of North Carolina Alumni Association. "UNC, Nike Sign New 10-Year Contract." July 7, 2009. https://alumni.unc.edu/news/unc-nike-sign-new-10-year-contract/.

USA Basketball, Women. 1994 Women's R. William Jones Cup. Taipei, Japan. August 4–12.

https://www.usab.com/history/additional-usa-basketball-history/r-williams-jones-cup-team/1994-womens-r-william-jones-cup.aspx.

Utter, Jim. "Tar Heels, Purdue Have Their Tradition: Bracket Matches These Two for the Third Time in Four Years." *Charlotte Observer* (NC), March 23, 2009.

Velliquette, Beth. "Team, Woman Share Gift of Hope." *Herald-Sun* (Durham, NC), November 11, 2001.

Vernon, Jeremy. "Questions Abound for the North Carolina Women's Basketball Team." *Daily Tar Heel* (University of North Carolina, Chapel Hill, NC), June 25, 2015.

Vinella, Susan. "Learning to Win: UD's Haskins Goes Full Speed in Hectic off Season Schedule." *Dayton Daily News* (OH), July 5, 1995.

Voepel, Mechelle. "Auriemma: Most Coaches 'Afraid' of Their Players." espnW.com. April 4, 2019. https://www.espn.com/womens-college-basketball/story/.

_____. "Is North Carolina Really Committed to Returning Women's Basketball to the Top?" espnW.com. May 1, 2019. https://www.espn.com/womens-college-basketball/story/.

_____. "UNC Has Potential to Repeat." *Daily Press* (Newport News, VA), December 2, 1994.

Von Kreisler, Kristin. *The Compassion of Animals: True Stories of Animal Courage and Kindness.* Rocklin, CA: Prima, 1997.

Wainstein, Kenneth, A., Joseph Jay, III, and Colleen Depman Kukowski. "Investigation of Irregular Classes in the Department of African and Afro-American Studies at the University of North Carolina at Chapel Hill." October 16, 2014. https://carolinacommitment.unc.edu/files/2014/10/UNC-FINAL-REPORT.pdf.

Walker, Richard. "Afterglow." *Charlotte Observer* (NC), April 8, 1994.

_____. "In Her Element: Hatchell Delights in Basketball Talk." *Gaston Gazette* (NC), July 18, 2006.

Walker, Teresa M. "North Carolina Believes Late Game Shook off Rust." Associated Press, March 20, 2009.

_____. "North Carolina Opens with 85–80 Win Over UCF." Associated Press, March 21, 2009.

Wall, Kathryn Lynn. "'We Always Loved to Play Basketball': A Window of Opportunity for Working-Class Women's Sports, Winston-Salem and Elkin, North Carolina, 1934–1949." MA thesis, University of North Carolina at Chapel Hill, 1994.

Warner, Pete. "Talented, Tenacious UNC Turns Back Black Bears." *Bangor Daily News* (ME), March 20, 2000.

Warnock, William Elliott. "Carolina Dismantles Davidson in Opener." *News & Observer* (Raleigh, NC), November 20, 2005.

_____. "It's the Only Game in Town." *News & Observer* (Raleigh, NC), March 13, 2002.

_____. "Picking Up Where Things Left off Before." *News & Observer* (Raleigh, NC), February 19, 2003.

_____. "A Short Season Remains." *News & Observer* (Raleigh, NC), February 12, 2006.

_____. "Tar Heels Take Classic Against Wolfpack." *News & Observer* (Raleigh, NC), January 17, 2001.

_____. "Tigers, Tar Heels to Bump Heads Again Today." *News & Observer* (Raleigh, NC), February 16, 2003.

_____. "UNC Getting an Earful About Duke." *News & Observer* (Raleigh, NC), January 8, 2003.

_____. "UNC Rides Bubble into Tournament." *News & Observer* (Raleigh, NC), February 28, 2001.

_____. "UNC Women Rise and Shine After Loss." *News & Observer* (Raleigh, NC), January 20, 2002.

Watson, Laurie. "The 1983 World University Games Opened Friday with Lavish." United Press International, July 1, 1983.

Way, Dan E. "Freshmen Lead Heels, Spartans in Battle." *Herald-Sun* (Durham, NC), March 25, 2014.

Weiss, Dick. "Stanley Might Coach U. S. Women in '88." *Philadelphia Daily News* (PA), July 30, 1985.

Wheelock, Helen. "Women's Basketball Timeline—Since 1891." Women's Hoops Blog. https://womenshoopsblog.wordpress.com/womens-basketball-timeline-since-1891/.

Whicker, Mark. "Marion Jones: Catch Her Act ... If You Can." *Orange County Register* (CA), May 14, 1993.

White House Briefing. "President Clinton Meets with University of North Carolina NCAA Women's Basketball Team." Federal News Service, July 27, 1994.

Whittaker, Celeste E. "Chapil [*sic*] Hill N. C. Tar Heel Women's Team Nets Hoopla." *Atlanta Journal-Constitution* (GA), March 22, 1994.

_____. "Clinton Gets Strategy Tips from NCAA Champions." *Atlanta Journal-Constitution*, July 30, 1994.

_____. "UNC Signs Top Recruits to Ease Loss of Jones." *Atlanta Journal-Constitution*, November 9, 1997.

Wilco, Daniel. "Calder Called up in Hatchell's Absence." *Daily Tar Heel* (University of North Carolina, Chapel Hill, NC), October 15, 2013.

_____. "Sylvia Hatchell and Kennedy Meeks Stole the Show at Late Night with Roy." *Daily Tar Heel* (University of North Carolina, Chapel Hill NC), October 6, 2014.

Wilcox, Ryan. "Hatchell Under Investigation for Racist Remarks, *Washington Post* Reports." *Daily Tar Heel* (University of North Carolina, Chapel Hill, NC), April 1, 2019.

Williams, Dick, and Bill Plaschke. *No More Mr. Nice Guy: A Life of Hardball.* Orlando: Harcourt Brace Jovanovich, 1990.

Williams, MaryEllen. *TRIUMPH: Inspired by the True Life Story of Legendary Coach Kay Yow.* LuLu.com, 2012.

Winkeljohn, Matt. "A Pair of Peaches Are the Pick of the State's Crop: Morrow's Lawrence Dials Long Distance." *Atlanta Journal-Constitution* (GA), March 17, 1991.

Wise, Dione L. "UNC's Hatchell Notches 800th Victory of Career." *Greensboro News & Record* (NC), January 12, 2009.

Wiseman, Steve. "Breland 'Dug Deep' for Special Run to ACC Final." *Herald-Sun* (Durham, NC), March 5, 2011.

_____. "Marion Jones Kept an Eye on the Guards." *Herald-Sun* (Durham, NC), October 28, 2010.

Witt, Gerald. "Carolina's Breland Benches Her Cancer." *Greensboro News & Record* (NC), March 4, 2011.

_____. "The Comeback Win." *Greensboro News & Record* (NC), March 3, 2011.

Zgoda, Jerry. "Back in Black? It's a Long Way off for Iowa Women." *Star Tribune* (Minneapolis, MN), December 14, 2005.

Index

*Numbers in **bold italics** indicate pages with photographs*